An Introduction to the

Canadian LABOUR MARKET

Helmar Drost

York University

H. Richard Hird

Durham College

Nelson
Thomson Learning™

Australia • Canada • Denmark • Japan • Mexico • New Zealand • Philippines
Puerto Rico • Singapore • South Africa • Spain • United Kingdom • United States

1120 Birchmount Road
Scarborough, Ontario M1K 5G4
www.nelson.com
www.thomson.com

Canadian Cataloguing in Publication Data

Drost, Helmar
An introduction to the Canadian labour market

Includes bibliographical references and index.
ISBN 0-17-616772-2

1. Labor market – Canada.   I. Hird, H. Richard.   II. Title

HD5728.D76 2000   331.12'0971   C99-933102-7

Editorial Director	Evelyn Veitch
Executive Editor	Tim Sellers
Project Editor	Mike Thompson
Production Editor	Natalia Denesiuk
Production Coordinator	Hedy Later
Marketing Manager	David Tonen / Anthony Rezek
Art Director & Cover Design	Angela Cluer
Interior Design	Julie Greener
Senior Composition Analyst	Zenaida Diores
Copy Editor	Madeline Koch
Proofreader	Wendy Thomas
Printer	Webcom

Printed and bound in Canada
    2   3   4   03   02   01   00

To Maria

H.D.

To my students

R.H.

BRIEF CONTENTS

Detailed Contents

CHAPTER 6: UNEMPLOYMENT 133

CHAPTER 9: LABOUR MARKET DECISIONS OF FIRMS   245

TABLE OF CONTENTS

CHAPTER 12: EDUCATION, TRAINING, AND EARNINGS DIFFERENTIALS 323

PREFACE

The tremendous growth in the field of human resource management has fuelled a growing interest in the Canadian labour market. Human resource (HR) professionals must have an understanding of the market conditions that influence the determination of earnings and the hiring and training of employees. The professional HR manager also needs to know how changes in government legislation are likely to affect the labour market. In the last 50 years, governments have been very active in implementing policies designed to regulate working conditions. Laws have been written concerning pay equity, severance pay, safety in the workplace, and so on. Knowledge of the Canadian labour market has become essential and, for this reason, human resource professional associations have made an understanding of labour economics mandatory before an individual can receive a designation.

An Introduction to the Canadian Labour Market introduces the prospective human resource professional to the economic issues affecting the market for workers. The book is also suitable as a reference for other professionals as well as students in business and commerce schools interested in the labour market.

This book has four goals. The first is to inform the reader about the major trends and developments in the Canadian labour market. The second is to provide some explanation for these real-world developments and labour market outcomes. Why, for example, do unemployment rates differ among employees depending on their age, gender, occupation, or location of work? Why have annual hours of work declined throughout most of this century but have levelled off more recently? What factors are responsible for the earnings gap between men and women? Since these questions often have more than one answer, the third goal is to show why economists sometimes disagree. Finally, the fourth goal is to teach the reader to apply labour market theory to analyses of current events and labour policy issues and in so doing learn to assess the relevance of theory.

The text is divided into three parts.

- **Part I: Introduction and Overview (Chapters 1 to 3)**
  Many HR students taking a course in labour economics have no previous exposure to the discipline of economics. The introduction provides an overview of how economists approach real-world problems. The central concept of a market is explained and the principles underlying demand and supply. The unique features of the

labour market are outlined and an explanation is given of how labour markets interact with other markets in the Canadian economy. International influences are also discussed. The third chapter presents the legislative and institutional framework of the labour market. It reviews the role of government in regulating the labour market, various labour legislation, and the extent of unionization of the Canadian labour force.

- **Part II: Trends and Recent Developments in the Canadian Labour Market (Chapters 4 to 7)**
  This part presents the major labour market trends and developments in Canada since World War II. The purpose is to establish those macroeconomic developments in the Canadian labour market that will be explained in later chapters. The trends cover the growth of the Canadian labour force and changes in employment, unemployment, and labour compensation.

- **Part III: Microeconomic Theory of the Labour Market (Chapters 8 to 12)**
  This part of the text explains the labour market behaviour of households and business firms. Households represent the supply side of the labour market and offer their services to employers. Business firms represent the demand side of the labour market. Business firms want the services of workers in order to provide goods and services to the marketplace. The interaction of the buyers and the sellers in the labour market determines the wage rate. Since workers and jobs are not the same, wages differ. The final chapters of the text shed some light on the reasons for these wage differentials. Special attention is paid to the impact of education, training, and discrimination on wage rate differentials.

Labour economics has become increasingly technical over the last two decades. It has also come to be distinguished by the use of highly sophisticated statistical techniques. Most textbooks on labour market economics are aimed at the student who has a solid background in economic principles. However, individuals entering the human resource management field often lack this extensive background in economics and statistical analysis. This text addresses the needs of those with no, or very little, previous economics training. The concepts and economic relationships are presented in non-technical language without relying on mathematical equations. The text, however, does use graphs and figures to illustrate economic trends and labour market principles. Although we use them sparingly, we believe that students should become accustomed to using graphs in their analysis of labour market issues. If you can trace one variable in a time series graph and plot relationships in a coordinate system distinguishing between positive and negative relationships, your knowledge of graphs is sufficient for this text.

This book will help the reader understand the aspects of the labour market that play a central role in the determination of employment and earnings in Canada. Toward that end, various learning tools appear throughout the book.

- **Objectives:** Every chapter begins with a list of learning goals. These objectives provide a good study guide and help students to focus on the key lessons presented in the chapter.

- **Key Terms:** When important concepts are introduced in the text, they are bold-faced. A list of key terms appears at the end of each chapter and a glossary defining each key term appears at the end of the text.

- **Summaries:** Each chapter ends with a brief summary that reminds students of the most important lessons that they have just learned. The chapter summaries provide a review for exams.

- **Boxes:** Economic theory is useful and interesting only if it can be applied to understanding actual events and policies. The boxes throughout the book contain interesting issues and applications of the theory.

- **Exercises:** At the end of each chapter are questions for review and discussion as well as for learning. Students can apply their newly acquired knowledge to these exercises. They can also be used for examination preparation.

As with all co-authored books, we realized it was necessary for one of us to take the lead role in authoring each chapter. Helmar tackled chapters 1, 4, 5, 6, 7, and 12, while Rick's primary work revolved around chapters 3, 8, 9, and 10. Chapters 2 and 11 were such that they could be written jointly. To maintain a consistent level of presentation, all chapters were read and commented on by both of us. In terms of lead authorship, then, it would be fair to say that Helmar took the lead in authoring the chapters related to trends and recent developments in the Canadian labour market, while Rick was the primary author of the chapters covering the microeconomic theory portion of the book. That being said, as authors we have done everything possible to write a book that reads as one voice, and we hope we have accomplished that objective.

ACKNOWLEDGEMENTS

A textbook is rarely the product of the authors alone. Our book is no exception. In writing this text we have benefited greatly from the comments, suggestions, and support of a number of people. We owe a special debt to Monica Belcourt who, after much hesitancy on our part, convinced us to write a labour economics text for the Nelson Series in Human Resource Management. Her encouragement in the early phase of the project was instrumental in keeping us on track. We and the publishers would particularly like to thank the following people, who provided their valuable comments and suggestions during the development of this book: Mary MacKinnon, McGill University; Stephen Havlovic, Simon Fraser University; Richard Delaney, Fanshawe College; Peter Fortura, Algonquin College; Ihor Sokolyk, Humber College; and Michael Walker, Georgian College.

Mike Thompson and Natalia Denesiuk of the Higher Education publishing team at Nelson offered careful and effective editorial assistance. Thanks also to the many others who worked behind the scenes to help produce this book.

Finally, there are our families. Their patience and emotional support, which made everything go more smoothly, was greater than we had any right to expect.

ABOUT THE AUTHORS

HELMAR DROST Dr. Helmar Drost is Professor of Economics and Social and Political Thought at York University. He received a Master of Arts in economics from the University of Cologne in 1965 and a Ph.D. in economics from the University of Bochum in 1968. He joined the faculty at York University in 1969 after a year as post-doctoral fellow at the University of Toronto.

He has held appointments as Full Professor at the Technical University of Berlin, as Visiting Professor at the University of Toronto at Scarborough and the University of Konstanz, and as director of York's Graduate Program in Social and Political Thought. He has acted as consultant to the federal governments of Canada and Germany.

Dr. Drost has taught introductory and advanced courses in microeconomic and macroeconomic theory, labour economics, the economics of education, and business cycle and growth theory. His research has primarily been in the areas of labour economics and macroeconomics. His current research focuses on unemployment in Canada, in particular unemployment of minority groups, and the links between the educational system and the labour market. He is the author of two books on social policy and growth theory as well as numerous articles in professional journals in Europe and North America.

H. RICHARD HIRD Mr. Hird is a Professor of Economics and Statistics in the Business Division at Durham College in Oshawa, Ontario. He earned his Bachelor's and Master's degrees in economics at the University of Windsor, where he specialized in labour economics. Prior to joining Durham College in 1977, he was an economist with the Ontario Ministry of Labour, the Ontario Ministry of Community and Social Services, and the Canada Department of Manpower and Immigration. Mr. Hird has helped draft legislation in the area of employment standards, written research reports on the labour market, and evaluated government initiatives in the labour market.

Mr. Hird has taught at Atkinson College, York University. He is the author of an introductory economics text (*Working With Economics*, 5th edition) and the co-author of an introductory statistics text (*Understanding Business Statistics*). He is a consultant to the Certified General Accountants Association of Canada, the Human Resources Professional Association of Ontario, and the Durham Regional Police.

Part I

Introduction and Overview

PART I

INTRODUCTION AND OVERVIEW

Many people like to dip their toes into the swimming pool to test the water temperature. They do not want to jump in without any information about the condition of the pool. Your introduction to the Canadian labour market is analogous to dipping your toes in the water. The first three chapters establish a framework for analyzing the labour market. Chapter 1 explains the differences between human resources management, labour relations, and labour market analysis. It provides an overview of the economist's way of thinking by showing the similarities and differences between the methods that economists and natural scientists use to explain real-world problems.

The labour market is one of several markets in the economy. Before analyzing the labour market in detail, we must first understand how markets work in general. Chapter 2 introduces the concept of a market and the two major components of any market: demand and supply. The labour market has special features that distinguish it from other markets; Chapter 2 discusses these features and places the labour market into the context of the national and global economy. The Appendix to Chapter 2 introduces some basic economic concepts, which will prove helpful in understanding the subsequent material.

Governments and unions play a major role in regulating the labour market. Chapter 3 outlines the legislative framework of the labour market. It refers to legislation concerning employment standards, human rights, health and safety, workers' compensation and employment insurance. For a significant portion of the Canadian labour force, wages and other conditions of employment are determined by collective bargaining. Union–management relationships as well as changes in union membership are discussed in the concluding part of the chapter.

1

THE WAY ECONOMISTS THINK

OBJECTIVES

After completing this chapter, you should be able to:

1. identify the differences between human resources management, labour relations, and labour market analysis;
2. describe the characteristics of scientific reasoning;
3. explain the three requirements of the scientific method;
4. assess the difficulties involved in making predictions in economics;
5. discuss the problems associated with carrying out experiments in economics;
6. distinguish between positive and normative economics.

THE STUDY OF EMPLOYMENT RELATIONSHIPS

"With Good Jobs Scarce, More Young People Stay in School," "Middle Income Families Losing Ground," "Hockey Star Signs Multi-million Contract," "Federal Government Tightens Eligibility for Unemployment Insurance Benefits," "Canadian Union of Public Employees Threatens with Strike."

Barely a day goes by without a newspaper headline or radio or TV report relating to the labour market. Understanding how the labour market works is important for several reasons. From a national viewpoint, the labour market is the largest market in Canada, with wages, salaries, and fringe benefits accounting for more than 70% of total income received in Canada. From the viewpoint of the individual, events in the labour market and related government policies have an impact on everyone's daily life. They affect wages and salaries, hours of work, and health and safety standards, as well as the chances of finding or losing a job. These work issues constitute an essential part of the relationship between employer and employee. Not only is the employment relationship central to one's ability to provide income, but it also plays an important part in shaping one's self-esteem and role in society.

The study of the relationship between employers and employees can be separated into three fields: human resources management, labour relations, and labour market analysis. Human resources management (HRM) deals with an organization's structure and processes aimed at attracting, motivating, and retaining employees of an organization. HRM views the relationship between an individual organization (the employer) and an individual employee from the perspective of the organization and aims at increasing the efficiency of its employees. HRM involves recruitment, performance assessment, compensation methods, training, job design, and health and safety.

Labour relations, or industrial relations, focuses on the interaction between an employer, or a group of employers, and the representatives of the employees (the union or professional association). Labour relations studies how employers and unions structure their relationship through the collective bargaining process. Topics covered include dispute resolution and the contents of collective agreements. While HRM focuses on improving the productivity of employees, labour relations tilts toward the equity aspect of the employment relationship. Historically, the lack of a balance between equity and efficiency in the workplace was a major factor in the rise of unions: their goal has been to promote equitable, or fair, treatment of their members by employers.

Labour market analysis is concerned with the interaction of employers and employees in the labour market. A market is where buyers and sellers get together to exchange a good or a service; the quantity of the good to be exchanged is determined and the price is set in the market. In the labour market, the buyers are the employers and the sellers are those who are seeking employment. The price is the wage rate, or salary, that is agreed upon by both parties. Thus, labour market analysis involves the determination of wage rates and the level of employment.

Labour market analysis constitutes the core of modern labour economics. Since the subject of this book is labour economics, we focus on the analysis of Canadian labour markets. Before plunging into the substance and details of labour economics, however, it is helpful to have an overview of how economists approach the complex problems of the real world. What is distinctive about how economists tackle a question? What does it mean to think like an economist?

THE SCIENCE OF ECONOMICS

Economists try to think like scientists think. The word "try" is used because there are important differences between the ways of thinking applied in the natural sciences, such as physics and chemistry, and those used in economics. Economists try to reason in scientific ways.

Scientific reasoning has several characteristics.

OBSERVING AND COLLECTING FACTS. At the basic level, science is concerned with facts. Scientists observe and collect facts. To a scientist, a fact is an item of experience that another scientist can be expected to detect in the same way. Religious revelations, for example, are of no concern to a scientist. These may be very important in a person's life, but they cannot be observed and measured in the exact way that facts can be.

EXPLAINING FACTS. Scientific reasoning tries to explain facts in terms of laws. The objective of science is not merely to observe and collect facts, but to explain these facts. By explain, a scientist usually means an attempt to detect a "law" at work. By **law**, scientists mean a regular and repeatable pattern of events, or a relationship between events. Balloons expand when they heat up, so scientists look for laws about the properties of gases. Objects fall, like the apple from the apple tree, a fact that led Isaac Newton, the 17th-century scientist, to develop the law of

law a regular and repeatable pattern of events

hypothesis tentative
generalization that tends
to fit the facts

gravity. Laws are not definitive explanations of how the universe works. Laws are only well-established **hypotheses**—tentative generalizations that seem to fit the facts. Laws or hypotheses never can be assumed to be absolutely true. The law of gases says that molecules move faster when energy (heat) is applied to them. The law of gravitation is a generalization that masses attract each other in a certain way. Since we have not observed every situation and every fact in the universe, we cannot say that our laws or hypotheses are absolutely true. We might discover molecules moving faster when they are put in a freezer, or we might discover circumstances in which an apple falls up. But insofar as we have been able to judge, certain generalizations about the natural universe seem to be true. As long as we have not experienced facts that contradict these generalizations we call them laws.

PREDICTING FUTURE EVENTS. Scientific reasoning uses laws to predict. The purpose of establishing laws is to explain past events and to anticipate their future course. Using the law of gases we predict an explosion—a very fast expansion—if we apply a flame to gasoline vapour. Based on the law of gravity, we predict that the next stone we drop will fall at a certain speed. In predicting, we assume that the new facts will behave like the previous ones, and we hope that the hypothesis explaining the facts accumulated up to this point will hold also for the new facts. If it does not, our hypothesis will have to be changed, because the facts, obviously, cannot be changed. If we predict a planet to be in a particular position relative to the earth at a particular time and we observe the planet to be at a different position, we cannot hold on to the hypothesis and claim that the observation is wrong.

scientific method
experimentation and
explanations about the
outcome of experiments

In applying this reasoning, scientists employ the **scientific method**. This method involves experimentation and explanations about the outcome of experiments. It is a method that has three critical requirements:

1. Experiments must be performed in ways that can be repeated and reconfirmed—or disproved—by other scientists. The reason that teacup reading is not a science is that the "experiments" of one fortune teller do not yield the same results as the experiments of another. Rather, each fortune teller has secrets. A scientific experiment conducted in secret ways cannot be checked by other scientists and, therefore, is not an acceptable experiment.

2. Scientific experiments must be run in ways that permit them to fail. The essence of an experiment is that it may not confirm the expected outcome. An experiment that could not produce negative results

would not be a true scientific procedure. We will see shortly that this requirement has particular relevance for economists.

3. Scientific experiments have to allow for disturbing influences from the outside. Experiments to test the law of gravity must allow for the resistance of air; they cannot only be conducted in a vacuum.

Finally, what is the meaning of theory in science? What do we mean by a theory of gravitation or a theory of evolution by natural selection? A hypothesis that can be generalized to explain many kinds of events is called a **theory**. The hypothesis of gravitation does not apply only to an apple falling to the earth but to any two objects in the universe. Thus the hypothesis of gravity becomes the theory of gravitation. Put differently, theories are hypotheses that have stood the test of time. They have been subjected to frequent tests and have passed them. Voodoo priests sacrificing chickens to pleasure spirits of the dead are probably working with a theory. So are millennarian cultists watching the skies for signs of the Second Coming. But scientific theories are fundamentally different. Their statements are designed to be tested through observation and experiments. They are constructed specifically to be disregarded if proven wrong. Science is littered with discarded theories. As the American economist Paul Samuelson once stated, science advances from funeral to funeral.

> **theory** an idea or set of ideas that can be generalized to explain many kinds of events

This detour through scientific reasoning and scientific method brings us closer to an understanding of economic reasoning. Economists pride themselves on reasoning like natural scientists. But economists are not concerned with factual aspects of the physical universe that attract the attention of physicists, chemists, biologists, and the like. Economists are concerned with society. Thus, economics is a social science.

ECONOMICS AS A SOCIAL SCIENCE

How does a social science like economics compare with a natural science? Social science, like natural science, is concerned with facts. However, these are not the facts of nature, but the facts of society. **Social science** studies the ways in which people behave. Economics, for example, mainly observes certain kinds of facts having to do with the way society organizes its economic activities; that is, how it produces and distributes goods and services. Like natural science, social science tries to explain facts by laws. The formulation of laws or theories, however, is a great deal more difficult than for a natural scientist, but the

> **social science** the study of the ways in which people behave

objective to detect patterns of regularity is the same. Social science also tries to predict. Suppose that economists observe that the level of prices always increases when the quantity of money in a society increases by a larger percentage than the percentage increase in the production of goods and services. That may lead to the hypothesis and the prediction that inflation will arise when governments print too much money. Can economists predict events with the same degree of success that natural scientists can? Unfortunately, they cannot, and it is important to understand why this is so.

PREDICTION AND FREE WILL

Economists are dealing with people, and people have a unique attribute: conscious will. Natural scientists make their predictions about molecules, planets, bacteria, and other objects that do not have conscious purpose. Human behaviour, which economists observe, is based on intentions, expectations, desires, hopes, and fears. Social events take place because human beings want to achieve certain ends and avoid others. Planets have no choice about continuing their trajectory. Bacteria multiply whether they will it or not. But humans do not necessarily behave in given ways. They have the capacity and will to change their behaviour. Behaviour depends on one's state of mind, and one can suddenly change one's mind. As difficult as prediction in meteorology is, weather forecasters do not have to contend with winds and clouds changing their mind. Thus, prediction in economics is immensely complicated because humans may change their ways of thinking about events or reacting to them.

THE DIFFICULTY OF CONDUCTING EXPERIMENTS

We have seen that natural science relies on experiments to confirm or to disprove its hypotheses. Economics, however, can rarely rely on experiments. While recent years have witnessed an increasing number of economic experiments, such as testing different welfare systems to determine their impact on work behaviour, social experiments are difficult to conduct on a large scale. Physicists studying gravity can drop many objects in their laboratories to generate data to test their theories. In contrast, there is no way of "trying out" social changes just to collect data. For example, it is not possible to implement a policy of large-scale temporary tax cuts just to generate the data for an experiment. Once implemented, the tax cuts become part of life. They cannot be changed quickly if they are unsuccessful.

Furthermore, experiments undertaken in economics cannot easily be controlled. In the natural sciences, the environment in which experiments are conducted is carefully controlled in a laboratory. The temperature of the liquid can be monitored. Precise amounts of each liquid can be combined. Experiments in economics must be undertaken in the real world, where external influences are difficult to control. Suppose that some economist established a hypothesis that inflation was the result of lowering the interest rate. How would we test it? Assume we did lower the interest rate, and prices rose. Does that experiment confirm the hypothesis? Unfortunately, it does not. First, we must be certain that the lower interest rate was the *only* new change occurring in the economic situation. There might have been crop failures. The government might have changed its tax policy, or business people, in a surge of optimism, might have increased investment spending. Any of these events, rather than the reduction in interest rates, may have caused prices to rise.

To find a substitute for laboratory experiments, economists pay close attention to the "natural experiments" offered by history. When the oil-producing countries in the Middle East formed a cartel in 1973 in response to the Yom Kippur war with Israel, prices of crude oil skyrocketed around the world. In 1990, when East Germany and West Germany became one country again, industrial production in East Germany collapsed to half the level of the previous year and the unemployment rate soared to 30%. For economists, these sudden historical events are valuable because they allow us to evaluate our theories. An example of a natural experiment in labour economics would be the use of a random sample of identical twins with different levels of schooling to study the effect of the level of education on earnings. Since identical twins share the same inherited characteristics, earning differentials due to genetic differences would be excluded. To isolate the effect of schooling on earnings, however, other factors affecting earnings such as work effort, occupational choice, or union membership must be controlled. Unfortunately, natural experiments in economics are relatively rare. How, then, do economists test their theories? Economists rely mainly on data analysis and statistical techniques to test their theories.

THE ROLE OF VALUES

The final point in the comparison of social and natural science concerns the role of values in scientific reasoning. Scientific reasoning tries to exclude an aspect of thinking that is often the dominant element in non-scientific thought. This is the element of personal likes and dislikes, of moral judgements, that we call values. When science examines its facts or develops a theory, it does not accept some facts because they are considered "good" and rejects others because they are considered "bad." Science does not categorize facts by the preferences of the observer. It behaves toward its research object with impartiality and disinterest. At least, this is what science claims to do. Scientists are fallible, however, like all humans. Social scientists, moreover, are placed in an unusual position when they seek to be value free. Social science, as we have seen, reasons about society, of which the researcher is a member. Few social scientists are indifferent to the outcome of their research. It is not a matter of indifference to them if the world works this way or that way. Many social scientists are interested in changing the world—that is, in policy—not merely in observing and explaining the world. Economists want to probe into the causes of such problems as unemployment, poverty, and the inequality of incomes in order to correct them. Explaining the world and changing the world are often so closely related that it is difficult to separate the role of scientist and policymaker. Let us look at the two roles using the field of labour economics as an example.

ECONOMISTS AS POLICYMAKERS

Often labour economists are asked to explain the causes of economic events. For example, why are equally productive men and women paid different wages? Why is the unemployment rate for teenagers higher than for adult workers? Sometimes labour economists are asked to recommend policies to improve labour market outcomes. What, for instance, should the government do to reduce the wage discrepancies between men and women? What should it do to reduce unemployment of certain groups in the labour market? When labour economists are trying to explain labour market events or outcomes, they act as scientists. When they are trying to improve outcomes, they are policymakers.

To help clarify the two roles that economists play, let us look at the example of minimum wage laws. An economist trying to explain teenage unemployment may come up with the following statement: "Minimum wage laws cause teenage unemployment." In a debate on how to improve the situation of the working poor, another economist may state: "The government should raise the minimum wage." Note what the two economists are trying to do. The first economist is making a claim about what causes teenage unemployment; that is, on how the world works. That economist takes on the role of a scientist. The second economist is making a claim about how to improve the situation of a particular group; that is, how to change the world. This economist takes on the role of a policymaker. Note also the difference in language used by both economists. The first statement is descriptive: it includes a claim about how the world *is*. We call this type of statement a **positive statement**. The second statement is prescriptive: it includes a claim about how the world *ought to be.* We call this statement a **normative statement**.

positive statement
a statement about how the world is

normative statement
a statement about how the world ought to be

EVALUATING POSITIVE AND NORMATIVE STATEMENTS

The central difference between positive and normative statements is how we judge their validity. As we saw in the previous section, scientific statements or positive statements might be right or wrong. They are formulated in such a way that they can be confirmed or rejected by examining evidence. There are many studies, for example, in which economists have tested the relationship between minimum wages and teenage unemployment by using data on changes in minimum wages and unemployment over time or across different groups of teenagers. To find out whether minimum wages increase teenage unemployment does not involve a value judgement. The answer to the question carries no implication as to whether the government should go ahead with increasing the minimum wage.

In contrast, evaluating normative statements involves not only facts but also values. Deciding whether increasing the minimum wage is good or bad policy involves personal values. Some working poor may receive an increase in wages as a result of the minimum wage increase. Others may lose their jobs as a result of the minimum wage increase. How do we know if it is a good idea to increase minimum wages when there will be winners as well as losers? If there were only winners, normative statements and the government policies to which they lead would not be controversial. Economic policies, however, very rarely see only winners. They usually involve tradeoffs, and some people gain at the expense of others. If the gains made by the winners are greater than the losses of the losers, is it a good idea to proceed with a minimum wage increase? Should the winners compensate the losers to have an acceptable policy? Clearly, the answers to these questions involve value judgements. They depend on our personal ethical, religious, or philosophical views.

BOX 1.1 Efficiency versus Distribution: A Matter of Value Judgement

Policies, as we saw in the example of minimum wages, nearly always result in some people gaining and some losing. Whenever some groups win and others lose, value judgements must be made in assessing the policy. Immigration policy is a case in point.

Whose economic well-being should Canada try to improve when it sets immigration targets: the well-being of people born in Canada (native-born Canadians) or that of immigrants? Suppose that the objective of immigration policy is to improve the well-being of the native-born population. What aspect of well-being should be the focus of immigration policy: the income per person or the distribution of income?

Immigration may increase the income per person in the native-born population but that does not mean that all native-born Canadians will gain.

Immigrants increase the number of workers in the economy. Because they increase competition in the labour market, the wages of some native-born workers will fall. At the same time, however, Canadian firms gain, because they can hire workers at lower wages. Also, native-born consumers gain when they use the goods and services produced by immigrants, because lower labour costs lead to less expensive goods and services.

Immigration not only changes the size of the economic pie (which economists call "efficiency") but also changes how the pie is sliced up (the distribution). Immigration policy, therefore, must be judged in terms of its impact on both dimensions: efficiency and distribution. The importance that Canadians attach to these two dimensions depends on their particular values. The science of economics provides no guidance on how to rank the two.

Links Between Positive and Normative Economics

The example of the minimum wage indicates that positive and normative statements are often related. Our positive views about how the world works affect our normative views about what policies are desirable. If economists establish that minimum wages cause teenage unemployment, that might lead them to reject the view that governments should increase minimum wages in order to ameliorate the situation of the poor. Yet, logically, the normative conclusion cannot be derived from the positive statement alone. It requires a value judgement to come to the conclusion that the loss of those suffering unemployment outweighs the gain of those whose income increases because of an increase in the minimum wage. Policy recommendations, therefore, should not be presented as if they were the sole outcome of scientific analysis. Whenever economists make normative statements, they are crossing the line from science to policymaking.

The relation between positive statements and normative judgements does not run just one way. We have seen in the above example how the result of a scientific inquiry may lead to a particular value judgement. Normative views, however, also affect the way we do science. Facts do not organize themselves into concepts and theories just by being examined. Questions must be asked before answers can be given. The questions are an expression of our interest in the world; they are, at bottom, valuations. Economists are guided by moral, political, or ideological values in their selection of problems. When the 19th-century English economist David Ricardo stated that the principal problem in economics is to determine the laws that regulate the distribution of income, he expressed a personal value judgement about what he considered to be the most important subject to be researched by economists. Values are thus necessarily involved already at the stage when we observe facts and carry on analysis. They do not only come into play when we draw political conclusions from facts and valuations.

Values also sometimes enter positive analysis through the language, concepts, and metaphors chosen by economists. The concept of market equilibrium, for example, was adopted by early economists to convey the idea that a market in balance reflected a natural state of harmony in which individuals pursuing their own interest would bring the price to a level at which both buyers and sellers were satisfied. While in modern economics, the conditions for a market equilibrium are often expressed in "value free" mathematical language, the term implicitly carries a value.

We can begin to see why it is very difficult even for economics, which is often called the queen of social science, to duplicate exactly the reasoning of natural science. Nor is there any reason why it should. Social science is about society. The essences of human life are wish and motive and purpose. Unless we think that men and women are like inert matter, there is no reason to think that human behaviour can be explained and predicted in the same way scientists explain and describe facts in the natural world. Indeed, it is astonishing how much of society, not how little, lends itself to scientific reasoning.

SUMMARY

The employment relationship is essential to our daily lives. The majority of Canadians depend on income from employment. The employment relationship is studied in three related fields: human resources management, labour relations, and labour market analysis. Labour economics deals primarily with labour market analysis.

Economists follow a way of thinking developed in the natural sciences. They observe and collect facts and try to explain facts with the help of laws. Laws are also used to make predictions and the predictions are tested.

Economics is a social science. It deals with human behaviour. The application of the scientific method in the social sciences encounters difficulties, which relate to making predictions and conducting experiments. Predictions and controlled experiments are more easily performed in the natural sciences.

Positive economics uses theories to explain and to predict labour market behaviour. Normative economics is concerned with changing certain aspects of the labour market. Positive economics describes "what is" and normative economics describes "what should be." Claims about how the world works often affect our views of how the world ought to be. Likewise, normative views often enter the way we try to explain the world.

KEY TERMS

law   7

hypothesis   8

scientific method   8

theory   9

social science   9

positive statement   13

normative statement   13

EXERCISES

1. For each of the following issues, determine whether it falls under the field of human resources management, labour relations, or labour market analysis:

   a. termination for just cause
   b. training and development
   c. causes of unemployment

   d. seniority rights
   e. pay equity

2. How valid do you think the laws of economic behaviour are? If the laws are not valid, why do economies function and not collapse? If they are valid, why can economists not predict more accurately?

3. If science is supposed to be free of values, can a scientist have strong moral beliefs? What do we mean by "value-free" scientific work?

4. A policy that redistributes income from one group to another always involves comparing the welfare loss of some people against the welfare gain of others. Whether the redistribution is equitable or just cannot be resolved with scientific methods but requires a value judgement. True or false? Explain.

5. Classify each of the following statements as positive or normative. Explain.

   a. Each Canadian family should have access to free child care.
   b. A reduction in the rate of growth of money will reduce the rate of inflation.
   c. Lower payroll taxes encourage firms to employ more people.
   d. An unemployment rate of 11% is too high.
   e. Employers should subsidize the work clothing of their employees.
   f. The deficit reduction of the federal government affects poor people unfairly.

REFERENCES

Barbash, J. (1989). Equity as Function: Its Rise and Attrition. In J. Barbash and K. Barbash (Eds.), *Theories and Concepts in Comparative Industrial Relations.* Columbia: University of South Carolina Press, 114–122.

Belcourt, M. L. (1999). *Managing Human Resources* (2nd Canadian ed.). Scarborough: ITP Nelson.

Craig, A. W. J., and Solomon, N. A. (1996). *The System of Industrial Relations* (5th ed.). Scarborough: Prentice Hall.

Mankiw, N. G. (1998). *Principles of Economics.* Orlando: The Dryden Press.

Meltz, N. (1989). Industrial Relations: Balancing Efficiency and Equity. In J. Barbash and K. Barbash (Eds.), *Theories and Concepts in Comparative Industrial Relations.* Columbia: University of South Carolina Press, 109–113.

Myrdal, G. (1953). *The Political Element in the Development of Economic Theory.* London: Routledge.

2

OVERVIEW OF THE LABOUR MARKET

OBJECTIVES

After completing this chapter, you should be able to:

1. describe the concept of a market;
2. describe the conditions under which both demand and supply curves are drawn;
3. explain how demand and supply curves can shift to a new position;
4. explain how the market eliminates shortages and surpluses;
5. explain how the labour market differs from other markets;
6. describe the flow approach to the labour market;
7. explain the circular flow model of the economy;
8. discuss how globalization affects the labour market.

The Market Mechanism (or How the Market Works)

Approximately 14 million people are employed in Canada, either part time or full time. There are close to 1.8 million registered business establishments and a multitude of government and non-profit agencies that provide jobs for these people. How do all these individual workers and organizations get matched up with one another? How are their employment relationships determined in terms of hours of work, rate of pay, annual vacations, and so on? To answer these questions economists have developed the concept of the labour market.

The labour market is one of several markets in the economy. Generally, a **market** exists whenever there is a good or service that buyers and sellers want to trade. The interaction between the buyers and the sellers results in an exchange of the good or service and in the establishment of a price. The market exchange is completed when both the buyer and the seller agree to the price and the quantity of the good or service to be exchanged. These exchanges can occur in geographically defined areas where buyers and sellers meet each other physically, as at farmers' markets or in retail stores. The location of some other markets is not so easy to identify. For example, the markets for gold, crude oil, or wheat are international in nature. The buyers and sellers in these markets are not likely to meet face to face.

In the **labour market**, labour services, such as those of carpenters or computer programmers, are exchanged. In these markets, the price agreed to by the buyers and the sellers is called the **wage rate**. As with product markets, some labour markets are local while others are national or international in scope. The market for retail clerks is likely of a local nature while the market for airline pilots is national and the market for those who can extinguish oil fires is worldwide.

Before studying the labour market in more detail, let us review how a market operates.

As mentioned, the interaction between buyers and sellers results in an exchange of a product or service, and a price is established. The establishment of a price is the primary function of a market. The price carries a different name in different markets. It may be called the interest rate, which is the price set in money markets. In the rental housing market, the price is called the rent. The exchange rate is the price at which the Canadian dollar exchanges for another currency. This price is set in the foreign exchange market. This text deals with the labour market. The price established in this market is the wage rate.

market the interaction of buyers and sellers, in which a price is established and a product or service exchanged

labour market the interaction of buyers and sellers of labour services

wage rate the price established in the labour market

The buyer's side of the market is called the demand side and the seller's side of the market is the supply side. For the purposes of analysis, we will discuss the two sides separately, starting with the demand side. Following our discussion of the supply side of the market, both sides will be joined and the process of price determination will be discussed.

THE DEMAND SIDE

The demand for a product or service represents the willingness and ability of consumers to purchase that product or service. Several factors influence demand. These are:

- the price of the product or service;
- the price of related products or services;
- income levels;
- expectations about future prices and income;
- tastes and preferences;
- the number of buyers.

It is difficult to analyze the demand for a product or service while attempting to consider all of the above factors at once. Therefore, to simplify our discussion, we will review the response of the quantity demanded to a change in the price, assuming that all other factors that influence demand remain constant. This assumption is temporary; once the relationship between the price and the quantity demanded is established, the other factors that influence demand will be allowed to vary.

As the price of the product decreases, the quantity demanded increases. There are two reasons for this. First, as the price falls, consumers are able to buy more of this product with their current income. This is referred to as the **income effect**. Second, as the price falls this product may be substituted for more expensive products. This is referred to as the **substitution effect**. As the price of the product increases, the quantity demanded declines. Income and substitution effects now work in the opposite direction. As prices increase, consumers can buy less of the product with their current income, and they substitute other products for this higher priced product.

The inverse relationship between the price and the quantity demanded is known as the law of downward-sloping demand. On a graph this relationship is referred to as the **demand curve** (see Figure 2.1). The demand curve depicts the quantities demanded of the product at various prices. The relationship depicted by the demand curve will

income effect (demand) the effect of changes in price on how much a consumer can buy with a given income

substitution effect (demand) changes in price encourage consumers to substitute one product for another

demand curve a graph of the relationship between the prices of a good and the quantity demanded

FIGURE 2.1   THE DEMAND CURVE

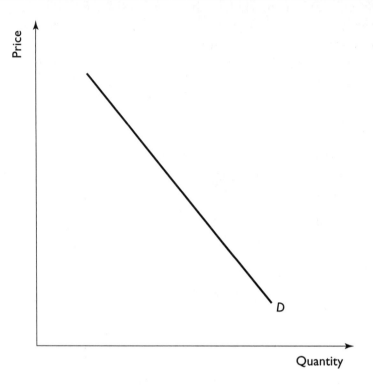

change if there are changes in any of the other factors that influence demand. For example, if consumer incomes are increasing, the quantity of a product demanded will likely increase at a given price. This change will shift the demand curve to the right (see Figure 2.2a). If the price of a substitute product falls, the demand curve will shift to the left (see Figure 2.2b).

THE SUPPLY SIDE

Supply represents the willingness and ability of firms to sell a product or service. Several factors influence supply, namely:

- the price of the product;
- production costs;
- the prices of related products or services;
- expected future prices;
- the state of technology;
- the number of suppliers;

FIGURE 2.2   INFLUENCES ON THE DEMAND CURVE

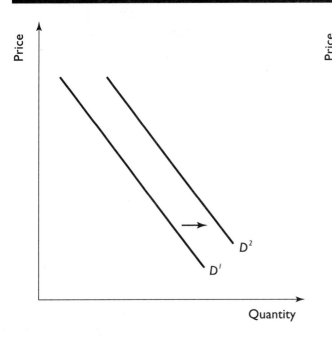

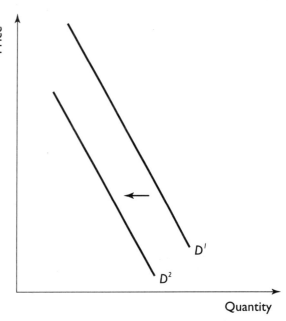

a. An increase in income shifts the demand curve to the right.

b. A decrease in the price of a substitute shifts the demand curve to the left.

- government regulations;
- weather conditions.

As with the demand side, it is difficult to analyze the supply side of the market with all these factors constantly changing. Therefore, for the purposes of this discussion we assume that the factors other than the price remain constant.

What happens to the quantity supplied as the price increases? If everything else remains the same, the quantity supplied increases as the price increases. In other words, the quantity supplied is positively related to the price. The positive relationship exists because of the relationship between output and costs. Economists define the **short run** as a period of time during which at least one factor of production is fixed and cannot be changed. The **long run** is defined as a period of time in which all factors of production can be changed. We will focus here on the change in production cost in the short run.

In the short run, if we assume there is fixed capital (given plant size, machinery, and tools), production can be increased by hiring more workers. Initially, this improves the efficiency of the operation. As workers are hired, jobs can be specialized and productivity improved.

short run a period of time during which at least one factor of production remains fixed

long run a period of time during which all factors of production can be changed

There will come a point, however, when the additional output created by adding one more worker is less than the addition to total output achieved by the hiring of the previous worker. The new workers have less of the fixed factor of production to work with. Economists refer to the decrease in additional output gained from hiring one more worker as **diminishing returns**. When diminishing returns set in, costs of production go up. To produce an additional unit of a product or service, more hours of work or number of workers must be paid. To cover the increasing cost, firms only supply more goods or services if prices increase.

diminishing returns additional output decreases as a result of hiring one more worker, when other factors are fixed

The positive graphical relationship between the price and the quantity supplied is referred to as the **supply curve** (see Figure 2.3). If one of the factors other than the price changes, the supply curve will shift. For example, if production costs increase because of an increase in wages paid to employees, the supply curve will shift to the left (see Figure 2.4). At the same price, quantity supplied will be less: there has been a decrease in supply.

supply curve a graph of the relationship between the price of a good and the quantity supplied

Since the axes for the demand and the supply curves are the same, we can draw both curves on the same graph (see Figure 2.5). The combination of the demand and the supply curves is the representation of

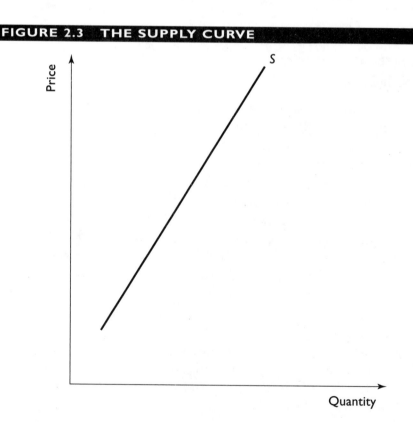

FIGURE 2.3   THE SUPPLY CURVE

FIGURE 2.4 INFLUENCES ON THE SUPPLY CURVE

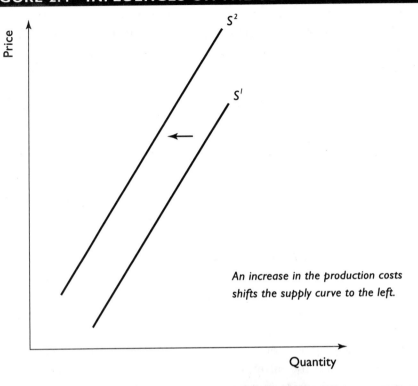

An increase in the production costs shifts the supply curve to the left.

FIGURE 2.5 THE MARKET

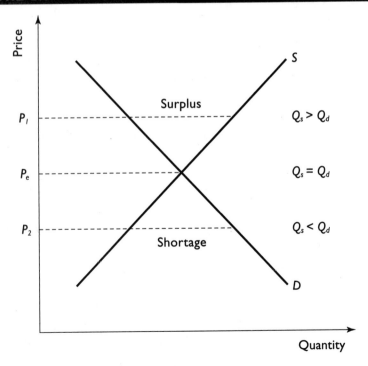

the market for a particular product or service. When we analyze the market, we refer to the graph with both curves.

It is easy to draw curves on a page, but it is more difficult to determine the real demand and supply curves for a particular product or a service. In the real world, the demand and supply curves are forever changing, and pinning them down can be difficult. Nonetheless, we can use the concept of demand and supply to predict the result of changes in the marketplace.

PRICE DETERMINATION

Suppliers try to gather information on the demand for their products. Unfortunately, this information is rarely perfect. In light of what information is available, they must select a price for the product or the service. Assume that the suppliers charged a price represented by P_1 in Figure 2.5. At this price the quantity demanded by consumers is less than the quantity supplied by the producers. A **surplus** or excess supply exists. To get rid of the surplus, the price is lowered. As the price falls, the quantity demanded increases and the quantity supplied decreases. As long as there is a surplus, the price will decline.

Assume that the suppliers charged a price represented by P_2 in Figure 2.5. At this price, the quantity supplied is less than the quantity demanded. There is a **shortage.** The price rises as a result of the shortage. As the price increases, the quantity supplied increases and the quantity demanded decreases.

What if the price charged is the one at P_e? At this price, the quantity demanded is equal to the quantity supplied. There is neither a surplus nor a shortage. Therefore, there is no reason for the price to change. The market is in a state of balance. The price determined by the intersection of the demand and the supply curves is known as the **equilibrium price**. When something is in equilibrium, it is not likely to change. If the price is not at equilibrium, it will change and move toward equilibrium. When you see prices changing in the marketplace, you are seeing the mechanism that brings the market into balance.

The equilibrium price changes when there is a change in either demand or supply. That is, a shift in either curve will result in a change in the equilibrium price. In Figure 2.6, an increase in income has shifted the demand curve to the right. If we assume that the market was in equilibrium prior to the shift, the quantity demanded is now greater than the quantity supplied at the previous equilibrium price (P_1). The price increases until it reaches the intersection of the new demand curve and the supply curve: a new equilibrium price is established (P_2).

surplus a situation in which the quantity demanded by consumers is less than the quantity supplied

shortage a situation in which quantity demanded is greater than quantity supplied

equilibrium price the price at which the quantity demanded equals the quantity supplied

AN INTRODUCTION TO THE CANADIAN LABOUR MARKET

BOX 2.1 Electronic Data Interchange and the Market Mechanism

We have seen how the market mechanism generally forces the price toward its equilibrium level. If there is a surplus, competitive price-cutting among producers will push the price down. If there is a shortage, because customers are unable to buy the quantities they want, they will outbid one another; this pushes the price up. Sometimes, the adjustment process can take a long time. However, as computer-based technologies are transforming the retail sector, markets are moving more rapidly toward an equilibrium. An example is electronic data interchange (EDI), a computer-based communication system that allows companies to adjust their supply rapidly to changing market conditions.

For example, Nancy works at a cash register in a building supply store in Calgary. Each item in the store has a product code, which is displayed on the merchandise. As a customer wheels eight bundles of cedar shingles to the counter, Nancy moves an electronic reader along the code on one of the bundles. Within seconds, eight bundles of cedar shingles are automatically deducted from the store's inventory. This triggers a rapid reaction down the supply chain. EDI notes that shingles have to be ordered. One day later, a truck leaves a lumber company in B.C. bound for the building supply store in Calgary.

EDI eliminates the time-consuming exchange of paper documents between suppliers and customers. The immediate recording of changes in inventory as well as just-in-time manufacturing and delivery make the supply of goods adjust much faster. As a result, shortages and surpluses in the market tend to disappear more quickly than in earlier times.

FIGURE 2.6   THE EQUILIBRIUM PRICE

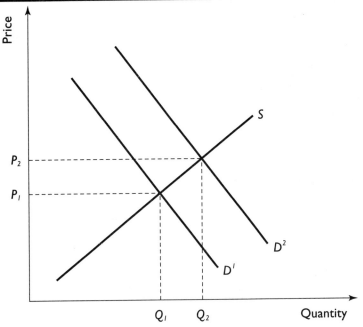

An increase in demand has raised the equilibrium price from P_1 to P_2.

Similarly, a shift in the supply curve will result in a new equilibrium price.

SPECIAL FEATURES OF THE LABOUR MARKET

Up to this point in our discussion, all markets have been treated in a similar manner. Although the labour market has the typical features of a market, it nevertheless differs from the commodity and other markets in several respects.

LABOUR SERVICES ARE INSEPARABLE FROM PEOPLE. The first feature that distinguishes the labour market from other markets is that the item being exchanged—labour services—is embodied in human beings. If one buys commodities (such as a suit, a car, or a dozen bagels) or assets (for example, stocks, bonds, or gold), ownership and possession of the purchase are transferred from the seller to the buyer. In most societies, workers cannot be owned; their services can only be rented. The high degree of control that ownership generally entails does not exist in the labour market. Because workers cannot be owned, managers and business owners try to exert control through other means. The rise of trade unions and labour legislation can be seen as responses to the persistent attempts of employers to gain control over workers. The legalization of collective bargaining between trade unions and management, as well as other labour legislation, has led to many constraints that shape the employment relationship. For example, the number of hours of work per week is subject to rules regulated by government or by negotiation between union and management. Other legislation guarantees a minimum wage rate. Some governments have enacted regulations requiring advance notice of employment termination and severance pay for job loss. Most governments state a minimum age for employment. Legislation regarding employment standards and union-management relations is discussed in Chapter 3.

Because the service provided by labour is inseparable from the person performing it, there is a direct, personal relationship between the supplier (the worker) and the purchaser (the employer). Generally, when a commodity is transferred, neither party has an interest in the personal characteristics of the other party. In contrast, workers have definite preferences with respect to their working conditions. Employers have preferences regarding the characteristics of their potential employees. The decisions made by both parties are based on a complex set of considerations, including not only the wage rate but also a host of non-monetary factors associated with the job or worker. These factors include work environment and the personalities of co-workers and managers, and are often considered as important as the wage rate. The aspect of fairness is probably more important in the labour market than in any other market. Workers want fairness in hiring, promotion, and layoff procedures, and they want "just" or "fair" wages. Employers want a "fair day's work" from their workers and the freedom to earn a "fair return" on their capital investment. Employers' perceptions of fairness are likely to vary from employees' perceptions.

EMPLOYMENT RELATIONS LAST LONGER. A second distinguishing feature is that employment relationships often last relatively long. Exchanges of products are generally of short duration; exchanges of labour services established through employment contracts usually last much longer, from months to many years. Employers, for example, find it to their advantage to maintain a stable core workforce, since they may have made substantial investments in workers in the form of hiring, training, and experience. Likewise, individual workers, as they get older, find it to their advantage to remain with one employer for a considerable time. The reason is partly economical, since wages and fringe benefits normally increase with tenure on the job. However, there are also psychological reasons for favouring a lengthier employment relationship: people generally place a value on security and familiar surroundings.

A significant implication of the long-term employment relationship is that it reduces the sensitivity of wages to changes in demand and supply. Prices rise and fall daily only in certain commodity markets. In the barley market, for example, an excess supply quickly leads to a drop in price as sellers underbid each other to attract a buyer. Buyers, in turn, have little reason not to switch from one seller to another, since bushels of barley are much the same. In the labour market, however, an excess supply of labour typically does not quickly lead to a fall in wage rates. Although unemployed workers might offer to work for lower wages, most firms would find it unprofitable to hire them because the costs of hiring and training, as well as the potentially negative effect on morale, would far outweigh the savings in lower wages. Thus, while in many commodity markets prices fluctuate to restore a balance between demand and supply, wage rates in the labour market change more slowly. The change is particularly slow in a downward direction. Firms may find it costly to terminate employees and hire employees at lower wage rates. The resulting sluggishness creates an imbalance between the demand and supply of labour, which may persist for a considerable time before wage rates change enough to bring about the necessary adjustments in the labour market. In those labour sub-markets where the employment relationship is short term and turnover costs are minimal—for example, in the market for day labourers—wage rates exhibit a flexibility similar to other markets.

WORKERS AND JOBS ARE HIGHLY DIVERSE. The third special feature of the labour market is closely related to the first feature. Because labour services are embodied in human beings and because each person is unique, there is extreme diversity in the characteristics of the "good" being exchanged. Such diversity does not occur in other markets. For many items, such as agricultural products or semi-finished products such as steel, each unit is fairly similar, if not identical, and the decision to buy or to sell is made predominantly on the basis of price. Consumer goods (such as dairy products, cars, or textiles) or final investment goods (such as metal stamping machines, construction cranes, or computer hardware systems) are more differentiated; the decisions to buy and sell these products are influenced by non-price factors as well as by price. The differentiation in the characteristics of workers and jobs is greater than in other markets. Individual workers differ by age, gender, race, education, experience, and skills. They also differ in psychological and social traits, such as self-confidence, motivation, and congeniality. Employees are faced with a similar diversity in characteristics of potential employers; employers differ, for instance, in the type of work, health and safety standards, commuting distance, and their labour relations, as well as in wages and fringe benefits.

This differentiation complicates the search and evaluation of information required by both buyers and sellers before an exchange can take place. Because each bushel of barley is alike, buyers need only to acquire information about the price demanded by various sellers; in the labour market, however, both buyers and sellers must invest much more time and effort in evaluating the many non-pecuniary, intangible characteristics that distinguish each worker and job. The exchange is more costly to undertake and less likely to result in the most efficient match of buyer and seller, compared to markets in which the product is more standardized. If the job or the worker turns out to be a disappointment, the employee and firm may look for more attractive opportunities. The result is turnover and search for new possibilities. In short, the labour market has more uncertainty and incomplete information than do other markets.

LABOUR MARKETS ARE HIGHLY FRAGMENTED. A fourth distinctive characteristic of the labour market is the number of individual sub-markets.

There is not just one national or regional labour market: there are many individual labour markets characterized by geographical location, occupation, and skill level. When we analyze how wage rates are determined, we must distinguish between the labour market for air pilots, brick layers, and corporate lawyers. Each occupation has different supply and demand conditions. Likewise, geographical location gives rise to distinct labour markets. The demand and supply for French-speaking high school teachers in Alberta is likely to be different from the demand and supply in New Brunswick. For some occupations, such as hockey players, computer analysts, or academics, the labour market may be national or even international. Few other markets are as fragmented as the labour market, in part because it is not always easy to move from one labour market to another. Movement among markets becomes more difficult the greater the geographic distance or the disparity in skills.

Of what significance are these special features of the labour market? Are the differences between the labour market and other markets so great that we cannot use the general theory of the market in this context? Labour economists differ in their answers to this question.

One position taken by many labour economists is that the labour market should be treated like any other market. Economists should focus on the mechanism that balances supply and demand through the variations in wage rates, rather than study the sociological, institutional, and regulatory details of the labour market. Such abstraction from those details is a necessary part of understanding. The English philosopher John Austin once remarked that one would be inclined to call oversimplification the occupational disease of philosophers, were it not their occupation. But the same applies for theorists of all kinds, including economists. Like all scientists, economists struggle with the complexity of real life by concentrating on crucial aspects of economic processes. Unless we separate the many institutional details from our study of the market, we cannot even begin to understand its basic functioning. Suppose that economists analyzing the fish market insisted on obtaining all the institutional details on the fisheries—are these details necessary to understand price fluctuations for seafood? Does one need to know the ins and outs of the construction trade in order to predict changes in prices? Knowing a great deal about the trades and municipal bylaws may help little in understanding the functioning of the new housing market.

The opposite position is held by some labour economists: one cannot equate the labour market with other markets. The idea that the labour market acts like a machine to equate the supply of labour and demand for labour by varying wage rates, in their view, is taking abstraction too far. These economists argue that regulatory and institutional elements are more important in the labour market than in other markets. Regulations imposed by governments and by collective bargaining between labour and management play a significant role in the determination of employment and wages, and institutions affect the balance of power between workers and management. Unions, works councils, quality circles, and other aspects of worker participation in the governance of companies fall into this category. Also, the fact that high unemployment persists over extended periods of time shows that the labour market does not readily equate supply and demand. If one treats the labour market like any other market, one is prone to misunderstand unemployment and other outcomes of the labour market.

Can the two positions be reconciled? Unfortunately, there is no ready answer. If we set the level of abstraction so high that institutional realities drop out of focus, important aspects of contemporary labour markets can easily move out of the picture. On the other hand, if we change the focus to highlight detailed institutional characteristics, we may end up with a newspaper account of economic life without any discernible patterns. The art of theorizing is to simplify the detailed complexity of daily life without losing the essential elements one wants to explain. The aim, therefore, is to set a middle level of abstraction that reflects the dominant institutional facts of the labour market. What does this mean for our analysis of the Canadian labour market? We will use the theory of supply and demand to explain earnings and employment levels in the labour market. We will also discuss important institutional aspects of the labour market and how they affect demand and supply.

THE LABOUR MARKET AND THE NATIONAL ECONOMY

circular flow model
a visual model of the economy that shows how goods and services and money flow between households and firms via markets

factors of production
the inputs used to produce goods and services (labour, land, and capital)

The millions of exchanges of labour services that occur daily in the labour market are not taking place in isolation from the rest of the economy. The labour market is but one of several markets interacting with each other. Figure 2.7 offers an illustration of how the labour market fits into the overall economy. This diagram represents the **circular flow model** of the economy. In this model there are two types of decision makers—households and firms. Firms produce goods and services using various inputs, such as labour, land, and capital (building, machines, tools). These inputs are called **factors of production**. Households own the factors of production and they consume the goods

FIGURE 2.7 THE CIRCULAR FLOW MODEL

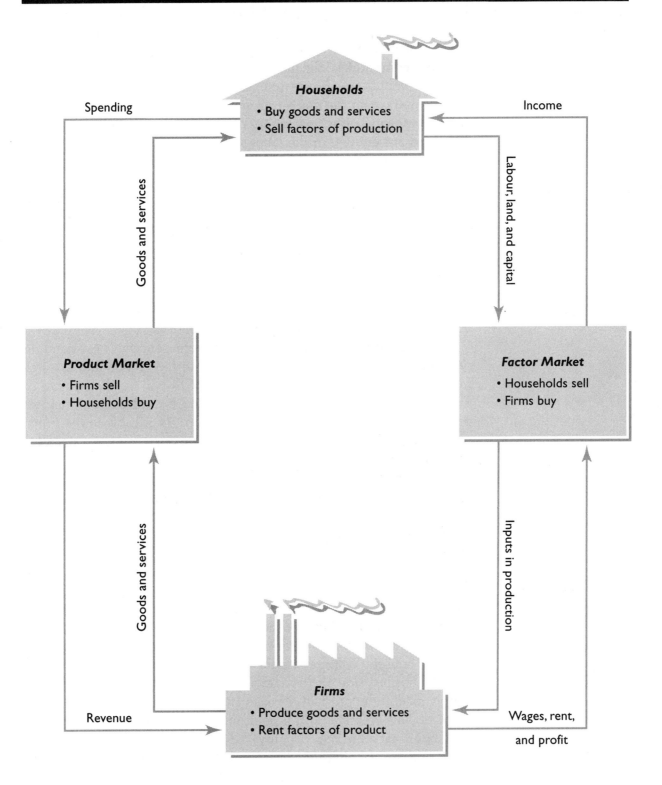

factor market   the
market in which factors of
production are exchanged

product market   the
market in which goods
and services are
exchanged

and services produced by firms. The market in which the factors of production are exchanged is called the **factor market**. The labour market is
a factor market in which labour services are offered in exchange for
wages. The market in which goods and services are exchanged is called
the **product market**, or the market for goods and services.

Households and firms interact in both the factor market and
product market. In the market for goods and services, households are
buyers and firms are sellers. In the factor market, households are sellers
and firms are buyers. In the labour market, for example, households
provide firms with the labour services that the firms use to produce
goods and services.

The inside clockwise arrows of the diagram represent the flow of
goods and services between households and firms. Let us start with the
households at the top: they sell the use of their labour, land, and capital
to firms in the factor markets. The inputs sold in the factor markets are
then used by firms to produce goods and services. These goods and services are sold to households in the markets for goods and services. The
services of factors of production flow from households to firms, and
goods and services flow from firms to households.

The outside counterclockwise arrows represent the corresponding
flow of money. Households spend money to buy goods and services
from firms, which use some of that revenue to pay for the services of
factors of production, such as the wages for their employees. Money not
paid out for factors of production are the profits payable to the firms'
owners. It should be noted that the owners of businesses are members
of households.

With every market transaction, goods and services move in one
direction, and money moves in the other. When a household makes a
purchase, money moves from the hands of households to the hands of
firms, and goods move from firms to households. If a firm purchases
the services of a factor of production, money moves from business to
the owners of these factors—wages and salaries to the owners of labour,
rent to landowners, profit or interest to owners of capital resources.
Hence, the factor markets not only facilitate the exchange of production
factors but they also organize the distribution of income.

Thus there is a link between the product markets and the factor
markets: households represent the demand side in the product markets
and the supply side in the factor markets, and firms represent the
supply side in the product markets and the demand side in the factor
markets. This link is a central point in understanding the operation of
the labour market in the economy. For example, a sustained increase in
the spending of households on goods and services—that is, a rising

demand in the product markets—leads firms to increase their production. In order to do so, firms will hire more labour. So an increase in the demand in the goods markets leads to an increase in the demand in the labour market. The demand for teachers is linked to the demand for educational services, and the demand for car mechanics is related to the demand for automobiles. For this reason, the demand for labour, like the demand for other production factors, is called a **derived demand**. Changes in the demand for labour, in turn, will feed back into the product market. For example, if job vacancies increase and are filled with unemployed people, incomes increase and the demand of households for goods and services will rise.

derived demand the demand for workers that is derived from the demand for goods and services

Clearly, the circular flow model in Figure 2.7 is a simplified version of the economy. Several sectors in the economy have been omitted. In the diagram, the flow of goods, services, and payments that takes place between business firms is omitted. For example, automobile manufacturers buy hundreds of parts from other companies. The government sector of the economy, which sells services in the goods and services market and buys inputs in the factor markets, is also omitted. Nevertheless, the circular flow model provides a first abstract view of the economy as a system of buyers and sellers interacting in different markets. It demonstrates how the labour market is linked with the rest of the economy.

THE FLOW APPROACH TO THE LABOUR MARKET

Now let us take a closer look at the structure of the labour market. When we talk about the structure of the labour market we are interested in the components of labour demand and labour supply and how changes in these components permanently reconstitute demand and supply.

To begin, we must distinguish between two types of variables: **stock variables** and **flow variables**. A stock is a quantity measured at a given point in time; a flow is a quantity measured per unit of time. The bathtub is a typical example used to illustrate stocks and flows. The amount of water in the tub is the stock: it is the water in the tub at a given time. The water pouring from the faucet into the tub is the flow: it is the quantity of water being added to the tub per unit of time. Clearly, the measure of the stock and the flow of water differ. We say that the bathtub contains 100 litres of water, but that water is flowing from the faucet at 10 litres per minute. In this example, stocks and flows are related. The stock of water in the tub represents the accumulation of

stock variable a variable whose quantity is measured at a given point in time

flow variable a variable whose quantity is measured per unit of time

the flow out of the faucet. As the flow increases in volume so does the stock, assuming the drain is plugged. If the bathtub is unplugged, the stock of water depends on the volume of water flowing into the tub and the volume of water flowing out.

The image of the water in a bathtub can help us to visualize the labour market as a system of stocks and flows. At any given moment, a certain number of people are employed or unemployed and a certain number of job openings are available to be filled. The stocks of job vacancies and employed workers together constitute the **demand for labour**—workers would not be employed if there was no demand for them. The stocks of unemployed and employed workers constitute the **supply of labour**—there would be no employment if workers did not supply their services.

The number of employed and unemployed people changes according to the flows in and out of employment and unemployment. Workers enter the pool of the employed through recalls or by being matched in the labour market with job vacancies (new hires). Workers leave employment as a result of quits, layoffs, and retirements. If the flows out of employment exceed the flows into employment, the stock of employed people will decline. As people leave employment because of quits or layoffs, they enter the pool of the unemployed. Thus some outflows from employment become inflows into unemployment. Workers also move into the ranks of the unemployed as they graduate from school or give up full-time housework and cannot find jobs. Workers who are recalled or newly hired constitute outflows from unemployment. Workers may also withdraw from the labour market altogether because they may have become discouraged as a result of unsuccessful job searching, or they may have decided to go back to school full time. If the flows into unemployment exceed the flows out, the stock of unemployed people will rise.

Although only relatively small changes in the stocks occur from month to month, the gross flows that account for these changes are much larger. As shown in Figure 2.8, over a period of 16 years the average monthly flow into employment, for example, is almost half a million: 240 000 from unemployment and 250 000 from those not in the labour force. The average monthly flow out of employment is 470 000: 190 000 to the pool of unemployed plus 280 000 to those not in the labour force. The average net change in employment per month is only 20 000.

Even when the size of a stock remains constant over time because the flow in is offset by the flow out, the composition of the stock changes. This is the reason why the number of people who have expe-

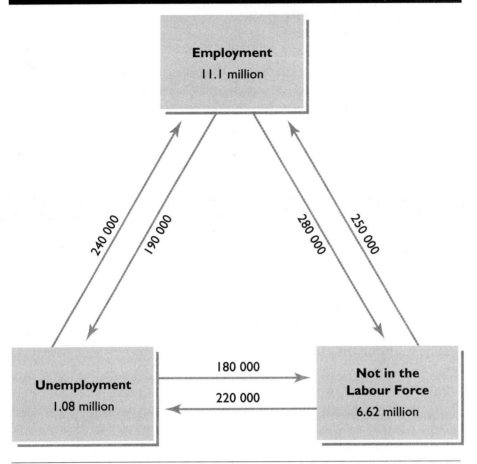

Source: Adapted with data from Stephen R. G. Jones (1993).

rienced unemployment, or who have had employment during a particular period, is substantially larger than the total number who are employed or unemployed at a given time. Recall the difference in measures of the stocks and flows mentioned earlier: the stock of unemployed people is measured at a particular moment. The flows of workers entering and leaving the state of unemployment are measured per unit of time (a week, a month, or a year).

Until the early 1970s, labour economists predominantly applied a stock approach to the labour market. They were interested in measuring the number of employed and unemployed people at a given time and in explaining the changes in the stocks over time. Over the last three decades, labour economists have increasingly turned to a flow approach. Flow analysis has distinct advantages over stock analysis. It provides insights into movements between the different labour force states (employment, unemployment, and being outside of the labour market). The flow approach also offers much more detailed information on the causes of the net changes in the stocks. For example, in studying the reasons for changes in the flows (layoffs, quits, re-entrants, or new entrants to the labour market), we gain a better understanding of the conditions that bring people into unemployment. Did unemployment increase in a particular year because more people were laid off or quit their jobs, or because a large cohort of school leavers entered the labour market for the first time? With a flow approach to the labour market, these and other questions can be tackled more effectively.

LABOUR MARKETS IN A GLOBAL ECONOMY

Previously, we discussed the labour market in the context of the national economy. National boundaries, however, are increasingly breaking down with respect to economic activities. Industrialized nations like Canada have become increasingly integrated through the growth in foreign direct investment and foreign trade—a process known as **globalization**. In general, globalization is understood as the process by which markets and production in different countries are becoming more interdependent due to international trade in goods and services and the transfer of capital and technology. The spread of international production across national boundaries has been accelerating due to the rapid growth of multinational corporations. Multinational corporations are companies that operate production facilities in different countries. Much international trade involves the shipment of products between divisions of the same multinational corporation. Foreign-controlled businesses are an important component of the Canadian economy. Many major employers in Canada are foreign-owned companies. Foreign-controlled companies accounted for about 35% of total corporate revenue generated in Canada in 1997. Foreign ownership is particularly high in the manufacturing sector. A recent study on the globalization of Canadian merchandise trade reported that of the 2000 manufacturing and wholesale enterprises covered in the study, foreign-controlled firms represented over one half of overall operating revenue (Olineck & McMechan, 1996).

Globalization is facilitated by the move toward reducing trade barriers between nations. Canada is a member of the World Trade

globalization the integration of countries through the growth in foreign trade and foreign investment

AN INTRODUCTION TO THE CANADIAN LABOUR MARKET

Organization (WTO). This organization represents most of the nations in the world and is committed to reducing trade barriers. Canada, the United States, and Mexico have signed the North American Free Trade Agreement (NAFTA), an agreement that eliminates many barriers to trade between these countries. The activities of multinational corporations and freer international trade are having important effects on the Canadian labour market. They affect the level of employment and unemployment in many industries and the type of skills demanded throughout the economy. They also influence organizational structure, human resources management, and employment standards of companies in Canada.

IMPACT OF GLOBALIZATION ON ORGANIZATION AND HUMAN RESOURCES MANAGEMENT. Intensified international competition together with an accelerating pace of technological change has changed the direction of competition between businesses toward continuing innovation. Continuing innovation involves not only constant improvement in products, production processes, and materials, but also changes in organizational structures and human resources management. Competition based on innovation requires an organizational structure and a human resources base geared toward maximizing the ability to learn. Knowledge has become the strategic resource and learning the most important process.

This shift in emphasis toward constant acquisition of new skills has sometimes been termed the move from Fordism to Toyotism. **Fordism** generally describes a mass production system—the assembly line in car manufacturing is a typical example of mass production—that combines a small group of highly skilled managers and technically trained personnel with a workforce of relatively low education and vocational skills, organized in a vertical hierarchy. The Fordist organizational model resembles a military command model with layers of middle managers who pass information and commands up and down the hierarchy. Such an organization is relatively inflexible, but well suited to mass production in capital-intensive sectors, where large-scale production is essential to competitiveness. **Toyotism** denotes an organizational model involving more flexible management forms of semi-independent groups linked laterally rather than vertically. Employees have more autonomy and responsibility within the organization. As a result, Toyotism requires an increase in the competence of employees across the board, which is accomplished through continual training and upgrading. Toyotism also puts pressure on union–management

Fordism a mass production system that combines a small group of highly skilled managers and technically trained personnel with a workforce of relatively low education and vocational skills organized in a vertical hierarchy

Toyotism an organizational model involving flexible management forms of semi-independent groups linked laterally rather than vertically

Globalization pitches the work practices of companies in developing countries against those of companies in developed economies. It also allows a multinational corporation to use the relocation of production facilities as leverage to make its plants in different countries conform to one common standard.

The German car maker BMW set up a manufacturing plant in the United States. It used the U.S. plant as a threat in bargaining with its German union to change work practices in Germany. Flexible shifts were introduced in Germany, which enables the company to operate plants on weekends when necessary to meet rising demands. The switch to flexible shifts reduced capital cost by a quarter. BMW

workers have a company account into which their pay for hours worked on weekends is deposited. When demand declines, workers who are redundant can draw pay for the hours they have accumulated on their accounts. Overtime is not paid unless it becomes apparent that total hours of work in a year will exceed the standard amount of hours.

BMW, which bought Rover in Britain, is now introducing the practice of flexible shifts in its Rover plants. British workers have been told that they must reduce the 30% productivity gap between themselves and the German workers. It doesn't take much for the British workers to realize that if they don't accept flexible shifts, production will be moved elsewhere.

relations to change from an adversarial relationship to one of cooperation and consensus.

IMPACT OF GLOBALIZATION ON EMPLOYMENT STANDARDS. The trend toward globalization also exposes differences in labour employment standards between countries. Workers in Canada work with more regulation and protection than their counterparts in the United States, but with much less protection than European workers. Differences in employment regulations are particularly large between Canada and developing countries in Latin America and Asia. Does increased economic integration imply that employment standards regulations in Canada must match those in the countries it trades with? Must Canadian governments relax labour standards in order to keep Canadian firms competitive in world markets?

Canada and the United States agreed that NAFTA would not be signed unless a side agreement was approved to guarantee Mexico's adherence to standards in areas such as minimum wages, child labour law, and occupational safety and health. Pressure for requiring Mexico to improve its labour market standards stemmed from at least two concerns: first, the concern for the well-being of children and mainly low-skilled workers in Mexico, and second—and probably more important—concern for Canadian and U.S. workers whose jobs may be threatened because of lower wages and what some perceive as Mexico's cost advantage due to its lower labour standards.

Do differences in labour standards in fact lead to differences in labour costs? This question is more difficult to answer than it first appears. It is neither conceptually nor empirically clear that higher employment standards necessarily mean higher labour costs. Some regulations may reduce costs or raise productivity: health and safety regulations that save lives, for instance, or regulations that establish work councils. Some regulations may increase cost or reduce productivity. The same regulation may add to efficiency in one setting but not in another; it may have a big effect, positive or negative, in one setting but not in another.

Even when higher labour standards imply higher labour costs, it is often not clear from the outset who will bear these costs. Costs nominally placed on companies may partly or fully be shifted back to workers. For example, an increase in the cost of labour due to mandated employer-purchased health insurance shifts the demand for labour down, which at existing wages would cut down employment. But if the provision of mandated employer-purchased health insurance makes work more attractive, that benefit will increase the supply of labour, so that the long-term cost will fall partly on workers as well as on employers. As long as employers do not carry the regulatory costs solely, these costs may not affect plant location and investment decisions negatively.

The threat, however, remains that companies will relocate in countries with less stringent employment standards and lower wages. Given freer trade and capital mobility, governments are under increasing pressure not to enact or enforce employment standards or labour relations laws. Do more stringent employment regulations increase labour costs? To what extent do labour costs affect plant location and investment decisions? Has the threat of companies relocating production outside of Canada influenced the willingness of governments to implement employment regulations and standards? Many questions still remain unresolved. Nonetheless, it is clear that increased globalization has an impact on the Canadian labour market.

SUMMARY

In a market, buyers and sellers get together to exchange a product or a service. The buyer's side of the market is referred to as demand and the seller's side is referred to as supply. The interaction of the demand and supply sides of the market leads to the setting of a price. In the labour market, the price is known as the wage rate.

The relationship between the quantity demanded of a good or service and its price is generally negative. This leads to a downward-sloping demand curve. On the supply side, there is a positive relationship between the price and the quantity supplied. The supply curve slopes upward to the right. The equilibrium price is determined by the intersection of the supply and demand curves. As the two curves shift, the equilibrium price changes.

The labour market has several features that distinguish it from other markets. Employers buy the services of workers; they do not buy the workers. A great deal of legislation has been enacted to regulate the relationship between employers and employees. That employment relationship often lasts a long time, and its long-term nature implies that wages are less flexible than prices in other markets. Wages are particularly sticky in a downward direction. Because wages do not adjust quickly, imbalances in labour markets can persist over longer periods of time. In the labour market, the services provided by individuals differ from one person to the next, whereas in many product markets the product being exchanged is identical. Exchanges in the labour market, therefore, involve a lot of uncertainty. The labour market is highly fragmented along geographical and occupational lines.

The labour market is just one market in the overall economy. It is a factor market in which labour is exchanged. In the labour market, households represent the supply side and businesses represent the demand side. In product markets, households represent the demand side and businesses represent the supply side. The links between the labour market and the rest of the economy can be illustrated in a circular flow model. In this model, labour services flow from households to firms and goods flow from firms to households. In exchange, money travels from businesses in the form of income to households and then back to businesses as households spend income on goods and services.

The flow approach to the labour market focuses on changes in the components of labour demand (number of job vacancies and employed workers) and labour supply (number of employed and unemployed workers). The number of employed people changes depending on the inflows to employment (new hires and recalls) and the outflows from employment (quits, layoffs, and withdrawals from the labour force). Quits, layoffs, and entrants to the labour force who cannot find jobs increase unemployment. Hires and withdrawals reduce unemployment.

The labour market is increasingly affected by the trend to globalization. The pressure to innovate requires more flexible forms of management and the constant acquisition of new skills. International competition also puts pressure on governments to adjust legislated labour standards to those of Canada's trading partners.

KEY TERMS

market   20

labour market   20

wage rate   20

income effect (demand)   21

substitution effect (demand)   21

demand curve   21

short run   23

long run   23

diminishing returns   24

supply curve   24

surplus   26

shortage   26

equilibrium price   26

circular flow model   32

factors of production   32

factor market   34

product market   34

derived demand   35

stock variable   35

flow variable   35

demand for labour   36

supply of labour   36

globalization   38

Fordism   39

Toyotism   39

EXERCISES

1. Describe the features of labour markets that distinguish them from other markets.

2. If human beings could be bought or sold like commodities such as barley or gold, how would it change the operation of the labour market? Would the supply of labour become more or less sensitive to the non-monetary aspects of employment? Why?

3. a. Where does the labour market belong in the circular flow model depicted in Figure 2.7? Can you draw it in?

   b. In the circular flow model, show the flows that correspond to the following activities:
      1) Nadja earns $7.50 as a raft guide on the Ottawa River.
      2) Daniel pays a car dealer $23 000 for a pick-up truck.

3) Agnes spends $12.75 on a meal in a fast food restaurant.
4) Paul earns $3000 in dividends from stocks of Canadian companies.

4. Discuss the distinction between a stock variable and a flow measure of employment and unemployment.

5. Give an example of a company or an industry that follows the organizational model of Fordism or Toyotism.

6. Using demand and supply curves, draw a market diagram to illustrate the impact of the following:

   a. an increase in lumber prices on the market for new houses;
   b. the aging of the baby-boom generation on the market for health care;
   c. an increase in consumer incomes on the market for restaurant meals;
   d. a freezing spell in Florida on the market for orange juice in Canada.

7. Why is the equilibrium price the price at which the quantity supplied equals the quantity demanded?

8. Suppose hamburgers and pizza are substitutes. What is the effect on the price of a hamburger and the quantity of hamburgers sold if:

   a. the price of pizzas increases;
   b. the cost of producing pizzas increases.

9. The cost of producing microchips has fallen dramatically over the years. Using a supply and demand diagram, show the effect of the cost decline on the equilibrium price in the market for computers.

10. Will economic integration through NAFTA force Canada, Mexico, and the United States to harmonize their labour standards, regulations, and payroll taxes? Discuss.

REFERENCES

Betcherman, G., and Gunderson, M. (1990). Canada-U.S. Free Trade and Labour Relations. *Labour Law Journal, 41:* 454–560.

Blank, R. (Ed.) (1994). *Social Protection versus Economic Flexibility: Is There a Trade-Off?* Chicago: University of Chicago Press.

Gagnon, E. (1997). *Free Trade in North America: The Impact on Industrial Relations and Human Resources Management in Canada.* Kingston: IRC Press, Queen's University.

Jones, S. R. G. (1993). Cyclical and Seasonal Properties of Canadian Gross Flows of Labour. *Canadian Public Policy, 19:* 1–17.

Kaufman, B. (1993). *The Origins and Evolution of the Field of Industrial Relations in the United States.* Ithaca: ILR Press.

Mankiw, N. G. (1998). *Principles of Economics.* Orlando: The Dryden Press.

Olineck, C., and McMechan, J. (1996). The Globalization of Canadian Merchandise Trade. In *Insights On...*, pp. 7–10. Ottawa: Statistics Canada. (Catalogue no. 61F0019XPE)

Solow, R. (1990). *The Labour Market as a Social Institution.* Oxford: Blackwell.

Appendix A

SOME BASIC ECONOMIC CONCEPTS

This appendix is written for those students with no previous background in economics.

OBJECTIVES

After completing this appendix, you should be able to:

1. describe how society deals with the scarcity of resources;
2. explain the concept of opportunity cost;
3. define the price elasticity of demand and supply;
4. discuss the factors that influence price elasticity.

ECONOMICS AND SCARCITY

Almost everything in this world has a limit. There are only 24 hours in a day. There is only so much money in your pocket, or in your bank account. Companies have only so much space within which to manufacture products. There is only so much land in Canada. Economists refer to the limitation of supply as **scarcity**.

scarcity limitation of a society's resources

As a result of scarcity, decisions must be made. You must decide how you will use the 24 hours in a day. You must decide what you will do with your money. Companies must plan how to use the space available to them. Canadians must decide how to use the land that we have available. Economics is the study of how these decisions are made.

opportunity cost value of the best forgone alternative when a decision is made

Any decision on the use of a scarce resource implies that something must be given up. Economists define **opportunity cost** as the value of the item that has to be given up. For example, if you decide to spend 12 hours in class per week then you give up the opportunity to spend these 12 hours playing tennis or browsing on the Internet. The value you attach to those 12 hours is the opportunity cost of attending class. If you spend some money on lunch, you cannot spend the same money on another item. If you spend money from your bank account, you lose the opportunity to earn interest on the money.

When you spend money on an item, you may argue that there are many other ways to dispose of your money. What is the opportunity cost when there are many alternatives? The opportunity cost represents the value of the best, or most valuable, forgone alternative. For example, the opportunity cost associated with spending money on an item is the amount of interest that could have been earned had that money been left in the bank.

Note that you cannot escape opportunity costs. Every time you make a decision to use your resources in a specific way, you sacrifice the alternative. If you decide, for example, to pursue a career as a human resources professional, you will sacrifice the opportunity of a career in some other field. A knowledge of opportunity cost encourages you to consider all the alternatives.

Societies must contend with the scarcity of resources available to them. All societies face a limited amount of land, people, machinery, and equipment. If Canadians use land to build a college, for example, the land cannot be used for an apartment building at the same time. When decisions regarding the use of resources are made by the state, it is referred to as a **command system**. In command economies, there is very little individual freedom and the society's resources are owned by the state; decision making is centralized. In societies where decisions about resource use are made by individuals, a **free-market system** exists: resources are privately owned and the decision-making process is decentralized. Free-market economies are characterized by a great deal of individual freedom. These two approaches are extreme, and no country takes either one or the other. All economies combine the command system with the free-market system in what is referred to as a **mixed economy**: the state makes some of the decisions regarding the use of resources and individuals make the rest.

command system a system in which the decisions about resource use are made by the state

free-market system a system in which the decisions about resource use are made by individuals

mixed economy a combination of the command system and the free-market system

Canada has a mixed economy and this is evident in the labour market. Individuals are basically free to pursue careers of their choice. Governments in Canada, however, have put restrictions on the number of people who can practise in certain occupations. For example, there are restrictions on the number of dentists, physicians, or veterinarians who can practise their profession as there are restrictions on the number of taxi-cab operators and people who fish for lobster. Governments also impose restrictions on the employment arrangement. Laws have been enacted to set minimum wage rates, restrict hours of work, regulate safety conditions, and so on. Much of the discussion about labour markets in this text focuses on the impact of government regulation.

PRICE ELASTICITY

This section on price elasticity expands on the discussion of demand and supply curves introduced earlier in the chapter. You will recall from that discussion that the demand curve slopes down to the right. It is important to learn more about the demand for a product than to state simply that there is an inverse relationship between price and quantity demanded. How much does the quantity demanded increase when the price decreases? For some products, the price is an important factor in the decision to buy a product. If the price decreases, the quantity increases significantly. For other products, the price is not an important factor in the buying decision; changes in the price of the product will have little impact on the quantity demanded. Economists use the term **price elasticity of demand** to describe the responsiveness of quantity demanded to a change in the price.

price elasticity of demand   the responsiveness of quantity demanded to a change in price

If the percentage change in the quantity demanded is greater than the percentage change in the price, the demand is said to be elastic. For products with an elastic demand, the price is an important factor in the decision to purchase the product. If the percentage change in the quantity demanded is less than the percentage change in the price, the demand is said to be inelastic. For products with an inelastic demand, the price is not an important factor in the decision to purchase the product. Economists compute the price elasticity of demand as the percentage change in the quantity demanded divided by the percentage change in the price.

The formula to determine the price elasticity of demand is:

$$\text{coefficient of elasticity} = \frac{\text{\% change in the quantity demanded}}{\text{\% change in the price}}$$

If the above fraction is greater than one, the demand is elastic. If the fraction is less than one, the demand is inelastic.

The concept of price elasticity is useful, for example, in calculating what happens to total revenue when the price changes. The total revenue is the price multiplied by the quantity purchased. If the demand is elastic, a price decrease will result in an increase in total revenue. The percentage drop in price is more than offset by the percentage increase in quantity demanded. A price increase results in a decrease in total revenue. The percentage increase in price is larger than the percentage decline in demand. If the demand is inelastic, a price decrease reduces total revenue. The percentage drop in price is larger than the percentage increase in quantity demanded. A price increase raises total revenue.

The percentage increase in price exceeds the percentage fall in the quantity demanded.

There are three main factors that affect the elasticity of demand.

- *The number of substitutes.* For products with many substitutes, such as chocolate bars, the demand is more elastic. For products or services with few substitutes, such as cigarettes, hair cuts, or gasoline, the demand is inelastic.

- *Luxury versus necessity.* Necessities tend to have an inelastic demand. Basic telephone service is considered a necessity in North America. The elasticity is less than one. Diabetics need insulin to survive. The demand for insulin is very, if not totally, inelastic. Luxuries such as exotic travel tend to have elastic demand curves.

- *Percentage of income spent on product.* If a product takes up a large percentage of consumers' income, the demand tends to be elastic. Purchases of cars, household appliances, and furniture constitute major household expenditures. The price elasticity of demand for these items is greater than one. If only a small fraction of income is spent on a good, then a change in its price has little impact on the consumer's overall budget. The purchase of a pack of chewing gum does not have a significant impact on a household's budget. The demand for chewing gum is usually price inelastic.

The concept of price elasticity can also be applied to the supply side of the market, and is known as the **price elasticity of supply**. If the percentage change in the quantity supplied is greater than the percentage change in the price, the supply is said to be elastic. If the percentage change in the quantity supplied is less than the percentage change in the price, the supply is said to be inelastic.

price elasticity of supply the responsiveness of quantity supplied to a change in price

The formula for the price elasticity of supply is:

$$\text{coefficient of elasticity} = \frac{\% \text{ change in the quantity supplied}}{\% \text{ change in the price}}$$

If the above fraction is greater than one, the supply is said to be elastic. If the fraction is less than one, the supply is inelastic.

On the supply side of the market, a special case of elasticity sometimes occurs. A vertical supply curve indicates that the quantity supplied does not change in response to a change in price. This is a perfectly inelastic supply curve and carries a coefficient of zero. Examples of a perfectly inelastic supply are a limited edition of art prints or the amount available of a crop after harvest.

The main determining factor in the elasticity of supply is the time factor. The longer the period of time we are talking about, the more elastic the supply curve. Over a longer period of time suppliers have more opportunities to adjust the quantity supplied in response to the change in price. Car manufacturers can build additional plants, farmers can increase or reduce their livestock, and banks can add or close branches or change office space.

KEY TERMS

scarcity   46

opportunity cost   46

command system   47

free-market system   47

mixed economy   47

price elasticity of demand   48

price elasticity of supply   49

3

INSTITUTIONAL ASPECTS OF THE LABOUR MARKET

OBJECTIVES

After completing this chapter, you should be able to:

1. outline the jurisdictional responsibilities of the federal and provincial governments with respect to the labour market;
2. list the labour standards that have been enacted by various levels of government;
3. describe the history of employment insurance in Canada;
4. discuss the trends in union membership in Canada;
5. discuss the characteristics of union membership in Canada;
6. discuss the arguments for and against severance pay.

The previous chapter indicated that regulatory and institutional elements are more prevalent in the labour market than in most other markets. The first part of this chapter discusses government intervention in the Canadian labour market, and the responsibilities for the federal and provincial governments are reviewed. The regulations imposed by governments in Canada are discussed in the second part. These regulations can be grouped into the following categories: employment standards, human rights, health and safety, workers' compensation, employment insurance, and union–management relations. The chapter ends with a discussion of trends in union membership in Canada.

JURISDICTION

Labour markets in Canada are heavily regulated by government. Both levels of government, federal and provincial, have enacted legislation that affects the labour market. The powers and responsibilities associated with each level of government are outlined in the *Constitution Act, 1867*. With respect to the labour market, the federal government is responsible for labour legislation in certain industries and the provinces for the remaining industries. The federal government has the authority to regulate and control those industries of an interprovincial, national, and international nature such as railways, airlines, banks, grain elevators, shipping companies, radio and television stations, communication industries including telephone companies, uranium mining, and flour and feed companies. Interprovincial railways, bus lines, and trucking companies also fall under federal jurisdiction. The federal government also regulates the working conditions of employees who work for the federal government and for Crown corporations such as the Canadian Broadcasting Corporation. Companies with operations that have been declared to be of general advantage for Canada, or for two or more provinces, also fall under federal jurisdiction.

CLC jurisdiction

Canada Labour Code
labour standards and practices for industries that fall under federal jurisdiction, and for their employers and employees

The **Canada Labour Code** legislates employment standards and labour relations practices for industries that fall under federal jurisdiction, and for their employers and employees. Since the employees of federally regulated industries represent only a small percentage of all employees in Canada, the various provincial labour laws regulate the working conditions of most Canadians.

According to the Canadian constitution, the provinces are responsible for property matters and civil rights. This authority permits provincial governments to impose conditions on the relationship between employers and employees. This intervention varies by province and takes several forms. One form is legislation regulating labour relations, that is, union–management negotiations. Labour relations legislation covers the establishment of a union, negotiation of a collective agreement, certain aspects of a collective agreement, and the rules for the settlement of disputes. In addition to labour relations legislation, all provinces have legislation outlining basic employment standards such as minimum wage rates, vacations with pay, maximum hours of work, severance pay, and so on. Some provinces may have enacted certain employment standards that others do not. For example, not all provinces require employers to give advance notice to employees regarding termination of employment. Employment standards that are common to all provinces, such as the minimum wage rate and maximum hours of work, may also vary from province to province.

The territories in Canada are under federal government authority and are administered by the Department of Indian Affairs and Northern Development. Certain powers in the area of labour legislation have been delegated to the territories by the federal government.

Governments in Canada also interfere with the operation of labour markets by imposing payroll taxes on employers and employees. For example, employment insurance and the Canada Pension Plan are financed by employer and employee payroll deductions. Some provinces levy payroll taxes for other purposes. For example, in Ontario a payroll tax provides revenue for health care. The impact of payroll taxes on wages and employment is covered in Chapter 10.

GOVERNMENT INVOLVEMENT IN THE LABOUR MARKET

Government regulation of the employment relationship falls into the following categories:

- Employment standards
- Human rights
- Health and safety
- Workers' compensation
- Employment insurance
- Union–management relationships

EMPLOYMENT STANDARDS

All jurisdictions in Canada have enacted minimum employment standards. These standards are sometimes found in one piece of legislation, often called the Employment Standards Act; sometimes they are contained in several pieces. For example, there may be special legislation regulating hours of work, or there may be legislation specific to an industry such as construction or trucking. A discussion of the most common standards follows.

MINIMUM AGE.   All jurisdictions other than Quebec have minimum age requirements. That is, the legislation specifies an individual must be a minimum age before he or she can be hired. In general, the minimum age applies to all industries in a jurisdiction but some provinces have special considerations for specific industries. The minimum age requirements range from a low of 14 in Nova Scotia to a high of 17 for the federal government and the three territories. Six provinces have set the minimum age at 16, and Alberta and British Columbia have set the age at 15.

HOURS OF WORK.   All jurisdictions except New Brunswick place a statutory limit on the number of hours of work in a day or a week. (New Brunswick has a restriction only for those under 16 years of age.) Four provinces set only a weekly maximum. This maximum ranges from 40 hours per week in Newfoundland and 44 hours per week in Quebec to 48 hours in Nova Scotia and Prince Edward Island. The other jurisdictions specify both daily and weekly maximums. They establish eight hours per day as the maximum but the weekly maximum again varies

BOX 3.1 Homeworkers Enforcing Employment Standards

The federal and provincial governments hire employment standards officers to investigate complaints that companies are not complying with the minimum standards in compensating their employees. In order to carry out investigations into alleged violations, officers have the authority to enter a company's premises and to inspect payroll records.

In some industries, employees do not work on the company premises but operate from home. One industry that is making increasing use of homeworkers is the garment industry. The capital equipment (sewing machine) can be easily installed at home. The material is brought to the worker's home. Workers need not travel to a factory to sew clothes.

The drawback of homework for the individual worker is the lack of enforcement of employment standards. Homeworkers are covered under the legislation, but officers are not permitted to enter private homes unless invited. How do governments guarantee that employee compensation complies with the legislation? Homeworkers in the garment industry are paid "piece rate." That is, they are paid for each piece of clothing produced. The piece rate must be set so it at least matches the minimum hourly wage rate in the province. How can officers ensure that homeworkers are compensated fairly when the hours worked by homeworkers is not monitored?

from 40 to 48 hours. In some situations such as seasonal industries, the weekly maximum hours can be extended.

Mandated weekly rest periods are also provided in most jurisdictions. For some provinces, at least 24 consecutive hours of rest must be given in a period of a week; in others a longer consecutive rest period is prescribed. Most jurisdictions also mandate a meal break of one half hour after five consecutive hours of work.

OVERTIME PAY. All jurisdictions have legislated a requirement that employees receive a premium rate of pay for working an excessive number of hours in a day or a week. The definition of an excessive number of hours varies by province. Seven jurisdictions provide for a premium rate of pay after eight hours in a day in addition to having a weekly limit on hours before the overtime rate kicks in. Seven jurisdictions have legislated that overtime pay be earned after 40 hours in a week. Four jurisdictions have set 44 hours and two jurisdictions have set 48 hours as the weekly limit before the premium pay begins to apply. The most common premium rate of pay is 1.5 times the regular rate of pay. Newfoundland states that employees must receive at least $7.12 per hour for every hour worked in excess of 40 in a week. British Columbia has legislated that two times the hourly rate must be paid for hours worked in excess of 48 in a week in addition to the requirement that 1.5 times the hourly rate be paid for hours worked in excess of 40 per week.

VACATIONS WITH PAY. Granting employees an annual paid vacation is a relatively recent employment standard. After World War II, one week's paid vacation began appearing in collective agreements. Following the lead of provisions inserted in collective agreements, governments imposed annual paid-vacation requirements. At present, all jurisdictions provide for at least two weeks of paid vacation after one year of employment. In addition to the two weeks' vacation time, employers are usually required to give the employee a minimum of 4% of the employee's annual earnings. Saskatchewan is alone in legislating a minimum of three weeks' vacation and payment of 3/52 of one's annual earnings after one year of employment; the province has also legislated four weeks' annual vacation after 10 years of service with an employer. The following jurisdictions have provisions for three weeks' vacation: the federal government, Northwest Territories and Nunavut, Quebec, British Columbia, and Alberta.

STATUTORY HOLIDAYS. In addition to annual paid vacations, certain days are designated as statutory holidays. Employees are entitled to the day off and, in most cases, are entitled to be paid for the day as well. All jurisdictions have the following statutory holidays: New Year's Day, Good Friday, Canada Day, Labour Day, and Christmas Day. The federal government and Ontario have declared Boxing Day to be a statutory holiday. Victoria Day is a statutory holiday in all jurisdictions with the exception of New Brunswick, Nova Scotia, and Newfoundland. The first Monday in August is a holiday in British Columbia, New Brunswick, Saskatchewan, the Northwest Territories, and Nunavut. Some provinces have designated Remembrance Day and Thanksgiving Day as statutory holidays.

MINIMUM WAGE RATE. All jurisdictions have legislated a minimum wage rate, although there are numerous exceptions and not all employees are entitled to receive a minimum hourly wage rate. For industries that fall under federal jurisdiction, the minimum wage rate is aligned with the equivalent in the province where the employees work.

Economic conditions vary by province. The industrial composition of the economy also varies by province. As a result, the minimum wage rates vary greatly by province, from \$5.00 per hour to \$7.00 per hour. During poor economic times, the minimum wage rate is rarely adjusted; when the economy is expanding, the minimum wage rate is increased more frequently.

PAY EQUITY. Concern over the difference in wages that has existed between men and women has prompted governments to enact legislation that attempts to address the situation. Initially provinces simply stated that equal pay must be given for equal work. The legislation was altered to state that equal pay must be given for similar or substantially similar work. The latter requirement applies in Alberta and British Columbia and in the private sector in Manitoba, Newfoundland, New Brunswick, Nova Scotia, Prince Edward Island, Saskatchewan, the Northwest Territories, Nunavut, and the Yukon. Since in many situations men and women do not do the same job, some jurisdictions have legislated that equal pay must be given for work of equal value, or **pay equity**. This approach requires that a definition of a job's value be developed, and has been adopted by the federal government and by the public sector in the Yukon.

The implementation of pay equity legislation relies on the complaint system. That is, if a worker believes that he or she is underpaid, the worker can file a complaint to have the situation investigated.

pay equity equal pay for work of equal value

Several provinces, however, are taking a proactive approach that shifts the burden of implementation from the employee to the employer, on the assumption that reasons for the male–female wage differential are deeply rooted in the economy and cannot be remedied by complaints alone. Employers must review their compensation procedures to ensure that their practices comply with the legislation. This compulsory review has been adopted in both the private and public sector in Ontario and Quebec and in the public sectors in Manitoba, New Brunswick, Newfoundland, Nova Scotia, and Prince Edward Island.

A discussion of the impact of pay equity legislation on the labour market appears in Chapter 11.

OTHER STANDARDS. Several other employment standards have been enacted across the country. These standards include maternity leave and adoption leave, bereavement leave, **severance pay**, and advance notice of termination.

severance pay a lump-sum payment to an employee upon termination of employment

BOX 3.2 The Rationale for Severance Pay

During the period of high unemployment in the 1980s, many unions negotiated severance pay clauses with their employers. Upon termination of employment, the employee received a lump-sum severance package, the size of which depended on the person's tenure with the company. As more collective agreements contained provisions for severance pay, and as unemployment persisted, pressure was put on governments to include some form of severance pay in employment standards legislation. Is there a valid argument for government-legislated severance pay? Upon termination should the employee receive a financial payment?

The first argument in favour of paying severance pay is based on the belief that employees earn ownership of their jobs. The longer an employee works at a job, the more the job belongs to the employee. If the employee is terminated from a job, the employee

should be compensated. This argument parallels that of government confiscation of one's property. If your property is expropriated for a new highway or airport, you should be compensated for the loss of something that you own. Similarly, if your job is taken away from you, compensation should be forthcoming.

In collective agreements and legislation, employees with more seniority are entitled to more severance pay. It can be argued that seniority rules benefit the company as well as the employee. When benefits are provided to those with more seniority, there is less turnover in the labour force. Employees tend to remain with the company, knowing they are eligible for a severance package if their employment is terminated. Thus, hiring and training costs are reduced.

BOX 3.2 The Rationale for Severance Pay (Continued)

A second argument in favour of severance pay is that employees are usually paid less than they are worth in the first years of employment with a company. In their last years with the company, employees are usually paid more than would be warranted by their productivity. If an employee stays with a company until retirement, the years of underpayment are usually matched by the years of overpayment. If an employee is terminated before the age of retirement has been reached, there will be more years of underpayment that are not matched by years of overpayment. Therefore, employees should be compensated for those years of underpayment.

The counter-argument claims that many employees are overpaid in their initial years with a company. While learning a job, productivity is low. Employees are paid more than they are worth in order to attract good employees and establish a stable workforce. Overpaying new employees may be a characteristic of firms that promote from within the organization. The firm expects to get more productivity once the employee has experience with the firm. Therefore, if an employee is terminated before retirement, there is no need for further compensation since the years of overpayment have outnumbered the years of underpayment.

The type of training received on the job provides another argument for severance pay. If the training is specific to the company, and only to that company, it may be difficult for the employee to find other employment upon termination. The employee has invested in learning this skill and the company has benefited, so the employee should be compensated for the loss of the job. A counter-argument asserts that the return on any investment is uncertain. Some people lose money on their investments. Why should the same logic not apply to investing in a career? Maybe the career investment will pay off, and maybe

it will not. If the terminated employee were highly trained in a company-specific skill, the salary previously earned by that employee may have been relatively high. The high salary would be a sufficient return gained on the investment in learning a skill.

Not all training given by companies is specific. If the training received by the employee is general in nature, it can be transferred to other companies so the likelihood of finding new employment is much improved. Under these circumstances, there may be no obligation for the company to give the employee a severance package.

In occupations with a high likelihood of termination, the wage rate often compensates for this unattractive feature. Employees in these jobs earn more than they would in jobs with a lower risk of termination. Under these circumstances, the argument in favour of severance pay is not strong. Conversely, those analysts who argue in favour of severance pay believe that one's weekly paycheque does not include payment for a possible loss of employment.

Arguments for severance pay can also be made on the basis of income distribution. Some employees may be terminated because of advances in technology; with the introduction of new technology, some benefit while others are harmed. For example, the public may benefit because the product is improved and available at a lower cost. The company may benefit from more sales and higher profits. Should those who benefit from the new technology compensate those who are hurt (by loss of employment) by that technology? Unfortunately, it may be difficult to identify the winners and losers in such situations. Furthermore, if all society benefits from an innovation, should the company that introduces the innovation be expected to bear the entire burden of paying severance pay?

Should severance pay be awarded if worker termination comes from a change in government policy? For example, the Canadian government has pursued a policy of freer trade with other nations. Trade barriers have been dropped. Industries and workers once shielded from international competition are now forced to compete. Who should compensate these workers if they are terminated because of their company's inability to compete? If they were protected from international competition in the past, their earnings were probably higher than they otherwise would have been. Should the workers also be compensated for loss of employment? Some countries have established redundancy funds to pay those who have been terminated because of changes in government policy and technology. Other countries offer retraining, counselling, and assistance with mobility.

HUMAN RIGHTS

In 1948, the United Nations adopted the Universal Declaration of Human Rights, which states the principle of equal rights for all individuals regardless of race, religion, gender, or language. Canadian jurisdictions followed suit by passing legislation prohibiting discriminatory practices in employment. The legislation covers employers, employer and employee associations, and employment agencies. Employment discrimination is defined as any preference or exclusion that impairs the equality of opportunity in employment or in conditions of employment. Legislation in all jurisdictions in Canada prohibit discrimination based on race, place of origin, colour, religion, marital status, physical and mental disability, and gender.

All jurisdictions forbid employment discrimination based on age, although not all jurisdictions apply the same age range. In Alberta, individuals 18 years of age and older are covered by human rights legislation. In British Columbia and Newfoundland, those who are between 19 years and 65 years of age are covered. In Ontario and Saskatchewan, the legislation covers individuals between 18 and 65 years of age. The other provinces make general references to age in terms of the minimum and maximum ages for employment.

Freedom of political belief, conviction, and opinion are covered in human rights legislation in British Columbia, Manitoba, Newfoundland, Prince Edward Island, Quebec, and the Yukon. All provinces with the exception of Prince Edward Island prohibit discrimination based on sexual orientation. In the jurisdictions of Ontario,

Quebec, the Northwest Territories, and the federal government, discrimination against those who have been pardoned for an offence is forbidden.

Closely related to human rights is legislation aimed at achieving **employment equity**. The goal is to create a work environment in which all barriers to employment have been removed and equitable treatment of employees exists. The push for employment equity came from the concern over employment issues facing women, racial minorities, aboriginal people, and people with disabilities. Human rights legislation deals with intentional discrimination. Employment equity regulations aim at both intentional and systemic discrimination, which can occur in human resources practices and policies that on the surface appear to be neutral. The regulations are proactive as opposed to dealing with complaints.

At present, only the federal government has mandatory employment equity regulations. Ontario has a voluntary Equal Opportunity Plan whereby government will help employers diversify their workforces. The federal government and Quebec have regulations that require those who do business with the government to practise employment equity. The remaining provinces handle employment equity through affirmative action programs.

employment equity
a work environment in which all barriers to employment have been removed and equitable treatment of employees exists

HEALTH AND SAFETY

All jurisdictions have a form of health and safety legislation for the workplace. The common practice is to give the government the right to enforce regulations regarding safety in the workplace. The regulations require employers to help ensure the safety of an employee. In all provinces except British Columbia, occupational health and safety legislation is separate from workers' compensation legislation. A common element of safety legislation is the right of an employee to refuse to perform unsafe work.

One outcome of governments' efforts in this area is the Workplace Hazardous Materials Information System (WHMIS). It is based on the belief that employees have the right to be informed about the handling, storage, and disposal of hazardous chemicals in the workplace.

WORKERS' COMPENSATION

Ontario was the first jurisdiction to introduce workers' compensation in 1915. All provinces now have workers' compensation, although Prince Edward Island did not introduce it until 1949 and Newfoundland did not until 1951. This legislation provides that workers who sustain personal injuries on the job or are disabled by industrial diseases are entitled to compensation. The compensation fund is financed by contributions from employers. In return, employees give up the right to take legal action against employers.

EMPLOYMENT INSURANCE

The introduction of employment insurance in Canada required a change to the constitution. In 1935, the federal government introduced the *Employment and Social Insurance Act,* which was later found to be unconstitutional as it interfered with provincial jurisdiction in the areas of property and civil rights. The change to the constitution, introduced in 1940, gave the federal government exclusive jurisdiction in the field of unemployment insurance legislation. The initial legislation was updated in 1955 and named the *Unemployment Insurance Act.* It provided income support for individuals during a temporary interruption of earnings, with an emphasis on returning to the ranks of the employed as soon as possible. Contributions to the unemployment insurance fund were paid by both employers and employees. Contributions and benefits were based on the individual's insurable earnings, with a ceiling on the amount that was insurable.

In 1971, the legislation was redrafted to cover more employees: 90% of the labour force was covered against loss of employment income. An individual could now receive up to two thirds of his or her insurable earnings; however, benefits became taxable, so the net income gain from benefits was reduced. Eligibility requirements were reduced to as low as eight weeks of employment and the maximum benefit period increased. Benefits were provided to those whose employment was interrupted by illness or pregnancy. A lump-sum payment was made to individuals who retired from employment.

After 1971, more changes were made to the legislation, including basing eligibility requirements on the unemployment rate in the area, reducing benefits to 60% of earnings, and including pension income and severance pay as earnings. It also improved maternity leave, introduced adoption leave, and granted paternity leave to fathers in the event of the mother's death or incapacity.

Because the contributions from employers and employees were not enough to meet the obligations of the fund in the past, the federal government subsidized the unemployment insurance fund. In 1992, the government stated that it would no longer do so: the fund was now to be fully financed by employer and employee contributions. In addition, the number of weeks of employment to qualify for benefits was increased and no lump-sum payment was to be made to those 65 years of age and above. In 1993, quitters were disqualified from receiving benefits, and the benefits for new claimants was reduced to 57% of earnings.

Effective January 1, 1997, the *Unemployment Insurance Act* became the *Employment Insurance Act*. Employers were required to withhold employment insurance premiums from all employees—full time, part time, and casual. Benefits were now based on hours of work rather than weeks of employment. The minimum number of hours ranged from 420 to 700 hours in the previous year, depending on the unemployment rate in the area, an increase from the minimum 15 hours per week previously required. New entrants into the labour force needed 910 hours of work to qualify for benefits. Individuals who received less than $200 a week in benefits could earn up to $50 a week without a reduction in benefits, and benefits were increased for low-income individuals with children. Individuals who made frequent claims would receive reduced benefits. The responsibility for the administration of the employment insurance program was given to Human Resources Development Canada.

Union–Management Relationships

All jurisdictions regulate the interaction between employers and the representatives of the employees, be they craft unions, industrial unions, or professional associations. Whereas individuals can negotiate employment conditions with employers, groups of employees need special legislation for those negotiations. Once workers are represented by trade unions, they can no longer negotiate as individuals.

Union Membership

Many of the employment standards discussed so far have been established only recently. Before these were legislated, employees relied on group pressure—mainly from trade unions—to force management to improve the working conditions. In fact, many standards were copied from the wording of collective agreements.

Only one third of Canadian employees are represented by a union. The percentage varies considerably between the public and private sectors and between industries. As shown in Table 3.1, approximately 76%

TABLE 3.1 EMPLOYEES (IN THOUSANDS) COVERED BY A UNION CONTRACT, CANADA, 1998

INDUSTRY	TOTAL EMPLOYEES	NUMBER OF EMPLOYEES COVERED BY A UNION CONTRACT	PERCENT OF EMPLOYEES COVERED BY A UNION CONTRACT
Total	11 801.2	3906.4	33.1
Public sector	2086.7	1591.5	76.3
Private sector	9714.5	2314.9	23.8
Agriculture	138.0	5.5	4.0
Other primary	229.7	65.0	28.3
Manufacturing	2137.2	742.0	34.7
Construction	484.1	141.7	29.3
Utilities	135.8	93.5	68.9
Transportation, storage, communications	801.8	384.4	47.9
Trade	1995.2	262.4	13.2
Finance, insurance, and personal services	4413.5	1574.8	35.7
Business services	739.9	58.6	7.9
Educational services	928.5	676.8	(72.9) _Highest_
Health and social services	1312.4	693.8	52.9
Accommodation and food services	815.8	66.8	8.2
Other services	616.9	78.9	12.8
Public administration	794.3	564.9	71.1

Source: Adapted from Statistics Canada. (1999, January). *Labour Force Update: An Overview of the 1998 Labour Market.* Ottawa: Statistics Canada, p. 35. (Catalogue no. 71-005-XPB).

of public sector employees belong to a union compared to about 24% of private sector employees. Public sector employees account for approximately 18% of the labour force but represent over 40% of the total trade union membership in Canada. As a percentage of the labour force, union membership ranges from 4% in agriculture to 72.9% in educational services. Heavily unionized industries, apart from those already mentioned, include utilities and health and social services.

Union membership varies according to gender. There are more male union members than female union members, although the number of women in unions is growing and the number of men is declining. In the 1960s, about 80% of union members in Canada were men. In the 1990s, that percentage had fallen to about 55%. About 30% of male workers belong to a union while the percentage for females is approximately 33%. The decline in the percentage of male membership is partly due to the shift in employment from goods-producing industries, which are heavily unionized and where men are over-represented, to the service sector of the economy, which is less unionized.

Union density is the ratio of the number of employees who belong to a union to the total number of paid employees. In 1967, union density in Canada was 33.2%, with 40.9% for men and 15.9% for women. By 1997, union density had fallen overall to 31.1%. It had fallen to 32.4% for men but had increased to 29.6% for women. Union density also varies by province: Newfoundland has the highest at 39% while Alberta has the lowest at 22%.

There are also age and educational differences in union membership. Only 11% of employees under 24 years of age are unionized; 44% of employees between 45 years and 54 years are unionized. The rate is higher among workers with higher levels of education.

union density ratio of the number of employees belonging to a union to the total number of paid employees

SUMMARY

Both the federal and provincial governments have jurisdiction over working conditions in Canada. The federal government has the authority to regulate and control those industries of an interprovincial, national, or international nature. The provinces are responsible for civil and property rights in Canada, which allows them to impose conditions on the employment relationship. The territories fall under federal government jurisdiction and are administered by the Department of Indian Affairs and Northern Development.

Government regulation of the employment relationship falls into the following categories: employment standards, human rights, health and safety, workers' compensation, employment insurance, and union–management relationships.

Only about one third of all employees in Canada belong to a labour union. Approximately 76% of public sector employees belong to a union, compared to only 24% of private sector employees. Since 1990, union membership has declined slightly. Union density in Canada is just over 30%.

KEY TERMS

Canada Labour Code 52

pay equity 56

severance pay 57

employment equity 60

union density 64

EXERCISES

1. List the labour legislation in your province or territory.

2. Write a brief summary of a relatively unknown labour statute in your province or territory. You may come across legislation that applies only to certain industries. For example, students in Ontario may review the *Industrial Standards Act.*

3. Human rights legislation aims to prevent discrimination based on age, yet the Supreme Court has upheld the rights of employers to force employees to retire at age 65. In your opinion, is this practice discriminatory?

4. The number of weeks that an individual is permitted to receive employment insurance benefits varies according to the number of weeks of insured earnings and the region in which the individual resides. What are the maximum weeks of benefits in your area?

5. If you are currently employed, determine whether your working conditions are regulated by federal or provincial legislation.

6. What industries other than the garment industry frequently use homeworkers?

REFERENCES

Akyeampong, E. B. (1998). The Rise of Unionization Among Women. *Perspectives on Labour and Income, 10*(4): 36–39.

CCH Canadian Limited. (1993, regularly updated). *Canadian Labour Law Reporter.* Don Mills, Ontario.

Craig, A. W. J., and Solomon, N. A. (1996). *The System of Industrial Relations in Canada* (5th ed.). Scarborough: Prentice Hall.

Mainville, D., and Olineck, C. (1999). Unionization in Canada: A Retrospective. Supplement to *Perspectives on Labour and Income.* Ottawa: Statistics Canada.

Part II

Trends and Recent Developments in the Canadian Labour Market

PART II

TRENDS AND RECENT DEVELOPMENTS IN THE CANADIAN LABOUR MARKET

This text explores the operation and outcomes of the Canadian labour market. Before we study how the labour market works in detail, we will outline the major trends and developments in the Canadian labour market since World War II.[1] The purpose, at this point, is to establish the developments and labour market outcomes that will be explained in later chapters. The importance of providing first observations on the labour market before developing theories is important. As Sherlock Holmes says, "It is a capital mistake to theorise before all facts are in. Insensibly one begins to twist facts to suit theories, instead of theories to fit facts."

What kind of information do labour economists use to develop and test their theories? Casual personal observation provides one source. For example, someone looking for a job learns whether, and under which conditions, firms are hiring. A member of a collective bargaining team gains particular insight into how wages are determined at the local level. Most of us work for pay at some time in our lives, so most of us have some sense of how the labour market operates; however, although our own experience may provide some insight, personal experience cannot cover all aspects of the labour market. We must therefore be careful not to rely solely on personal experience when analyzing the Canadian labour market.

Statistics provide a more systematic and objective source of information about the labour market than personal experiences can. This information is mostly obtained from government-run surveys of households and businesses. The statistics are like a snapshot and summarize the state of the labour market at a particular time point.[2] Most of the data presented in the following chapters come from these surveys.

---

1. Unfortunately, trends for several variables cannot be traced back to the mid or late 1940s. This is due to lack of appropriate surveys in earlier years or due to revisions in survey questionnaires that resulted in inconsistent data over time. For example, some of the time series considered in this text start in 1976 because the Labour Force Survey questionnaire was significantly changed in 1975.

2. In Appendix B to Part II we provide a brief guide to the most important surveys and the type of data derived from them.

When we look at this information over a number of years, we can identify trends in the Canadian labour market.

Part II of the text is divided into four chapters. The order of presentation of the chapters is related to the concepts of demand and supply. To paraphrase the late British economist Alfred Marshall, it takes both demand and supply to determine market outcomes as it takes two blades of a pair of scissors to cut cloth. In Canada, important structural changes on both the supply side and the demand side have been transforming the Canadian labour market and the nature of work.

Chapter 4 discusses the trends in the labour force, which represent the supply side of the labour market. Trends on the demand side are presented in Chapter 5 with the emphasis on employment, which is only part of the demand side; job vacancies are the other part. However, because we have no data on vacancies, we use employment as a proxy for demand. Chapters 6 and 7 consider the outcomes of the interaction between demand and supply: long-run changes in unemployment and the level of compensation for those who are employed.

4

GROWTH OF THE CANADIAN LABOUR FORCE

OBJECTIVES

After completing this chapter you should be able to:

1. evaluate the factors that bring about changes in the labour force;
2. explain changes in domestic population;
3. discuss reasons for changes in net immigration;
4. explain changes in the labour force participation rates for men and women;
5. explain the impact of the "baby boom" on the labour force;
6. describe changes in the gender composition of the labour force.

THE LABOUR FORCE

In order to determine the amount of labour available to the economy, it is necessary to distinguish between the quantity and the quality of labour supplied. The quantity depends on the size of the population, the proportion of the population that desires work, and the hours of work that individuals are willing to make available per year. The quality depends on such factors as the level of education, skills, and the health of the workforce, which we will discuss in Chapter 12. The total labour supply in an economy includes those who are working (the employed) and those seeking work (the unemployed). The sum of all employed and unemployed individuals in a country is called the **labour force,** which we use throughout this text to mean the total labour supply. That is:

labour force = total labour supply = number of employed + number of unemployed

How is the size of the labour force established? Each month, Statistics Canada releases statistics based on a survey of households, called the Labour Force Survey (LFS).[1] For each survey, about 1 in every 200 Canadian households is asked a series of questions about the labour market status of its members. Based on the answers, each adult (aged 15 and older) in each surveyed household is placed into one of three categories:

Employed

Unemployed

Not in the labour force

A person is considered **employed** if he or she did any work at all for pay or profit during the week prior to the week of the survey (the reference week). The definition also includes any household member who worked without pay in a family enterprise. To be counted as **unemployed**, a person must be without work, must be available for work, and must have actively looked for work within the past four weeks. Individuals who have not searched for work but who expect to start working soon, either because they are on temporary layoff or they are waiting to start a new job within four weeks, are also counted as unemployed. A person who is neither employed nor unemployed is **not in the labour force**. These are people who are either retired, who are in school full time, who are at home looking after their own children, or

labour force the total number of workers, including both the employed and unemployed

employed describes a person who works for pay or profit during the reference week of the Labour Force Survey

unemployed describes a person without work, available for work, and looking for work

not in the labour force describes a person who is neither employed nor unemployed

---

1. See Appendix B to Part II for more information on the Labour Force Survey. Appendix C is the questionnaire.

who are not looking for work for some other reason. Adding the total number of employed and unemployed people from the LFS, Statistics Canada computes the labour force for every month.

Since the end of World War II, there have been two outstanding developments on the supply side of the labour market. The first relates to the growth in the size of the labour force; the second reflects major changes in the age and gender composition of the labour force. The growth of the labour force will be discussed first.

Figure 4.1 shows the growth of the Canadian labour force over the last five decades. In 1947, 4.9 million people were members of the labour force. By 1998, the labour force had grown by about 220% to

FIGURE 4.1 LABOUR FORCE GROWTH, 1947–98

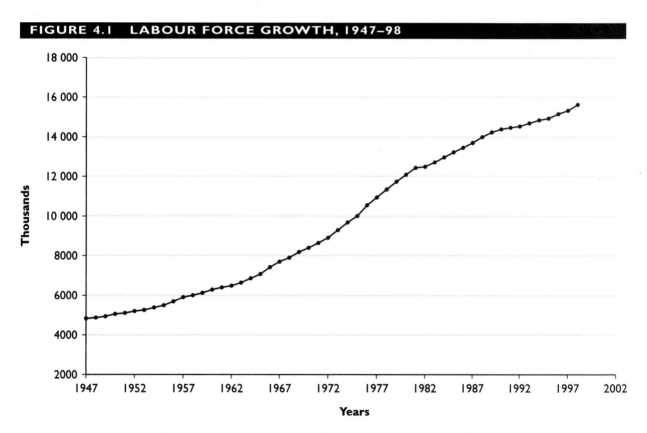

Notes: Annual data prior to 1950 exclude Newfoundland.

Estimates prior to 1966 are based on persons aged 14 and over.

Estimates from 1966 include persons aged 15 and over.

Estimates from 1966 to 1974 have been adjusted to conform to current concepts. Estimates prior to 1966 have not been revised.

Sources: For 1947–94, adapted from Statistics Canada. (1995). *Canadian Economic Observer, Historical Statistical Supplement 1994/95*. Ottawa: Statistics Canada. (Catalogue no. 11-210); for 1995–98, adapted from Statistics Canada. (1999, July). *Canadian Economic Observer, Statistical Summary*. Ottawa: Statistics Canada. (Catalogue no. 11-010).

15.6 million people. From 1950 to 1980, the Canadian labour force experienced growth rates unsurpassed among western industrialized countries. Growth was particularly strong between 1966 and 1978, with annual growth rates varying from 3.3% to 3.7%. In the last two decades of the century, growth slowed down. Annual average growth rates were 1.8% in the 1980s; during the 1990s the rates averaged only about 1%.

Part of the decline in the growth rate of the labour force can be attributed to the fact that growth is an exponential phenomenon. The growth rate is calculated based on the labour force of the previous year, which is constantly increasing. As the labour force grows each year, the number of entrants required to maintain a constant growth rate must also grow exponentially. The difference between an annual growth rate of 3% and 1% becomes clear if one realizes that growth at 3% a year implies a doubling of the labour force in about 23 years.[2] If the growth rate falls to 1%, the doubling time drops to 70 years.

Figure 4.2 outlines the factors that determine changes in the labour force. Let us start with the **working-age population**, also called the labour force source population. The LFS defines the working-age population as the Canadian population aged 15 years or over, excluding members of the Armed Forces, institutional residents such as inmates in prisons or psychiatric hospitals, persons living on Indian reserves and residents of Yukon, Nunavut, and the Northwest Territories.[3]

The percentage of the working-age population participating in the labour force, either through employment or the search for employment, is called the **labour force participation rate** (LFPR):

$$\text{labour force participation rate} =$$
$$(\text{labour force} \div \text{working-age population}) \times 100$$

For example, in 1998, the working-age population comprised 24 012 million people of whom 15 632 million were in the labour force (14 326 employed and 1305 unemployed), resulting in an LFPR of 65.1%.

The labour force grows as the population increases. As shown in Figure 4.2, the growth in the working-age population results from increases in the domestic population and changes in international migration.[4] The country's domestic population is affected by fertility and mortality rates. The right side of Figure 4.2 shows the withdrawals

working-age population (labour force source population) the Canadian population aged 15 years and over excluding members of the Armed Forces, institutional residents, persons living on Indian reserves, and residents of the Yukon, Nunavut, and the Northwest Territories

labour force participation rate the percentage of the working-age population that is in the labour force

---

2. The convenient way to calculate how long it takes for a quantity to double, if we know its exponential growth rate, is to divide the growth rate into the number 70.

3. These exclusions account for roughly 2% of the population of working age.

4. Changes in international migration are the net result of subtracting the number of emigrants from the total number of immigrants.

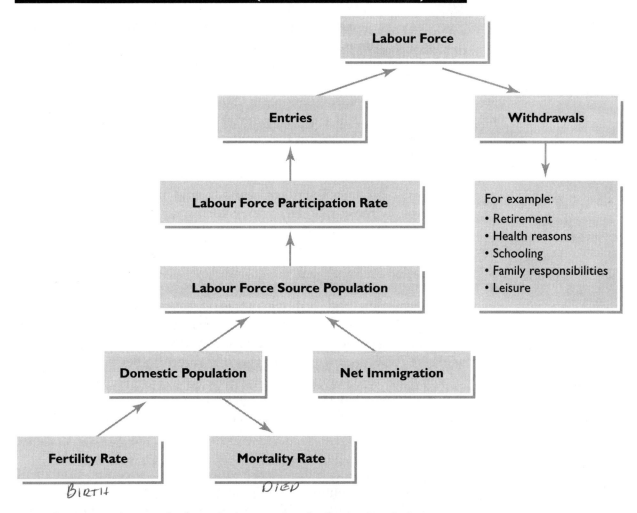

FIGURE 4.2   LABOUR FORCE (SUPPLY OF LABOUR)

Labour Force

Entries

Withdrawals

Labour Force Participation Rate

For example:
• Retirement
• Health reasons
• Schooling
• Family responsibilities
• Leisure

Labour Force Source Population

Domestic Population

Net Immigration

Fertility Rate

BIRTH

Mortality Rate

DIED

from the labour force, which include people who have decided to retire or to return to school full time. It also includes those who are forced to quit work for health or family reasons. The net change in the labour force is determined by subtracting the withdrawals from the entries into the labour force.

THE POPULATION BASE

From 1947 to 1998, the working-age population in Canada grew from 9 million to 24 million, an increase of 167%. As mentioned above, the changes in the population base come from changes in the domestic population and from net immigration. Each of these changes is discussed below.

GROWTH OF THE DOMESTIC POPULATION

Since the early 1960s, domestic or natural population growth in Canada has declined almost without interruption from about 2% in 1961 to 1% in 1997. **Natural population growth** is the balance between the total number of births and deaths. The **birth rate**, that is, the number of births per 1000 of population, has fallen from 28 in the late 1950s to approximately 12 in 1997. This decline mirrors the decline in the **fertility rate**, which measures the number of births per 1000 women aged 15 to 49 years. In 1959, there was an average of 3.9 births per woman. In the 1990s, the fertility rate was approximately 1.7 births per woman. The lowest provincial fertility rate is found in Newfoundland (1.3) while the highest rate is in the Northwest Territories, including Nunavut (2.7).

The **mortality rate** is the number of deaths per 1000 persons. In the last 30 years, it has hardly deviated from the 7.0 mark (7.4 in the late 1960s and 7.2 in 1997). Since microbial disease is no longer frequently fatal, preventive and curative medicine has made great inroads in fighting cardiovascular diseases, which had been rising steadily since the beginning of the 20th century. While mortality rates for these causes of death have declined, rates of deaths due to other causes, such as cancer, have been rising.

The long-run decline in Canada's birth rate together with the small changes in the mortality rate have led to the continuous decrease in the net growth of Canada's domestic population. Since the aging of the population is accompanied by an increase in the number of deaths— even if the mortality rates were reduced—and since the number of births is likely to continue to fall, natural population growth is bound to decrease further. If Canada is to sustain its past population growth, it will have to rely more heavily on immigration.

IMMIGRATION

Net immigration is the difference between the number of immigrants and the number of emigrants. Net immigration has played a vital role in Canada's demographic, economic, social, and cultural development for more than a century. Immigrants have been an important source of labour supply. Their spending, which stimulates the demand for goods and services, has also contributed significantly to increases in the demand for labour. The level of immigration has varied considerably. It is estimated that over the last 100 years, net immigration has contributed one fifth of total population growth. Since World War II, immigration to Canada has been strongly related to the business cycle. If the

---

natural population growth   the balance between the number of births and deaths

birth rate   number of births per 1000 of population

fertility rate   the number of births per 1000 women aged 15 to 49 years

mortality rate   the number of deaths per 1000 of population

AN INTRODUCTION TO THE CANADIAN LABOUR MARKET

economy was booming, immigration was increasing. During the early and mid 1950s, when the resource sector of the economy was booming, one half of the growth of Canada's labour force came from immigrants. In the peak year of 1957, 282 000 immigrants entered Canada. In the late 1950s, the contribution of immigration to the overall labour force growth started to decline. By 1966, immigration accounted for only 12% of labour force growth; by 1975, the contribution had dropped to 6%.

Reflecting the slowdown in economic growth, the peaks in immigration following 1957 were lower. In 1967 and 1974, the numbers peaked at about 220 000 immigrants (see Figure 4.3). In 1980, the number of immigrants fell to 140 000. The severe recession in 1981/82, in combination with restrictive immigration policies in place since the end of 1982, resulted in a dramatic decline in immigration, which reached a low of 84 000 new arrivals in 1985.

recession a period during which the total production of goods and services falls

A period in which total production of goods and services in an economy falls is called a **recession**.[5] Recessions are associated with high

FIGURE 4.3   NUMBER OF IMMIGRANTS AND IMMIGRATION RATE, 1944–97

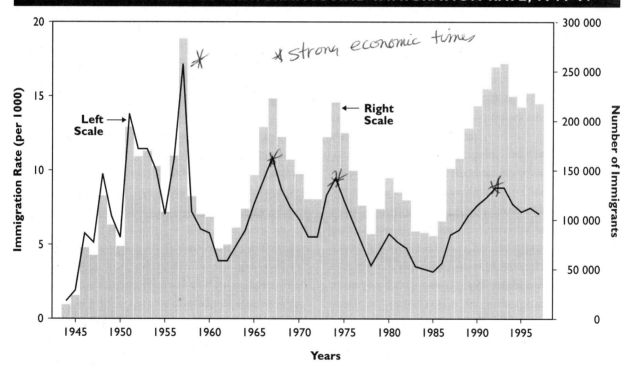

Note: Data are preliminary as of January 20, 1998.

Sources: Employment and Immigration Canada, *Immigration Statistics*, and after 1993, Citizenship and Immigration Canada, unpublished data. Reproduced with the permission of the Minister of Public Works and Government Services Canada, 1999.

---

5. By standard definition, a recession occurs when the real gross domestic product declines for at least two consecutive quarters. There are other more complex definitions. For a survey of how some of these apply to Canada, see Cross (1996).

unemployment as firms reduce hours of work and lay off workers to adjust their production levels to the declining demand for their products. As unemployment among domestic workers rises, the federal government generally reduces the annual target number of immigrants accepted to Canada. After reaching a trough in 1985, immigration rose sharply again, doubling in three years to almost 161 000 in 1988. Between 1990 and 1997, Canada granted permanent resident status to more than 1.8 million people, representing an annual average of close to 230 000 persons. Not since the settlement of the Prairies before the outbreak of World War I has there been such a sustained period of strong immigration. Although the deep recession of 1990/91 again led to a fall in the number of immigrants, the decline was less steep than in previous recessions. In each of the following four years, new immigrants still numbered between 210 000 and 220 000. In 1997, an estimated 216 000 immigrants entered Canada. The strong influx of immigrants coincides with the slower pace in the domestic population growth raising once more the importance of immigration in demographic terms. During the period of 1991 to 1997, more than half (51.4%) of the Canadian population growth was attributable to international migration.

Historically, the majority of immigrants to Canada originated in European countries. However, sources of immigration have shifted away from Europe toward the Pacific Rim countries. This has significant implications for the skill, demographic, and cultural mix of the labour force. A comparison of the differences between the immigration intake in 1969 and 1988, two years in which Canada accepted almost the same number of people, yields interesting results: In 1969, 22 countries produced more than 1000 immigrants each, accounting for 132 000 of the 161 000 persons accepted. In 1988, 37 countries produced more than 1000 immigrants each, for an almost identical total of 133 000 of the 161 000. For the first time, Asia supplied more than half (51.4%) of these immigrants. Only seven countries on the 1969 list were developing countries. By 1988, six countries, including Australia and four in Europe, were no longer major sources of immigrants to Canada, and the 1988 list included some 15 other developing countries. These changes illustrate the rapidly growing diversity in the source countries of new Canadians. Throughout the 1990s, countries such as the former Hong Kong, China, Philippines, and India continued to increase their share of total immigration. In 1996, immigrants from Asian countries represented 64% of total immigration.

Canadian immigration policy has been shaped by economic self-interest and humanitarian concerns. These two dimensions are reflected in the division of immigrants into two classes: the assessed and non-assessed classes. The assessed classes include all immigrants admitted to Canada on the basis of their likely positive contribution to the Canadian economy. The assessed classes are now referred to as economic classes, which include the traditional independent immigrants (admitted according to a point system based mainly on educational and occupational skill levels), the business class (entrepreneurs, inventors, and self-employed), assisted relatives (evaluated according to the assessment unit system for their skill qualifications but rewarded additional points for having relatives in Canada), and others (admitted under special occupational programs, for example, nannies and domestic services). The non-assessed classes include immediate family members and refugees. Immigrants in the non-assessed classes are

BOX 4.1 How Do Immigrants Fare After Their Arrival in Canada?

Two recurrent issues in the debate over Canada's immigration policy have been how many immigrants should be admitted and what kinds of people should they be. Economic factors alone are not resolving the debate, but they play a significant role.

What have immigrants contributed to the Canadian economy? Part of the answer to this question depends on the labour market outcomes of immigrants compared to those of people born in Canada. During the 1960s and 1970s the outcomes have been largely positive. Immigrants had higher labour force participation rates and lower unemployment rates than native-born Canadians. A higher proportion of immigrants worked "year round" than those born in Canada. Although most immigrants were at an economic disadvantage at the time of their arrival, their economic conditions improved rapidly over time; within a decade or two their earnings usually overtook the earnings of native-born Canadians of comparable socioeconomic background. The evidence also suggests that immigrants did not adversely affect the employment opportunities of those born in Canada.

Since the early 1980s, however, labour market outcomes of new arrivals to Canada have deteriorated. Recent immigrants have lower participation rates than earlier immigrants. They experience unemployment rates above those of native-born Canadians and their rate of assimilation in terms of earnings has declined. Given that immigrants start out at an economic disadvantage, their relatively slower earnings growth may result in their earnings never reaching parity with the earnings of native-born Canadians. The empirical evidence thus paints a far less optimistic picture of the economic contribution of recent immigrants to the Canadian economy.

The reasons for this relative decline are not yet fully understood. Perhaps they are to be found on the supply side—are changes in the age, educational, and skill composition of immigrants the cause? Or perhaps the reasons are on the demand side. Have recent immigrants increasingly been confined to low-paying, dead-end jobs? Since a growing proportion of recent immigrants are visible minorities, has discrimination possibly played a role? Time may tell as these questions are increasingly researched.

admitted strictly on humanitarian grounds without any consideration of their potential economic contribution.

Two observations are worth noting with respect to relative changes in immigrant classes. While the number of refugees admitted to Canada has not shown any significant upward trend, the family class has steadily grown in numbers. Throughout the 1980s and into the early 1990s, immigrants in the non-assessed classes outnumbered those in the economic classes. Only recently has this pattern begun to reverse, reflecting the government's renewed focus on the economic aspects of immigration. In 1996, immigrants in the assessed classes made up close to 56% of all landed immigrants. Economic downturns affect the economic classes more than the family and refugee classes. Though the total intake of immigrants generally declines during and shortly after a recession, it is the class of independent immigrants that bears the main brunt of the adjustment.

Fewer immigrants are entering Canada under the skills-oriented point system and more are entering as part of the family reunification program. It is more difficult for those immigrants admitted according to family reunification criteria to be absorbed into the labour market. To what extent slower integration will affect overall unemployment and wages has not yet been documented.

CHANGES IN LABOUR FORCE PARTICIPATION

An increase in the working-age population does not necessarily imply an increase in a country's labour supply. As the adult population has increased, more people are staying in school longer and more workers are retiring earlier. Staying in school and early retirement can lead to a decline in the labour force participation.

From the early 1950s to the mid 1960s, labour force growth almost entirely resulted from an increase in the working-age population. From the mid 1960s on, increased labour force participation became increasingly important in the overall growth of labour supply. Increases in the working-age population continued to have the largest impact on labour force growth during the period of 1966 to 1979, largely due to the baby-boom generation entering the labour force. Throughout the 1980s, however, increased labour force participation became the dominant contributing factor to the growth in the labour force.

Changes in the LFPR from 1947 to 1998 are shown in Figure 4.4. During this period, the LFPR increased by about 10 percentage points, from 54.9% (1947) to 65.1% (1998). Three phases can be distinguished:

FIGURE 4.4 LABOUR FORCE PARTICIPATION RATES, 1947–98

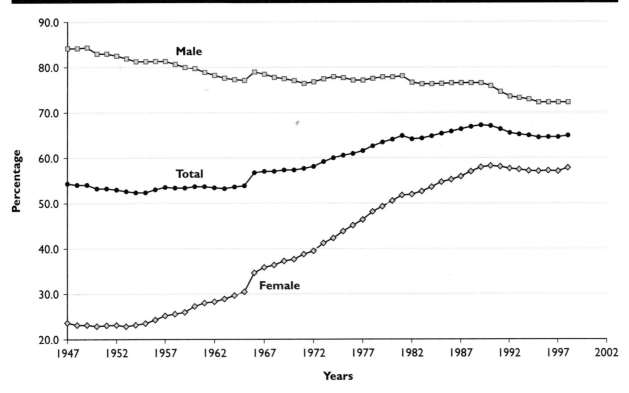

Notes: Annual data prior to 1950 exclude Newfoundland.

Estimates prior to 1966 are based on persons aged 14 and over.

Estimates from 1966 include persons aged 15 and over.

Estimates from 1966 to 1974 have been adjusted to conform to current concepts. Estimates prior to 1966 have not been revised.

Source: For 1947–94, adapted from Statistics Canada. (1995). *Canadian Economic Observer, Historical Statistical Supplement 1994/95*. Ottawa: Statistics Canada (Catalogue no. 11-210); for 1995–98, adapted from Statistics Canada. (1999, July). *Canadian Economic Observer, Statistical Summary*. Ottawa: Statistics Canada. (Catalogue no. 11-010).

no trend increase in the first 20 years from 1946 to 1966, a strong trend increase from the mid 1960s until the peak year of 1989, and a decline in the 1990s. As demonstrated in Figure 4.4, the long-run net increase in the LFPR has been the result of two opposite trends: the decline in the male participation rate and increase in the female participation rate. For males, the participation rate dropped from 85.1% in 1947 to 72.4% in 1998, whereas the LFPR of women more than doubled from 24.1% to 58.1% over the five decades. The two trends offset each other, leaving the overall LFPR nearly unchanged until the mid 1960s. Beginning in 1966, the rise in the female LFPR was so strong that it dominated the fall in the male LFPR. As a result of the converging LFPR of men and women over the years, women have gradually increased their share of the labour force: in 1998, they made up 45% of all people active in the labour force.

LABOUR FORCE ACTIVITY OF MEN

The downward trend in the male participation rate has resulted mainly from the decline in the participation rate of men aged 55 to 64 years. Initially, the percentage of men in this age group who were in the labour force declined slowly from 85% in 1954 to 80% in 1974. But in the 24 years that followed, the decline in labour force participation was much more rapid, dropping about 10 percentage points each decade to about 58% in 1998. This decline has come about because men are retiring from employment at an earlier age; the median age of retirement for men was still close to 65 in the late 1970s, and it has decreased steadily over the past couple of decades. It is not clear how much of this trend toward earlier retirement is voluntary and how much is involuntary. With the restructuring of the economy leading to declines in relative employment in the goods-producing sector, older men may be increasingly forced into retirement by job losses and bleak prospects for re-employment. Other reasons for early retirement are the growth in real wages in the 1960s and 1970s, the appreciation in the value of home ownership between the 1970s and 1980s, and the growth of pension plans with relaxed criteria for retirement with full pension.

The LFPR of men is also decreasing as the life expectancy of males increases. As men live longer, a greater percentage of men is classified as "not in the labour force." As the denominator of the LFPR-ratio rises, the ratio declines.

FEMALE PARTICIPATION TRENDS

The decades-long uninterrupted growth in the labour force participation rate of women has been one of the most remarkable features of the Canadian labour market since World War II. The increase occurred among women of all working ages, with those between 25 and 54 years being the main contributor. As women have aged, their LFPR has moved like a wave through the age groups. While women aged 25 to 44 years increased their participation to the greatest extent during the 1970s, those aged 45 to 54 were the leading group during the 1980s. The most significant change was for women in their childbearing years. Historically, women entered the labour force in two phases. The first phase was in the young adult period when they left school and were unmarried or were married without children; the second phase reflected women's return to the labour force once their children were older and in school or had graduated from school. This sequence created the traditional "double-peak" pattern resembling an inverted W, with labour force participation peaking in the 20 to 24 and the 45 to 54 age groups.

However, over the last two decades, the sharp dip and rebound in female participation rates have disappeared. In the 1950s, 65% of women who interrupted their paid work for the birth of their first child returned to work, but only 8% did so within two years of the start of the interruption. The average interruption lasted 12 years. By the early 1990s, 78% of new mothers who interrupted their paid work returned after the birth of their child; 56% of the new mothers returned within two years of the interruption. The average interruption was only one year. The pattern of age-specific participation rates for women now more closely resembles that of men, as the labour force participation rates of the two groups have converged.

Many factors, often classified as demand and supply factors, are cited for the growing presence of women in the workforce. When we summarize them, it becomes clear that any distinction between supply-related factors and demand-related factors is to some degree artificial. The long-term increase in women's participation in the workforce reflects the complex interaction of forces emanating from both sides of the market. The chief factors that have encouraged female labour force participation, especially for married women, are discussed below.

THE CHANGE IN SOCIAL ATTITUDES. Social attitudes concerning the appropriateness of women working outside of the home, especially when married with small children, have undergone a remarkable transformation. Prior to World War II, strong social barriers, often in form of social taboos, existed against women working outside of the home. Many social scientists consider World War II as the crucial event that changed attitudes against women's work in the labour market. With many men serving in the military, women replaced them on the factory floor. The fact that women filled "male jobs," and often performed extremely well in them, revealed the taboo as what it was—a social custom intended to exclude women from better paying jobs and thus from obtaining economic influence and power. Other researchers see the women's movement as the central social force that changed attitudes considering women's work.

There remains considerable debate, however, about whether the change in social attitudes has been the cause or the consequence of the movement of women into the workforce. Most labour economists tend to argue that the underlying determinants of the rise in female participation are economic in nature, and changing attitudes are simply the consequence of a process that has its roots in changes of the economy. Other social scientists, mainly sociologists and social psychologists, claim that changes in attitudes have played an important role. A comparison of labour force participation trends across different countries may lend support to the latter position. For example, in Japan and West Germany, two of the most economically advanced countries in the world, the female LFPR declined from the late 1950s to the mid 1970s and early 1980s, respectively, and have shown only very modest increases since then. Meanwhile in Canada, Sweden, and the United States, the female LFPR increased rapidly throughout this period.

THE RISING EDUCATIONAL LEVEL OF WOMEN. More women than men complete secondary education and women now constitute the majority of undergraduate students in Canadian universities. There is a strong, positive relationship between years of education completed and the probability of participation in the labour force. In the early 1990s, women with a university degree at the bachelor's level or higher had participation rates close to those of men. Conversely, women with no post-secondary degree, certificate, or diploma had a much lower participation rate, both absolutely and relative to males. There are several reasons why more education fosters labour force participation. First, higher education is often undertaken as an investment, in the sense that a person deliberately incurs the large direct cost (tuition fees, books, etc.) and opportunity cost (forgone earnings from work) of a post-secondary education with the expectation that these expenses will be recouped in the form of higher earnings and occupational attainment after graduation. To reap this return on higher education, however, requires a sustained period of participation in the labour force. Second, people with more education usually have more marketable skills and are, therefore, able to obtain higher paying and more stable jobs. As earnings rise progressively with educational attainment, the cost of time spent not working increases. Third, long-term improvements in education have shifted women's preferences in favour of work outside the home.

THE INCREASE IN EMPLOYMENT OPPORTUNITIES FOR WOMEN. While increased educational attainment widened job opportunities, employment possibilities improved independently of educational status. The increase in employment possibilities is reflected in the increase in the LFPR of women at all educational levels. Urbanization and the expansion of both the government and private service sectors of the economy have been especially conducive to participation of women in the workforce. Although women workers are still concentrated in relatively few occupational categories (clerical workers, nurses and health technicians, elementary and secondary school teachers, sales clerks in retail trade, and personal services such as hairdressers, waitresses, and dental hygienists), most of these occupational groups have grown over-proportionately in size since World War II. Another source of job opportunities for women has been male-dominated occupations such as management positions in natural sciences, engineers, lawyers and notaries, accountants, optometrists, chiropractors, and architects. Some of the more recent advances may have been the result of employment equity legislation enacted in the mid 1980s.

THE INCREASED FLEXIBILITY IN WORK-TIME SCHEDULING. As the service sector has grown, alternative work-time arrangements such as part-time work, flexible working hours, job sharing, compressed work weeks, and contracted work done in the home have become more common. These changing workplace practices have facilitated women's integration into the labour market because they have allowed women to combine household work with contractual work for pay.

THE RISE IN WOMEN'S REAL HOURLY EARNINGS. The monetary value of an hour's time is measured by the hourly real wage a person could earn. As real earnings per hour have increased substantially for women over the last 50 years, the price per hour, or the opportunity cost of not participating in the labour market, has increased as well. The increased opportunity cost of not working convinces many women to substitute labour force work for non-paid work.

THE DECLINE IN THE NUMBER OF CHILDREN PER FAMILY. For biological and cultural reasons, childbirth and child rearing have been the primary responsibility of the female parent. Given the strong negative relationship between the number of children in a family and the probability of participation of women with children, the decline in fertility rates and family size and increased flexibility in childcare arrangements have had a powerful positive impact on the labour market participation for women. Several factors have been responsible for the decline in fertility rates. One factor is improved birth control techniques since the 1950s, which have permitted couples to plan the number and the timing of their children. A second factor is the growing cost of raising children:

the cost includes the direct cost of food, clothing, and education, and the opportunity cost of the wife's time if she does not work for pay. The opportunity cost of raising children, in particular, has grown considerably as real earnings of women have increased, causing families to cut back on the number of children they desire. A third factor is the fact that many women delay childbearing until they have established their careers; this has allowed women to combine the role of wife and mother with a career and the accumulation of work experience.

THE DEVELOPMENT OF LABOUR-SAVING HOUSEHOLD TECHNOLOGY AND SUBSTITUTES FOR HOUSEHOLD PRODUCTS. Technical innovations, for example, in household appliances, and improvements in commercially prepared food and dry cleaning have greatly facilitated the entry of women into the workforce.

ADVANCEMENT OF LIVING STANDARDS. Among the economic factors that have brought women into the labour force is the attempt of couples to maintain and advance their standard of living in the face of several economic squeezes. One squeeze stemmed from the large increase in labour supply as the baby-boom generation entered the labour market, which resulted in a relative decline in nominal wages and salaries, particularly for entry-level positions. Another squeeze was the high rate of inflation during the 1970s and 1980s, particularly for housing. As growth in nominal earnings was dampened by job competition, inflation eroded real income. Since the mid 1970s, real average annual labour income has made almost no gains. (Changes in real income are discussed in Chapter 7.)

THE RISING INCIDENCE OF MARRIAGE BREAK-UPS. With the dramatic increase in the frequency of separation and divorce, more women have become sole supporters for themselves and often for their children, forcing them to seek employment in the labour market.

Labour Force Participation of Youth

Participation rates of youth, that is 15- to 24-year-olds, showed a decline during the 1950s up to the mid 1960s. From the early 1970s until 1989, there has been a continuous upward trend interrupted only during periods of recession. In 1969 the youth LFPR was 56%. By 1989, the peak year in the trend, it had increased to 70%. The rise in youth LFPR was attributable to two factors. The first factor was the increase in the overall proportion of students, especially those aged 15 to 19, holding

FIGURE 4.5 LABOUR FORCE PARTICIPATION RATES OF YOUTH, 1966–98

Sources: For 1966–94, adapted from Statistics Canada. (1995). *Canadian Economic Observer, Historical Statistical Supplement 1994/95.* Ottawa: Statistics Canada, 1995 (Catalogue no. 11-210); for 1995–98, adapted from Statistics Canada. (1999, July). *Canadian Economic Observer, Statistical Summary.* Ottawa: Statistics Canada (Catalogue no. 11-010).

part-time jobs while attending school. The second factor was the growing LFPR among young women.

Since the start of the 1990 recession, the overall participation rate of youth has been declining.[6] Most of the drop reflects the falling participation of both female and male youths. While a contraction of labour force activity is typical during recessions, particularly among young people, the magnitude of the decline in youth LFPR during the last economic downturn and its continuing fall during the period of recovery— a decline of almost 9 percentage points over 10 years (1989 to 1998)—has been unprecedented. Two factors may be responsible for this dramatic shift: the upswing in school attendance and the relatively poor job market for youth. For some time, young people have been staying in school longer, and full-time students are historically less

6. Only in 1998 did the LFPR show an increase. At the time of writing, it is too early to know whether the reversal marks the turnaround in the decline of youth LFPR.

likely to work or look for work than their non-student counterparts. Also, it is much more common now than a decade ago for youth to stay out of the labour force while studying full time, which is probably a reflection of the deteriorating labour market conditions for youths in the 1990s.

RECENT DECLINE IN LABOUR FORCE PARTICIPATION

Another group that has contributed significantly to the recent decline in the overall LFPR is men aged 55 and over. As noted earlier, the labour force participation rate of older men has been on a long-term decline. In earlier years the decline may have been largely due to voluntary early retirement, but in recent years involuntary job loss has probably been the main contributing factor for older men withdrawing from the labour force. Once laid off, older workers, especially those without post-secondary qualifications, face much greater difficulties in finding a replacement job compared to adults aged 35 to 54 years. Even the women's participation rate has been on a slight downward slope since 1991, mainly as the result of the declining LFPR of women aged 25 to 34, a group that showed strong gains in previous decades.[7] The decline in the total participation rate in the 1990s poses a challenge. The challenge is to determine whether the reversal in a long-standing pattern is an indication of the perceived weak labour market conditions in the 1990s or whether it reflects a change in social values and as such the beginning of a new trend.

Participation in the labour force reflects only part of the behavioural component of labour supply. Once people decide to become active participants in the workforce they must determine the level of their labour supply, which could be measured by the preferred hours of work per week or per year. Unfortunately, no continuous data exist on Canadians' work-time preferences. To substitute the number of hours actually worked would confuse the hours offered by labour force members with hours of work determined in collective bargaining agreements or set by companies. Clearly, the latter can deviate from the hours preferred. Trends in actual hours worked are described in Chapter 5, which deals with different aspects of labour demand.

In conclusion, the two outstanding trends on the labour supply side have been the increase in fertility rates during the baby-boom period (1947 to 1960) and the increase in the LFPR of females, particu-

---

7. The decline was reversed in 1998 as the female LFPR increased by a healthy 1.2%.

larly of adult females. The first trend accounted for a significant part of the rapid labour force growth in the 1960s and 1970s and the change in the age structure of the labour force. The second trend is the source of a fundamental change in the gender composition of the labour force.

CHANGES IN THE AGE COMPOSITION OF THE LABOUR FORCE

No other component of population movement has had a greater effect on the age structure of Canada's population than fertility. Over the course of the 20th century, the fertility rate has decreased by half, narrowing the base of the age pyramid and broadening its peak. The gradual aging of the population was interrupted for about 20 years by a phenomenon still not fully understood—the baby boom. Between 1946 and 1965, fertility soared, resulting in an increase in births that demographers had considered long past. At the peak of the baby boom in the late 1950s, annual births topped 460 000, more than double the number in the late 1930s. Around 1970, fertility returned to the levels it would have reached if the secular trend had continued unbroken, but the coming of age of those born in the baby boom fundamentally changed the age composition of the population and, with it, the labour force.

Canada's recent demographic past and its future are characterized by an aging population, which translates into an aging labour force over time. Figure 4.6 depicts how the baby-boom generation is transforming the age structure of the Canadian population from the typical population pyramid in 1951 to a barrel-like shape in the first three decades of the new century. As the baby boomers entered the labour force in increasing numbers since the mid 1960s, the share of younger people in the labour force increased, reaching a peak in the mid 1970s (in 1975 the share of youth in the labour force was 27.2%). Since 1982, the growth rate of youth has become negative and the share of youth has declined below the mid 1950s level. The maturation of the baby-boom generation and the renewed downward trend in fertility since the early 1970s have resulted in the smallest proportion of the population under the age of 14, and the largest share accounted for by the elderly in this century. It is estimated that by the end of the 20th century, close to one third of the labour force would be age 45 and older, compared to 21% in the mid 1980s. Barring a spectacular reversal in the secular trend of declining fertility, the aging of the population and the labour force

FIGURE 4.6 AGE PYRAMIDS OF CANADA FOR SELECTED YEARS

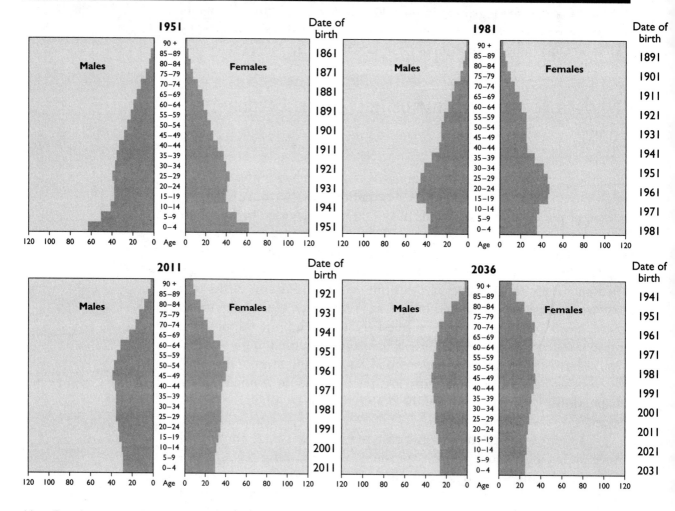

Note: Distribution in each age group for a total population of 1000.

Sources: For the 18th century, Coale, A. J., and Demeny, P. (1983). *Regional Model Life Tables and Stable Populations*. New York: Academic Press, pp. 86, 137. For 1861 and 1891, adapted from Census of Canada, *1931*, vol. I, table 9 respectively; for 1921, 1951, and 1981, adapted from Censuses of Canada. For 2011 and 2036, adapted from Perreault, J. (1990). *Population Projections for Canada, Provinces and Territories, 1989–2011*. Ottawa: Statistics Canada, pp. 150, 177, 187. (Catalogue no. 91-520).

will continue in the 21st century. By the year 2030, the last baby-boom cohorts will have passed the threshold of 65 years of age. By then, the age structure will be inverted and the elderly will account for one quarter of the total population.

The aging of the workforce is affecting the labour market in many different ways:

IMPLICATIONS FOR JOB ADVANCEMENT AND CORPORATE ORGANIZATIONAL STRUCTURE. Among the influences on the employment relationship is, for example, the phenomenon called "plateauing." As the workforce grows older, more workers compete for fewer senior positions and in turn block the advancement of younger colleagues. Changes in the organizational structure of corporations are also directly related to the changing age structure of the workforce.[8] As long as there are more younger workers than older ones, corporations structure their organizations to have fewer positions at the top and the bulk at the bottom. In other words, triangular corporate structures correspond to the triangular shape of the population's age pyramid. As the pyramid starts to take the shape of a barrel, organizations that maintain a pyramidal structure find themselves in trouble, with too many middle-aged employees and not enough entry-level people. As a result, many start to lay off employees in their forties because there are not enough middle and upper management positions to accommodate the large baby-boom cohorts. Other corporations adopt a more constructive approach by flattening their corporate structure. Realizing that the only way to fit a barrel up a triangle is to flatten the triangle, corporations begin to reduce the number of organizational levels and broaden each occupational level. Changes in the organizational structure, in turn, necessitate changes in career paths. The traditional linear promotion path to the top is increasingly replaced by a mix of lateral and promotional moves. Since lateral moves are often associated with changes in occupation and required skills, employees need more frequent re-education and retraining. This example demonstrates how the aging of the workforce through changes of corporate organizational structures will deeply affect the whole field of human resources management. Changes in organizational structures brought about by the aging labour force parallel organizational changes resulting from globalization, some of which were outlined in Chapter 2.

IMPLICATIONS FOR CANADA'S SOCIAL SECURITY SYSTEM. Debate has particularly intensified over whether or not the aging trend will increase the burden on the current and future labour forces to support social services, particularly elder care, health services, and pension support, to the expanding number of non-working elderly. Those who argue that the demographics of the baby boom will place an unbearable burden on the social security system point to the increasing dependency rate—the

8. The information in this section is based on Foot and Venne (1990) and an interview between D. Foot and D. Duchesne from Statistics Canada, reported in *Perspectives on Labour and Income* (1994).

increasing ratio of retired recipients to taxpaying workers. Their argument is reinforced by the fact that people live longer. If people continue to retire at the same age but live longer, then a larger percentage of their lives will be spent in retirement. One possible counter-argument is that the worker/beneficiary ratio is only one of two ratios on which the financing of much of the social security services depends; the other is the ratio of average workers' wages to average retirees' benefits. The worker/beneficiary ratio, for example, does not consider the effects of increasing productivity. As output per employed worker, called average labour productivity, increases, wages likely increase as well. Put differently, a rise in labour productivity means that it will take fewer workers to support each retiree. An increase in the ratio of average workers' wages to average retirees' benefits could offset a decline in the worker/beneficiary ratio; however, given the low productivity growth in Canada over the last 20 years, this does not seem to hold much promise. One general possibility to reduce the financial burden put on the working population would be more flexible work arrangements. Such arrangements would allow older workers to ease

BOX 4.2 Aging of the Labour Force and Absences From Work

In a recent study, Statistics Canada reported that in 1998 5.7% of all full-time workers were absent from work for all or part of a week because of illness, disability, or personal or family responsibilities. The cost to employers in terms of wages and benefits paid for work not done was estimated to be close to $10 billion.

Absences from work have been on the rise in recent years. One of the reasons suggested in the study is the aging workforce. Work days lost, for both men and women, tend to rise with age. In 1998, older workers (age 55 to 64) missed on average 12 work days, more than double the 5 days that young workers (age 15 to 24) were absent from work. Most of the difference can be attributed to illness or disability. Absences due to personal or family responsibilities did not differ much across age groups; they remained at about one day per employee with the

exception of women aged 25 to 44 who missed slightly more than 1.5 days.

As the first large cohorts of the baby-boom generation, now in their early fifties, move toward retirement age, the increase in absenteeism may continue for some years. It would, however, be too simplistic to attribute the higher absence from work only to the aging of the workforce. Days missed from work also vary by industry, union coverage, occupation, and province. Employees in the public sector miss more days than their counterparts in the private sector, professionals have much lower absenteeism rates than clerical workers, and workers in British Columbia lose more days than those in Alberta or Ontario. Since employment shifts occur between industries, occupations, and regions, these variations are prone to affect changes in absence from work over time.

gradually out of the labour force by working five days a week, then four days, then three days until they retire "full time."

OTHER IMPLICATIONS.   The growing labour force population over age 45 will likely have other effects on the labour market. Part-time work can be expected to increase substantially, since older workers are more frequently engaged in part-time work than workers aged 25 to 44 years. Long-duration unemployment is prone to rise because employers are reluctant to hire unemployed older workers they believe to be less healthy, less flexible, and less trainable than younger workers. The number of days of work lost per worker is likely to increase because older workers tend to lose more time from work because of illness or disability. On the positive side, job and labour force turnover rates probably will decline as older workers constitute a more experienced, stable workforce with less turnover.

CHANGES IN THE GENDER COMPOSITION OF THE LABOUR FORCE

The increased involvement of women in the paid workforce has been one of the most profound economic and social changes in Canada over the last five decades. Both long-run changes in demographic and labour force participation patterns account for the shift in the gender structure of the labour force. Women's share of the total population has grown steadily over the course of the century. Between 1971 and 1981, for the first time the size of the female population exceeded that of the male population. In 1951, the female population was predominantly young adults; by 1981 the largest age group was 40 years. In 1998, females accounted for 50.5% of the total population, up from 48.7% in 1941. The rising demographic trend is largely attributed to the fact that mortality rates among women are substantially lower than those among men. The dramatic increase in the labour force participation rate of women described earlier paralleled this trend. In fact, women have accounted for most of the growth in labour force participation since the mid 1970s and as a result, women currently represent almost half of the Canadian workforce.

The rise in female labour force participation has had dramatic effects on family structure. Within 30 years, from the mid 1960s to the mid 1990s, the dual-earner family changed from being the exception to being the rule. In a dual-earner family both spouses are engaged in paid work. In 1967, 33% of all husband-wife families were dual-earner families. By 1995, 62% of all husband-wife families were dual-earner families. While the predominance of the dual-earner family has implications for men's labour market behaviour, the consequences are more serious for that of women. Even when women are part of the paid workforce, they continue to spend considerably more time than their spouses on unpaid domestic work. This applies, in particular, to married women with children whose labour force participation rate has relatively increased most over the last decades. As a result, the provision of paid maternity leave and the availability of accessible, affordable child care have become central demands for women and their advocacy groups.

The proliferation of dual-earner families has had many economic ramifications. One is the negative effect on labour mobility, particularly geographical mobility. The costs of moving from one community to another are potentially much greater for the two-income family than for the family with only one working spouse. In case of the single-earner family, the non-working spouse (traditionally the wife) sacrifices financially relatively little in making a move, while the husband may be able to considerably advance his career and income. For the two-earner family, however, the income and career gains from moving for one spouse may be largely offset if the relocation results in lower earnings and career prospects for the other spouse.

The growing proportion of women engaged in paid work and the accompanying changes in family structure also have had far reaching implications for human resources management and public policy. The changes have put pressure on employers to offer, for example, flexible work time arrangements and paid or unpaid maternity leaves to accommodate family responsibilities. Dual-earner families may want a full-time job for one earner and a part-time job for the other. Workers may also be more reluctant to take on extra tasks at work if they conflict with household responsibilities. Employers likely face greater difficulties in recruiting and moving employees if they conflict with family responsibilities. The proximity of schools and the availability of accessible and affordable child care have become important factors in employees' choices of jobs.

SUMMARY

The labour force is the sum of the employed and unemployed workers in our economy. Over the last 50 years, the labour force has more than tripled in size. The sources of this tremendous growth have been increases in the domestic population, net increases in the number of immigrants, and the rise in labour force participation. The relative contributions of these factors to the overall growth of the labour force have varied over the years.

The participation rate refers to the percentage of the working-age population that is in the labour force. The participation rate for men has been declining mainly because of the tendency for men to opt for early retirement. The labour force participation rate for women has been increasing for a variety of reasons including changes in social attitudes, increases in educational levels and employment opportunities, changes in family structure, and the rise in real wages of women. The increase in the labour force participation of women has more than offset the decline in the labour force participation of men. The resulting change in the gender composition of the labour force has far reaching consequences for human resources management and public policy.

The coming of age of the baby-boom generation has led to a rapidly aging labour force. The changing age composition of the labour force has implications for job advancement, the organizational structure of companies, the financing of Canada's social security system as well as other labour market variables.

KEY TERMS

labour force   72

employed   72

unemployed   72

who — not in the labour force   72

working-age population   74

labour force participation rate   74

natural population growth   76

birth rate   76

fertility rate   76

mortality rate   76

recession   77

EXERCISES

1. Suppose you have to forecast the growth in the Canadian labour force over the next 20 years. What demographic factors would you consider to be essential? Explain.

2. Describe the major changes in the ethnic composition of immigration to Canada over the last 20 years. How does the growing ethnic diversity in Canada's urban

Fig 4-2 pg 75

labour force affect human resources policies?

3. The increase in the labour force participation rate of women was uninterrupted from the 1940s until 1990. Elaborate on some of the factors that played a role in this increase.

9 factors

4. Labour participation rates vary by province. For 1997 the rates were:

Low —Newfoundland 53.1%
Ontario 65.9%
Prince Edward Island 66.1%
Manitoba 67.1%
Nova Scotia 60.4%
Saskatchewan 66.3%
New Brunswick 61.1%
High — Alberta 71.8%
Quebec 62.0%
British Columbia 64.2%

a. How would you explain the high participation rate for Alberta compared to other provinces?

b. How would you explain the low participation rate for Newfoundland compared to other provinces?

5. Suppose you are working as a human resources professional in a company. Assess how the aging of the Canadian labour force may affect the policies and practices in your organization.

REFERENCES

Basset, P. (1994). Declining Female Labour Force Participation. *Perspectives on Labour and Income,* 6(2): 36–39.

Chaykowski, R. P. (1994). *Modern Labour Economics: The Canadian Context.* New York: Harper Collins College Publishers.

Cross, P. (1996). Alternative Measures of Business Cycles in Canada: 1947–1992. *Canadian Economic Observer.* Ottawa: Statistics Canada. (Catalogue no. 11-010)

Duchesne, D. (1994). David Foot Discusses Career Paths.

Perspectives on Labour and Income, 6(4): 13–21.

Foot, D. K., and Venne, R. A. (1990). Population, Pyramids and Promotional Aspects. *Canadian Public Policy,* 16(4): 387–398.

Ford, D., and Nault, F. (1996). Changing Fertility Patterns, 1974–1994. *Health Reports,* 8(3): 39–46. (Catalogue no. 82-003-XPB)

Green, A. (1995). A Comparison of Canadian and U.S. Immigration Policy in the Twentieth Century. In D. DeVoretz (Ed.), *Diminishing Returns.* Toronto: C. D. Howe Institute and Laurier Institution.

Gunderson, M. (1998). *Women and the Canadian Labour Market: Transitions Towards the Future.* Scarborough: Statistics Canada in conjunction with ITP Nelson.

Jennings, P. (1998). School Enrolment and the Declining Youth Participation Rate. *Policy Options, 19*(3): 10–14.

Statistics Canada. (1998). *Canadian Economic Observer, Statistical Summary.* Ottawa: Statistics Canada. (Catalogue no. 11-010)

Statistics Canada. (1998). *Labour Force Update. Older Workers.* Ottawa: Statistics Canada. (Catalogue no. 71-005-XPB)

Statistics Canada. (1998). *Report on the Demographic Situation in Canada 1997.* Ottawa: Statistics Canada. (Catalogue no. 91-209 XPE-97000)

Statistics Canada. (1995). *Canadian Economic Observer, Historical Statistical Supplement, 1994/95.* Ottawa: Statistics Canada. (Catalogue no. 11-210)

Statistics Canada. *The Labour Force,* various years. (Catalogue no. 71-001)

Statistics Canada. Target Group Data Bases. (1995). *Women in Canada: A Statistical Report* (3rd ed.). Ottawa: Statistics Canada.

Statistics Canada. (1998). *Annual Demographic Statistics.* Ottawa: Statistics Canada. (Catalogue no. 91-213XPB)

Sunter, D., and G. Bowlby. (1998). Labour Force Participation in the 1990s. *Perspectives on Labour and Income, 10*(3): 15–21.

5

....

EMPLOYMENT

OBJECTIVES

After completing this chapter, you should be able to:

1. describe the major trends in total employment over the last five decades;
2. explain the employment growth in the service sector relative to the other sectors of the economy;
3. describe the changes in the occupational distribution of the workforce;
4. evaluate the argument of the deskilling of the labour force;
5. discuss the trends in non-standard employment;
6. distinguish between different concepts of working hours;
7. describe and explain the trends in working hours.

AGGREGATE LABOUR DEMAND

As the number and characteristics of people wanting to work have changed significantly over the last 50 years, so have the number and characteristics of jobs that employers offer. The total number of jobs made available by firms and government agencies is called total labour

aggregate labour demand
the total number of jobs made available by firms and government agencies

demand, or **aggregate labour demand**. As indicated in the discussion of the flow approach to the labour market in Chapter 2, aggregate labour demand is measured by the number of employed workers plus the number of unfilled vacancies.[1] Statistics on unfilled vacancies at the national level are unfortunately no longer available since the Job Vacancy Survey was discontinued in 1978. At present, the Help Wanted Index is used as an indicator of changes in vacancies. This index is based on Statistics Canada's count of help-wanted ads published in 22 metropolitan-area newspapers across the country. The Help Wanted Index, however, has serious shortcomings for labour market analysis. Only a fraction of job vacancies tend to be publicly advertised, as many companies use internal recruitment patterns to fill vacancies. Also, blue-collar jobs are generally underrepresented in the Help Wanted Index. As a result, the trend in the index may be upward biased in relation to the trend in vacancies because of the long-run decline in the ratio of blue-collar job openings to white-collar ones. Therefore, we will concentrate here only on the long-run changes in employment as an indicator of aggregate labour demand.

Two caveats seem appropriate at this point. First, to take employment as an approximation of aggregate labour demand is to some degree artificial, because the employed portion of the measured labour force reflects the continuous interaction of forces operating on both the supply and demand sides of the labour market. That is, the level of employment is determined by the interaction of demand and supply in the labour market. Second, care must be taken not to confuse employment with the number of jobs. Equating changes in employment with changes in jobs distorts the extent of job creation or loss. Since the Labour Force Survey (LFS) measures employment by counting employed workers rather than occupied jobs, a newly created job taken by someone already working does not increase employment. Likewise, the loss of a job previously held by a multiple jobholder (moonlighter) does not reduce the number of workers.

CHANGES IN LEVEL OF EMPLOYMENT

Employment in an economy can be assessed by asking two questions: How many people are working, and how many hours are they

---

1. Employment is defined here as any work for pay or profit in the "formal" market economy. It consists of paid work in the context of an employer-employee relationship or self-employment. It also includes unpaid family work, that is, unpaid work that contributes directly to the operation of a farm or business owned or operated by a family member.

AN INTRODUCTION TO THE CANADIAN LABOUR MARKET

FIGURE 5.1 EMPLOYMENT GROWTH, 1947–98

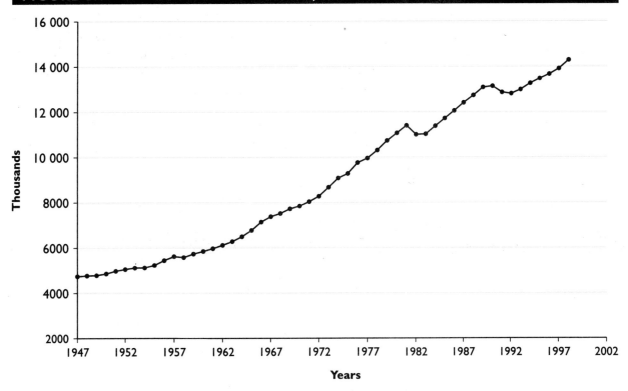

Sources: For 1947–94, adapted from Statistics Canada. (1995). *Canadian Economic Observer, Historical Statistical Supplement 1994/95*. Ottawa: Statistics Canada (Catalogue no. 11-210); for 1995–98, adapted from Statistics Canada. (1999, July). *Canadian Economic Observer, Statistical Summary*. Ottawa: Statistics Canada (Catalogue no. 11-010).

working? Figure 5.1 illustrates the dramatic expansion of employment in Canada from 4.8 million in 1947 to 14.3 million in 1998. This change represents an increase of 198%. Expressed in growth rates, employment increased over five decades at an average annual rate of 2.2%. However, over the last two decades average annual growth rates of employment have sharply declined. In the decade of 1970–80 employment grew on average 3.6% per year, but employment growth between 1980 and 1990 was only half that (1.8%), and during the 1990s it averaged just 1% per year.

Part of the increase in employment can be explained by the increase in the number of people of working age. However, employment numbers have risen faster than the working-age population. This difference is illustrated in Figure 5.2, which shows the trend in the proportion of people 15 years and older who have at least some paid employment. The ratio of employment to working-age population is

FIGURE 5.2 EMPLOYMENT RATE, 1947–98

Sources: For 1947–94, adapted from Statistics Canada. (1995). *Canadian Economic Observer, Historical Statistical Supplement 1994/95.* Ottawa: Statistics Canada (Catalogue no. 11-210); for 1995–98, adapted from Statistics Canada. (1999, July). *Canadian Economic Observer, Statistical Summary.* Ottawa: Statistics Canada (Catalogue no. 11-010).

employment rate the ratio of employment to working-age population

called the **employment rate**. In Figure 5.2, three main developments in the employment rate are discernible over the past 50 years. From 1947 to the early 1960s, the rate showed a downward trend, from about 54% to just a little over 50%. Upward movements in the employment rate of adult women failed to offset the rate decline of youths and adult men. Thereafter, the overall rate began an upward trend—driven mainly by increases in women's employment rate—to reach 60.4% at the onset of the 1981/82 recession. Following a brief slide in 1982 and 1983, the ratio resumed its climb in 1984, rising to its peak of 62.4% in 1989, just before the last recession. The baby boom, high immigration levels, and the aging of the population all had the potential to lower the employment rate (by increasing the denominator of the ratio).

Still, the ratio continued upward during most of the 1960s, 1970s, and 1980s, suggesting that the economy was able to generate more jobs than were required to keep up with the growth in the working-age population. With the onset of the 1990/91 recession, the ratio dropped once more, and since then has remained fairly steady around 59%. As Figures 5.1 and 5.2 indicate, total employment and the employment rate fall in recessions because fewer workers are needed when production is reduced. The decline in the average annual growth rate of employment over the last two decades that was noted earlier was largely due to the negative effect of the two recessions in the early 1980s and 1990s on employment.

As discussed in Chapter 4, one of the most dramatic changes has been the growth in the employment rate of women, which tripled after World War II. In 1946, fewer than one in five (17.9%) adult women were working; by 1970 the ratio had risen to almost one in three (32.9%). Since 1987 more than one in two adult women have had jobs. The employment rate of men displayed a starkly different trend over the last 50 years. With few exceptions, men's employment rate decreased steadily while women's rate rose. In 1946, about 87% of adult men were employed; by 1970, the level had fallen to 80%, and by 1998, it was 68.5%. Most of the decline was due to the withdrawal—voluntary or otherwise—of older, poorly educated men from the employed labour force.[2]

Compared to adult men and women, the employment rate of youths (both sexes combined) has shown the greatest sensitivity to the ups and downs in economic activity. Starting at 54.5% in 1946, it declined to roughly 44% in the first half of the 1960s. It shifted upward to 53% following the LFS's exclusion of 14-year-olds from the working-age population in 1966, but then continued its decline until 1970 (50.3%). Movements in the youth ratio between 1971 and 1989 followed closely the business cycle, although the overall trend was upward. However, after hitting its peak in 1989 (62.7%), the ratio declined by more than nine percentage points to 53.5% in 1998. Considering the large decline in the youth labour force participation rate mentioned in Chapter 4, this is a strong indication of the declining employment opportunities for young people. During the recent economic upturn, the rate has improved little. Faced with poor job prospects, many young Canadians seem to be opting to remain in school.

SHIFTS IN THE COMPOSITION OF EMPLOYMENT

Quantitative changes in the overall level of employment, or the employment rate, hide many different features of labour demand.

---

2. For example, the employment rate for men aged 55 or over with fewer than nine years of schooling fell from 36.7% in 1976 to only 19.4% in 1995.

These features include the mix of jobs (for example, full-time/part-time), the quality of jobs (for example, in terms of job stability or working conditions), and the distribution of jobs (for example, by industry or occupation). As the demand for goods and services shifts over time, so does the demand for labour. While some industries and occupations expand, others contract, which leads to large changes in the skills and geographic and industrial locations required of workers. These compositional changes in labour demand are the focus of the next two sections.

THE SHIFT TO SERVICE-SECTOR EMPLOYMENT

Historically in Canada, the most important change in the distribution of employment has been the shift in employment away from the goods-producing industries[3] to the service-producing industries. The shift from primary-resource industries, particularly agriculture, to manufacturing and service industries has coincided with the rise of a modern industrial economy. The proportion of employment in agriculture declined continuously from roughly 33% of the employed labour force in 1921 to 18.4% in 1951, to the very low 2.9% in 1998. In addition to the relative decline of employment in agriculture, employment has shifted from the goods-producing sector to the service industries. The share of manufacturing and construction in total employment dropped from 42.5% in 1961 to 27% in 1998.

Until the 1950s, the employment gains in non-government services were very gradual. Major non-governmental services are listed in Table 5.1 under "Dynamic Services" and "Traditional Services." Within 30 years, from 1921 to 1951, employment in these services rose from 25.2% to 35.1%, that is, by 10 percentage points. Since then the growth has accelerated. Between 1951 and 1991, service employment in the non-government sector increased by 24 percentage points, at an annual rate of about 1.3%. However, employment growth in government services (including municipal, provincial, and federal administrations) during the same period was relatively flat.

The shift to services is the outstanding feature on the demand side of the Canadian labour market. By 1998, about 72% of Canadian workers were employed in the service sector (non-government plus government services). This shift, however, is not unique to Canada; the transition has been one of the most consistent features of economic

---

3. Goods-producing industries include manufacturing, mining, forestry, construction, transportation, utilities, and communication.

TABLE 5.1 THE STRUCTURE OF THE SERVICE SECTOR

Dynamic Services

Transportation, communications, and utilities
- Air, rail, and water transport
- Ground transportation
- Pipelines
- Storage and warehousing
- Broadcasting—radio, television, cable
- Telephone systems
- Postal and courier services
- Utilities—electricity, gas, water, and sewage systems

Wholesale trade

Finance, insurance, and real estate
- Banks and trust companies
- Credit unions and mortgage companies
- Insurance companies
- Investment dealers
- Real estate operators

Business services
- Employment agencies
- Advertising services
- Architectural, scientific, engineering, and computing services
- Legal services
- Management consulting

Traditional Services

Retail trade
- Food stores
- Drug stores and liquor stores
- Shoe and clothing stores
- Furniture, appliance, and auto repair shops
- Department stores
- Jewellery stores and photographic stores

Personal services
- Hotels
- Restaurants and bars
- Film, audio, and video production and distribution
- Movie houses and theatres
- Barber and beauty shops
- Laundries and cleaners
- Funeral services
- Machinery and car rental companies
- Photographers
- Repair shops (excluding auto)
- Building security services
- Travel agencies

Non-market Services

Education services
- Schools, colleges, and universities
- Libraries, museums, and archives

Health services
- Hospitals
- Nursing homes
- Doctors and dentists
- Medical laboratories

Social services
- Day care, meal services, and crisis centres
- Psychologists and social workers
- Religious organizations

Public administration

Note: For data-related reasons, this classification scheme has been organized within the framework of Statistics Canada's Standard Industrial Classification.

development in all major industrialized countries, although it occurred over a much longer period in most. The sectoral redistribution of employment over time was succinctly stated by Colin Clark some 40 years ago: "A wide, simple and far-reaching generalisation in this field is to the effect that, as time goes on and communities become more economically advanced, the numbers engaged in agriculture tends to decline relative to the numbers in manufacture, which in their turn decline relative to the numbers engaged in services" (Clark, 1957, p. 492). The shift from agriculture to services is sometimes described as the shift from the primary to the tertiary sector. Others who like to describe the present with the prefix "post" have called it the arrival of the "post-industrial" state. The relatively faster growth in service-sector employment is the result of several interrelated factors.

DIFFERENCES IN PRODUCTIVITY GROWTH RATES. Significant differences in productivity growth rates between the goods-producing industries and the service-sector industries have been cited as a major cause for the growth in the service sector. The level of output in any industry depends on its production factors and the production technology. As mentioned in Chapter 2, the primary production factors are labour and capital. The contribution of labour to growth in output depends on the increase in labour, measured as a percentage change in hours of work or number of employed workers, times the marginal productivity of labour. In economics, the word "marginal" means extra or additional; thus, the **marginal productivity of labour** indicates the extra output obtained by adding one more worker or having a worker work one more hour. Similarly, the contribution of capital depends on changes in capital times the marginal productivity of capital. The marginal productivity of capital is calculated as the change in output over the change in capital by one unit. Even if the quantities of labour and capital remain constant, output still could change if technological progress takes place. For the same amount of inputs, we get more output today than we did in the past. This increase in output is attributed to a change in **total factor productivity**.

Primary-resource industries and most manufacturing industries saw much more rapid gains in productivity—individual factor or total factor productivity, or both—in the 1950s and 1960s in comparison to the service industries. In the 1970s, when productivity growth started to slow down in the goods-producing industries, the service sector showed an even greater decline in growth rates. Do productivity gains in an industry create jobs or destroy them? For the overall economy, productivity gains have generally been associated with positive effects on output and employment. Productivity gains lead to a rise in real wages or profits, or both, all other things being the same. Increases in real income stimulate total consumption and investment. Increased spending, in turn, has a positive effect on production and employment. What applies to the economy at large, however, may not apply for each

marginal productivity of labour extra output obtained by adding one more worker or having a worker work one more hour

total factor productivity the increase in output obtained from the same amount of inputs into the production process

AN INTRODUCTION TO THE CANADIAN LABOUR MARKET

BOX 5.1 Are All Industrial Nations Becoming Service Economies?

The answer is yes. Employment data for the 10 leading industrial nations show that in every country the share of the labour force employed in services has increased significantly. During the last 30 years, in countries such as Japan and Germany, which are associated with a strong manufacturing sector, the proportion of workers in service industries grew even more than in Canada.

Productivity plays a key role in explaining the similar development. Throughout the industrial world, productivity has grown much faster in manufacturing than it has in most services. Several service industries, such as telecommunications, use highly sophisticated equipment and their productivity has grown rapidly. But in most other services productivity growth has been very slow.

The role of productivity in the employment shift to the service industries can be made clear with a simple example. Suppose productivity in the steel industry doubled as the result of mechanization and output rose by 50%. There must have been a 25% reduction in the number of workers employed in that industry. If, over the same period, productivity in the real estate industry remained constant while sales volume rose by 50%, that industry must have employed 50% more workers than before. With both industries expanding their outputs by the same percentage, some workers must have moved out of the steel industry into the real estate industry. While the share of output produced in manufacturing generally has not declined, its share of employment has fallen. It is in this sense that all industrial countries are becoming service industries.

industry that experiences productivity gains. For example, industries that experienced large productivity gains in the first decades after World War II, such as mining and oil, communication, and agriculture, channelled some of the gains into increasing the capital stock. Much of the increase in the capital stock has been in the form of labour-saving equipment. Considering the shift of employment to the service sector, one could argue that the relatively higher productivity growth in the goods-producing industries lowers employment opportunities in those industries relative to the service industries.

INCREASES IN REAL INCOME. How much people spend depends on their real income: as real income per person rises, expenditures rise. The increases in real income that occurred between the end of World War II and the late 1970s, however, are associated with an over-proportionate growth in the demand for services. The demand for consumer services tends to grow faster than the demand for consumer goods. For example, as real income rises, people tend to eat more restaurant meals instead of buying food to prepare at home. The demand has increased particularly in the areas of medical care, education, recreation, communication, and transportation.

The relationship between an increase in real income and a more than proportional increase in the demand for services was established in the 19th century by the Prussian statistician Ernst Engel. **Engel's law** states that expenditures on necessities such as food take a decreasing proportion of income as real income increases, while expenditures on clothing and rent remain constant and expenditures on luxuries increase over-proportionately. Many services are classified as luxuries. Economists define a luxury as a good or service with an income elasticity of demand greater than one. The **income elasticity of demand** measures how the quantity demanded changes as consumer income changes. Like the price elasticity, which is discussed in the Appendix to Chapter 2, the income elasticity is a ratio of two percentage changes: the percentage change in quantity demanded divided by the percentage change in income. If income increases by 1% and the percentage change in the quantity demanded of a certain service—for example, the number of consultations with chiropractors—is greater than 1, the income elasticity of demand for chiropractor services is greater than 1. The validity of Engel's law is clearly borne out by a comparison of estimates for the income elasticity of various goods and services. The income elasticity, for instance, for food items (mean value in Canada for the period of 1926 to 1989) has been 0.39. Beer has a very low income elasticity of 0.06. High income elasticities apply for many services, for example airline travel (5.82), movies (3.41), and restaurant meals (1.71). For medical services the elasticity has been 1.95.[4]

CONTRACTING OUT OF COMPANY INTERNAL SERVICES. The shift to service-sector employment partly reflects the growing trend of companies in the manufacturing sector to contract out. Much of the business-services sector is devoted to providing services to goods producers: advertising services, accounting audits, legal advice, engineering expertise, etc. Firms in the manufacturing sector have increasingly turned to specialized firms for these services rather than using their own employees. When a manufacturer stops using in-house staff and hires a specialized firm to provide a service such as advertising, employment in the manufacturing sector falls and rises in the service sector. The shift may not affect the total number of people in an economy producing advertising

---

4. The estimate for medical services implies that as real income increases by 1%, the demand for medical care increases by 1.95%.

services, however: advertisers were formerly counted as employees in the manufacturing sector and are now enumerated in the service sector.

INTERNATIONAL COMPETITION. Imported goods often compete with domestically produced goods on the basis of price, quality, and design. This competition, often from countries where wages are low, has been particularly strong in the Canadian manufacturing sector and has contributed to the rapid decline of that sector's share in total employment. Canada is a highly **open economy**, which means that imports and exports represent a large percentage of overall economic activity. Canadians spend almost 30% of total income on imports. In contrast, American spending on imports is just over 11%. _– closed economy_

open economy an economy in which imports and exports represent a large percentage of overall economic activity

omit **INCREASE IN THE DEMAND FOR SERVICES AS INPUTS.** The Betcherman report (Economic Council of Canada, 1991) claims that all the factors we have discussed so far account for only a small part of the shift in employment to the service sector. The report argues that the major force behind the transition has been the increase in the demand for services as inputs into the production of the goods-producing industries. The authors of the report claim that the stimulative influence of the goods-producing industries on services has been increasing over time. Of the 28 goods-producing industries, 25 had more stimulative power on the service sector in 1981 than in 1971. By 1985, most goods-producing industries had a significant influence on output in the service sector. Manufacturing and resource industries were important sources of demand for service inputs. In contrast, the stimulative power of the service industries on goods production was generally weak.

The report focuses on the relationship between the goods-producing industries and the dynamic services (see Table 5.1). Dynamic services are services with relatively high growth rates. Six service industries, which together make up the bulk of the dynamic-service sub-sector, were particularly dependent on demand from the goods industries for their output: finance and real estate, wholesale trade, business services, utilities, transportation, and communications. The links between the goods sector and the transportation, utilities, and wholesale trade industries have always been strong. One of the most striking changes in the overall structure of the economy, however, has involved business services, financial services, and communications. These industries have shown strong employment growth and significant increases in their links with the goods sector. Technological change has played an important role in these developments by increasing the demand for information and by providing the means for satisfying that demand through those information-based services.

OCCUPATIONAL SHIFTS

Given the extensive shifts in the industrial composition of employment, one would expect commensurate changes in the distribution of employment across occupations. Table 5.2 shows the occupational distribution of the Canadian labour force for the period of 1948 to 1998. Major increases in employment occurred in white-collar jobs, with the managerial and professional group exhibiting the greatest change. Taken together, the share of the labour force in white-collar jobs (including managerial and professional, clerical, sales and service) increased from 38.6% in 1948 to 70.7% in 1998. In contrast, the combined share of employment in the primary and processing occupations declined from 45.1% in 1948 to only 16.7% in 1998.

The decline of primary and manufacturing jobs and the growth of service jobs have raised concern among those who believe that the decline of the manufacturing sector implies a decline in the availability of skilled, unionized, well-paid blue-collar jobs and that the new jobs provided by the expanding service industries are largely low-skilled, low-wage jobs. The claim of a "deindustrialization" or a "deskilling" of the labour force often conjures the image of a nation of hamburger flippers. For example, two leading exponents of this hypothesis describe in a study that "automobile workers who lose their jobs in this high productivity industry are found two years later to be in jobs that pay on average 43% less. Even six years after losing their jobs, these workers have recovered only five sixths of the salaries they would have been earning had they not been laid off. Similar long-term losses are recorded for steelworkers, meat packers, aircraft employees, and those who refine petroleum, produce flat glass, and make men's clothing. These are not merely personal losses, for when a worker is forced out of a high productivity job into a low productivity job, all of society suffers. Real productivity goes down when an experienced, skilled autoworker ends up buffing cars in the local car wash" (Bluestone & Harrison, 1982, p. 111).

Even though there is a disproportionate number of well-paying blue-collar jobs in manufacturing industries, the decline in the employment share of the manufacturing sector as such does not allow us to draw conclusions about changes in the skill composition of the labour force. The link between sectoral shifts in employment and the skill level of the workforce is tenuous because most industries consist of high-

TABLE 5.2 OCCUPATIONAL DISTRIBUTION OF THE CANADIAN CIVILIAN LABOUR FORCE, 1948–98

	1948	1951	1961	1971	1981	1991	1998
Managerial, professional	10.9%	14.9%	19.1%	23.9%	23.7%	31.6%	33.4%
Clerical	10.2	11.2	13.3	15.1	17.7	16.4	13.6
Sales	8.0	6.4	7.4	7.1	10.3	9.7	10.2
Service	9.5	9.7	11.8	13.2	13.4	13.3	13.5
Primary occupations	26.7	22.7	13.4	7.9	6.2	4.9	4.2
Processing	18.4	17.7	24.2	24.1	15.2	11.8	12.5
Construction	5.2	6.3	NA	NA	6.0	5.3	5.3
Transportation	6.8	6.5	5.8	4.5	3.8	3.6	3.8
Materials handling	4.1	4.6	5.0	4.3	3.8	3.3	3.4

Note: Data are derived from Statistics Canada's Labour Force Survey. Because of changes in survey frequency, questionnaire, and occupational classification, care should be exercised in making comparisons across time.

Sources: For 1948–51: Statistics Canada. (1983). *Historical Statistics of Canada* (2nd ed.). Ottawa: Statistics Canada. (Series D355-382). The occupation categories have been adjusted as follows to fit the current breakdown as reported in Statistics Canada's *The Labour Force:* Communication, financial, and service workers are classified as "service"; manufacturing and mechanical trades workers are classified as "processing"; labourers and unskilled workers are classified as "materials handling"; agricultural, fishing, logging, and trapping workers are classified as "primary occupations." For 1961–71, Statistics Canada. (1983). *Historical Statistics of Canada* (2nd ed.). Ottawa: Statistics Canada. (Series D383-412). Farmers and farm workers, loggers and related workers, fishers, trappers, hunters, and miners are classified as "primary occupations"; craftspeople are classified as "processing"; labourers and unskilled workers are classified as "materials handling." For 1981–91, Statistics Canada. (1987, 1992). *Historical Labour Force Statistics* (1987: pp. 143–147; 1992: pp. 161–171). Ottawa: Statistics Canada (Catalogue no. 71-201). For 1998, Statistics Canada. (1999). *Labour Force Update.* Ottawa: Statistics Canada (Catalogue no. 71-005-XPB).

skilled, high-paying jobs as well as low-skilled, low-paying jobs. Some service workers flip hamburgers, while others hold highly skilled, well-paid professional, managerial, or administrative jobs.

No clear conclusion about overall trends in the skill intensity of employment is possible at present; however, it does not appear that the skill level of the workforce is declining. Technological and organizational changes seem to have increased the literacy and numeracy requirements across the workforce. Employers look for an understanding of abstract principles, analytical and problem-solving abilities, and communication and interpersonal skills.

Some inferences about the changing skill structure of jobs can be drawn by looking at the demand shifts for more or less skilled (educated) workers. Data on educational qualifications show that the quantity of jobs requiring better educated workers (that is, workers who hold secondary and post-secondary certificates) has increased compared to the quantity of jobs employing less educated workers. To the extent that jobs filled by better educated workers require higher skills than jobs filled by less educated workers, the skill level of jobs has been increasing. The fact that real wages of higher skilled workers have increased relative to lower skilled workers suggests an increase in the skill structure of these jobs on average. The stronger growth of wages in high-skill occupations relative to low-skill occupations is not what one would expect if the skill level across the workforce were deteriorating. The decrease in the relative earnings of low-skilled workers—a topic covered in more detail in Chapter 7—would also indicate that changes in technology, trade patterns, and the ways in which work is organized bias employment in favour of the more skilled and educated worker.

Another aspect of the changing skill profile of the labour force is the growing emphasis on information-based work. The central role of information technology in today's economy is captured in phrases such as "the knowledge-based economy" or the "information economy." According to estimates, more than half of all Canadians are employed in occupations that are primarily concerned with the creation and use of data and knowledge. Information-based work accounts for two thirds of net employment growth since the early 1970s. The skill distribution in information-based employment is particularly polarized in the service sector. However, there has been an acceleration of highly skilled jobs in the finance, business, and non-market services. The share of managerial, administrative, professional, and technical occupations rose from 23.9% to 31.6% of overall employment from 1971 to 1991. Nonetheless, employment in traditional services such as retail and personal services, even where it is related to information-based jobs, tends to have a lower skill level. These jobs are predominantly involved in routine handling or production of data. The shift in employment to the service sector would thus contribute to a polarization of the skill distribution of the workforce rather than a lowering of the skill level in general.

THE GROWTH OF NON-STANDARD EMPLOYMENT

non-standard employment employment that is not full time for a full year

Linked to the relative growth of the service sector is another significant trend on the demand side of the labour market: the rise in **non-standard employment**. A non-standard job is one that is not full time for the full year. Although the majority of Canadian workers are still employed in full-time permanent jobs, rates of non-standard work arrangements increased throughout the 1980s and into the 1990s.[5] Non-standard employment accounted for about 50% of all new jobs in the 1980s. It is estimated that the various forms of non-standard employment now represent nearly 30% of total employment in Canada (25% in the United States). While non-standard employment was already widespread in social services, retail, and other consumer services for some time, by 1994 it had also become more prevalent in the remaining service sectors and in the goods-producing industries. We will focus here on four—not mutually exclusive—types of non-standard work.

Part-time Work

The most important category of non-standard work is part-time employment, defined as the number of workers who worked less than a total of 30 hours at all jobs during the week referenced by the Labour Force Survey. Part-time work has been increasing since the middle of the century, though the trend has accelerated since the mid 1970s. The proportion of part-time workers climbed from 4% of total employment in 1953 to 18.7% in 1998. Between 1976 and 1998, part-time employment increased by 120% whereas full-time employment grew by 36% (see Figure 5.3). Data on part-time employment figures understate the growth of part-time jobs, however, since many individuals holding several part-time jobs were until recently classified as full-time workers if their hours at all jobs totalled 30 or more per week. For example, the LFS defines a person with two part-time jobs who works a total of at least 30 hours per week as one full-time worker, while someone whose total hours at all jobs amount to less than 30 per week is considered a part-timer.[6] As the number of multiple jobholders grows, the number of part-time workers will increasingly deviate from the number of part-time jobs. In 1994, for example, 23% of all jobs were part-time, although only 17% of all workers were classified as such. As the example demonstrates, assessing the actual part-time work generated by the economy requires estimating the number of existing jobs, not only the number of people occupying them. Since 1975, the number of part-time jobs has increased at an average annual rate of 4.5% for a total growth of more than 120%. In comparison, full-time jobs increased by only 23% (1.2%

---

5. Full-year full-time jobs are jobs that provide at least 49 weeks per year at 30 or more hours per week.

6. Beginning in 1997, LFS publications no longer define part-time work according to total hours of all jobs for multiple jobholders but according to hours on the main job only. A worker's main job is the one with the greatest number of hours worked in the reference week.

FIGURE 5.3 TYPE OF EMPLOYMENT, 1976–98

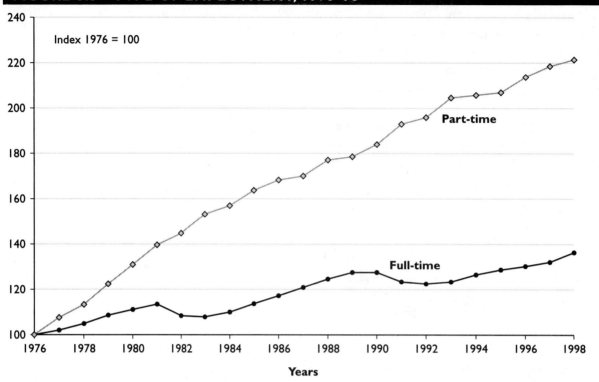

Source: Adapted from Statistics Canada. (1999). *Canadian Economic Observer, Historical Statistical Supplement 1998/99.* Ottawa: Statistics Canada, table 8. (Catalogue no. 11-210).

annually) over the two decades. As a result of the different growth rates, part-time jobs accounted for 23% of all jobs in 1994, compared with only 14% in 1975.

Where are part-time jobs most likely to be found? Part-time work is mostly a service-sector phenomenon. By the mid 1990s, about 75% of part-time workers were employed in the service sector. As Table 5.3 shows, the three service industries with the highest proportion of part-time employment are retail trade, other consumer services (especially accommodation, food, and beverage services), and social services. These industries experience uneven consumer demand, for instance, peak hours in shopping, entertainment, and restaurants and peak demand periods such as holidays and seasonal sales. The powerful fluctuations provide strong incentives to businesses for using part-time workers.

Who are the part-time workers? Part-time employment displays a strong gender and age bias. In 1994, 24% of all women with jobs worked part-time. In comparison, just 8% of employed men held part-time jobs.

TABLE 5.3 NON-STANDARD EMPLOYMENT AMONG 15- TO 64-YEAR-OLDS BY INDUSTRY*

IN 1000s

	TOTAL EMPLOYMENT		PART-TIME		TEMPORARY**		MULTIPLE JOBHOLDERS		OWN ACCOUNT***	
	1989	1994	1989	1994	1989	1994	1989	1994	1989	1994
All industries[t]	12 468	12 799	1905	1972	799	970	635	944	858	1147
Agriculture	278	369	—	50	—	—	—	—	124	190
Natural resource-based	818	759	—	—	28	58	—	—	—	—
Manufacturing	1779	1560	71	62	73	90	88	75	39	32
Construction	626	671	35	52	69	95	—	58	81	151
Distributive services	1320	1366	89	105	50	72	54	75	86	120
Business services	1337	1556	135	179	50	78	78	107	123	229
Social services	2050	2317	484	521	184	273	143	225	77	86
Public administrative	1124	908	74	47	90	99	41	54	—	—
Retail trade	1628	1613	515	472	88	52	59	160	117	91
Other consumer services	1337	1584	424	456	136	128	130	124	152	219
% of total employment[tt]										
All industries	100	100	15	15	8	9	5	7	7	9
Agriculture	100	100	—	14	—	—	—	—	5	51
Natural resource-based	100	100	—	—	4	8	—	—	—	—
Manufacturing	100	100	4	4	4	6	5	5	2	2
Construction	100	100	6	8	17	22	—	9	13	23
Distributive services	100	100	7	8	4	6	4	5	6	9
Business services	100	100	10	12	5	6	6	7	9	15
Social services	100	100	24	22	10	13	7	10	4	4
Public administrative	100	100	7	5	8	11	4	6	—	—
Retail trade	100	100	32	29	7	4	4	10	7	6
Other consumer services	100	100	32	29	13	11	10	8	11	14

Sources: Adapted from Statistics Canada. (1989). *Education and Work.* Ottawa: Statistics Canada. (Catalogue no. 12M0004); and Statistics Canada. (1994). *Education, Work and Retirement.* Ottawa: Statistics Canada. (Catalogue no. 12M0009).

* For industry inclusion, see methodology and definitions in sources listed above.   ** Excludes self-employment   *** Self-employed workers without paid employees

[t]Includes workers who did not state their industry of employment   [tt]For temporary workers, this calculation excludes the self-employed

In the same year, 69% of all part-time workers were female, a figure that has changed little over the past two decades. Young people are more likely to work part-time than adult workers.

The rise of part-time employment has raised concern among some labour market analysts who view changes in the proportion of part-time workers as evidence of a fundamental restructuring of the job market. They argue that part-time jobs are inferior to full-time jobs because they provide lower earnings and fewer fringe benefits. Also, because they are mostly non-unionized, part-time jobs offer diminished job security. This concern has gained support due to the rising number of people who work part-time because they cannot find full-time jobs. The involuntary part-time workers are **underemployed** in that they are obliged to take part-time jobs although they would prefer to work full-time. In 1994, underemployed workers accounted for 36% of all part-time employment, more than triple the proportion in 1975. The largest group is found among women aged 25 to 54.

When trying to reach a conclusion about trends in the rate of underemployment (which is defined as the number of involuntary part-

underemployed
describes workers who are obliged to take part-time jobs although they prefer to work full time

---

BOX 5.2 Four Young People and Ten Jobs

Adam, Daniel, Naomi, and Winston rent a small townhouse in Whistler, B.C. They came to this resort town to combine work with pleasure—that is, the outdoors. Since the cost of living in Whistler is very high, however, they find themselves working many more hours than they had anticipated. For most of them, little time is left for their favourite sports activities.

Adam, a history major from Quebec, rises every day during the week at 5:30 in the morning to start his shift as a bus driver. In the afternoon, he works with a landscaping company tending gardens in the summer and removing snow in the winter. Daniel, who did his undergraduate studies in physical geography, works during the winter as a ski instructor. Four times a week, after the ski lessons he puts in several hours of work in a sports store fitting ski boots and repairing skis. In the summer he juggles jobs as a raft guide and safety kayaker with different

rafting companies. Naomi, a trained teacher from Ontario, holds two jobs throughout the year. During the day she is a cashier in a supermarket and four nights a week she works as a waitress in a pub. Winston, who holds a fine arts certificate from a college in Nova Scotia, is self-employed. He does freelance work as a photographer for receptions and tour groups. He runs his own little company producing and distributing photo cards of groups of nude, male ski bums chasing down the slopes of Whistler. In addition, he does layout work for a local magazine.

When asked whether they prefer this pattern of employment to holding a stable, full-time job, the answers are mixed. Adam and Naomi would like to pursue full-time careers but claim that there is no full-time work for them in Whistler. For Daniel and Winston, their work suits their preferences, at least at this point in their lives.

time workers as a proportion of all part-time workers), one must keep in mind that any such conclusion depends on the years chosen as starting and cut-off points of the time series. Non-standard employment is highly cyclical. As with unemployment, involuntary part-time employment is tied to the business cycle. In times of recession, full-time employment generally decreases and involuntary part-time employment and unemployment increase. During economic recovery, the two measures are expected to fall. The unemployment rate did indeed decline during the expansion years between 1983 and 1989 to its pre-recession level of 1980, and again after the 1990/91 recession from 1994 onward. In contrast, the involuntary part-time employment rate hovered well above its 1980 level, revealing persistent underemployment. If one interprets changes in voluntary part-time employment to reflect changes in the relative supply of part-time workers and changes in involuntary part-time employment to reflect changes in the demand by firms for part-time workers, a rise in the rate of involuntary part-time employment could be seen as an indicator of the reduced availability of "good" jobs.

MULTIPLE JOBHOLDING

Growth in part-time work is only one dimension of a more extensive transformation of the labour market. Partly due to the rise in part-time employment, multiple jobholding, or **moonlighting**, has also become more common. During the mid 1970s, moonlighting was not very common: just 1 out of every 50 workers held more than one job. Over the following 20 years, the number of moonlighters more than tripled, by far outpacing the 40% growth in employment in general over the same period. By 1997, about 723 000 workers, or just over 5% of working Canadians, were holding two or more jobs.

moonlighting multiple jobholding

Who are the moonlighters? In 1977, moonlighting was much more prevalent among men than women. Barely one quarter of all moonlighters were women. By 1997, women slightly outnumbered men as multiple jobholders. The rising number of female moonlighters is not just a reflection of women's increasing participation in the workforce. The incidence of multiple jobholding has increased much more rapidly for women (from 1.7% in 1977 to 5.9% in 1997) than for men (2.8% to 4.6%).[7] Young adults (aged 20 to 24), both men and women, have the highest rate of moonlighting (7%). Although this is partly the result of

---

7. The rate of incidence of multiple jobholding shows the number of multiple jobs in a group as a percentage of all workers in that group.

the difficulties young people encounter in finding full-time jobs, it may also reflect their preferences for flexibility and for broadening their work experience. It has become increasingly common to stitch together several part-time jobs rather than supplement a full-time job with part-time work. The majority (51%) of moonlighters are well educated, holding either a post-secondary certificate or diploma or a university degree, compared to 45% of single job holders. The proportion of highly educated moonlighters is particularly high among those holding several part-time jobs compared to part-timers holding only one job. The overrepresentation in this group of moonlighters indicates that some of our most highly trained people may be unable to secure suitable full-time jobs.

Where are the second jobs mostly found? According to the Survey of Work Arrangements (SWA), in November 1991 more than 70% of moonlighters who were paid employees in both jobs reported that their second jobs were in one of the following five categories: retail trade (18%), health and social services (14%), education services (14%), accommodation, food, and beverage services (12%), and other services (12%). Moonlighters in education services, health and social services, or retail trade were most likely to have their second job in the same industry as their first. In contrast, moonlighters with a main job in manufacturing rarely had their second jobs in the same industry.

Own-Account Self-employment

More and more Canadians are starting a business on their own. Since the mid 1970s, year-over-year increases in self-employment have been higher than the average growth rate in paid employment. As a result, the self-employed grew from 10% of total employment in 1976 to 18% in 1998. During this period, the nature of self-employment has changed. Between 1976 and 1989, 53% of the growth of self-employment was among business owners with paid help (employees). In sharp contrast, self-employed persons with paid help represented only about 10% of the net growth in self-employment between 1989 and 1997. Nine tenths of the growth in self-employment in the 1990s has come from entrepreneurs without employees (**own-account self-employment**). Of the 2.3 million business owners in 1996, well over half were their own boss without the additional help of employees.

Own-account self-employment continues to be the preserve of older workers, perhaps because they have more of the experience, skills, capital, and contacts required to succeed in their own business. In

own-account self-employment entrepreneurs without employees

some cases, older displaced workers may have more difficulty than younger individuals in finding paid employment, with self-employment the only alternative. Own-account self-employment was very high in agriculture, followed by construction, services to business (particularly computer, accounting, advertising, engineering, and management consulting services), and personal and household services. With the exception of the consumer services, where large numbers of young workers are employed, this industry pattern generally mirrors the age-distribution of self-employment.

NON-PERMANENT WORK

Changes in the definition of what constitutes a permanent or a temporary job combined with the lack of surveys providing data in the past make it impossible to establish long-run trends on temporary work arrangements. The General Social Survey (GSS), conducted in 1989 and 1994, provides data on temporary or contract workers, defined as paid workers with a specified end-date for their job or completion of a task or project. The GSS included only employees because the concept of a temporary job is not particularly meaningful for the self-employed. In 1989, 8% of employees identified themselves as temporary workers. Five years later, almost one million or 9% of all 15- to 64-year-old employees were in temporary or contract positions. Younger employees were more likely than middle-aged or older employees to be in temporary or contract jobs. By 1994, roughly one in six employees aged 15 to 24 were in limited-term jobs. Low rates of temporary employment were found in manufacturing, distributive services, and business services. In contrast, high rates were seen for employees in construction, social services, and other consumer services, as well as in public administration. The relatively high rates of temporary employment in social services (13% in 1994) and public administration (11%) are noteworthy. Together, these two non-market sectors accounted for 30% of all employees aged 15 to 64 but 38% of all temporary or contract workers. The public sector appears to have become more reliant on this form of non-standard work. A survey of temporary or contract workers found that 41% are in this type of work because they could not find full-time jobs.

The Survey of Work Arrangements (SWA), conducted in November 1995, expanded the relatively narrow definition of contingent work used in the GSS by adding to temporary or term and contract work, seasonal jobs, casual and on-call jobs, and work done through a temporary help agency.[8] These four types of temporary work arrangements are defined in the SWA as non-permanent jobs.[9] According to the SWA, 12% of all Canadian paid workers in November 1995 described their main job as non-permanent. The most common non-permanent work arrangements were temporary, contract, and term jobs (50%), followed by casual and on-call jobs (33%), and seasonal jobs (14%). Temporary help agency workers constituted the smallest segment. Seasonal jobs are largely determined by the annual fluctuations in labour demand of such industries as agriculture, fisheries, forestry, construction, and tourism. For example, two out of three non-permanent jobs in primary industries were seasonal, as were nearly half (47%) in construction and 39% in transportation. Although seasonal jobs have been an important form of work in Canada for most of the 20th century, the increased frequency of the other forms of non-permanent work is of more recent vintage.

There is a common perception that workers in non-permanent jobs are young, low-skilled people in clerical, service, and manual jobs with low hourly rates of pay and few if any fringe benefits. According to the SWA, however, the picture is much more diverse. Workers with non-permanent jobs include men and women of all ages and levels of education in many different occupations and industries. While one third of paid workers with non-permanent jobs were between 15 and 24 years of age—compared to only 14% of permanent job holders—by far the majority (62%) were adults in the 25- to 54-age range. More than half held a post-secondary certificate or diploma or university degree and more than one third were working in professional, managerial, and technical occupations, mostly in commercial, business, and personal services and in sales. Rates of hourly pay in non-permanent jobs were lower than in permanent jobs and fewer fringe benefits, such as pension plans, supplementary healthcare plans, dental insurance, paid sick leave, and paid annual vacation leave, were provided by the employer. In fact, 65% of permanent jobs in Canada boasted at least three of the five benefits in 1995, whereas 60% of the non-permanent positions offered none of them. To establish whether lower hourly pay and fringe benefits are causally linked to job permanency, however, would require

8. The work hours for casual and on-call jobs vary substantially from one week to the next. There are no pre-arranged schedules (employees are called to work as need arises), there is no usual pay for time not worked, and there are limited prospects for regular work over the long term.

9. In January 1997, the redesigned LFS began to provide monthly estimates of permanent and non-permanent jobs. In both the SWA and the LFS, the distinction between a permanent and non-permanent job relates to the job and not to the worker's intentions. For example, a student working at a permanent job is considered permanent even if he or she plans to stay in the job only temporarily.

statistical analyses that control for possible effects of other factors on the pay and benefit differential such as industry type, firm size, union membership, and collective agreement coverage, region, and the age, sex, and occupation of workers in these two job categories.

WHY HAS NON-STANDARD EMPLOYMENT BEEN ON THE RISE?

The current status of non-standard employment results from the coincidence of various trends on the supply and demand side of the labour market.

DEMOGRAPHIC CHANGES. On the supply side, the demographic shifts toward larger labour force shares of younger people (until the late 1970s) and of women facilitated the growth of non-standard jobs.

Young people, aged 16 to 24, often consider the early phase of their labour market experience as an experimental phase. Many do not want to commit themselves to jobs that will lock them into long-run careers. Instead, they prefer job hopping, which entails short work experiences on different jobs, in order to find out which career suits them better. Fringe benefits, such as health and life insurance, or private pensions, do not rank very high on the priority list of young people. The flexible jobs offered in non-standard employment often fit the bill of younger workers.

For women the picture is more varied. Many are committed to a long-term career and many have the educational background to pursue such a career. For them, disposable jobs are of little interest. Some women have been pushed into the workforce, perhaps owing to divorce or widowhood. For them, contingent employment may be the only alternative to welfare. There are also many women for whom flexible jobs with few fringe benefits are attractive. Many women with children at home prefer part-time work or work at home to supplement their spouse's income without interrupting family life. Women are often covered by their husband's benefit programs and are therefore willing to make concessions on the benefit side.

RISING UNCERTAINTY IN THE BUSINESS ENVIRONMENT. On the demand side, the growth of the service sector has been a major source for the rising number of non-standard jobs. In addition, the rise in non-standard employment reflects one of several strategies adopted by firms to adjust the level of labour input to changing market conditions. It is said that strategies such as the greater use of temporary employees, part-time employment, and the other forms of non-standard employment described earlier reflect the increase in the need for firms to have more flexible staffing arrangements. Long-run contracts that were preferred by employers in the stable 1950s and 1960s to assure themselves of a loyal and skilled workforce have become more risky since the 1970s.

One reason has been the increase in the scope and intensity of international and national competition due to liberalization in trade and the formation of larger trading blocks, as well as the large fluctuations in exchange rates. The exchange rate is the relative price of the currency of two countries. For example, if the exchange rate between the Canadian dollar and the U.S. dollar is 68 cents U.S. per Canadian dollar, one can exchange one Canadian dollar for 68 cents U.S. in foreign currency markets. An American who wants to obtain Canadian dollars would pay 68 cents U.S. for each dollar. A Canadian who wants to obtain U.S. dollars would pay $1.47 for each U.S. dollar. When people refer to the exchange rate between two countries, they usually mean the *nominal* exchange rate, which is the relative price of two currencies. Liberalization in trade with large fluctuations in exchange rates has led to increasing uncertainties regarding production cost. A declining value of the Canadian dollar against the U.S. dollar, for example, makes imports from the United States more expensive. If the Canadian dollar declines from 68 to 63 cents U.S., the price of a U.S. dollar in Canadian funds rises from $1.47 to $1.59. If U.S. imports, such as machines or computer software programs, are used by Canadian firms in the production of goods and services, production cost will rise. To compensate for increases in production cost caused by unpredictable exchange rate changes, firms often reduce their labour cost by replacing permanent employment contracts with more flexible work arrangements.

In particular, rising imports from East Asian countries have led firms in North America to seek ways to reduce labour cost and to achieve higher flexibility to react to overseas competition. East Asian countries generally produce goods with significantly lower labour cost per unit—lower wages or higher productivity, or both—and a traditionally high share of contingent workers. Canadian firms in the goods-producing sector are increasingly imitating the two-tier workforce of Japan and other East Asian countries, in which a core of workers possesses the polyvalent skills required to ensure functional flexibility in labour deployment. **Functional flexibility** refers to internal labour market rules that give employers greater freedom to move employees from one job to another within the firm. Traditionally, well-defined job ladders produce employees who are well qualified for higher level positions in their specialties, but these same employees may be less qualified to assume a different set of positions. Providing employees

functional flexibility
internal labour market rules that give employers greater freedom to move employees from one job to another within the firm

AN INTRODUCTION TO THE CANADIAN LABOUR MARKET

with a variety of experiences may prove to be functional when the company's needs are more difficult to predict in advance. In the two-tier system, the core workforce is supplemented by a pool of "just-in-time" workers who provide the numerical flexibility required to meet the unforeseen changes in sales or demand. **Numerical flexibility** refers to a company's practice of contracting out and making greater use of temporary or part-time workers to improve flexibility in its workforce.

Another reason for increased uncertainty is that technological developments are changing in shorter and shorter intervals. Among these changes are developments in new production materials (for example, ceramics and plastics replacing metals), production technologies (such as laser techniques, electronically guided machinery, and tools or robotics), and new products. These rapid changes shorten production cycles and the life cycle of products, which makes any long-term planning in production and sales more and more difficult.

A third reason, until recently, was relatively high inflation, especially in the mid and late 1970s and in the late 1980s, which locked many employers into expensive wage contracts because of COLA (cost of living allowance) clauses.[10] Also, accounting techniques designed for periods of basically stable prices were unable to cope with the added tax liability imposed through inflation. After-tax profits fell sharply, depleting the reserves that were often used to cover labour cost in downturns. Starting in 1988, the Bank of Canada embarked on a zero-inflation policy using tighter monetary policy. The inflation rate has since dropped sharply, eliminating most of the uncertainties arising from rising price levels.

While non-standard forms of employment increase companies' numerical flexibility, for workers they mostly entail unstable employment, low wages, lack of fringe benefits, and minimal opportunities for training and promotion. The growth in non-standard jobs is seen by some analysts as a major contributor to the creation of a large group of second-class workers mired in low-paying, unstable jobs and a resulting wage polarization. In an analysis of the labour market of the 1980s, the Economic Council of Canada stated: "Two quite distinct growth poles account for virtually all of the employment expansion in the 1980s: one includes highly skilled, well-compensated, stable jobs while the other consists of non-standard jobs with relatively low levels of compensation and stability" (Economic Council of Canada, 1990, p. 17; for similar views, see Bluestone & Harrison, 1986, 1988).

> **numerical flexibility**
> a company's practice of contracting out and making greater use of temporary or part-time workers to improve flexibility in its workforce

---

10. COLA clauses generally require companies to raise their nominal wages in line with rising price levels, normally measured by the Consumer Price Index.

The growth of the polar ends of the occupational and earnings distribution and the decline of middle-wage jobs are often described as the "disappearance of the middle class." This notion will be covered in more detail in the next chapter.

Also, since investment in training is discouraged by workers and employers alike due to the transient nature of the employment relationship, long-term productivity growth may be hampered. As a result, this type of employment may lead to the inability to compete in high technologies in the long run.

HOURS OF WORK

Measuring employment by the number of workers reflects only one component of labour demand. The other component is the hours worked on a job. The volume of employment in an economy is defined as the product of the number of employed workers times the hours of work per employed person. Adjustments in employment can thus occur as a result of changing the number of people employed, that is, through hiring and firing, or through changes in hours of work. The recent renewed debate over shortening the hours of work as a possible means to reduce unemployment is just one example illustrating the importance of this labour demand aspect.

To trace the long-term trend of working hours in Canada one must decide between different dimensions of work time, for example, hours per day or week, days per week, or weeks per year. To complicate matters, there is a set of at least three quite distinct measures of hours to choose from: standard or normal hours, actual hours worked, and hours paid. Taking one week as reference period, a count of **standard working hours** is based on the notion of a standard work week as established through law, collective agreement, or company policy. This measure is not affected by *temporary* changes in work schedules due to factors such as overtime, holidays, vacations, illness, and strikes. The total number of hours actually worked (**actual working hours**) reflects increases or decreases in work hours due to factors just mentioned. The total actual hours as well as the average hours worked per week are always lower than total or average standard hours because net time lost from work is always greater than net hours worked in excess of the regular schedule.[11] The number of **hours paid** is the hours for which

standard working hours
the number of hours in a standard work week as established by law, collective agreement, or company policy

actual working hours
total hours actually worked

hours paid hours for which workers are paid regardless of whether they were working or not

---

11. For example, between 1976 and 1996 the average actual hours per week calculated for all employed persons was about 2.5 to 3.5 hours lower than average usual hours.

workers are paid regardless of whether they are working or not. Each of these three measures may exhibit a different trend, since each responds to a somewhat differing set of determining factors. Since the concepts of these three measures have changed over time, as has the coverage, no consistent data set is available to track weekly work hours for the Canadian economy as a whole over more than two decades.[12]

The longest consistent data on hours worked covering the period 1901 to 1981 pertains to the manufacturing sector (see Figure 5.4).[13] This information reflects the widespread declining trend in the standard hours of work in Canada. At the beginning of the 20th century, workers in manufacturing typically put in 59 hours per week spread over six days. By 1957, the standard work week was reduced to 40 hours over five days. Compared to the dramatic decline in normal work hours that occurred during the first six decades of this century, Canadian workers have not seen much reduction in standard work time since then. As Figure 5.4 illustrates, the decline in standard weekly hours in manufacturing was not a steady one, as the sharpest drops occurred in the first 20 years of the century and from 1946 to 1957. Between 1901 and 1921, the standard manufacturing work week fell by eight hours, that is, each year by half an hour. From 1921 to 1946, the trend continued downward but at a much slower pace. In fact, over the more than 20 years the work week fell by only 1.5 hours. The period between 1946 and 1957 saw a dramatic change of nine hours, a drop of more than three quarters of an hour a year. Since the early 1960s, the decline levelled off. From 1961 to 1981, weekly manufacturing hours fell just by slightly more than an hour to approximately 39 hours per week.

Since that time the length of the standard work week has changed very little. According to the Labour Force Survey, the average number of hours usually worked in manufacturing in 1997 was 39.6, compared to 35.3 in the service sector and 36.8 in the economy as a whole.

---

12. The most recent example of a redefinition of standard, normal, or usual hours of work is the revision introduced by the Labour Force Survey in 1997. Between 1976 and 1996, usual hours referred to hours worked in a typical week. Thus, if paid overtime or unpaid extra hours were typical of the worker's schedule, they would be included in the estimates of usual hours. Since 1997, usual hours for employees are defined as those normally worked in a week for regular pay rates. Information on overtime hours, paid or unpaid, is now collected separately. The change was introduced to improve understanding of standard work schedules and overtime behaviour.

13. The series covering the period 1901–71 was put together from different data sources by Ostry and Zaidi (1979). Most of their primary data came from the Survey of Working Conditions, from which the figures for 1981 were added. Unfortunately, the series could not be updated to more recent years since the survey was discontinued in the early 1980s.

FIGURE 5.4 STANDARD WEEKLY WORKING HOURS IN MANUFACTURING, 1901–81

The survey containing the most recent data used for this table was discontinued in the early 1980s. Nevertheless, the table illustrates the most significant changes of the twentieth century; the length of the standard work week has changed very little since 1981.

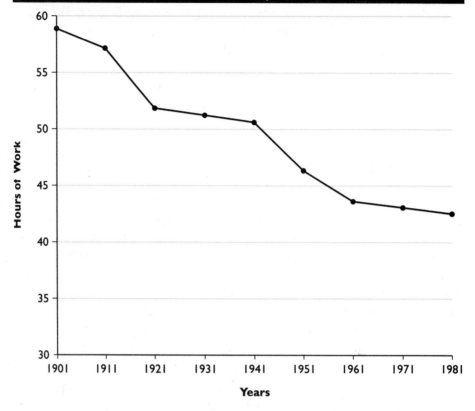

Sources: For 1901–71, Ostry, S., and Zaidi, M. (1979). *Labour Economics in Canada* (3rd ed.). Toronto: Macmillan, pp. 80–81; for 1981, Canadian Department of Labour, Wage Rates, Salaries, and Hours of Labour.

WHAT CAUSED THE CHANGES IN STANDARD WORKING HOURS?

The decline in the length of the standard work week during the first 60 years of the 20th century was largely due to increased productivity and growth in real wages. As technology advanced, workers produced the same amount in less time. Both employers and employees enjoyed the benefits of growing productivity in the form of higher profits and higher real wages. Rapidly rising real wages allowed workers to trade some of the real wage gains for more leisure and still experience an increase in their standard of living. As long as productivity grew fast enough to keep reduced hours cost-neutral, it was in the employers' interest to accommodate worker and union demands for more free time.

After 1960, the length of the standard work week "stabilized" despite strong growth in productivity, which lasted until the late 1960s, and continued growth in real wages, which lasted until the mid 1970s. These had been the very conditions that had led to the decline of the standard weekly working hours in the first half of the century. Labour economists offer a variety of supply-and-demand explanations for this levelling-off.

On the supply side, workers were investing in more years of education. Once they were employed, the pressure to recoup the cost of schooling and forgone wages as quickly as possible made them less likely to trade wage gains for shorter hours. At the same time, the trend to earlier retirement shortened the portion of the life cycle devoted to paid work. This left fewer earning-years during which workers could save for comfortable retirement. Also, workers increasingly opted to take their share of increased productivity in the form of more vacations and other non-wage benefits, rather than shortening further the standard work week. For example, the average annual vacation in manufacturing rose from 2.7 weeks in 1959 to 3.6 weeks in 1979. Improvements were made in other non-wage benefits as well. Employers' payroll contributions to health care, dental care, and pension plans and to mandatory programs such as unemployment insurance, the Canada and Quebec Pension Plans, and workers' compensation almost doubled from 4.6% of labour income in 1961 to 8.7% in 1979.

On the demand side, employers had little incentive to reduce the standard work week below 38 to 40 hours, since further reductions were unlikely to yield a proportionate increase in productivity. Shorter hours could even have a negative effect on productivity as daily "gearing up" and "gearing down" would take a greater proportion of paid work hours.

Many of the factors underlying the stability of the standard hours in the 1960s and 1970s persisted into the 1980s and 1990s. Fringe benefits have continued to increase as a share of labour income, educational attainment has continued to rise, and early retirement has become even more common. Most importantly, however, real wages of full-time, full-year workers have increased only very modestly. Thus workers have had no major wage gains to trade for added leisure. Employers were also unlikely to support a reduction in work hours without a proportionate reduction in wages, since the growth in productivity continued to be slow throughout the 1980s. Furthermore, with rapid technological change, employers have increased their investment in job-specific training of full-time staff. Shorter hours of work for these workers would mean a smaller return on that investment.

CHANGES IN THE DISTRIBUTION OF STANDARD WORKING HOURS

Although the standard work week has changed little over the last three decades, substantial changes have occurred in the underlying distribution of hours worked, particularly since the 1981/82 recession. As the proportion of workers with standard hours (35 to 40 hours) declines, the proportions with short hours (fewer than 35) and long hours (41 and over) rises. This shift away from the middle is known as "hours polarization." While the share of workers with standard hours fell by 10.7 percentage points between 1976 and 1995 down to 54%, the share of workers with shorter work weeks increased from 16% to nearly 24%, and those with longer working schedules rose from 19% to 22%. The polarization in the distribution of working hours is likely to be an important factor explaining the growing inequality in earnings as highly paid workers increased their weekly hours while low-paid employees decreased their weekly hours.[14]

More years in school may account for some of the increase in below-standard hours. Part-time employment is usually more feasible than longer work schedules for people attending school. As mentioned earlier, youths who have left school are having an increasingly difficult time finding full-time employment. In 1995, 3 out of 10 non-student youths worked less than standard hours, triple the rate in 1976. Although the rise in the frequency of shorter work weeks may partly reflect the response of firms to rising costs and competition, the increasing incidence of above-standard work weeks may be part of the same response. Part-timers and casual workers enable an enterprise to meet shifting levels of demand with minimal current and future costs, but not all tasks are easily divisible and not all workers are substitutable. Long work weeks may be required of those with special skills or management responsibilities. As the proportion of men and women working in professional and managerial occupations has grown so has the tendency for this group to work above standard hours. In the case of skilled blue-collar occupations, given administrative and overhead considerations, firms may find it more cost efficient to offer paid overtime than to hire and train new workers.

---

14. See Morissette, Myles, and Picot, 1994.

SUMMARY

The number of Canadians employed has almost tripled over the last five decades. The employment rate is affected by changes in the population and by economic conditions. The rapid growth in the employment rate of women has been a major characteristic of the Canadian job scene. In contrast, the employment rate of men has been steadily declining since the 1940s. There has been a major shift in the composition of employment with a shift toward employment in the service sector, away from resource and manufacturing industries. The relatively faster growth in the service sector can be attributed to a variety of factors, including differences in productivity growth in the goods- and services-producing industries, increases in real income, contracting out of services, intensified international competition, and the increased demand for services by firms in the goods-producing industries.

There have also been shifts in the occupational composition of the labour force, with the greatest employment gains being made in white-collar occupations. There are some indications that the skill structure of the labour force is becoming more polarized between higher skilled and less skilled workers.

Growth in non-standard employment, that is part-time work, moonlighting, self-employment, and non-permanent work, has been accelerating in relation to full-time permanent work. The rise in non-standard employment reflects demographic changes in the Canadian labour force as well as changes on the demand side. Firms are increasingly replacing long-term employment contracts with more flexible staffing arrangements to compensate for uncertainties caused by increased foreign and domestic competition and rapid technological change.

Standard hours of work declined up to the early 1960s. Since then, the decline has levelled off, largely due to the slowdown in productivity and the decline in real wages. Recently, the distribution of hours worked has been changing with the proportion of workers working standard hours declining and the proportion of workers working shorter and longer hours rising.

KEY TERMS

aggregate labour demand 100

employment rate 102

marginal productivity of labour/marginal physical product 106

total factor productivity 106

Engel's law 108

income elasticity of demand 108

open economy 109

non-standard employment 112

underemployed 116

moonlighting 117

own-account self-employment 118

functional flexibility 122

numerical flexibility 123

standard working hours 124

actual working hours 124

hours paid 124

EXERCISES

1. The most important change in the distribution of employment in Canada has been the shift in employment away from the goods-producing industries to the service-producing industries. Explain how Engel's law might apply to this shift.

2. One of the reasons provided for the shift in employment has been the difference in productivity gains between the manufacturing and service sectors. If productivity rose more in the manufacturing sector than in the service sector, what effect would this have on employment in the manufacturing sector?

3. The decline of jobs in the primary and manufacturing sectors and the growth of service jobs have led to the claim that the skill level of the labour force is declining. Assess the validity of the "deskilling" hypothesis.

4. What is meant by non-standard employment? Describe some of the changes in non-standard employment over the last 20 years.

5. It is claimed that the growth in non-standard employment reflects the need for firms to have more flexible staffing arrangements. Why would the need for these arrangements be greater in recent years than in earlier years?

6. While the proportion of employees working standard hours (35 to 40 hours per week) is declining, the proportion working short hours (fewer than 35) and long hours (41 and over) is increasing. What factors may have con-

tributed to the rising polarization in work hours?

7. The decline in standard weekly working hours has slowed down over the last 30 years. Assess some of the factors that may have contributed to the slowdown.

REFERENCES

Akyeampong, E. (1996). Another Measure of Employment. *Perspectives on Labour and Income, 8*(4): 9–15.

Bluestone, B., and Harrison, B. (1982).*The Deindustrialization of America: Plant Closings, Community Abandonment and the Dismantling of Basic Industries.* New York: Basic Books.

Bluestone, B., and Harrison, B. (1986, December). The Great American Jobs Machine. Study prepared for the U.S. Joint Economic Committee.

Bluestone, B., and Harrison, B. (1988). The Growth of Low-Wage Employment: 1963–86. *American Economic Review,* pp. 124–128.

Chaykowski, R. P. (1994). *Modern Labour Economics. The Canadian Context.* New York: HarperCollins College Publishers.

Clark, C. (1957). *The Conditions of Economic Progress.* London: St. Martin's Press.

Economic Council of Canada. (1991). *Employment in the Service Economy* (The Betcherman Report). Ottawa: Minister of Supply and Services.

Cohen, G. L. (1994). Ever More Moonlighters. *Perspectives on Labour and Income, 6*(3): 31–38.

Economic Council of Canada (1990). *Good Jobs, Bad Jobs: Employment in the Service Economy.* Ottawa: Minister of Supply and Services.

Economic Council of Canada. (1989). *Legacies: Twenty-Sixth Annual Review.* Ottawa: Minister of Supply and Services.

Grenon, L., and Chun, B. (1997). Non-permanent Paid Work. *Perspectives on Labour and Income, 9*(3): 21–31.

Krahn, H. (1995). Non-standard Work on the Rise. *Perspectives on Labour and Income, 7*(4): 35–42.

Manser, M. E., and Picot, G. (1999). Self-employment in Canada and the United States. *Perspectives on Labour and Income, 11*(3): 37–44.

Morissette, R., Myles, J., and Picot, G. (1994). Earnings Inequality and the Distribution of Working Time in Canada. *Canadian Business Economics, 2*(3): 3–16.

Noreau, N. (1994). Involuntary Part-timers. *Perspectives on Labour and Income, 6*(3): 25–30.

Ostry, S., and Zaidi, M. (1979). *Labour Economics in Canada* (3rd ed.). Toronto: Macmillan.

Sunter, D. and Morissette, R. (1994). The Hours People Work. *Perspectives on Labour and Income, 6*(3): 8–13.

Sussman, D. (1998). Moonlighting: A Growing Way of Life. *Perspectives on Labour and Income, 10*(2): 24–31.

Statistics Canada. (1997). *Labour Force Update. Hours of Work.* Ottawa: Statistics Canada. (Catalogue No. 71-005-XPB)

Theil, H., Cheung, C.-F., and Seale Jr., J. L. (1989). *Advances in Econometrics. Supplement 1, International Evidence on Consumer Patterns.* Greenwich, CT: JAI Press.

6

······································

UNEMPLOYMENT

OBJECTIVES

After completing this chapter, you should be able to:

1. describe how the amount of unemployment is measured;

2. discuss the problems that arise in interpreting the official unemployment rate;

3. distinguish between the frequency of unemployment and duration of unemployment;

4. describe the main features of unemployment in Canada;

5. discuss the gap in unemployment rates between Canada and the U.S.;

6. distinguish between various types of unemployment;

7. discuss the factors that may have led to the increase in the natural rate of unemployment.

In Chapters 4 and 5 the steady increase in both the labour force and the level of employment over the last 50 years was described. Has employment matched labour force growth over the years? If we compare the development of the labour force (labour supply) and employment (labour demand) in Figure 6.1, we notice that the overall trend increase

FIGURE 6.1   LABOUR FORCE AND EMPLOYMENT GROWTH, 1947–98

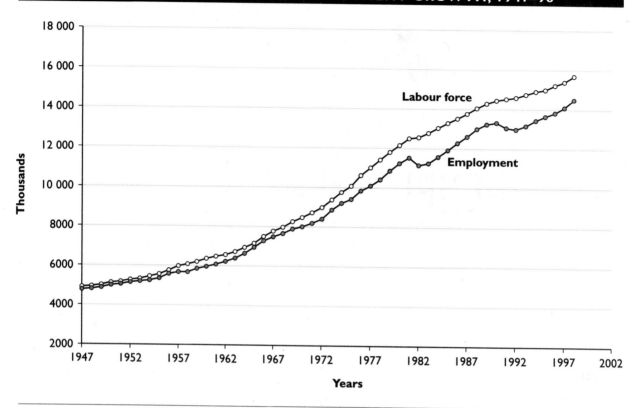

Sources: For 1947–94, adapted from Statistics Canada. (1995). *Canadian Economic Observer, Historical Statistical Supplement 1994/95*. Ottawa: Statistics Canada. (Catalogue no. 11-210); for 1995–98, adapted from Statistics Canada. (1999, July). *Canadian Economic Observer, Statistical Summary*. Ottawa: Statistics Canada. (Catalogue no. 11-010).

in employment has been lower than the trend increase in the labour force. One reason can be found in the fact that recessions have a relatively larger negative impact on labour demand than on labour supply. Note the large declines in employment during the last two recessions in 1981/82 and 1990/91 as compared to the relatively minor changes in labour supply.

Since unemployment is the difference between the quantity of labour supplied and the quantity of labour demanded, differences in the growth of the labour force and employment must affect the level of unemployment. Before looking at unemployment in Canada and the reasons behind the phenomenon, we consider how unemployment is measured and what problems arise in interpreting unemployment statistics.

HOW IS UNEMPLOYMENT MEASURED?

Different countries use different methods for estimating the number of unemployed. For example, in France, Germany, and the United Kingdom, a person is recorded as unemployed if he or she is registered with one of the employment offices as a claimant for unemployment insurance benefits. Canada and the United States have not opted for the registration approach primarily because it leads to serious underestimation of unemployment rates. For example, young people or adult women who enter the labour force for the first time and cannot find employment would not be registered as unemployed because they are not eligible for employment (or unemployment) insurance benefits. Likewise, long-term unemployed individuals who have exhausted their claims and are not receiving benefits are not included in this count.

Canada and the United States use the survey method to collect unemployment data.[1] As mentioned in Chapter 4, the Canadian unemployment statistics released each month are based on the Labour Force Survey conducted by Statistics Canada. To be counted as unemployed a person must be without work, must be available for work, and must have actively looked for work within the past four weeks. The criterion "actively looking for work" is defined as making some effort to find work, for example, answering a want ad, going for a job interview, or asking friends for job leads. The condition of active job search is waived for persons on temporary layoff and for people with a new job scheduled to start in four weeks or less. In both cases, it is assumed that the only reason these people are not looking for work is that they already have a job and would have worked in the reference week had work been available. As noted, a person must be available for work in order to be classified as unemployed. One would naturally expect that most people looking for work are in fact available for work, but although this is generally true, there are exceptions. For example, students looking for full-time summer jobs during the spring months are not currently available for work. Until they are free to take a full-time job, they are not part of the labour supply and are accordingly counted as not in the labour force.

The **unemployment rate** is the percentage of the labour force that is unemployed:

unemployment rate
percentage of the labour force that is unemployed

$$\text{Unemployment rate} = \frac{\text{Number of unemployed people}}{\text{Labour force}} \times 100$$

---

1. The different ways unemployment data are collected make international comparisons difficult.

In 1998, the labour force contained 15.632 million people, 14.326 million of whom were employed and 1.306 million were unemployed. The unemployment rate was thus 8.4 percent:

$$\left(\frac{1.306}{15.632}\right) \times 100 = 8.4\%$$

DO THE OFFICIAL UNEMPLOYMENT FIGURES MEASURE WHAT THEY OUGHT TO?

Measuring the amount of unemployment in the economy appears to be a straightforward task. In fact, it is not. There are several reasons why the official statistics may not accurately reflect the true amount of unemployment.

INACTIVE JOB SEEKERS

The unemployment rate may overstate the extent of unemployment by including individuals who have only a weak attachment to the labour force. For example, some of those who report being unemployed may, in fact, not have been engaged in serious job search; when asked directly if they looked for work, they might give a positive answer even though they may have at best answered one newspaper ad during the survey month, or gone for one interview to tender an application. They may be calling themselves unemployed in order to qualify for one of the government programs that provide financial assistance to the unemployed. It may be more realistic to view some of these people as out of the labour force.

DISCOURAGED WORKERS

discouraged workers
persons who want a job but have given up the search for a job

hidden unemployed
discouraged workers who do not show up as unemployed on the Labour Force Survey

The officially reported unemployment rate may understate the true unemployment level in the labour force because it excludes the **discouraged workers**. These are people who are available and willing to work but have given up looking for work because they believe nothing suitable is available. People who decide to stop looking for work are classified as having dropped out of the labour force rather than as unemployed. Discouraged workers are not counted in the official unemployment statistics, even though they are interested in working. The number of discouraged workers is referred to as **hidden unemployment**.

AN INTRODUCTION TO THE CANADIAN LABOUR MARKET

A simple example shows how the discouraged-worker effect lowers the unemployment rate. Assume there are 1.5 million unemployed out of a labour force of 15 million. This would mean an unemployment rate of 1.5/15 = 0.10 or 10%. If 100 000 of these 1.5 million unemployed people simply stop looking for work and drop out of the labour force, there would be 1.4 million unemployed out of a labour force of 14.9 million. The unemployment rate would have dropped to 1.4/14.9 = 0.094 or 9.4%.

Statistics Canada produces data on the discouraged worker from two sources. The first is the Labour Force Survey; the second is an annual supplement to the Labour Force Survey called the Survey of Job Opportunities. Discouragement in the labour force is measured through a series of questions. The survey asks willing and available workers who are not searching for work why they are not actively looking. One possible response is that the respondent believes no work is available. In 1997, 108 000 individuals chose this response. If these discouraged workers had been counted as unemployed instead of being as outside of the labour force, the officially recorded unemployment rate would have increased from 9.2% to 9.9%.

The discouraged-worker effect is generally larger in times of recession, when unemployed people often become so discouraged that they stop looking for work. They are then classified as having dropped out of the labour force rather than as being unemployed. As a consequence, the increase in the official unemployment rate during a recession is smaller than would be the case had the discouraged workers been counted as unemployed. Similarly, during expansions, people become encouraged about their job prospects. Once they begin looking for jobs they are considered part of the labour force. As a result, the decline in the unemployment rate, particularly in the early state of a recovery, is smaller than it would be had these people remained outside the labour force.

UNDEREMPLOYED WORKERS

The official unemployment account may also understate the true unemployment situation because those involuntarily employed part-time are recorded as employed rather than partly unemployed. "Unemployed" includes only those who did not work at all during the reference week. The group of those who work up to 30 hours in total, regardless of the number of jobs, but who would prefer to work full time (i.e., the involuntary part-time worker) can be very large. This group is referred to as

Mary, age 47, lives in Freshwater, Nfld. She worked for several years as a fishplant weigher in the local fish plant. She liked her job. Not only did it provide a steady income but it also strengthened her ties to the community. The plant was like an extended family. Everybody knew everybody. In July 1992, shortly after the federal government declared a two-year moratorium on northern cod fishing, the plant closed and Mary was permanently laid off. Her husband Patrick, a 49-year-old fish cutter, was also among the 210 workers who lost their jobs.

Mary considered taking a retraining course, but her age and knowledge of the regional labour market, in the end, made her decide against it. If young people with degrees could not find jobs, she reasoned, how would she be able to find employment? After one year of unsuccessful job searching, she gave up. Patrick also left the labour force because he believed that no jobs were available.

Mary and Patrick are obviously not alone. In 1998, Newfoundland had an unemployment rate of 18%, the highest in the country. If the number of discouraged workers had been added to the official unemployment figure, the jobless rate would have increased to 23%. Newfoundland had as many discouraged workers (16 000) as Ontario, which has a labour force 25 times bigger.

underemployed workers. As stated in Chapter 4, involuntary part-time employment has shown a marked increase over the last 20 years.

When sales decline, employers often react by reducing the hours of work bef... g to lay off workers. This reduction can take var... is to change full-time jobs into part-time jobs. employment tends to follow the business cycle. the number of full-time jobs decreases, while ork increases. Faced with the prospect of unem- have no choice but to accept part-time posi- would prefer full-time work. Thus labour ization of employed labour, can imply a loss that does not show up in the official unem- these record only head counts. The unem- of involuntary part-time employment are ame direction. Both indicators declined etween 1983 and 1989; however, although ined significantly, the involuntary part- remained well above what it had been in the overall improvement in the labour market as shown by the declining unemployment rate, the involuntary part-time rate revealed persistent underemployment.

In addition to involuntary part-time unemployment, underemployment can also take the form of individuals doing work for which they are overqualified, for example, a historian with a Ph.D. who rides a bike for a courier service.

MARGINAL WORKERS

Marginal workers are workers with a weak labour force attachment. Typically, young people (aged 15 to 24) belong to the group of marginal workers. Their tenuous attachment to the labour force is reflected in the frequent moves into and out of the labour force. Of those who are still in school, some may work sporadically during the school year; others seek employment only during the summer months. Among those not in school, many are not interested in, or cannot find, longer term employment, and change frequently between casual jobs and non-market activities.

marginal workers workers with a weak attachment to the labour force

The ever-changing balance between market and non-market activities among marginal workers makes it difficult to draw lines between the three categories of employed, unemployed, and not in the labour force. The behaviour of marginal workers severely complicates the interpretation of standard labour market statistics. Several labour economists have adopted the viewpoint that the distinction between a person who is unemployed and a person who is not in the labour force becomes meaningless for marginal workers because the behaviour of most of the unemployed and many persons outside the labour force is functionally indistinguishable. They suggest combining the unemployed with those not in the labour force in a category of non-employed or jobless and focusing, for example, in the case of youths, on the analysis of youth non-employment rather than merely on youth unemployment. Similar proposals replaced the old classification with two new categories: economically active (employed, those engaged in household work, and enrolled students) and the economically inactive (unemployed and all others). Whether the categories "unemployed" and "not-in-the labour force" are behaviourally distinct labour force states is ultimately an empirical question. Some preliminary tests have rejected the idea that the two categories are meaningless in terms of behaviour. It would seem that our understanding of the group of marginal workers is still too limited to justify a revision of the conventional classification of labour market status. Nevertheless, the discussion reflects some doubts that the unemployment rate is a useful measure of unused labour for certain groups in the labour force.

The conclusion we can draw is that there is no easy way to fix the unemployment rate to make it a more accurate indicator of the conditions in the labour market. The official unemployment rate reflects one of many possible ways of defining unemployment and the labour force. To complement the official unemployment rate, Statistics Canada has developed the following eight additional measures of unemployment:

- R_1: people unemployed 14 weeks or more as a percentage of the labour force;
- R_2: unemployment rate of people heading families with children under 16 years of age;
- R_3: unemployment rate excluding full-time students;
- R_4: unemployment rate including full-time members of the Canadian Armed Forces;
- R_5: official unemployment rate;
- R_6: unemployment rate of the full-time labour force;
- R_7: unemployment rate including people not in the labour force who sought work in the past six months but, for reasons related to the labour market, are not now looking for work;
- R_8: underutilization rate based on hours worked and hours lost to the economy through unemployment and "visible" underemployment;
- R_9: unemployment rate of the part-time labour force.

Using some of the supplementary measures in conjunction with the official unemployment rate provides a more complete picture of the underutilization of labour in the economy.

THE UNEMPLOYMENT RATE AS A MEASURE OF ECONOMIC HARDSHIP

The unemployment rate is used not only to measure the extent of unused labour but also as an indicator of economic hardship. Economic hardship occurs when the level of income is not enough to provide for minimum consumption requirements. An unemployed person does not receive any income from work. The larger the number of unemployed people in an economy, the greater the loss of earnings. There are several reasons, however, to suggest that hardship associated with unemployment has weakened over the last decades.

One reason is the change from the single-earner family to the dual-earner or multi-earner family, a change we described in Chapter 4. In earlier times when the single-earner family dominated, the family's economic well-being depended on the employment of the single breadwinner, usually the man in the family. As more and more women enter the labour force on a permanent basis, the family relies less on the employment income of any one member. In recent times, the majority of families with one member unemployed have at least one employed member, and many have two or more employed. Another reason has been the increase in income transfer programs, in particular the availability of employment insurance benefits. In the absence of such programs, the standard of living depends on the availability of employment and the adequacy of earnings. With the creation of the unemployment insurance system in the early 1940s and the growth of payments and coverage, particularly since 1971/72, families became more protected against loss of income due to unemployment. Although the level of benefits and the eligibility period have been reduced in recent years, the system still provides a substantial buffer against financial hardship caused by unemployment.

The degree of financial hardship caused by unemployment depends on many factors. Whether, for example, a person is unemployed for 4 weeks or for 40 weeks, or whether a family experiencing unemployment has no children or several children significantly affects the economic strain caused by unemployment. An aggregate figure, such as the official unemployment rate, clearly cannot reveal all these factors. Two of the measures in the list above of supplementary unemployment rates, R_1 and R_2, are more indicative of possible hardship associated with unemployment. R_1 relates to longer term unemployment. The underlying assumption of this measure is that, all other things being equal, longer term unemployment induces greater economic hardship. As the proportion of long-term unemployed people has been growing in Canada for some time, the associated increase in hardship is not indicated in the official unemployment rate (R_5). Relative increases in R_2, which focuses on families with children under age 16, may indicate increased hardship.

AN ALTERNATIVE MEASURE OF THE UTILIZATION OF LABOUR

The unemployment rate is supposed to measure the proportion of people who are without work and are actively seeking work. It measures the degree of *underutilization* of labour. An alternative way to assess the tightness or slack in the labour market is to focus on the *utilization* of labour. One measure is the employment rate or the employment-population ratio (E/P). As mentioned in Chapter 4, the employment rate measures the proportion of the civilian population of working age that is employed:

$$\text{Employment rate} = \frac{\text{Total number of employed}}{\text{Population of working age}} \times 100$$

The employment rate has at least two important advantages over the unemployment rate. One is that employment figures in the numerator represent a more reliable statistic than the unemployment figures in the numerator of the unemployment rate. It is easier to establish whether a person is employed as opposed to whether a person is unemployed.

The other advantage of using the employment rate is that it makes the sometimes hazy distinction between being in the labour force and not being in the labour force redundant. The unemployment rate uses the labour force as its base, whereas the employment rate uses the total civilian population, excluding certain age groups and people in institutions. In this way, the sometimes difficult distinction between being in or out of the labour force need not be made. Also, the employment rate is a more consistent measure to compare over time. The population as a denominator is a more stable base than the labour force, because the working-age population hardly changes over the business cycle. In contrast, the labour force expands or contracts over the business cycle as people drop out of and move back into the labour force in response to changes in employment opportunities. As a result, unemployment rates change significantly due to changes in the denominator, thus giving a possibly wrong picture of the labour market situation. Take the case of an economic recovery during which the labour force participation rate increases significantly, and the unemployment rate declines. Focusing on the unemployment rate would understate the strength of the recovery if the employment gain exceeds the unemployment reduction.

Although the employment rate is undisturbed by the shifts of workers into or out of the labour force, the measure is not without its own problems. Estimates of unemployment focus on a problem, similarly to statistics on illness, crime, and poverty. The unemployment rate reports the number of people who cannot find work. For them, the economy has failed since it has not provided a job. The employment rate stresses a strength in the economy, namely its capacity to create jobs. Labour economists are divided over the question whether the employment rate is a better indicator of the state of the labour market than the unemployment rate. An increase in the labour force participation rate (LFPR), for example, can be associated with a simultaneous increase of employment and unemployment:

AN INTRODUCTION TO THE CANADIAN LABOUR MARKET

$$\text{LFPR} = \frac{\text{Number of employed + Number of unemployed}}{\text{Working age population}}$$

In this case, the increase in the employment rate and the unemployment rate gives a very different picture of the strength in the labour market. The increase in the employment rate captures only the employment effect and ignores the unemployment effect, thereby understating the weakness in the labour market. If one adopts the view that the strength of a labour market should be measured by the ability of job seekers to find jobs, then a rising unemployment rate would indicate that the labour market is not strong enough to provide jobs to all who look for work. If both indicators increase simultaneously, there is clearly some ambiguity as to whether or not the economy is doing well in providing jobs.

There is growing awareness that the unemployment rate and the employment rate should be used in conjunction with each other. For instance, if the employment rate and the labour force participation rate increase simultaneously and the unemployment rate is stable or even declines, this would indicate that the labour market is creating a sufficient number of jobs. If, however, the employment rate and the unemployment rate both increase, a look at the size of the increase in the LFPR would be necessary to assess the strength in the labour market.

CHARACTERISTICS OF CANADIAN UNEMPLOYMENT

Figure 6.2 shows the post-war history of the unemployment rate. Two features stand out. Since World War II, the unemployment rate has been on an upward trend. Unemployment seems to fluctuate around an increasing average rate: 4% in the 1950s, 5% in the 1960s, close to 7% in the 1970s, slightly more than 9% in the 1980s, and close to 10% in the 1990s (1990–98).

Second, there are large fluctuations in the unemployment rate; the unemployment rate has fluctuated between 2% and 12% since 1947. These fluctuations are closely related with recessions and expansions. Note that the increases in unemployment were much steeper in the last two recessions than in earlier recessions. Unemployment peaked at 11.9% in the recession of the early 1980s and at 11.3% in the recession of 1990/91.

The unemployment rate officially published by Statistics Canada represents a snapshot of only limited information. Looking at the

FIGURE 6.2 UNEMPLOYMENT RATE, 1947–98

Notes: a) Annual averages from 1950 onward include Newfoundland.

b) Population aged 15 and over from 1966. Data prior to 1966 are based on population aged 14 and over.

c) Estimates prior to 1966 have not been adjusted to conform to current concepts.

Sources: For 1947–65, adapted from Statistics Canada. (1985, November). *The Labour Force.* Ottawa: Statistics Canada. (Catalogue no. 71-001); for 1966–98, adapted from Statistics Canada. (1999). *Historical Labour Force Statistics, 1966–1998.* Ottawa: Statistics Canada. (Catalogue no. 71-201).

unemployment rate tells us little about how people become unemployed, or how long they stay unemployed. As we pointed out in the discussion of the flow approach in Chapter 2, we can learn a lot from an analysis of labour market dynamics. Figure 6.3 shows the flows among the three labour market states of employment (E), unemployment (U), and not-in-the-labour force (N).

THE INCIDENCE OF UNEMPLOYMENT

In any month, many people become unemployed and many others leave the state of unemployment. People become unemployed if they

FIGURE 6.3   FLOWS AMONG THE THREE LABOUR MARKET STATES

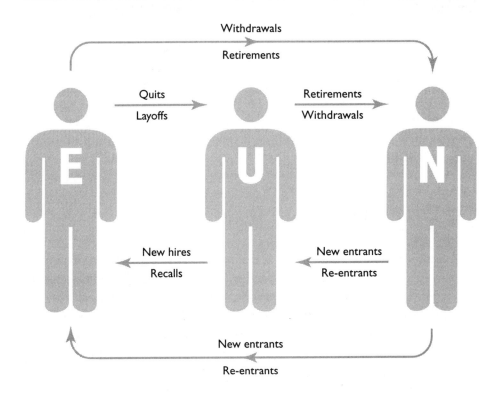

lose their jobs, leave their jobs, or enter or re-enter the labour force and cannot find a job. The proportion of people in the labour force who become unemployed in a given period is called the **incidence of unemployment**. As people constantly enter unemployment, others leave unemployment to take a job or because they are recalled from a layoff. They also may leave unemployment if they withdraw from the labour force.

Figure 6.3 illustrates the flows between the three labour market states that affect the number of unemployed people at any given time. When we break down unemployment by reason for becoming unemployed, we can see that job losers—that is, people who are laid off either permanently or temporarily—are the biggest source in the incidence of unemployment. Their number fluctuates greatly over the business cycle. In the recession of 1990/91, on any given day in Canada, almost 1 million of the 1.6 million unemployed people were job losers. In contrast, in the business cycle peak year of 1989, fewer than 500 000 of the 1 million unemployed were job losers. Entrants and re-entrants—that

incidence of unemployment   the proportion of people in the labour force entering the state of unemployment in a given period

is, people who enter the labour force for the first time (after leaving school for example) or re-enter the labour force after a temporary absence—constitute the second largest component of the unemployed. On any given day, around 300 000 unemployed people are entrants or re-entrants. Job leavers—that is, people who have voluntarily quit their jobs (because they were dissatisfied, had to move geographically, etc.)—are the smallest and most stable group among the unemployed. On any given day, around 200 000 people are job leavers. Although this number is relatively constant, it fluctuates slightly according to the business cycle: a larger number of people quit their jobs in good economic times than in bad times.

THE DURATION OF UNEMPLOYMENT

duration of unemployment the average time each person spends unemployed

The unemployment rate depends not only on the proportion of people becoming unemployed but also on the average time each person spends unemployed (the **duration of unemployment**). The simplest way to calculate the duration of unemployment is to look at the average duration of unemployment for those currently unemployed. Since these spells are in progress rather than completed, this duration measure is only an approximation.

It is essential to distinguish between the relative contribution of duration and incidence changes to the overall unemployment rate in order to assess the economic and social impact of unemployment. A yearly unemployment rate of 9%, for example, may indicate that 9% of all members of the labour force are unemployed for one year. (The unemployment rate can be approximated by the product of the incidence of unemployment and the average duration of unemployment. In our example, 9% would be the incidence and 52 weeks would be the average duration, so the product is $0.09 \times 52/52$). A 9% unemployment rate, however, could also describe a situation in which 80% of the labour force experiences unemployment once a year for six weeks ($0.80 \times 6/52$). An overall unemployment rate of 9% is thus consistent with considerably different durations and incidences of unemployment.

If turnover among the unemployed is rapid and an increase in unemployment occurs because more people are experiencing brief spells of unemployment, this situation poses a less serious problem than one in which the burden of unemployment is borne mainly by people experiencing longer spells of unemployment. Workers unemployed for many months or even longer than a year are more likely to suffer economic and psychological hardship. Prolonged unemployment saps the will and initiative of the unemployed and furthermore leads to loss of valuable work experience. Employers tend to use the unemployment record as a screening device, eliminating job applicants with longer spells of unemployment. As an individual's duration of unemployment grows, the probability of finding employment declines.

The average duration of unemployment has increased significantly in Canada since the early 1980s: from 15 weeks in 1981 to 18 weeks in 1989, to 24 weeks in 1996. At the same time, the incidence of unemployment declined from 2.6% of the labour force in 1981 to 2.1% in 1996. Thus the rise in the unemployment rate over this period is largely accounted for by a rise in unemployment duration.

Although the average duration of unemployment has increased, most people who become unemployed in any given month nevertheless remain unemployed for only a short time. In 1996, for example, 53% of unemployed people in Canada were unemployed for fewer than 14 weeks.[2] Approximately one third of the unemployed leave unemployment within one month. The observation that most unemployment spells are short, however, does not imply that most unemployment is due to short spells. The mean duration of unemployment spells does not indicate the fraction of overall unemployment attributable to unemployment spells of different duration. Both measures tell very different stories.

Consider the following example. Assume that 20 spells of unemployment begin each week, each lasting three weeks, and that 1 spell begins each week lasting 30 weeks. The mean duration of unemployment is approximately 4 weeks (90 weeks divided by 21 spells). However, one third of total unemployment is due to one spell. While the majority of unemployment spells in Canada are still of relatively short duration, the relative importance of long-term unemployment in total unemployment has increased significantly.

For an eight-year period, from 1989 to 1996, the proportion of unemployed people without work for six months or more increased from about 20% to 27%. Unemployment has become more concentrated among a subset of workers in the labour force. Who are the long-term unemployed? The unskilled members of racial minorities, workers

---

2. To measure the duration of unemployment by the mean length of unemployment spells may be misleading. For example, many of the discouraged workers withdrawing from the labour force will re-enter the labour force at a later point when economic circumstances appear to have improved. If we count the time outside the labour force as unemployed, the average duration of unemployment clearly would increase.

nearing retirement age, and people who live in economically depressed areas most frequently have problems finding employment.

The overall unemployment rate not only conceals how long people are unemployed but also conceals large differences in unemployment rates among various groups and regions.

DEMOGRAPHIC DIFFERENCES IN UNEMPLOYMENT

The English political economist Thomas R. Malthus once referred to the unemployed as "those unhappy persons who in the great lottery of life draw a blank." The reference to a lottery might evoke the idea that every participant has the same chance of drawing a blank. The conception of a random draw, however, would be wrong. The lottery of unemployment is heavily biased. As Figure 6.4 shows, some groups in our society are much more prone to unemployment than others.

YOUTH UNEMPLOYMENT

The unemployment rate of youths (people aged 15 to 24 years), particularly of teenagers, is always much higher than for the other age groups. For instance, in 1997 the overall unemployment rate was 9.2%. For the 15–24 age group, the rate was 16.7%, while for adults it was 7.8%. As mentioned in earlier chapters, there are several reasons why young people experience consistently higher unemployment. First, movement from job to job is particularly common for young workers as they try to find out what kind of work is best suited for them.

Second, movement into and out of the labour force is also much more frequent as young people alternate between work, schooling, and other non-market activities. Many young people are not ready to settle into permanent employment immediately after leaving school. To interpret the higher job and labour force turnover of youth as a reflection of weaker work attachment, however, only tells part of the story. Many firms that offer stable employment, higher wages, and good working conditions are reluctant to hire youth. Young people are, therefore, often forced into jobs that involve low wages, poor working conditions, and little opportunity for skill acquisition and advancement within firms. From the worker's viewpoint these types of jobs are very much alike; changing between them does not entail noticeable advantages or disadvantages. Whatever the reasons for the frequent job changes and movements into and out of the labour force are, they often are associated with spells of unemployment.

AN INTRODUCTION TO THE CANADIAN LABOUR MARKET

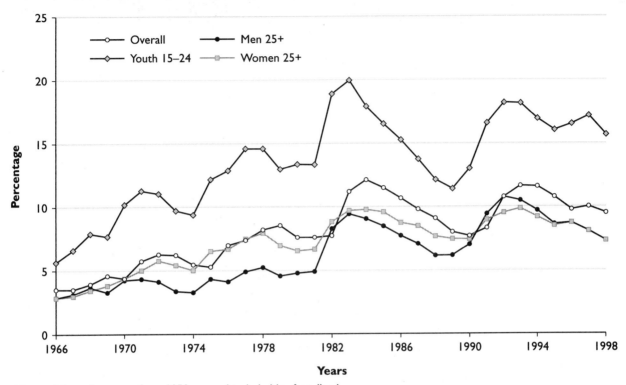

FIGURE 6.4 UNEMPLOYMENT RATES ACROSS DEMOGRAPHIC GROUPS, 1966–98

Notes: a) Annual averages from 1950 onward include Newfoundland.

b) Population aged 15 and over from 1966. Data prior to 1966 are based on population aged 14 and over.

c) Estimates prior to 1966 have not been adjusted to conform to current concepts.

Sources: For 1947–65, adapted from Statistics Canada. (1985, November). *The Labour Force*. Ottawa: Statistics Canada. (Catalogue no. 71-001); for 1966–98, adapted from Statistics Canada. (1999). *Historical Labour Force Statistics, 1966–1998*. Ottawa: Statistics Canada. (Catalogue no. 71-201).

A third reason for relatively high youth unemployment is that firms often hire young people on a short-term trial basis. Consequently, the rate of job loss is higher for youths than for adult workers. In cases of temporary or permanent layoffs where the seniority principle is applied, young people who have little seniority are the first laid off.

Last, young people also have more difficulty finding jobs because they often lack training or work experience.

FEMALE UNEMPLOYMENT

In most of the years since 1947, the unemployment rate for adult women has been higher than that of adult men. The gap generally narrows substantially during recessions. The service sector, where most women are employed, is generally less sensitive to business cycle influences than is the manufacturing sector. In the 1991 recession, for the first time the unemployment rate for adult women was less than that for men. Since then, the unemployment rate for adult women has stayed slightly below the one for men.

It is not yet clear whether the reversal is a temporary phenomenon or whether male-female differences in unemployment rates are a thing of the past. One of the reasons cited for the relatively higher unemployment of youth also applies for adult women: the relatively high proportion of re-entrants in the female labour force. Among unemployed adult females, an average of roughly one third are re-entrants who had been out of the workforce for longer than one year. Female re-entrants typically have had work experience interrupted by family responsibilities, especially child rearing.

Employment possibilities for this group are significantly worse than for those with longer term labour force experience. Aside from this structural factor, the proportion of entrants and re-entrants always rises with the rate of increase of the labour force participation rate. A certain amount of female unemployment, therefore, is the result of the rapidly expanding female workforce.

OTHER FACTORS

Factors other than age and gender bias the unemployment lottery. Members of ethnic minorities are much more likely to be out of work than the rest of the population. Canada's aboriginal peoples, for instance, suffer unemployment rates nearly three times as high compared to the national average. Educational attainment level is another factor that affects the incidence and duration of unemployment. Unemployment rates are lowest for those with university degrees, followed by those who hold other post-secondary diplomas and certificates. High school dropouts experience unemployment rates 2.5 times higher than their age counterparts with a completed high school certificate.[3]

---

3. As shown in Chapter 12, the level of education affects the incidence and duration of unemployment as well as the level of earnings.

REGIONAL DIFFERENCES IN UNEMPLOYMENT

Unemployment rates also differ across regions of the country. These differences have persisted over the last 50 years. Unemployment tends to be highest in the Atlantic region, followed by Quebec and British Columbia. The lowest unemployment rates are found in Ontario and on the Prairies. Although the unemployment rate in the Atlantic region has been consistently higher than in the rest of the country, the difference has grown since the early 1970s. In 1998, the unemployment rate ranged from a low of 5.7% in Alberta to a high of 18.4% in Newfoundland. Even within provinces, there can be significant variation by area. Ontario, for example, had an overall unemployment rate of 7.2% in 1998. This rate included unemployment of 9.1% in Thunder Bay and 5.2% in Hamilton. Nova Scotia's unemployment rate was 10.7%, but in Halifax it was 7.4%.

In the Atlantic provinces and Quebec, with the exception of the few metropolitan areas, labour markets are relatively small. The range of jobs available to job seekers is limited, and employers have a less varied pool of skills to draw from. The recent collapse of the fishing industry in the Atlantic provinces has limited the number of jobs available even further. In addition to the limited size of the labour market, higher job and labour force turnover in these regions result in a higher incidence of unemployment. These higher rates stem from at least two related sources. Many people are accustomed to pursuing a way of life that involves employment in several, often seasonal industries such as fishing, small farming, and logging during the course of a year, with the relatively high chance to experience unemployment in between. At the same time, low-paying casual jobs are in relatively greater supply than regular, more stable employment, making continuous attachment to the labour force more difficult.

Migration has not alleviated the problem of regional differences in unemployment. Workers often cannot, or will not, move to take advantage of job opportunities in other parts of Canada. Migration patterns sometimes reinforce unemployment in the high unemployment regions. When unemployment increases across the country, when people who have migrated in previous years lose a job, they often return to their province of origin (known as return migration). Unemployment is often easier to endure in a familiar environment. As return migration increases during recessions, the rate of migration in the other direction (out migration) often drops because the pull factor of higher wages is outweighed by the higher risk of not finding a job in the new province.

Industries in British Columbia are mostly natural resource industries and rely heavily on exports. Since these industries are more affected by the business cycle, British Columbia experiences heavier fluctuations in economic activity than most other provinces and accordingly reports relatively large fluctuations in unemployment. The Asian economic crisis of the 1990s, for example, hit the British Columbia economy and its labour market particularly hard.

Unemployment generally tends to be lower in agricultural regions. Canada is no exception. The largely agricultural prairie provinces of Manitoba and Saskatchewan traditionally experience the lowest unemployment rates in the country.

UNEMPLOYMENT IN CANADA AND THE UNITED STATES COMPARED

An important labour market development in the past 20 years has been the growing gap between the Canadian and U.S. unemployment rates. As Figure 6.5 shows, from 1947 to the beginning of the 1980s the unemployment rates in Canada and the United States were remarkably similar both in their levels and the timing of their rises and falls. Economists are divided over whether to date the beginning of the divergence in 1977 or in 1982. In the 1980s, the Canada-U.S. unemployment rate gap was about 2 percentage points. Since 1992, the gap has increased to 4 percentage points or more. The unemployment differential has affected both men and women, all regions, all age groups, all industries and occupations, and all educational attainment groups.

Why has Canada more recently experienced unemployment well above the level in the United States? A definitive explanation is still outstanding. A number of key points, however, are emerging from recent research.

MACROECONOMIC PERFORMANCE

Both countries experienced recessions in the early 1980s and 1990s but, for the first time, the recessions were deeper in Canada than in the United States. It therefore seems reasonable to attribute the relative increase in Canadian unemployment to the greater severity of the two recessions in Canada. The economic recovery and expansion in the

FIGURE 6.5 UNEMPLOYMENT RATES, CANADA AND U.S., 1947–98

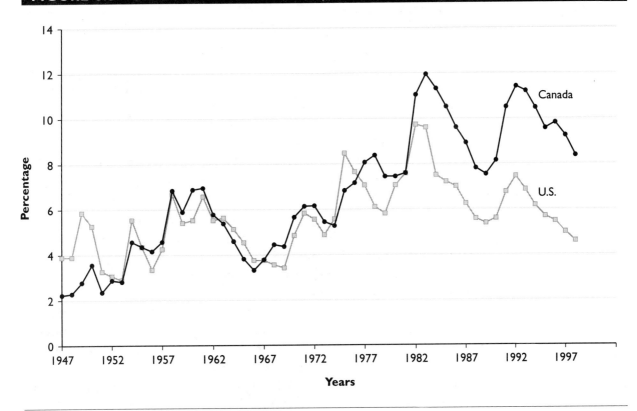

Sources: For 1947–65, adapted from Statistics Canada. (1985, November). *The Labour Force.* Ottawa: Statistics Canada. (Catalogue no. 71-001); for 1966–98, adapted from Statistics Canada. (1999). *Historical Labour Force Statistics, 1966–1998.* Ottawa: Statistics Canada. (Catalogue no. 71-201). For United States: for 1947–66, U.S. Bureau of Labour Statistics. (1968). *Employment and Earnings 13,* January 1967, Table A-1. Washington: U.S. Government Printing Office; for 1967–98, United States. President. (1999). *Economic Report of the President.* Washington, DC: U.S. Government Printing Office.

latter part of the 1980s, however, was stronger in Canada than in the United States. The simultaneous increase in the labour force participation rate and the employment-population ratio throughout the 1980s also indicates a strong employment performance in Canada. It is, therefore, difficult to explain the persistent unemployment gap during the 1980s as simply a weaker performance by the Canadian economy.

The situation in the 1990s is markedly different. Between 1989 and 1996, the performance in terms of real output growth was much weaker in Canada compared to the United States, and both the participation rate and the employment-population ratio dropped significantly compared to the United States. All three measures of economic activity indicate a substantial deterioration in the Canadian economy. Thus, in contrast to the 1980s, the further widening in the Canada–U.S. unemployment differential during the 1990s can be explained mainly, if not entirely, by the very poor performance of the Canadian economy and labour market.

EMPLOYMENT INSURANCE

Because a relatively weaker economic performance is not a convincing explanation for the persistence of the unemployment gap during the years of economic expansion that occurred in the 1980s, other reasons must account for it. One reason frequently pointed to is Canada's more generous employment insurance (EI) program, which was known as unemployment insurance until 1997. Differences between the systems in Canada and the U.S. date back to the 1971/72 revisions in the Canadian program and the tightening of the U.S. program in the early 1980s, in particular with regard to the probability of receiving benefits, the amount of benefits, and the duration of benefit claims.

A generous EI system can increase unemployment for a number of reasons. It makes forgoing employment to search for a new job less costly to the individual, so that people are induced to enter unemployment more often and to stay in it longer. It makes it easier for employers who lay off workers regularly to find people willing to accept this working condition. And it may encourage people who otherwise would not have participated in the labour market to enter the labour force in order to qualify for benefits after the required period of unemployment.

A few features of the Canadian employment insurance system may have been particularly important in the 1980s. For one, it was much easier for Canadians who voluntarily left their jobs to receive insurance benefits. This may explain why the share of unemployment accounted for by people who quit their previous job or were recently out of the labour force was significantly higher in Canada than in the United States. Another feature relates to the regional provisions introduced to the Canadian program in 1978; these tied the maximum length of time a person can collect unemployment benefits and the minimum hours a claimant must work in order to become eligible in part to the unemployment rate in the area of residence. Under the current system, workers who live in a region where the unemployment rate exceeds 16% must work 420 hours to become eligible for 32 weeks of insurance. Workers who live in a region where the unemployment rate is no more than 6% must work a minimum of 700 hours to become eligible for 14 weeks of insurance. As a result, when a recession increases the unemployment rate across regions, the employment insurance program becomes more generous. This encourages prolonged job searching and, by increasing unemployment duration, may raise the overall unemployment rate. As the unemployment gap appears to have emerged around the same time as the 1981/82 recession, this feature seems particularly relevant.

DIFFERENCES IN THE MEASUREMENT OF UNEMPLOYMENT

Although both Canada and the United States use the same concepts and ask very similar questions in their labour force surveys, some differences in the measurement of unemployment exist that can affect the unemployment gap. In both countries, a person who is classified as unemployed is without work, is available for work, and has actively looked for work. The difference lies in the way active job search is measured. In Canada, people satisfy the requirement of active job search if they are just looking at want ads in the newspaper or listings on the Internet, picking up job applications (even if they do not return them), or placing the occasional call to friends to inquire about job vacancies. These people are counted as unemployed. In the United States, these search methods are classified as "passive methods." In contrast, "active methods," such as answering ads, placing calls to employment agencies or companies, could potentially lead to a job offer. People who use only passive search methods are excluded from the U.S. unemployment count. When these differences in measuring active job search are accounted for, the unemployment gap in the 1990s is reduced by 0.7 percentage points. Obviously, this leaves much of the gap of 4% to be explained by other factors.

Another difference exists in the measurement of the working-age population. In the United States, this population includes people aged 16 and over. In Canada, the cutoff is 15 years. Fifteen-year-olds who are in the labour force and unemployed are included in the Canadian unemployment count; in the U.S. they are excluded. Removing this group from the labour force, however, reduces the unemployment gap by less than 0.1 percentage point, as most 15-year-olds attend school full time.

TYPES OF UNEMPLOYMENT

We have described how unemployment is measured in Canada and have discussed some of the problems related to interpreting unemployment statistics. We have also presented some of the distinctive features and contributing factors of unemployment in Canada. None of this, however, systematically explains why economies experience unemployment. In most markets in the economy, prices adjust to bring the quantity supplied and the quantity demanded into balance. In an ideal labour market, wages would adjust to balance the quantity of labour supplied and the quantity of labour demanded. This adjustment would ensure that all workers are employed. Why does reality differ so much from this ideal?

As Figure 6.2 revealed, the unemployment rate is never zero even in boom times. For example, in 1989, when the economy was in the seventh year of the expansion that followed the 1981/82 recession, and overall production was close to maximum capacity, the unemployment rate never fell below 7.4%. The first step in finding out why there always exists some unemployment in an economy is to distinguish between four main types of unemployment:

- frictional unemployment;
- seasonal unemployment;
- structural unemployment; and
- cyclical unemployment.

FRICTIONAL UNEMPLOYMENT

Labour turnover is a normal feature of the labour market. People are constantly entering the labour force—young people leave school, mothers return to the labour force, formerly discouraged workers try once more to find a job. At the same time, other people retire and create job vacancies for new entrants and re-entrants. Also, there is the constant change of businesses offering jobs. Some firms reduce production or close down for good, laying off workers; others expand or start up and hire workers. The constant flow of workers into and out of the labour force as well as the constant creation and destruction of jobs require people to search for jobs and firms to search for workers. Firms do not usually hire the first person who applies for a job and unemployed people do not usually take the first job offered to them. Instead, both firms and workers spend time searching for what they believe will be the best match available. Unemployment that occurs as the result of this constant churning in the labour market is called **frictional unemployment** or search unemployment. One can think of frictional unemployment as unemployment resulting from short-run job-matching problems: Suitable job vacancies exist, but it takes time to match jobs and job searchers appropriately. Usually, frictional unemployment is of

frictional unemployment unemployment that is inevitable even in a well-functioning labour market

relatively short duration. The time spent looking for work is frequently a month or less.

In contrast to other types of unemployment, frictional unemployment entails some economic benefits. For the individual worker, a short spell of unemployment allows a more intensive and wide-ranging job search. For the economy, a certain amount of frictional unemployment is necessary for the job-matching process to allocate workers to jobs efficiently. Not all frictional unemployment, however, is beneficial. Moving from one dead-end job to another, for example, can be highly demoralizing for the individual involved.

There are several ways that public policy can reduce frictional unemployment. One is to improve the information on available jobs, their rates of pay, location, etc. This could be done through computerized, nation-wide or regional job banks, an improved public employment service, and job fairs. Another way is to eliminate undesirable causes of job and labour force turnover, perhaps by reforming those features of the employment insurance system that lead to increased frequency of unemployment.

BOX 6.2 Commercial Employment Agencies

One of the functions of the labour market is to match job seekers with employment opportunities. Matching vacant jobs with qualified and willing workers is not always made quickly because information is not perfect. That is, workers do not always know what jobs are available, and employers do not always know where to find the workers to fill job vacancies. The role of the employment agency is to bridge the information gap and bring workers and employers together. The employment agency is a labour-market intermediary.

The federal government operates a no-cost employment referral service. Its goal is to facilitate the matching process and reduce frictional unemployment. Yet many Canadians find employment through commercial employment agencies. Why do workers and employers use commercial agencies when a no-cost agency exists? Perhaps it is because commercial agencies are often specialized both on an occupational basis and on a geographic basis. For example, an agency might specialize in placing accountants or might operate in a defined geographic area.

Also, commercial employment agencies often assist firms that contract out some of their tasks. Firms may find it expensive to hire full-time workers to perform certain functions and it may be easier to contract out these services on a temporary basis. Temporary workers can be found through a commercial employment agency. It may be cheaper, in the long run, for firms to use a specialized employment service rather than rely on the no-cost federal service, which is not specializing in temporary placements. Some economies of scale may be achieved by firms that specialize in a certain type of job. Even though the agency may charge the employer a fee, the quick results provided by the firm may reduce costly bottlenecks in human resources within the firm.

Seasonal Unemployment

seasonal unemployment
unemployment resulting
from the decline in the
number of jobs at certain
times of the year

Some jobs are only available during certain seasons of the year. In most parts of Canada, construction, fishing, and farming generally close down during the winter months. Unemployment that arises because the number of jobs has declined due to the season is called **seasonal unemployment**. We have seen earlier that the Atlantic provinces have unemployment rates above the national average. Part of the problem in this region is the high seasonal unemployment. For people working in tourism, farming, and fishing during the summer months, it is very hard to find seasonal work during the winter. For example, in Prince Edward Island, the unemployment rate during the winter months is generally twice as high as in summer.

Official unemployment rates compiled by Statistics Canada are defined as seasonally adjusted or unadjusted. The seasonally unadjusted figures report the actual unemployment rate in a particular month. The seasonally adjusted figures show the unemployment rate that would have existed had there not been high or low seasonal demand conditions in a particular month; these rates permit comparisons of unemployment rates from month to month taking out the seasonal influences.

Structural Unemployment

Another reason for substantial unemployment even in an economy operating at full capacity is that not all labour sub-markets are in equilibrium at the same time. As we saw in the introduction, instead of a single labour market, there are a great number of sub-markets for particular jobs with specialized skills and qualifications. As a result of structural changes in the economy, there will be more vacancies than unemployed workers (excess demand) in some markets coexisting with an excess of workers over vacancies (excess supply) in others. The markets with excess supply of labour contribute positive amounts of unemployment. In contrast, those with excess demand cannot have negative unemployment. The average unemployment rate must always be positive. Vacancies and unemployment do not simply cancel each other out: they coexist.

Structural changes refer to changes in the industrial and occupational mix of an economy as well as to changes in its workforce. Employers may be having trouble finding software engineers, but construction workers may be out of work in large numbers. When technological changes such as the introduction of robotics in the automotive industry or budget cuts in health care lead to job losses in these sectors, there may be other industries, such as electronics or fibre-optics, that are rapidly growing and creating new jobs. Job vacancies in these industries may not be filled by unemployed job searchers over an extended period of time because the workers lack the right skills or live in the wrong location. Unemployment due to the matching problems that arise from such structural changes in the economy is called **structural unemployment**. Since it arises from long-run adjustment problems, it can last for many months and as such is a more serious problem than frictional unemployment.

structural unemployment unemployment resulting from a mismatching of workers and job opportunities based either on skills or geography

It is often not easy to establish a clear distinction between frictional and structural unemployment. In both cases a sufficient number of jobs exist in the economy and both involve job search. The main difference is the speed with which the job-matching process is completed—relatively quickly in the case of frictional unemployment, but slowly for structural unemployment.

There are several ways in which public policy might reduce structural unemployment. One way is for governments to provide training programs or subsidize training in private companies through direct payments or tax incentives. Recent reforms to the employment insurance program have allocated funds away from the payments of benefits to the unemployed and toward the funding of training. Another possibility is to facilitate the movement of unemployed workers out of depressed regions through payments of reallocation allowances. A third possibility could be for the government to act as employer of last resort by offering employment in the public sector to people who suffer persistent unemployment.

Economists describe the unemployment rate that prevails under normal conditions, i.e., when the economy operates at full capacity, as the **natural rate of unemployment**. The term appears rather misleading as there is nothing natural about unemployment. Economists chose the term to remind us that friction in the labour market and structural changes in the economy are unavoidable. Since there is always some unemployment, what do we mean then by full employment? **Full employment** occurs when the actual unemployment rate equals the natural rate of unemployment. At full employment all unemployment is frictional, structural, or seasonal.

natural rate of unemployment the unemployment rate that exists when the economy is functioning at full capacity

full employment when the actual rate of unemployment equals the natural rate of unemployment

The natural rate of unemployment is not a fixed number. It changes over time as labour market conditions change. Since the natural rate of unemployment cannot be observed directly, there is some dispute about its level at any time. Estimates of the natural rate of unemployment for the late 1980s varied between 6.5% and 8%; for 1997, the estimates ranged from a high of 9% to a low of 7%. However, there is a general consensus among economists that the natural rate of unemployment has followed an upward long-run trend, more than doubling over the last 30 years. Some of the reasons for the increase are discussed in the next section.

CYCLICAL UNEMPLOYMENT

cyclical unemployment (demand-deficient unemployment) unemployment that arises because the economy does not generate enough jobs for those seeking one

Often, the observed unemployment rate deviates from the natural rate. The difference between actual unemployment and the natural rate of unemployment is generally defined as **cyclical unemployment**. When the observed unemployment rate equals the natural rate, the economy is operating at full employment and cyclical unemployment is zero. Cyclical unemployment arises from inadequate demand in an economy, so it is also called **demand-deficient unemployment**. Since the demand for labour depends on the demand for goods and services, declining demand for output leads to declining demand for labour. As an economy moves into a recession, sales decline and, as a result, firms cut back on production. When production levels decline, fewer hours of work are needed and fewer workers are employed. Frictional unemployment and structural unemployment arise because of job-matching problems. Cyclical unemployment occurs because the economy does not generate enough jobs for all who want to work.

Public policy might reduce cyclical unemployment in several ways. The most widely used approach is to use fiscal and monetary policy to stimulate economic growth. *Fiscal policy* refers to the government's decision regarding the level of government spending or taxes. When the economy slows down, the government can increase its own spending on goods and services: it can build new schools or hospitals, repair roads, or expand its own research facilities. It can also cut taxes to increase the spending of households or companies. *Monetary policy* refers to changes in the supply of money by the Bank of Canada, which affect the interest rates in the economy. If a recession looms, the Bank of Canada can increase the money supply in order to reduce interest rates. As interest rates decline, bank loans become less expensive. This consequently stimulates spending by households and firms. Government intervention in the form of fiscal or monetary policy, or both, can limit the severity of an economic downturn and the resulting cyclical unemployment.

To break total unemployment down into frictional/structural and cyclical unemployment is an attractive method for distinguishing the effects of the business cycle from those associated with frictional and structural changes in the labour market. Nonetheless, the actual breakdown of unemployment into these categories is often not as straightforward because the sources are not independent of each other. An increase in cyclical unemployment can, over time, lead to increased structural unemployment. One reason has to do with the fact that unemployment duration increases during recessions: as time spent unemployed increases, skills, work attitudes, and habits deteriorate, which results in increased matching problems. Another reason is that a contraction in economic activity means companies spend less on physical capital, such as machinery and office equipment. When the economy recovers, the reduced capital stock becomes fully utilized before the unemployed are re-employed; this constitutes structural unemployment due to insufficient capital.

WHY HAS THE NATURAL RATE OF UNEMPLOYMENT SHIFTED UPWARD?

We noted earlier that the natural rate of unemployment has increased over time, although the exact amount is debated. In the remainder of this chapter we explore the question of why the rates of frictional and structural unemployment have increased.

DEMOGRAPHIC SHIFTS

Labour turnover is a major source of unemployment. One factor that may have led to higher labour turnover is the changing composition of the labour force. As mentioned earlier, two labour force groups with above-average job and labour force turnover rates are youth and women. As a result of the baby boom and rising labour force participation, the share of young people in the labour force increased from 22% in 1960 to 27% in 1975. The increase in the proportion of adult women in the labour force was even more dramatic and sustained. It rose from 22% in 1947 to almost 50% in 1998.[4]

These demographic shifts can have increased the natural rate of unemployment in two ways. The first is referred to as the *weights effect* of demographic changes on unemployment. The overall unemployment rate is a weighted average of the unemployment rates of the

---

4. See Chapter 4 for a discussion of the significant changes in the age and gender composition in the Canadian labour force over the last 50 years.

various demographic sub-groups. Unemployment can be expected to rise if the groups with relatively high unemployment rates, such as youth and women, increase their share (weight) in the labour force.[5]

Another possibility is that the entrance of large numbers of young people and women into the labour force can lead to crowding in the labour market of these two groups. If relative wages were flexible in a downward direction, the increase in supply of youth and women would decrease their wages relative to adult men, making it profitable for firms to provide employment for them. Because relative wages do not fall easily, the result is relatively higher rate of unemployment for young people and women as scarce jobs are rationed among a large pool of job seekers. This effect has been termed the *cohort-overcrowding effect*. The weight effect is based on the relatively higher rates of labour turnover in the two groups, and the crowding effect refers to a more serious structural problem, namely an imbalance between the supply of young and adult female workers and the number of jobs available for these two groups.

Empirical studies indicate that demographic changes working through the weight effect have had a minimal impact on overall unemployment. In contrast, the cohort-overcrowding effect seems to have contributed to the increase in the natural rate of unemployment, at least during the 1960s and early 1970s. Since the mid 1970s, however, the explanation of higher unemployment relying on demographic shifts has lost much of its force. In 1976, the share of youth in the labour force started to decline and by the late 1980s it had fallen below the level of 1960.[6] The share of adult women in the labour force is still rising but the corresponding unemployment rate has been below that of adult men since 1991.

EMPLOYMENT INSURANCE

Considerable attention has focused on the growth of income-transfer programs in Canada as a cause of increased frictional unemployment. To the extent that most people prefer leisure to work, it is the pressure of financial necessity that encourages job acceptance and discourages excessive turnover. Government transfer payments reduce the incentive to work, leading to an increase in both unemployment and non-participation in the labour force.

---

5. As noted earlier, unemployment rates of women have been either lower or equal to unemployment rates of men since 1991.

6. In 1998, the share of young people in the labour force was only 16%, 6 percentage points less than in 1960.

AN INTRODUCTION TO THE CANADIAN LABOUR MARKET

The transfer program that has received most attention is employment insurance. As discussed earlier in this chapter, one explanation offered for the higher unemployment rate in Canada compared to the United States is the relatively greater generosity of the Canadian employment insurance system. At various times through the 1970s and 1980s, the insurance program was extended and benefits and eligibility periods increased. These changes could have led to an increase in the natural rate of unemployment in a number of ways.

EFFECT ON THE DURATION OF UNEMPLOYMENT. An increase in the duration of unemployment among recipients would increase the natural rate of unemployment. By providing unemployed workers with income support, their costs of not working and thus of job searching are reduced. As a result, recipients of benefits may stay unemployed longer, thereby increasing the natural rate of unemployment.

EFFECT ON LAYOFFS. An increase in the number of layoffs leads to higher unemployment. In seasonal and cyclically sensitive industries such as construction, forestry, and steel, firms frequently have slack periods when they have more workers than they need; as a result they might lay off part of their workforce, recalling them when sales and production pick up again. Two costs of a temporary layoff policy, however, limit its use. One is that firms must pay higher wages to attract workers to the industry given the higher risk of layoffs. The second is that some workers with valuable transferable skills may take jobs elsewhere, resulting in higher training costs for the firm. With an employment insurance system, both costs of layoffs are reduced. Since laid-off workers qualify for benefits, firms with a layoff policy need not pay such high wages to attract workers. Benefits allow laid-off workers to more easily sit out a spell of unemployment until the firm recalls them.

EFFECT ON THE SIZE OF THE LABOUR FORCE. The employment insurance program can increase unemployment by attracting additional persons, especially from demographic groups that have traditionally experienced higher unemployment rates, into the labour force. For young people or adult women, for example, the availability of employment insurance benefits may increase the attractiveness of market work over non-market activities. As more people join the labour force, the incidence of unemployment is likely to increase.

Over the last 20 years, a large number of studies have been conducted examining the size of the various effects of employment insurance on unemployment. The results of most studies confirm the link between features of the employment insurance system, length of job search, and unemployment duration. Several studies also have shown that the availability and generosity of benefits have a positive effect on the incidence of unemployment as the number of new entrants and re-entrants to the labour force increases.

The fact that there are strong indications that employment insurance causes higher levels of unemployment does not imply that employment insurance should be eliminated. The primary objective of the program is to provide insurance against the loss of income resulting from unemployment. As such, it eases the financial burden of those who find themselves unemployed. Also, employment insurance allows people to conduct a more thorough job search, thereby increasing the chances of a better job match and of receiving a higher wage than would otherwise have been the case. As often happens in cases of economic tradeoffs, economists disagree on whether the benefits of employment insurance in terms of providing income support and potentially improving job matching outweigh the cost in terms of higher unemployment.

Since 1990, several changes have been introduced with the objective to tighten the program. With the revised employment insurance plan enacted in 1996, the conditions for eligibility and duration of benefits are now more stringent than they were in 1971. As a result, the natural rate of unemployment could be expected to decline, all other things remaining the same.

INDUSTRIAL RESTRUCTURING

A factor often cited as contributing to greater structural unemployment is the substantial number of layoffs and plant closings due to deregulation and heightened foreign competition. These changes have coincided with the decline of blue-collar, often unionized, jobs in the manufacturing sector. Older workers in heavily unionized industries such as steel, car manufacturing, and machinery were particularly hard hit by industrial restructuring. For many of these displaced workers, the long duration of unemployment was due to several factors, including the lack of jobs in the local labour market, the reluctance to uproot their families to move to different parts of the country with better employment opportunities, and the unwillingness of many of the unemployed to accept low-paying jobs in alternative occupations.

TECHNOLOGICAL CHANGE

Technological change is a major force in the process of structural change. Since the beginning of the industrial revolution, workers have worried that technological change will destroy their jobs. Every major wave of technological innovation, from the steam engine to the automobile to the microchip, has raised fears of permanent mass unemployment. In his essay "Economic Possibilities for Our Grandchildren" published in 1930, the English economist John Maynard Keynes reflected on the implications of the tremendous productivity increases brought about by technological progress: "In quite a few years—in our lifetimes I mean—we may be able to perform all the operations of agriculture, mining, and manufacture with a quarter of the human effort to which we have been accustomed." For Keynes, the advances in productivity raised the spectre of **technological unemployment**, which he defined as "unemployment due to our discovery of means of economising the use of labour outrunning the pace at which we can find new uses of labour."

In order to analyze the relationship between technological change and unemployment, it is useful to distinguish between two related but separate dimensions of technological progress:

First, technological progress allows the production of more goods and services with the same number of workers. Alternatively formulated, technological change allows the economy to produce the same amount of output with fewer workers; when expressed in this manner, it reflects the fear of those who worry about technological unemployment. Since technological change increases labour productivity, a given output level requires fewer workers. The critical question then is this: As technological change increases productivity over time, does it also increase unemployment? If we look at the overall economy over longer periods, the answer is no. Periods of high productivity growth, such as the 1950s and 1960s, were associated with a lower unemployment rate; periods of low productivity growth, such as the 1980s and 1990s, have been associated with a higher unemployment rate. Instead of causing more unemployment, technological change seems to lower unemployment.

Second, technological progress leads to the rise of new industries and occupations and the disappearance of old ones. This structural dimension of technology seems to be at the heart of the fears of technological unemployment. Technological change implies a constant process of job destruction and job creation. New goods are developed, old ones disappear. New production techniques are invented, requiring

technological unemployment unemployment due to advances in technical and organizational know-how occurring at a faster pace than the ability to find new uses for labour

new skills and making old ones obsolete. The mechanical loom, for example, largely wiped out the jobs of the weavers during the 19th century but created many new jobs in the emerging textile industry. When the automobile replaced the horse and buggy, many occupations such as harness maker and blacksmith were destroyed, but many more new ones were generated, creating large numbers of new jobs. The petroleum and rubber industry, the car insurance industry, and road construction, to mention only a few, are industries that evolved as spin-offs. With the increased use of computers in large parts of the economy today, we are witnessing the latest example of what the Austrian economist Joseph Schumpeter called the process of "creative destruction." Although historically technological change has not created massive unemployment in the economy, technological unemployment is a serious problem for those groups of workers left with insufficient skills to fill the newly created jobs. The decline, both relative and absolute, in the wages of low-skill workers during the last 15 to 20 years reflects a decline in the demand for less skilled workers, and technological progress appears to be the main cause. Whether the wage decline will be sufficient to preserve a minimum number of jobs for low-skill workers is to be seen. We still know very little quantitatively how much technological change is contributing to structural unemployment.

SUMMARY

An unemployed person is someone who is not working but is looking for work. The unemployment rate is computed by Statistics Canada using data from the monthly Labour Force Survey. The official unemployment rate may not be an accurate indicator of unemployment because of the presence of discouraged workers, underemployed workers, and marginal workers. The validity of the unemployment rate as an indicator of economic hardship is increasingly questioned. While the unemployment rate measures the underutilization of labour in the economy, the employment rate measures the extent to which labour is utilized.

The proportion of people in the labour force entering unemployment in a given period is called the incidence of unemployment. Job losers represent the biggest group of those entering the ranks of the unemployed. The average time a person remains unemployed is called the duration of unemployment; the duration of unemployment has increased over time. The incidence and the duration of unemployment affect overall unemployment.

Since World War II, the average level of unemployment in the economy has been on an upward trend. The increase in the unemployment rate also has been much steeper in the last two recessions. Not all labour force groups suffer equally from unemployment. Youth and, until recently, female workers are more likely to be unemployed. Workers in the Atlantic provinces and Quebec are more affected by unemployment than individuals in other provinces. During the last 20 years, the unemployment rate in Canada has consistently been higher than the rate in the United States. The unemployment gap can be traced to differences in macroeconomic performance, the employment insurance system, and differences in the measurement of unemployment.

Economists distinguish between four types of unemployment: frictional, seasonal, structural, and cyclical (or demand-deficient). Frictional unemployment is associated with turnover in the labour market, and structural unemployment stems from a mismatch between workers and jobs. Seasonal unemployment is caused by seasonal fluctuations on the demand or supply side of the labour market. Cyclical unemployment, or demand-deficient unemployment, is related to fluctuations in aggregate demand for goods and services. The natural rate of unemployment is a combination of frictional and structural unemployment, and describes the unemployment that exists when the economy operates at full capacity. The natural rate of unemployment has increased over the years. The increase can be attributed to demographic shifts in the labour force, changes in the employment insurance system, industrial restructuring, and technological change.

KEY TERMS

EXERCISES

1. What is the difference between being unemployed and not working? Give some examples of people not at work who are not unemployed.

2. Is the official unemployment rate an inadequate measure of the underutilization of labour in the economy? Explain.

3. Explain how the employment rate and the unemployment rate can increase at the same time.

4. In 1975 the total working-age population was 16.323 million, the labour force participation rate was 61.1%, and the unemployment rate was 6.9%. In 1998, the working-age population was 24.012 million and the labour force participation rate had risen to 65.1%. How quickly would total employment have to grow from 1975 to 1998 to keep the unemployment rate at 6.9%?

5. There are two flows from employment to unemployment: layoffs and quits. How do they change over the business cycle?

6. Evidence shows that women and young people have more frequent spells of unemployment than adult men but that unemployment of these two groups is of shorter duration. What does this suggest as possible causes of unemployment for youth and women?

7. Why is frictional unemployment inevitable? How might the government reduce it?

8. Is a simultaneous increase in unemployment and job vacancies a sign of growing frictional, structural, or cyclical unemployment? Explain.

9. What type of unemployment are the following workers experiencing? Explain.

   a. Workers in a fish plant in Newfoundland lose their jobs when the cod fishery closes down.
   b. Ski lift attendants in British Columbia are laid off due to the lack of snow.
   c. A sales clerk in a video store loses her job when a new video store opens around the corner.
   d. Bank tellers lose their jobs as banks install automatic teller machines.

10. Over the last 50 years the unemployment rate has gradually crept upward. Why?

11. Some years ago, the federal government passed legislation that unemployment beneficiaries pay income tax on their unemployment benefits. Explain the effect this taxation of UI benefits might have on the unemployment rate.

REFERENCES

Akyeampong, E. B. (1992). Discouraged Workers—Where Have They Gone? *Perspectives on Labour and Income, 4:* 38–44.

Devereaux, M. (1992). Alternative Measures of Unemployment. *Perspectives on Labour and Income, 4:* 35–43.

Fortin, P. (1989). How High Is Canada's Natural Rate of Unemployment? *European Economic Review, 33:* 89–110.

Gera, S. (Ed.). (1991). *Canadian Unemployment. Lessons from the 80s and Challenges for the 90s.* Ottawa: Economic Council of Canada.

Jackson, G. (1987). Alternative Concepts and Measures of Unemployment. *The Labour Force* (pp. 85–120). Ottawa: Statistics Canada. (Catalogue No. 71-001)

Keil, M. W., and Simons, J. S. V. (1990). An Analysis of Canadian Unemployment. *Canadian Public Policy, 16*(1): 1–16.

Mankiw, N. G. (1998). *Principles of Economics.* Orlando: The Dryden Press.

Organization of Economic Development and Co-operation (OECD). (1996). *Canada: OECD Economic Surveys.* Paris: OECD.

Riddell, W. C., and Sharpe, A. (1998). The Canada–U.S. Unemployment Rate Gap: An Introduction and Overview. Special Issue. *Canadian Public Policy, 24:* 1–37.

Statistics Canada. (1998). *Labour Force Update. Canada–U.S. Labour Market Comparison, 2* (4). Ottawa: Statistics Canada. (Catalogue No. 71-005-XPB)

7

....

TRENDS IN LABOUR COMPENSATION

OBJECTIVES

After completing this chapter, you should be able to:

1. distinguish between wages, earnings, labour income, and total income;

2. describe the trends in total labour income and labour's share in national income;

3. evaluate the changes in average labour income;

4. describe the changes in weekly earnings and nominal and real hourly wages;

5. discuss the growing wage differential between skilled and unskilled workers.

INTRODUCTION

The determination of wage rates is at the core of labour economics. It is through changes in wage rates that labour services are allocated to their various uses and that a balance between demand and supply is maintained in the market. Employers are concerned with wages because they, together with labour productivity, largely determine labour cost per unit of output. Workers are concerned with wages because, for the majority of them, wages are the most important source of income. Their paycheques determine how much they actually can purchase in a given period in relation to the prices of goods and services. Workers are not only interested in their own wages, but they also are particularly concerned with how their wages compare with those of their fellow workers.

Few economic variables are as controversial and as hotly debated as is the wage rate. At the centre of the debate is often the notion of a "fair" wage. Is a bank CEO's contribution to the economy so much more than a chemist in a cancer research laboratory that it should justify the tremendous differences in their compensation? Is it "fair" that a cashier in a supermarket in Toronto earns significantly more than a cashier with similar work experience in a supermarket in Montreal? Is it "just" that female lawyers graduating from the same law school at the same time earn initially about 9% less than their male peers? These are difficult questions for which economists do not offer any answer. From the perspective of economic theory there is no "just" wage. A wage reflects the price an employer is willing to pay for a specified labour service in a particular location at a certain point in time. This does not imply, however, that a society has to accept wage levels and structures as determined by markets. Government labour regulations, taxation laws, and social programs are intended to redistribute earnings as determined in the market. In this chapter we are interested in the broad trends of labour income in Canada, labour's share in total national income, wage levels, and the growing polarization between high and low earnings.

Before examining these trends, it is useful to discuss briefly the meaning of wages and other components of labour compensation. To economists, the meaning of the term wage rate is intuitively obvious— it is the price of labour per hour of work. Measuring the actual wage rate, however, proves to be quite difficult. Also, labour compensation does not only consist of wages.

CONCEPTS AND MEASURES

There are essentially two ways to compute wages. One is on the basis of time (time wages), and the other is per unit of output (production wages or piecework). The great majority of Canadian workers are paid by the hour, day, week, month, or year. That is, they are paid by time. Workers paid by the hour or the day are usually referred to as **wage earners**, while those paid by the week or longer time periods are commonly referred to as **salaried workers**. In Canada, wage earners outnumber salaried workers.[1] Wages and salaries include bonuses, commissions, tips and gratuities, taxable allowances, and retroactive wage payments, in addition to basic pay. Estimates are usually calculated on a "gross" basis, that is, before deductions for income tax, employment insurance premiums, pension contributions, etc. **Net wages** or take-home pay is gross wages minus the deductions just referred to. While the term "wages" or "wage rate" refers to the payment for a unit of time, "earnings" refers to wages multiplied by the number of time units (typically hours or weeks) worked. Thus, earnings depend on both wages and the length of time the employee works.

Labour Income

Both wages and earnings are defined and measured in terms of direct monetary payments to employees. In addition to wages, workers receive non-cash benefits as compensation for their labour, benefits that are mostly payments in kind or deferred. Examples of payments in kind are employer-provided extended healthcare benefits such as dental and pharmaceutical insurance, where the employee receives a service or an insurance policy rather than money, and paid vacation time, since employees are given days off instead of cash. Deferred payments can take the form of employer-financed retirement benefits for which employers set aside money now to enable their employees to receive pensions later. Other non-wage benefits are the percentages of workers' salaries that employers must set aside so that staff is properly covered by employment insurance, the Canada or Quebec pension plan, and worker's compensation. These are all components of what is termed **supplementary labour income**. Total labour compensation or **labour income** then comprises earnings (wages and salaries) and supplementary labour income.[2] The individual's **total income** is the total command over resources of that person during a particular period (usually a year), including both labour compensation and unearned income. The latter can include income from stocks, bonds, debentures and other

wage earner worker paid by the hour or the day

salaried worker worker paid by the week or longer time period

net wages gross wages minus taxes and other payroll deductions

supplementary labour income non-wage benefits received by an employee

labour income earnings and supplementary labour income combined

total income the total of labour compensation and unearned income

---

1. According to the Labour Force Survey, in 1997 about 61% of employees worked on a per hour basis.

2. Ideally, labour compensation estimates should also include the monetary value of fringe benefits such as subsidized meals, uniforms and clothing, low-cost loans and housing, discounts on merchandise, and recreational, athletic and daycare facilities. However, no survey currently provides these data.

FIGURE 7.1 CALCULATING TOTAL INCOME

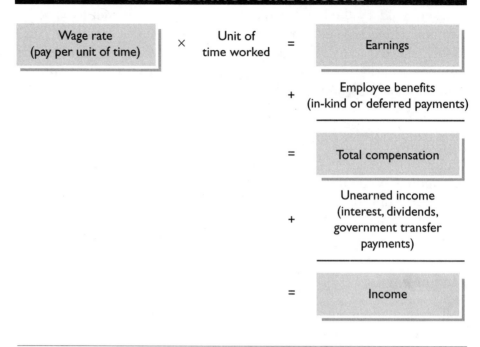

Source: Ehrenberg, R. G., & Smith, R. S. (1997). *Modern Labour Economics: Theory and Public Policy* (6th ed.). New York: Addison-Wesley.

investments, transfer payments received from the government in the form of welfare payments, employment insurance benefits, and the like. Figure 7.1 illustrates the relation between wages, earnings, labour compensation, and total income.

NOMINAL WAGES VERSUS REAL WAGES

nominal wage   the rate of payment to workers in current dollars

Another important distinction in any study of wages or earnings is that between money or nominal wages and real wages. The **nominal wage** denotes the rate of payment to workers in current dollars, e.g., $15 per hour or $550 per week. Nominal wages are most useful in comparing the pay of various workers at a given time. Compared over time, however, nominal wages lose much of their meaning as an indicator of the standard of living if the price level changes during the particular period. For example, a worker who earned $13.50 per hour in 1985 and $15 an hour 10 years later would receive a nominal wage increase of 11%. The worker would be better off in real terms only if the price level had increased by less than 11%. If the price level increased by more than 11%, the worker would be clearly worse off than before.

The relative changes in nominal wages and the price level are measured by real wages, which are nominal wages divided by some measure of prices. A rise in real wages suggests that more can be purchased with workers' nominal wages and vice versa. For example, if a worker earns $120 a day and a summer dress costs $60, one could say the worker earns the equivalent of two summer dresses a day (real wage = $120/$60 = 2). If the worker's daily pay rose to $150 over a period of 10 years and the price per dress increased to $70, the real wage would have increased to 2.14 (real wage $150/$70 = 2.14), that is, by 7%. The **real wage**, thus, measures the quantity of goods and services that can be bought with nominal wages.

real wage the quantity of goods and services that can be bought with the nominal wage

Calculations of real wages are especially useful in comparing the purchasing power of workers' earnings over a period of time when both nominal wages and product prices are changing. Thus, real wages are normally expressed as an index number, which compares the purchasing power of an hour of work to some base period (the base is set equal to 100). The base year in Table 7.1 is 1992. To understand how index numbers are constructed, refer to the next-to-last column, where the index of real hourly wages in 1998 is listed as 103. This means that hourly real wages were 3% higher in 1997 than in the base year 1992 $[(103 - 100)/100 \times 100]$.

To arrive at the index of real hourly wages requires the calculation of an index of nominal wages and an index of prices. An index of nominal wages can be constructed for each year (with 1992 as a base) by dividing the wage in each year by $15.38 (the hourly wage in 1992) and multiplying by 100. For the base year 1992, the nominal wage index is 100 $[(15.38/15.38) \times 100]$, and for 1998, the index is 111.9 $[(17.21/15.38) \times 100]$. The nominal wage index is not reported in Table 7.1.

Changes in prices of goods and services can be measured by the **Consumer Price Index** (CPI). The CPI measures the overall cost of goods and services bought by a typical consumer. It is used to monitor changes over time in the cost of living of a typical family. If the CPI rises, the typical family must earn higher nominal wages in order to maintain the same standard of living. As the fifth column in Table 7.1 indicates, the CPI in 1998 is 108.6. The cost of living between 1992 and 1998 thus has increased by 8.6%. If we divide the index for nominal wages in 1998 by the CPI and multiply by 100, we get the index of real hourly wages, as indicated in the seventh column $[(111.9/108.6) \times 100 = 103]$. While the nominal hourly wages increased by 11.9%, real hourly wages rose by only 3%. The difference between nominal and real wage changes is due to the increase in the price level. The increase in the overall level of prices is called **inflation**. We can write the relationship

Consumer Price Index (CPI) a measure of the overall cost of the goods and services bought by a typical family

inflation an increase in the overall level of prices in the economy

TABLE 7.1 AVERAGE WAGES AND EARNINGS OF PRODUCTION WORKERS IN CANADIAN MANUFACTURING, 1945–98

Year	Weekly Earnings (current dollars)	Average Weekly Hours Paid For	Average Hourly Wage (current dollars)	Consumer Price Index (1992 = 100)	Index of Real Weekly Earnings (1992 = 100)	Index of Real Hourly Wages (1992 = 100)	Annual Percentage Change in Real Hourly Wages Over Previous 10 Years
1945	30.98	44.1	0.67				
1950	45.94	42.1	1.06	14.9	47.2	46.2	
1955	60.53	41.0	1.44	16.8	55.2	55.7	
1960	72.39	40.4	1.77	18.5	60.0	62.2	3.5
1965	89.30	41.1	2.14	20.0	68.4	69.6	
1970	132.75	39.7	3.01	24.2	84.0	80.9	3.0
1975	213.43	38.6	5.06	34.5	94.8	95.3	
1980	342.19	38.5	8.19	52.4	100.0	101.6	2.6
1985	486.97	38.6	11.59	75.0	99.4	100.5	
1990	599.37	38.3	14.19	93.5	98.2	101.1	-0.05
1992	652.92	38.3	15.38	100.0	100.0	100.0	
1995	694.58	38.5	16.19	104.2	102.1	101.0	
1997	736.69	39.3	16.85	107.6	104.9	101.8	
1998	755.92	38.6	17.21	108.6	106.6	103.0	1.9

Note: The weekly earnings include overtime. The figures in this table are derived from several sources. Caution should be exercised in making comparisons over time.

Sources: For 1945–65, adapted from Statistics Canada. (1983). *Historical Statistics of Canada, 1945–1965,* 2nd ed. Ottawa: Statistics Canada. (Catalogue no. 11-516, Series E61-62, E131); for 1970–80, adapted from Statistics Canada. (1973–80, March issues). *Employment Earnings and Hours,* Vols. 51–58, Tables 14, 15, and 18. Ottawa: Statistics Canada. (Catalogue no. 72-002); for 1985–98, adapted from Statistics Canada. (1999, July). *Canadian Economic Observer, Historical Statistical Supplement 1998/99,* Vol. 7, Table 9. Ottawa: Statistics Canada. (Catalogue no. 11-210); for Consumer Price Index, adapted from Statistics Canada. (1999, July). *Canadian Economic Observer, Historical Statistical Supplement 1998/99,* Vol. 7, Table 12. Ottawa: Statistics Canada. (Catalogue no. 11-210).

between changes in the nominal wage rate, the real wage rate, and inflation in general as follows:

Change in the real wage rate = Change in the nominal wage rate – Inflation rate

So far we have focused attention on the worker, for whom wages are income. For the majority of the workforce, wages are the single largest determinant of living standards; however, for most employers, they are the single largest cost component in the production process. The crucial item for the company is not the amount of wages or compensation paid per hour but the labour cost per unit of output. Choosing an hour as the time reference, unit labour cost relates the hourly wage to the units of output a worker produces in an hour (average labour productivity):

$$\text{Labour cost per unit of output} = \frac{\text{Wage rate}}{\text{Output per worker (labour productivity)}}$$

For example, a company paying an hourly wage of $15 to workers producing 60 units of output per hour would have lower labour unit cost than a company paying $13 to employees who produce only 40 units per hour. In the former case, the labour cost per unit is 25 cents (15/60) while in the latter it is 33 cents (13/40).

When it comes to tracking the long-term changes in earnings and labour compensation in Canada, as in the case of work hours, there is a mix of data series, many of which are discontinued, scattered over different industrial sectors or labour force groups, and varying in definitions and coverage. Ideally, one would like to find a consistent time series on total labour compensation derived from a broadly based survey of well-defined occupations in specific industries and geographic regions. Unfortunately, no such source is available in Canada. Information on various components of labour income must be pieced together from various data sources. The following sections present three data sources to provide a picture of the main developments of various aspects of labour compensation over the last decades.

Changes in Total Labour Income and Labour's Share

The first source is Statistics Canada's National Income and Expenditure Accounts. Estimates of wages and salaries and supplementary labour income in the national accounts are primarily based on income tax records. At the end of the calendar year, all employers are required to submit T-4 forms to Revenue Canada. These forms provide information on company payrolls and personal income tax deductions that were remitted from employees regularly throughout the year. Quarterly and monthly estimates of labour income are derived by linking the annual tax data to related series generated from the Labour Force Survey or the Survey of Employment, Payrolls, and Hours.

Figure 7.2 describes the changes in total labour income, adjusted for inflation, from 1948 to 1998.[3] Over those 50 years, the trend in annual growth rates has declined. Labour income showed strong

---

3. In the National Income Accounting System, labour income is defined as all compensation paid to employees residing in Canada. This includes Canadians employed abroad, if their residence is listed as in Canada. Not included are earnings received by self-employed people such as independent professionals, proprietors of unincorporated businesses, and farmers.

gross national product (GNP) the total income earned by Canadians in a given year

growth throughout the 1950s and 1960s. Since the mid 1970s, largely due to the three recessions in 1974/75, 1981/82, and 1990/91, growth rates dipped. Growth in labour income closely followed the total income earned by Canadians, commonly defined as Canada's **gross national product** (GNP).[4]

FIGURE 7.2 TOTAL LABOUR INCOME, 1948–98

Sources: For 1947–94, adapted from Statistics Canada. (1995). *Canadian Economic Observer, Historical Statistical Supplement 1994/95.* Ottawa: Statistics Canada. (Catalogue no. 11-210); for 1995–98, adapted from Statistics Canada. (1999, July). *Canadian Economic Observer, Statistical Summary.* Ottawa: Statistics Canada. (Catalogue no. 11-010).

---

4. As a measure of total Canadian income, GNP is preferable to gross domestic product (GDP), which is total income earned domestically. Suppose a resident of Hong Kong works temporarily in Vancouver. The income that person earns is part of Canadian GDP because it is earned in Canada. But the income is not part of GNP because the worker is not a Canadian national. Although GNP excludes the income earned by foreigners in Canada, it includes the income that Canadians earn abroad. The use of GNP as a benchmark is consistent with the definition of labour income, which includes the earnings of Canadians working abroad. GNP is generally about 4% lower than GDP.

AN INTRODUCTION TO THE CANADIAN LABOUR MARKET

As a result, labour income as a ratio of total income (GNP), called **labour's share**, has fluctuated within a narrow band over the last five decades (see Figure 7.3). In 1947, the labour share was 0.49; 51 years later it was 0.55.[5] In other words, as output of the economy grew, employees (whose income is represented in labour's share) and owners of capital (who receive the remaining portion of total income) have shared equally in the growth of national income. Labour's share noticeably increased during recessions, starting with the 1953/54 recession and continuing the same pattern in the last three recessions of 1974/75, 1981/82, and 1990/91. Were it not for the cyclical movement of labour's

labour's share labour income as a ratio of total income (GNP)

FIGURE 7.3   SHARE OF LABOUR INCOME IN GROSS NATIONAL PRODUCT, 1947–98

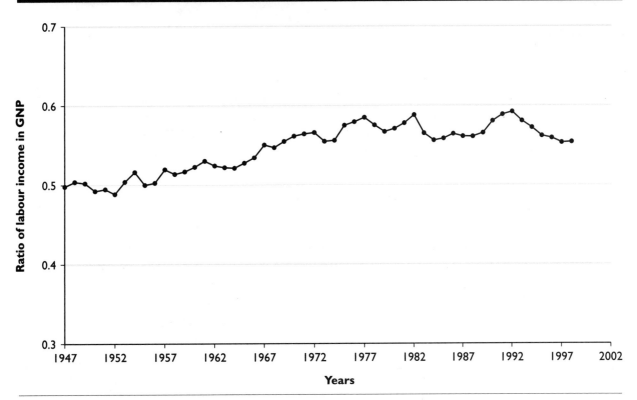

Sources: For 1947–94, adapted from Statistics Canada. (1995). *Canadian Economic Observer, Historical Statistical Supplement 1994/95*. Ottawa: Statistics Canada. (Catalogue no. 11-210); for 1995–98, adapted from Statistics Canada. (1999, July). *Canadian Economic Observer, Statistical Summary*. Ottawa: Statistics Canada. (Catalogue no. 11-010).

5. Total income or GNP is the sum of labour income, corporate profits before taxes, interest and investment income, and depreciation. If we exclude depreciation we obtain the net national product (NNP). We subtract indirect business taxes, such as sales taxes, which make up about 15% of NNP from the NNP to get the national income. Expressed as a percentage of national income instead of GNP, labour's share is much higher. In 1998, labour's share in national income was 71%, compared to labour's share in GNP of 55%.

share, the near constancy of the ratio over a long period would be more pronounced.

The approximate constancy of labour's share in national income is not unique to Canada. In fact, it has been observed in many other industrialized countries, such as Germany, Japan, and the United States. As long ago as 1927, the American economist Paul Douglas noticed to his surprise that the division of national income between capital and labour had been roughly constant in the U.S. over a long period.

The observed constancy of labour's share allows us to draw an interesting conclusion from the following simple equation.

$$\text{Labour's share} = L/Y = \frac{W \times E}{P \times y} = \frac{W/P}{y/E}$$

In this formula, L stands for labour income and Y for total income measured in current prices, or nominal GNP. Labour income is the average nominal labour income per worker (W) multiplied by the number of employed workers (E). Total income can be decomposed into its real component, that is the quantity of goods and services actually produced (y), and the price level (P).

The second ratio in the formula is just a different way of expressing the first ratio. The numerator (W/P) now denotes the average nominal labour income divided by the price level—the real average labour income. The denominator (y/E) is the real output produced in an economy divided by the number of employed workers. We call this ratio **average labour productivity**; it tells us how much, on average, an employed worker has produced within a certain period.[6]

A constant labour's share implies that nominal earnings and supplemental labour income rose over time in line with inflation plus average labour productivity. Put differently, real average labour income fully absorbed the gains in labour productivity made over the years. If workers had been paid less in real terms than what they had contributed to overall production—that is, if real average labour income were less than labour productivity—the share of labour income in national income would have declined.

average labour productivity   the output produced per worker in a given period

---

6. On page 176, we defined labour productivity as output produced per hour rather than per employee. This is more precise because it avoids possible biases in labour productivity caused by changes in hours of work and thus allows comparisons of labour productivity over time.

AN INTRODUCTION TO THE CANADIAN LABOUR MARKET

BOX 7.1 Labour's Share Rises in Recessions

In a recession, total output produced declines and unemployment rises. Why then does labour's share in total output rise during a recession? One reason is that in a cyclical downturn firms tend first to adjust their labour input by reducing hours of work. Initially, they try to hold on to their workforce, especially if they have invested substantial amounts in hiring and training. This investment would be lost if workers who are temporarily laid off were not available for recall when production returns to normal. This strategy is called *labour hoarding*. As firms retain workers who have little work to do, labour productivity falls. Only if a recession is deep and prolonged will firms lay off workers on a larger scale.

The other reason for the increase in labour's share is that firms cannot easily cut wages to adjust their labour cost to falling demand. They are often bound by wage contracts. Even if a wage contract were to expire during a recession, unions or individual employers would strongly resist wage cuts.

Rigid wages and falling labour productivity explain the rise of labour's share in recessions. In our formula for the labour's share, we can see that if wages (W) and employment (E) remain constant while real output ($P \times y$) declines, labour's share (L/Y) must increase. Or using the second expression, as labour productivity (y/E) declines relative to the real wage rate (W/P), labour's share rises.

When interpreting the constancy of labour's share, one must keep in mind that national accounts define labour income broadly, including cash compensation, the realized value of stock options, and the value of taxable fringe benefits such as the personal use of a company car. Likewise, as a factor of production labour includes a heterogeneous group of people: anyone who draws a wage or salary from a business is counted as an employee, from dishwashers paid minimum wage to car mechanics, doctors, and lawyers, to chief executive officers of corporations earning several million dollars a year. Furthermore, the meaning of labour's share becomes less clear in light of certain arbitrary legal definitions in the national accounts regarding the classification of income of business owners. For example, if two doctors are partners in an unincorporated medical practice, their income is counted as proprietor's income, but if they incorporate their business and draw a salary from their corporations (which, given the tax advantages, is likely) their income is counted as employee compensation. Because corporate officers control the firm's capital and in many cases are the owners of the firm, their compensation should be classified as capital income. Attributing the income of business owners to labour income may partly explain the long-run stability of the labour's share.

Some people are simultaneously members of the workforce and owner of capital, that is they derive income both from their labour ser-

functional income distribution the share of national income going to the owners of the factors of production, labour, and capital

personal income distribution the share of national income going to groups of families or individuals

vices and from owning capital. The income distribution by factors of production, also called factoral or functional income distribution, therefore, should not be confused with personal income distribution. **Functional income distribution** refers to the shares of national income owned by the factors of production, labour, and capital. **Personal income distribution** is concerned with how national income is distributed among groups of individuals or families ranked by the size of their annual incomes.

CHANGES IN AVERAGE LABOUR INCOME

While aggregated data on labour income can give a picture of how workers as a group fared over time, they convey little information about the compensation of individual workers. Changes in total labour income reflect changes in number of employed persons as well as compensation levels. To obtain a measure, albeit imperfect, of the compensation received by a worker, we divide total annual labour income by the average annual number of paid workers. Adjusted for inflation, this is called the **real average labour income**.

real average labour income total annual labour income, adjusted for inflation, divided by average annual number of paid workers

From the late 1940s throughout the 1950s, real average labour income grew at an average annual rate of about 4%. These significant income gains continued until the mid 1970s at an only slightly reduced average annual rate of 3.5%. From 1976 on, however, the picture started to change dramatically. With high inflation rates outpacing growth in average nominal labour income, changes in real average annual labour income became negative in 1978. They remained negative for 12 of the 18 years up to 1997 and, whenever positive, they showed only very small positive advances, with two exceptions (1987 and 1988). The overall result is that over the last 20 years no gains were made in real average labour income. Of interest are the opposing changes in the two components of labour income. Between 1977 and 1988, annual average real wages and salaries dropped by almost $1000 or 3.3%. In contrast, supplementary labour income, adjusted for inflation, grew by about 17% throughout the period of 1977 to 1988, offsetting about one half of the wage and salary decline.

Also of interest are the differences in labour income changes by sector. While average labour income increased in the goods-producing sector, it declined in the services-producing sector. The increase in the goods-producing sector resulted from a substantial increase in the supplementary income component ($881), which more than compensated for the slight loss in wages and salaries (–$260). In contrast, the labour income loss in the services-producing sector resulted from the large decline in real wages and salaries (–$963), surpassing the modest growth in supplementary labour income ($281). Several factors may account for the different patterns in the two sectors: the higher rate of unionization, the large share of adult men, and the slower employment growth in the goods-producing sector, versus the high levels of youth and female employment and the higher rate of part-time employment in the services-producing sector.

These factors point to a main difficulty in interpreting changes in average annual labour income figures. The problem is that this measure of compensation does not distinguish between factors that influence an individual worker's labour income and those that do not. Factors such as the number of hours worked, changes in labour statues (such as regulations governing minimum wages and overtime premiums), and the hourly, weekly, or monthly wage rate can affect the labour income of individual workers. Likewise, a change in legislation may extend coverage of various components of supplementary labour income to new groups of workers or increase supplementary labour income contributions made on behalf of existing workers.

On the other hand, there are factors that have no effect on an individual worker's labour income but may affect average labour income overall. These relate to the distributional aspects of employment in the labour market, for example shifts in the composition of employment within and between industries, regions, and occupational groups, or between full-time and part-time workers or persons holding more than one job. Substantial employment growth in low-wage service industries would be reflected in a decline of average labour income, although an individual worker's labour income might remain constant (assuming no job change).

To understand how shifts between industries affect the annual income per employee, suppose that there were only two industries in the economy, one that might be called the "goods" industry and the other the "services" industry. Half the employees worked in the goods industry and the other half worked in the services industry. Suppose also that all employees working in the goods industry received a labour income of $35 000 per year regardless of their occupation or the region they worked in, and that all employees in the services industry received $29 000 per year. The average annual income in the economy would be $32 000 [(35 000 × .5) + (29 000 × .5)]. Now suppose that labour income in both industries remained constant but that employment in the goods industry fell by 15% over a particular period, while employment in the services industry rose by 15%. The average annual income would fall to $31 550 [(35 000 × .425) + (29 000 × .575)] or by 1.4%, even though workers' labour income in both industries did not change. Similar effects would be observed if employment growth in part-time jobs was relatively higher than in full-time jobs.

CHANGES IN AVERAGE WEEKLY EARNINGS AND HOURLY WAGES

The Survey on Employment, Payrolls, and Hours (SEPH) collects data on labour compensation (see Appendix B). Although SEPH does not collect data on actual wage rates, the information it gathers can be used to calculate measures of average weekly earnings and hourly wages by dividing total earnings by total paid weeks or hours. The average hourly wage data from the SEPH have the advantage of being directly derived from a survey, but they are limited when compared to labour income estimates from the System of National Accounts. The information is available only from March 1983 on and is less comprehensive because it excludes compensation elements not directly reflected in the payrolls of firms, such as employers' contributions to pension funds, health, and insurance programs.

In 1983, Canadian employees in all industries were paid an average of $383 per week, including overtime premiums. Fourteen years later, in 1998, average weekly earnings had risen to $606, that is by 58%. Although weekly earnings increased at about 4% annually between 1983 and 1990, their growth dropped off sharply after the 1990/91 recession to an annual rate of 1.9%. If inflation is taken into account, real weekly earnings stagnated over the entire period of 1983 to 1998.

The weekly earnings figures for all industries hide marked differences in terms of levels and growth rates between the goods- and services-producing industries. In 1983, average weekly earnings in the goods-producing industries were $471, compared to the $351 in the services-producing industries. In other words, employees in service-producing industries earned 75 cents for every dollar earned per week by their counterparts in the goods-producing industries. By 1998, weekly earnings in the two sectors had changed to $776 and $554, respectively. That is, the gap had widened slightly to about 71 cents for every dollar earned in the goods-producing industries, indicating a larger overall growth in nominal weekly earnings in the goods-producing industries.

Because average weekly earnings are the product of average hourly earnings times average usual hours worked per week, an increase in weekly earnings may not reflect any gain in the reward for labour services but may just result from Canadians working longer hours compared to earlier years. Average hourly wages, therefore, is a preferable indicator. Average hourly wages computed for all industries grew from $9.83 in 1983 to $15.12 in 1998. On an hourly basis, the wage gap between the service- and goods-producing industries in 1983 was very much the same as the difference in weekly earnings, namely 74 cents for every dollar earned in an hour. The same gap applied in 1998: $13.51 in the services-producing industries as compared to $17.97 in the goods-producing industries, or 75 cents for every dollar.

These earnings estimates share a problem with the National Account estimates of labour income, namely that they are subject to the effects of compositional changes in employment that do not reflect changes in employees' hourly earnings. To correct partly for these problems, Statistics Canada constructed a series of average hourly earnings with fixed weights. Overtime compensation is omitted because it is an important source of income differences between industries. All employees are included on the assumption that salaried employees work their "standard work week."[7] The fixed weights are calculated using employee paid hours data for 1986, the base year for the series. Separate weights are applied for 258 three-digit industry categories to exclude the effects of shifts in the employment composition between these industries. Fixed weights are also applied separately within each of the provinces and territories, so that differential employment growth rates among these regions will not be a source of compositional variation in the earnings series. Finally, fixed weights are also used for employees paid by the hour and salaried employees. Significant shifts between these two employee groups, for example, can occur over the business cycle. Employers tend to retain highly qualified salaried employees during recessions partly because the hiring and termination costs for this group of employees are higher than for hourly paid workers.

Figure 7.4 shows the annual growth rates in the fixed-weighted nominal and real average hourly wages and the inflation rate (as measured by the CPI) from 1984 to 1998. Over the 15-year period, nominal wages and the inflation rate followed a similar path with the exceptions of the years 1991/92 and 1993/94, when the inflation rate dropped

---

7. The SEPH questionnaire defines the standard work week as the "average number of hours of work normally scheduled in a work week."

FIGURE 7.4   NOMINAL AND REAL AVERAGE HOURLY WAGES, 1984–98

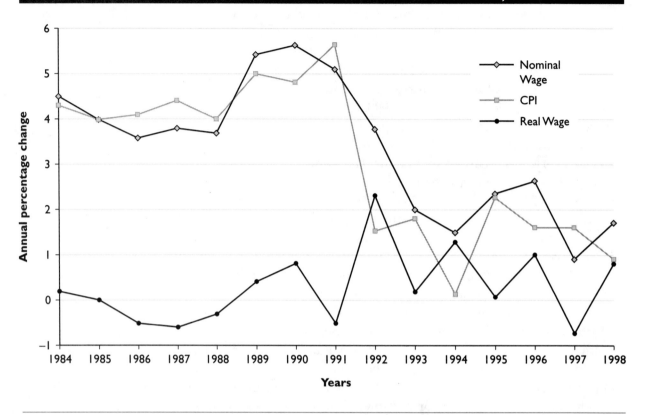

Source: Authors' tabulations based on Statistics Canada. (1999, July). *Canadian Economic Observer, Historical Statistical Supplement, 1998/99*, Tables 9 and 12. Ottawa: Statistics Canada. (Catalogue no. 11-210).

more than nominal wages raising real wages in these years by 2.3% and 1.3%, respectively. From 1997 to 1998, the growth rate in nominal wages increased while the inflation rate dropped further, leading to a modest positive increase in real hourly wages. In 7 of the 15 years, the growth rate in real wages was negative or zero, which offset most of the small gains made in the other years; as a result, over the entire period real hourly wages remained largely stagnant.

CHANGES IN NOMINAL AND REAL WAGE RATES

base wage rate the wage rate that applies to the lowest-paid classification for workers in a bargaining unit

The direct data source for wage rates is Labour Canada's series in base wage rates as negotiated in collective agreements. The **base wage rate** in a contract applies to the lowest-paid classification for workers in the bargaining unit. The data are available on a consistent basis over a rel-

FIGURE 7.5 NOMINAL AND REAL WAGE RATES, 1967–96

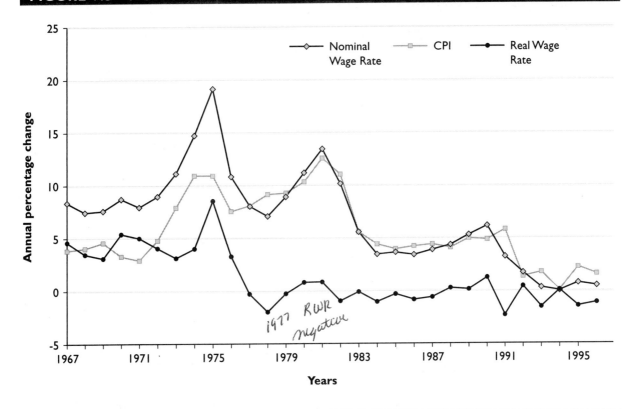

Source: Authors' tabulations based on Labour Canada. *Major Wage Settlements*, various issues. Ottawa: Bureau of Labour Information.

atively long period of time. However, they are only available for unionized workers and, within that group, only for workers covered by major collective agreements involving 500 or more employees. Figure 7.5 shows the year-to-year changes in the nominal wage rate, the inflation rate, and the real wage rate (the rate of change of nominal wages minus the inflation rate) for the period of 1967 to 1996. Nominal wage rate changes are the compound annual average percentage increase in base wage rates in major collective agreements over the duration of the contract. Only those collective agreements are included that do not contain COLA clauses.[8]

The picture that emerges from Figure 7.5 is similar to the one reported in Figure 7.4 on the rate of change in average annual real

---

8. Many contracts tie nominal wage changes to changes in the inflation rate. Such provision is called a cost of living allowance, or COLA. A COLA automatically raises the wage when the CPI rises.

labour income. Between 1967 and 1976, unions were able to obtain wage concessions that exceeded substantially the inflation rate. Real wage growth, as a result, was very high during this period, averaging 4.5% per year. By 1975, nominal wage increases exceeded 19% and inflation had reached almost 11%, leading to the largest increase in real wages in the past three decades.

Responding to the acceleration in wages and prices, the federal government introduced the Anti-Inflation Program (AIP) in October 1975. As a result of the wage and price controls of the AIP, wage settlements and prices declined substantially during the three years of the AIP, although prices declined less than wage settlements did. In 1977, for the first time real wage change was negative.

The lifting of the controls and the second major increase in OPEC oil prices in 1979 led to another round of wage and price increases, which reached two-digit levels in 1980. In contrast to the earlier wage and price escalation, however, nominal wage and price changes followed so closely that real wage growth remained below 1%. This time, the Bank of Canada responded with a forceful anti-inflation policy. As we mentioned in Chapter 6, the Bank of Canada can affect the overall level of economic activity through monetary policy. By reducing the supply of money, the central bank can raise interest rates, which discourages households and firms from spending money on goods and services. As overall demand declines, firms reduce their prices in order to sell their products or services.

When it raised nominal interest rates above 16%, the Bank of Canada created a severe recession in 1981/82. As economic activity drastically slowed down, inflation and nominal wage growth declined dramatically. Throughout most of the 1980s real annual wage change remained negative. Only toward the end of the decade did real wage growth become marginally positive when nominal wages and prices started to edge up again, with wages rising more rapidly than consumer prices. Average annual growth in real wages over the whole decade, however, remained in the negative range.

In 1988, the governor of the Bank of Canada announced that he was determined not only to prevent inflation from rising but also to reduce the inflation rate permanently to near zero. Later, in February 1991, the governor and the minister of finance agreed to set an inflation target of 2% by the end of 1995. The target was in fact reached by 1992. In its pursuit of the zero-inflation policy, the Bank of Canada was the main contributor to the 1990/91 recession, arguably the worst recession Canada has experienced since the Great Depression. By tightening monetary conditions, the central bank raised real short-term interest rates to close to 10%. The increase, together with the Canadian-U.S. exchange rate appreciation of almost 20%, caused annual real growth in the gross domestic product to decline sharply from a positive rate of 5% to a negative rate of 2%. The drastic decline in GDP and employment put such pressure on prices and nominal wages that both grew during the early and mid 1990s at the lowest rates experienced over the last 30 years. Since increases in wages were slightly below the inflation rate for most of the period 1990 to 1995, average annual growth in real wage rates was –0.5%.

In conclusion, the various measures of real worker compensation all show that average real wages have grown little over the last 20 years. Important differences, however, have appeared in the pattern of wages for different labour force groups.

EARNINGS POLARIZATION

So far, we have focused on the trends in levels or percentage changes of various earnings or compensation measures. Changes in average levels or percentages, however, do not tell us much about the structure of wages, namely the relationship of one wage rate to another. Wage differences can be analyzed with different focuses: regional, industrial, occupational, gender, age, and so on. For example, men and women have fared very differently since the early 1970s. Real earnings for men grew only 3% over the last 20 years; by contrast, women's earnings have grown much faster. In 1967, women earned 58 cents to each dollar earned by men; by 1998, the ratio had climbed to 78 cents.

Although earnings differentials declined between men and women, large differences in earnings have emerged based on age. In Canada, the gap between younger and older workers has widened considerably. From 1972 to 1980, the rate of growth of real income for both sexes did not vary much with age; since 1980, however, young workers have fared much more poorly. For example, while older male workers have more or less held their own, the real income of young male workers declined by almost 18%. In Chapter 11 we will analyze wage differentials in more detail. For now, we will only look at the recent trend in skill differentials, which mostly manifest themselves as occupational wage differentials.

One of the most important changes in the Canadian labour market has been the widening of the earnings distribution. The debate on the growing polarization of occupational earnings and the consequent shrinkage of jobs paying middle-class wages is sometimes referred to as the "declining middle class" or the "decline of middle-class wage jobs."

When we discuss issues of inequality we must be careful how we specify the variable we choose to compare earnings or incomes of groups. If we choose family income, this measure includes incomes of all family members and, as we saw earlier, includes income from other sources—for example, government transfer payments, dividends, or interest from bonds—in addition to labour earnings. A widening dispersion in earnings does not necessarily imply an increase in inequality of family income, especially if changes in spouses' incomes offset each other. In a recent study, Beach and Slotsve (1996) concluded that overall inequality in family income did not change significantly throughout the 1970s and 1980s, although the inequality in men's earnings widened sharply. The proportion of middle-class men (those with earnings between 50% and 150% of the median) declined over the last 25 years. At the same time, the proportions of both rich men (with earnings above 150% of the median) and poor men (with earnings below 50% of the median) increased. Among women, however, there was no evidence of a widening dispersion. The proportion of women in the middle class remained unchanged, while the proportion of poor women declined and that of rich women increased slightly.

Why has the distribution of men's earnings become more unequal? Because earnings are the product of wages and hours, perhaps the main reason is related to changes in hours rather than to wages. We have already seen that hours of work have polarized and that more people work more as well as less than the number of hours in the standard work week. Morissette et al. (1995), for example, report that, while real earnings among men in the bottom fifth of wage earners declined by 16% between 1973 and 1989, about half of this decline can be attributed to the decline in the number of hours worked. Still, among men who worked full-time for a full year, the real annual earnings of the bottom fifth fell by 7% over this period.

Where are the sources for the increasing inequality in wages? Do we have to look for explanations primarily on the supply or the demand side, or to institutional changes in the labour market? There is no consensus yet among economists. The various explanations can best be contrasted within the supply and demand framework of two labour markets: the market for skilled labour and the market for unskilled labour. Wages of unskilled workers might decline in relation to those of skilled workers because the relative demand for unskilled workers has declined or because the relative demand for skilled workers has increased. Alternatively, the skill differential could have grown due to a decline in the supply of skilled workers relative to the supply of unskilled workers.

One possible explanation is that changes in skill differentials over time have been driven by changes in the growth of the supply of higher educated workers. This dramatic increase in the 1970s led to the narrowing of the skill differential in that decade. The supply increase was mainly due to the large baby-boom cohorts and the large expansion of secondary and post-secondary education. In the subsequent decade, the relative supply growth decelerated significantly and the wage differential widened. The slowdown in the growth of graduates from the post-secondary sector was larger in the U.S. than in Canada. This may be one of the reasons why the widening in the skill differential has been smaller in Canada than in the U.S.

An alternative account is that the growing inequality of the earnings of skilled and unskilled workers has been driven by relative shifts in labour demand. One factor on the demand side has been increased international competition, especially from low-wage countries. Increased imports from these countries have reduced the demand for less skilled labour in Canada, causing wages to fall relative to skilled workers.

Another explanation attributes the demand shifts to technological change. Many economists believe that the most important force at work in shaping the relative compensation of skilled and unskilled workers has been skill-biased technological progress. New machines and new methods of production require skilled workers, today more so than in the past. Several recent studies point to the computer revolution as the main source of skill-biased technological change.[9] Office automation has become inseparable from the computer. Robotics is growing on the shop floor and the assembly line. Computer-assisted technology is rapidly advancing in every manufacturing or service industry. The advent of computer technology, and the design and manufacturing applications it has spawned, puts more demands on workers. The new methods of production require workers to be more flexible and do a variety of tasks. Firms have responded to the need for higher skilled workers by upgrading the skill level of their employees, displacing low-skilled workers in the process.

Yet another possibility, frequently advanced in the literature, hinges on the decline in labour market institutions mainly in the United States, such as union representation, minimum wage laws, employment

---

9. See, for example, Krueger (1993), and Berman, Bound, and Griliches (1994).

BOX 7.2 Bargaining Structure and the Relative Wage Decline among Unskilled Workers

Unions tend to protect or even raise wages of less skilled workers relative to those of skilled workers. Workers in the United States are less unionized than those in most other industrialized nations. This fact is, therefore, often cited as an explanation of why the level of wage inequality in the United States is higher than in comparable economies. In Canada, unionization rates have changed much less and the wage gap between skilled and less skilled workers has grown less sharply.

In France, union membership has also fallen drastically but declining unionization has not been associated with relative wage declines for low-skilled workers. One reason may be differences in the bar-gaining structure. Collective bargaining in France is highly centralized. It takes place at the industry level and provisions bargained by unions are often extended to non-union workers. In the United States and Canada, bargaining is decentralized. It takes place mostly at the firm or plant level where competitive forces are felt more directly.

Not only did the rate of unionization fall in the United States but bargaining also became even more decentralized. As unionization declined and collective bargaining agreements increasingly had to respond to market forces at the firm or plant level, unions' power to prevent the widening of the wage gap between skilled and unskilled workers weakened.

insurance provisions, etc. Traditionally, these institutions have compressed the wage structure or prevented the relative decline of workers at the bottom of the wage distribution.

Which of these various explanations is the more relevant is a matter of controversy. Although much of the literature treats changes in labour market institutions, foreign trade, and technological progress as separate factors, it should be stressed that they are likely interrelated processes. For example, in a context of stronger international competition, firms may come under increasing pressure to adopt new technologies quickly. Improved technologies, in turn, can make firms more competitive internationally, which can lead to an expansion of international trade.

Will the polarization of earnings between skilled and unskilled workers continue to increase? Nobody knows for sure. Most predictions point in the direction of a worsening of the earnings gap, yet one can think of reasons that would show in an opposite direction. First, the relative increase in demand for skilled workers may simply slow down. For example, one could think of computers in the future as becoming more and more user friendly, even for unskilled workers. One can even think of computers as replacing skilled workers, those whose skills involve primarily the ability to compute or to memorize. Second, how much firms spend on research and development and in what directions they direct their research efforts in developing new technologies depend on expected profits. The low relative wage of unskilled workers may lead firms to explore new technologies that take advantage of unskilled, low-wage workers. Market forces may cause technological progress to become less skill-biased in the future. Third, the large increase in the relative wages of more educated or skilled workers implies that the return to acquiring more education and training are higher than they were several decades ago. Higher returns to education and training may induce people to further their education thus increasing the relative supply of skilled workers. This would stabilize relative wages.

SUMMARY

In analyzing changes in labour compensation, one must distinguish between different concepts: nominal wages and real wages, earnings, labour income and total income. Over the last 50 years, labour income has followed very much the same trend as total national income. Labour's share in national income has changed very little, suggesting that workers as a group have been paid according to their productivity. While real labour income per worker grew rapidly in the three decades following World War II, average real labour income has stagnated since the mid 1970s.

Average real weekly earnings and real hourly wages showed a similar picture in that there have been no gains over the last two decades. The gap in weekly earnings and hourly wages between the goods-producing industries and the services-producing industries has slightly widened.

While earnings differentials between men and women have declined, differences in earnings between older and younger workers have increased considerably. The gap between the earnings of male skilled and unskilled workers has also been increasing. Explanations for the widening skill differential range from increased competition from low-wage countries to skill-biased technological progress, to a weakening of labour market institutions.

KEY TERMS

EXERCISES

1. Does the market distinguish between a "fair" and an "unfair" wage? Explain.

2. What is the difference between a person's labour income and total income?

3. You are given the following data on hourly wage rates for the Canadian manufacturing sector and on the Consumer Price Index (CPI):

Year	Average hourly rate	CPI
1985	$11.59	75.0
1990	$14.19	93.3
1992	$15.38	100.0
1995	$16.19	104.2
1998	$17.21	108.6

Construct the index of real hourly wages for the years given, starting with 1985 and ending with 1998. Use 1992 as the base year. What is the percentage change in the average hourly nominal wage between 1985 and 1998? What is the percentage change in the average hourly real wage?

4. Labour's share in national income has remained fairly constant over the last 50 years. What are the implications for the relationship between real average labour income and labour productivity?

5. Does an increase in the average annual labour income suggest that the individual worker's labour income has increased? Explain.

6. What has been the trend in the real wage rate over the last 30 years?

7. One of the most striking changes in the personal distribution of income has been the widening gap in the earnings between skilled and unskilled workers. Discuss some of the factors that could explain the growing inequality between these two groups.

REFERENCES

Atkinson, A. (1983). *The Economics of Inequality.* Oxford: Clarendon Press.

Beach, C., and Slotsve, G. (1996). *Are We Becoming Two Societies? Income Polarization and the Myth of the Disappearing Middle Class.* Social Policy Challenge, Vol. 12, Toronto: C. D. Howe Institute.

Berman, E., Bound, J., and Griliches, Z. (1994). Changes in the Demand for Skilled Labor within U.S. Manufacturing Industries: Evidence from the Annual Survey of Manufacturing. *Quarterly Journal of Economics, 109:* 367–397.

Blackburn, M., Bloom, D., and Freeman, R. (1990). The Declining Economic Position of Less Skilled American Males. In G. Burtless (Ed.), *A Future of Lousy Jobs?* Washington, D.C.: Brookings Institute.

Borjas, G., Freeman, R. B., and Katz, L. F. (1994). *Changing Futures in a Skill-Driven World.* Oxford: Clarendon Press.

Chaykowski, R. P. (1994). *Modern Labour Economics: The Canadian Context.* New York: HarperCollins.

Economic Council of Canada. (1990). *Good Jobs, Bad Jobs.* Ottawa: Minister of Supply and Services Canada.

Ehrenberg, R. G., and Smith, R. S. (1997). *Modern Labour Economics: Theory and Public Policy* (6th ed.). New York: Addison-Wesley.

Krueger, A. B. (1993). How Computers Have Changed the Wage Structure: Evidence from Microdata 1984–89. *Quarterly Journal of Economics, 108:* 33–60.

Morissette, R., Myles, J., and Picot, G. (1995). Earnings Polarization in Canada, 1969–1991. In K. Banting and C. Beach (Eds.), *Labour Market Polarization and Social Policy Reform.* Kingston: Queen's University School of Policy Studies.

Murphy, K. M., and Welch, F. (1992). The Structure of Wages. *Quarterly Journal of Economics, 107:* 285–326.

Pold, H. and Wong, F. (1990). The Price of Labour. *Perspectives on Labour and Income,* Vol. 2, pp. 42–49. Ottawa: Statistics Canada. (Catalogue 75-001E)

Smith, P. (1990). Recent Trends in Wages. *Perspectives on Labour and Income,* Vol. 2, pp. 41–49. Ottawa: Statistics Canada. (Catalogue 75-001E)

Appendix B

A GUIDE TO LABOUR MARKET DATA AND SOURCES

TYPES OF LABOUR MARKET DATA

Labour economists employ a variety of data in empirical analysis and policy evaluation. The following three types are the most commonly used.

Cross-sectional data can be described as a snapshot of a situation. They provide information for individuals at a given point in time, such as hours of work, compensation, or qualification. When a survey is carried out, its sample represents the population at that point in time. The following year, the same type of information can be collected from a different sample, which represents the population in that year. Because the population changes over time, cross-sectional data can only compare similar populations over time; they cannot trace the same population over time. For example, cross-sectional data can be used for comparing the population of 45-year-old women employed full-year full-time in 1981 with the population of 45-year-old women employed full-year full-time in 1991.

Longitudinal or panel data are derived from surveys that follow the same people over time. This makes it possible to track the changing circumstances of the same people. To illustrate, consider a standard business practice—the maintenance of personnel files. Events in an employee's career with a company are recorded over time, producing a long-term record of that individual's promotions, grievances, special leave, pension benefits, and so on. Longitudinal surveys are the equivalent of personnel files. Many questions in labour economics can only be settled with panel data, such as questions on job mobility. It is widely believed that workers must make frequent career changes during their working lives, but at the moment we do not know much about how often people change their occupations over the course of their working lives. Cross-sectional data can show, for instance, that 100 000 people worked in a specific occupation in 1985 and 80 000 worked in the same occupation in 1990. However, the data cannot identify the composition of this change: whether 100 000 new people entered the occupation and 120 000 left, or nobody entered and 20 000 left. These two interpretations tell radically different stories, with very different implications, and only longitudinal data can distinguish one from the other.

Time-series data provide information on variables such as the employment and unemployment rates, the degree of unionization, or the inflation rate, on a highly aggregated level, that is mostly on a national or provincial level. The data are usually reported on a monthly or annual basis and, therefore, allow to track changes in these variables over time.

DATA SOURCES

Much of the data that labour economists rely on are collected by government agencies, including Human Resources Development Canada, Labour Canada, and Statistics Canada. Most data are produced from surveys or as byproducts from administrative records. Surveys used as the source of statistical data may be either sample surveys or censuses. Sample surveys use the responses of a few to draw conclusions about the complete group or population.

Surveys conducted by various government agencies can be divided into the two categories of household surveys and surveys of business firms. When a survey collects statistical data by contacting private households, it is termed a household survey. When survey data are obtained from officials in business establishments, the surveys are called establishment surveys. Most current labour market surveys focus on the behaviour of households (the supply side of the labour market). Due to a well-developed set of household (worker) surveys, we have a solid data base on labour market outcomes for workers, such as wages, job stability and layoffs, training, and unemployment. Establishment surveys, which inform us about employers' behaviour (the demand side of the labour market), are more rare. This imbalance is reflected in the following guide to some of the main surveys.

HOUSEHOLD SURVEYS

LABOUR FORCE SURVEY. The main source of information on vital labour market data in Canada is the Labour Force Survey (LFS). Conducted by Statistics Canada, it covers some 58 000 representative households across the country involving about 106 000 respondents. Initiated in

1945, the LFS originally surveyed 30 000 households at quarterly intervals. Since 1952, it has been carried out monthly. In 1966, a more extensive stratification of provincial areas allowed estimates for all 10 provinces and the age of individuals surveyed was raised to 15. A major revision of the survey was implemented in 1976, when the number of households was increased to 56 000. The questionnaire was redesigned to allow more detailed estimates on the national and provincial level and to scrutinize the extent of active job searching more carefully. The revision resulted in discontinuities of some data series, although for most of the important ones the changes were not severe enough to distort overall trend. Another major redesign occurred in 1997. The most recent changes provide a number of improvements on data, including wages and union status, and more detailed information on job status and hours worked. A copy of the new LFS questionnaire (reformulated in the 1997 revisions) follows this appendix (see Appendix C).

A selection of data produced from the LFS is found in the following regularly produced publications:

- *Labour Force Information* (Catalogue no. 71-001P). This publication is available on the day the LFS results are released and provides a series of summary tables of seasonally adjusted estimates of previous monthly estimates and quarterly data. Each month a brief commentary highlights the main changes in the labour market.

- *The Labour Force* (Catalogue no. 71-001). This is the main publication available shortly after the release of monthly LFS results. It contains a large selection of data for the current month such as estimates of job tenure, educational attainment, employment and unemployment rates, and multiple jobholders.

- *Labour Force Update* (Catalogue no. 71-005-XPB). This quarterly publication features the latest information and trends on labour market issues.

- *Historical Labour Force Statistics* (Catalogue no. 71-201). This publication presents a selection of historical labour force statistics. Most series begin in 1966 or 1970; some start in 1975.

- *Perspectives on Labour and Income* (Catalogue no. 75-001E). Each quarter this publication brings together and analyzes a wide range of data. Articles follow recent labour market trends as well as current income and wealth issues. There is also news about products, surveys and research projects, and several pages of labour and income indicators by province.

Inquiries about the publication and statistics derived from the LFS can be directed to the Labour Force Survey Section of Statistics Canada (phone: 613 951-9448).

CENSUS OF POPULATION AND HOUSING. The other main source of labour market statistics is the Census of Population and Housing, generally known as the Census. Conducted every 10 years since 1871, it provides data on labour force status since 1921. Since 1971, the Census has been conducted every five years, the most recent one in 1996. It collects labour market information from a one-in-five sample of the entire population and as a result is more comprehensive than any other data source on labour market behaviour. Because of its size, the Census is the only source that provides reliable data on labour market behaviour and outcomes for numerically small groups of people and for small geographic areas. The use of Census data, however, is limited because it is only conducted every five years and most of its results are published with a time delay of one or more years. Statistics Canada now needs three years from the time the Census was taken to release the Census Public Use Sample File, which many researchers rely on for their own work.

Information from censuses is published in hundreds of different publications. The best guides on how to use census data are the following reference products, here cited for the 1996 census:

- *1996 Census Catalogue* (Catalogue no. 92-350-XPE). This catalogue provides full product descriptions including information on the release data, price, and catalogue numbers. Also included are descriptions of the various services available to census data users with a complete list of Statistics Canada contacts.

- *1996 Census Dictionary* (Catalogue no. 92-351-XPE). This essential reference tool helps users to understand and interpret the census data more easily. It provides information on all the concepts, variables, and geographic elements of the Census. Information on each variable includes the definition, related population, and the associated census question.

- *1996 Census Handbook* (Catalogue no. 92-352-XPE). This handbook offers a non-technical overview of the census and a brief history of Canadian censuses, and describes the data collection and processing activities. It discusses each census question, and includes a comparison with those questions asked in 1991.

SURVEY OF CONSUMER FINANCES. Every April, the Survey of Consumer Finances (SCF) collects data on the income of Canadians. Respondents in approximately 39 000 households are asked about the amount of income they received in the previous year and the sources of that income (earnings from employment, government transfer payments, pensions, investment, etc.). Because the SCF is conducted as a supplement to the LFS, it is able to link demographic and labour force characteristics to the income data. The SCF supports an extensive publications program. Six publications are released annually:

- *Income Distributions by Size* (Catalogue no. 13-207)
- *Earnings of Men and Women* (Catalogue no. 13-217)
- *Household Facilities by Income and Other Characteristics* (Catalogue no. 13-218)
- *Family Incomes: Census Families* (Catalogue no. 13-208)
- *Income After Tax* (Catalogue no. 13-210) and
- *Characteristics of Dual-Earner Families* (Catalogue no. 13-215).

Information about the SCF and its publications can be received from the Income and Housing Surveys Section of Statistics Canada (phone: 613 951-4633).

GENERAL SOCIAL SURVEY. Conducted annually since 1985, the General Social Survey (GSS) addresses a broad range of social issues, and although some are not directly related to employment, it collects data on work-related characteristics. The 1989 survey, for example, collected data on educational attainment, activities before starting and after completing education, job satisfaction and other material rewards from employment, and computer use at home and at work. The 1994 survey focused on work environment stress, work activities before and after retirement, work interruptions, computer use, and unpaid work. As of 1998, the GSS has been operating on a two-year rather than one-year cycle. The 1994 GSS contacted approximately 11 500 Canadians by telephone. The survey included a main sample of 10 000 respondents aged 15 and older and a sub-sample of 1500 individuals aged 55 to 74.

For information on the GSS contact the Housing, Family and Social Statistics Division of Statistics Canada at 613 951-9180.

SURVEY OF WORK ARRANGEMENTS. The Survey of Work Arrangements (SWA), which is sponsored by Human Resources Development Canada, was conducted twice by Statistics Canada, in 1991 and 1995, as a supplement to the Labour Force Survey. The 1995 SWA used a sample of approximately 29 000 households. About 42 000 individuals responded to the survey, either directly or by proxy response. Like the LFS, the SWA collected information on the labour market activities and demographic characteristics of the working-age population. It covered additional topics of interest such as place of work (home-based work), non-wage benefits, job permanency, multiple jobholding, work-time preferences, and union status.

SURVEY OF LABOUR AND INCOME DYNAMICS. The Survey of Labour and Income Dynamics (SLID) provides longitudinal data on changes in employment and unemployment, life-cycle labour market transitions (such as the transition from school to work or from work to retirement), and changes in family income, especially the dynamics of low-income families. The first panel of 15 000 households was drawn from the LFS in 1993 and was followed over six years. The second panel started up in 1996 and the third in 1999, when the first panel retired.

Reports based on data from the SLID are published annually in *Dynamics of Labour and Income* (Catalogue no. 75-201E).

LABOUR MARKET ACTIVITY SURVEY. Since 1986, the Labour Market Activity Survey (LMAS) has been the other major longitudinal survey in the labour field. It focuses on the frequency of job changes, the characteristics of jobs held, and socioeconomic/demographic profiles of groups of people who benefit from Human Resources Development Canada programs including training programs.

SURVEYS OF BUSINESS FIRMS

SURVEY OF EMPLOYMENT, PAYROLLS, AND HOURS. The Survey of Employment, Payrolls, and Hours (SEPH) is an employer-based survey that provides monthly estimates of payroll employment, paid hours, and earnings. The data are compiled at detailed industrial levels for Canada, provinces, and territories, and cover all employers except those in agriculture, fishing and trapping, private households, religious organizations, and the military. The survey reference period is the pay period that includes the last seven days of the month.

SEPH statistics are published monthly in *Employment, Earnings, and Hours* (Catalogue no. 72-002). Information on the SEPH and the publication can be obtained from the Labour Division of Statistics Canada (phone: 613 951-4090).

SUMMARY DATABASES

A good summary of current developments in the Canadian labour market and the Canadian economy in large is provided by the *Canadian Economic Observer,* published each month by Statistics Canada. The most comprehensive database of economic time series is made available by Statistics Canada through the Canadian Socio-Economic Information System (CANSIM). Access to CANSIM is by subscription only (universities usually have a licence agreement that allows students to access CANSIM without cost). CANSIM gives yearly data as far back as 1926 and quarterly data as far back as 1947.

If you need any information on data and their sources you can browse the Web page of Statistics Canada (www.statcan.ca). You can download various guides detailing the construction of various surveys such as the Labour Force Survey.

Appendix C

LABOUR FORCE SURVEY QUESTIONNAIRE[1]

Introduced January 1997

DEMOGRAPHIC INFORMATION

HOUSEHOLD MEMBERSHIP

10   **Hello, I'm (your name) from Statistics Canada. I'm calling regarding the Labour Force Survey.**

11   **Would you prefer to be interviewed in English or in French?**
If birth interview go to 12
If subsequent interview go to 20

12   Confirm the listing address.

13   Select the dwelling type.

14   **What is your correct mailing address?**

15   **What are the names of all persons who usually live here? (Begin with adults who have responsibility for the care or support of the family)**

16   **Is anyone staying here temporarily?**
Add a person unless he/she has a usual residence elsewhere.

17   **Are there any other persons who usually live here but are now away at school, in hospital or somewhere else?**
Go to 30

20   **Are you still living in the same dwelling as last month?**

21   **Do the following people still live or stay in this dwelling?**
Select a member and press Enter to change membership status.
Go to 21A if member selected
Otherwise go to 22 if F12 selected

21A   **Is ...**
Now a member
No longer a member
Deceased

22   **Does anyone else now live or stay there?**

---

1. Reprinted from Statistics Canada. (1999, January). *Guide to the Labour Force Survey*. Ottawa: Statistics Canada. (Catalogue no. 71-543-GIE).

INDIVIDUAL DEMOGRAPHICS

30   Select a member and press Enter to enter or update the demographic information. When the information is correct, press F12 to continue

Name Age Sex MS FID RR Ed1 Ed2 Ed3 Ed4

....

31   **What is ...'s date of birth?**

32   **So ...'s age last Saturday was (AGE).**
        Is that right?
        Yes, go to 34
        No, go to 33

33   **What is ...'s age?**

34   Enter ...'s sex.

35   **What is ...'s marital status?**
        (Read categories to respondent)

36   Enter ...'s family code: A to Z.
        Assign the same letter to all persons related by blood, marriage or adoption.

37   Determine a reference person for the family and enter ...'s relationship to that reference person. A reference person should be an adult involved in the care or support of the family.

38   **What is the highest grade of elementary or high school ... ever completed?**

39   **Did ... graduate from high school?**

40   **Has ... received any other education that could be counted towards a degree, certificate or diploma from an educational institution?**
        No, go to 30

41   **What is the highest degree, certificate or diploma ... has obtained?**
        Go to 30 to complete demographic information for all family members.
        When complete, go to 50

ARMED FORCES MEMBERSHIP

50   **Is anyone in this household a full-time member of the regular armed forces?**
        Select a member and press Enter to change the response indicated.
        Go to 50A if member selected

Otherwise go to 60 if F12 selected

50A **Is ... a full-time member of the Regular Armed Forces?**

60 **Is this dwelling owned by a member of this household?**
If rented, complete Rent questions and return.
**GO TO LABOUR FORCE INFORMATION
COMPONENT FOR EACH PERSON AGED 15+ AND
NOT A REGULAR MEMBER OF THE ARMED
FORCES**

Labour force information

PATHS

1 Employed, at work
2 Absent from work
3 Temporary layoff
4 Job seeker
5 Future start
6 Not in labour force, able to work
7 Not in labour force, permanently unable to work

JOB ATTACHMENT

100 **Many of the following questions concern ...'s activities last
week. By last week I mean the week beginning on Sunday,
[date], and ending last Saturday [date]. Last week, did ...
work at a job or business? (regardless of the number of
hours)**
Yes, PATH = 1, go to 102
No, go to 101
Permanently unable to work, PATH = 7, go to 104

101 **Last week did ... have a job or business from which he/she
was absent?**
No, go to 104

102 **Did ... have more than one job or business last week?**
No, go to 110

103 **Was this a result of changing employers?**
No, go to 110

PAST JOB ATTACHMENT

104 **Has ... ever worked at a job or business?**
No, go to 170

105 **When did ... last work?**

If subsequent interview and no change in 105 and PREVIOUS-PATH = 3, go to 131

If subsequent and no change in 105 and PREVIOUS-PATH = 4 to 7, go to 170

If not within last year, go to 170

If not last month, and PATH = 7, go to 131

If not last month and PATH not 7, go to 110

106 **Was that before or after Sunday, [date beginning last reference week]?**

If PATH = 7, go to 131, otherwise go to 110

JOB DESCRIPTION

110 **I am now going to ask some questions about ...'s [new] job or business [at which he/she usually works the most hours].**

Was ... an employee or self-employed?

If not "self employed," go to 114

111 **Did ... have an incorporated business?**

112 **Did ... have any employees?**

113 **What was the name of ...'s business?**

Go to 115

114 **For whom did ... work?**

115 **What kind of business, industry or service was this?**

116 **What kind of work was ... doing?**

117 **What were ...'s most important activities or duties?**

118 **When did ... start working [at name of employer]?**

If not last month, go to 130

119 **Was that before or after Sunday [date following last reference week]?**

Go to 130

ABSENCE - SEPARATION

130 *If PATH = 1, go to 150*

If 101 = No, go to 131

What was the main reason ... was absent from work last week?

Temporary layoff, go to 134

Seasonal layoff, go to 136

Casual, go to 137

Otherwise, Employed but absent, PATH = 2, go to 150

131   **What was the main reason ... stopped working at that [job/business]?**
       If not "Lost job or layoff," go to 137

132   **Can you be more specific about the main reason for ...'s job loss?**
       If PATH = 7, go to 137
       If not "Business conditions," go to 137

133   *If date last worked over one year ago, go to 137*
       Does ... expect to return to that job?
       No or "Not sure," go to 137

134   **Has ...'s employer given him/her a date to return?**
       Yes, go to 136

135   **Has ... been given any indication that he/she will be recalled within the next 6 months?**

136   **As of last week, how many weeks had ... been on layoff?**
       If 130 = "seasonal layoff" or absent more than 1 year, go to 137; otherwise, PATH = 3, go to 137

137   **Did ... usually work more or less than 30 hours per week?**
       If PATH = 3, go to 190
       Otherwise go to 170

WORK HOURS (MAIN JOB)

150   **The following questions refer to ...'s work hours at [name of main job].**
       [Excluding overtime], does the number of [paid] hours ... works vary from week to week?
       Yes, go to 152

151   **[Excluding overtime,] how many [paid] hours does ... work per week?**
       If PATH = 2, go to 158
       If not employee, go to 157
       Otherwise, go to 153

152   **[Excluding overtime,] on average, how many [paid] hours does ... usually work per week?**
       If PATH = 2, go to 158
       If not employee, go to 157

153   **Last week, how many hours was ... away from this job because of vacation, illness, or any other reason? (remember that [civic holiday] occurred last week)**
       0 hours, go to 155

154   **What was the main reason for that absence?**

155   **Last week, how many hours of paid overtime did ... work at this job?**

156   **Last week, how many extra hours without pay did ... work at this job?**

157   *If (employee and 150 = no) actual hours = 151 - 153 + 155 + 156, go to 158*

       Last week, how many hours did ... actually work at [name of main job]? (Remember that [civic holiday] occurred last week)

158   *If 151 or 152 > 29, and PATH = 2, go to 162*

       If 151 or 152 > 29, and PATH = 1, go to 200

       Does ... want to work 30 or more hours per week (at a single job)?

       Yes, go to 160

159   **What is the main reason ... does not want to work 30 or more hours per week (at a single job)?**

       If PATH = 2, go to 162

       Otherwise go to 200

160   **What is the main reason ... usually works less than 30 hours per week (at his/her main job)?**

       If not ("business conditions" or "couldn't find full-time") and PATH = 2, go to 162

       If not ("business conditions" or "couldn't find full-time") and PATH = 1, go to 200

161   **At any time in the 4 weeks ending last Saturday, [date], did ... look for full-time work?**

       If PATH = 2, go to 162

       Otherwise go to 200

ABSENCE

162   **As of last week, how many weeks had ... been continually absent from work?**

       If not (employee or incorporated owner), go to 200

163   **Is ... getting any wages or salary from his/her [employer/ business] for any time off last week?**

       Go to 200

JOB SEARCH - FUTURE START

170   *If PATH = 7, go to 500*

In the 4 weeks ending last Saturday, [date], did ... do anything to find work?

No, and age > 64, PATH = 6, go to 420
No, and age < 65, go to 174
Yes, PATH = 4

171 **What did ... do to find work in the past 4 weeks?**
Did ... do anything else to find work?

172 **As of last week, how many weeks had ... been looking for work? (since date last worked)**

173 **What was ...'s main activity before he/she started looking for work?**
Go to 177

174 **Last week did ... have a job to start at a definite date in the future?**
No, PATH = 6, go to 176

175 **Will ... start that job before or after Sunday, [date four weeks from survey week]?**
Before, PATH = 5, go to 190
On or after, PATH = 6, go to 420

176 **Did ... want a job last week?**
No, go to 420

177 **Did ... want a job with more or less than 30 hours per week?**

178 *If PATH = 4, go to 190*
What was the main reason ... did not look for work last week?
If not "Believes no work available," go to 420
Otherwise, go to 190

AVAILABILITY

190 **Could ... have worked last week [if he/she had been recalled/if a suitable job had been offered]?**
Yes, go to 400

191 **What was the main reason ... was not available to work last week?**
Go to 400

EARNINGS - UNION - PERMANENCE

200 *If not Employee (at main job), go to 300*
If subsequent and no change in 110, 114, 115, 116, 117, 118, go to 260

Now I'd like to ask a few short questions about ...'s earnings from (name of main job). Is ... paid by the hour?

201 Does ... usually receive tips or commissions?
If 200 = no, go to 204

202 [Including tips and commissions,] what is ...'s hourly rate of pay?
Go to 220

204 What is the easiest way for you to tell us ...'s wage or salary [including tips and commissions], before taxes and other deductions? Would it be yearly, monthly, weekly, or on some other basis?

205 [Including tips and commissions,] what is ...'s
to [weekly/bi-weekly/semi-monthly/monthly/yearly]
209 wage or salary, before taxes and other deductions?

220 Is ... a union member at [name of main job]?
Yes, go to 240

221 Is ... covered by a union contract or collective agreement?

240 Is ...'s job permanent, or is there some way that it is not permanent? (e.g. seasonal, temporary, term, casual, etc.)
Permanent, go to 260

241 In what way is ...'s job not permanent?
Go to 260

FIRM SIZE

260 About how many persons are employed at the location where ... works for [name of business/ his/her employer]? Would it be less than 20, 20 to 99, 100 to 500, or over 500?

261 Does [name of business/...'s employer] operate at more than one location?
No, or 260 = "over 500," go to 300

262 In total, about how many persons are employed at all locations? Would it be less than 20, 20 to 99, 100 to 500, or over 500?
Go to 300

CLASS OF WORKER - HOURS AT OTHER JOB

300 *If 102 = no, go to 400*
Now I have a couple of questions about ...'s [other/old]job or business. Was ... an employee or self-employed?
If not "self-employed," go to 320

301   **Did ... have an incorporated business?**

302   **Did ... have any employees?**

320   **Excluding overtime, how many [paid] hours [did/does] ... usually work per week at this [job/business]?**
       If PATH = 2, go to 400

321   **Last week, how many hours did ... actually work at this [job/business]? [Remember that [civic holiday] occurred last week.]**
       Go to 400

TEMPORARY LAYOFF JOB SEARCH

400   *If PATH not 3, go to 420*
       In the 4 weeks ending last Saturday, [date], did ... look for a job with a different employer?
       Go to 420

PREVIOUS SEPARATION

420   *If not (118 = survey month or 119 = since previous reference week) go to 500*
       If 103 = 1, go to 423
       Before ... started working at [name of main job], had he/she ever worked at a job or business [not counting the other [job/business] he/she also works at now]?
       No, go to 500

421   **When did ... last work at that job or business?**
       If prior to month preceding this survey, go to 500
       If this survey month, go to 423

422   **Was that before or after Sunday, [date of Sunday beginning last reference week]?**
       Before, go to 500

423   **What was the main reason ... stopped working at that [job/business]?**
       If not "Lost job or laid off," go to 425

424   **Can you be more specific about the main reason for ...'s job loss?**

425   *If 103 = 1, go to 500*
       At that job or business, did ... usually work more or less than 30 hours per week?
       Go to 500

SCHOOL ATTENDANCE

500   *If age > 64, go to END*
Last week, was ... attending a school, college or university?
No, go to 520

501   **Was ... enrolled as a full-time or part-time student?**

502   **What kind of school was this?**
Go to 520

SUMMER STUDENT CONTENT

520   *If survey month not May thru August, END*
If age not 15 to 24, END
If subsequent and PREVIOUS-520 = "no," END
If subsequent and PREVIOUS 520 = "yes," go to 521
Was ... a full-time student in March of this year?
No, END

521   **Does ... expect to be a full-time student this fall?**
END

Codes for demographic component

35

1   Now married or living common-law
2   Single, never married
3   Widow or widower
4   Separated or divorced

37

1   Reference person
2   Spouse
3   Son or daughter (natural, adopted or step)
4   Grandchild
5   Son-in-law or daughter-in-law
6   Foster child (less than 18 years of age)
7   Parent
8   Parent-in-law
9   Brother or sister
0   Other relative - Specify in Notes
0   Grade 8 or lower (Quebec: Secondary II or lower)
1   Grade 9 - 10 (Quebec: Secondary III or IV)
     (Newfoundland: 1st year of secondary)
2   Grade 11 - 13 (Quebec: Secondary V)
     (Newfoundland: 2nd to 4th year of secondary)

41

1   No postsecondary degree, certificate or diploma
2   Trades certificate or diploma from a vocational school or apprenticeship training
3   Non-university certificate or diploma from a community college, CEGEP, school of nursing, etc.
4   University certificate below bachelor's level
5   Bachelor's degree
6   University degree or certificate above bachelor's degree

Codes for labour force component

106 / 119 / 174 / 422

1   Before the date above
2   On or after the date above

110 / 300

1   Employee
2   Self-employed
3   Working in a family business without pay

130

01   Own illness or disability
02   Caring for own children
03   Caring for elder relative (60 years of age or older)
04   Maternity leave (females only)
05   Other personal or family responsibilities
06   Vacation
07   Labour dispute (strike or lockout)
08   Temporary layoff due to business conditions (Employees only)
09   Seasonal layoff (Employees only)
10   Casual job, no work available (Employees only)
11   Work schedule (e.g., shift work, etc.) (Employees only)
12   Self-employed, no work available (Self-employed only)
13   Seasonal business (excluding employees)
00   Other - Specify in Notes

131 / 423

01   Own illness or disability
02   Caring for own children
03   Caring for elder relative (60 years of age or older)
04   Pregnancy (Females only)
05   Other personal or family responsibilities
06   Going to school
07   Lost job, laid off or job ended (Employees only)

08	Business sold or closed down (Self-employed only)
09	Changed residence
10	Dissatisfied with job
11	Retired
00	Other - Specify in Notes

132 / 424

1	End of seasonal job
2	End of temporary, term or contract job (non-seasonal)
3	Casual job
4	Company moved
5	Company went out of business
6	Business conditions (e.g., not enough work, drop in orders, retooling, etc.)
7	Dismissal by employer (i.e., fired)
0	Other - Specify in Notes

154

01	Own illness or disability
02	Caring for own children
03	Caring for elder relative (60 years of age or older)
04	Maternity leave (Females only)
05	Other personal or family responsibilities
06	Vacation
07	Labour dispute (strike or lockout)
08	Temporary layoff due to business conditions
09	Holiday (legal or religious)
10	Weather
11	Job started or ended during week
12	Working short-time (due to material shortages, plant maintenance or repair, etc.)
00	Other - Specify in Notes

137 / 177 / 425

1	30 or more hours per week
2	Less than 30 hours per week

159

1	Own illness or disability
2	Caring for own children
3	Caring for elder relative (60 years of age or older)
4	Other personal or family responsibilities
5	Going to school
6	Personal preference
0	Other - Specify in Notes

AN INTRODUCTION TO THE CANADIAN LABOUR MARKET

160

1	Own illness or disability
2	Caring for own children
3	Caring for elder relative (60 years of age or older)
4	Other personal or family responsibilities
5	Going to school
6	Business conditions
7	Could not find work with 30 or more hours per week
0	Other - Specify in Notes

171

1	Public employment agency
2	Private employment agency
3	Union
4	Employers directly
5	Friends or relatives
6	Placed or answered ads
7	Looked at job ads
0	Other - Specify in Notes

173

1	Working
2	Managing a home
3	Going to school
4	Other - Specify in Notes

178

1	Own illness or disability
2	Caring for own children
3	Caring for elder relative (60 years of age or older)
4	Other personal or family responsibilities
5	Going to school
6	Waiting for recall (to former employer)
7	Waiting for replies from employers
8	Believes no work available (in area, or suited to skills)
9	No reason given
0	Other - Specify in Notes

191

1	Own illness or disability
2	Caring for own children
3	Caring for elder relative (60 years of age or older)
4	Other personal or family responsibilities
5	Going to school
6	Vacation
7	Already has a job
0	Other - Specify in Notes

204
1   Yearly
2   Monthly
3   Semi-monthly
4   Bi-weekly
5   Weekly
0   Other - Specify in Notes

241
1   Seasonal job
2   Temporary, term or contract job (non-seasonal)
3   Casual job
4   Work done through a temporary help agency
0   Other - Specify in Notes

260 / 262
1   Less than 20
2   20 to 99
3   100 to 500
4   Over 500

501
1   Full-time
2   Part-time

502
1   Primary or secondary school
2   Community college, junior college, or CEGEP
3   University

Part III

Microeconomic Theory of the Labour Market

Part III

Microeconomic Theory of the Labour Market

This part of the text applies the principles of demand and supply introduced in Chapter 2 to the labour market. The goal is to understand how wage rates and employment levels are determined. The reasons for wage rate differences between occupations are also examined.

Chapter 8 introduces the supply side of the labour market starting with the factors that influence one's decision to work for pay. It is assumed that individuals can only do two things with their time: work for pay or enjoy leisure. The impact on the labour supply of government social assistance programs, tax rates, education, retirement, and migration are discussed. The demand side of the labour market is represented by employers. The factors that influence the employer's demand for labour are introduced in Chapter 9. An important topic in this chapter is productivity, or the output per worker.

In Chapter 10, the demand and supply sides of the labour market interact. The result is an equilibrium wage rate and an equilibrium level of employment. We review the impact of government initiatives such as minimum wage rates and payroll taxes on the equilibrium position, as well as the impact of unions on the equilibrium wage rate and employment levels. The interaction of demand and supply in the labour market determines the level of employment. A consequence of this interaction is that some workers do not find work. The causes of unemployment are discussed in Chapter 10, following up on the discussion of unemployment in Chapter 6.

Not all workers earn the same wage rate. The reasons for these differences are explained in Chapter 11. The reasons can be categorized into three groups: adjustment lags, compensating wage differentials, and labour market barriers. The presence of discrimination—a labour market barrier—has prompted governments to enact pay equity legislation, which is discussed here. As an individual's skill level also affects his or her compensation in the marketplace, training and education are discussed in Chapter 12. The chapter focuses on the investment aspects of education. Do the returns to an investment in education exceed the costs of such an investment?

8

....

LABOUR MARKET DECISIONS OF HOUSEHOLDS

OBJECTIVES

After completing this chapter, you will be able to:

1. define and describe the following terms: normal good, income effect, substitution effect (supply), reservation wage rate, marginal tax rate, economic rent, and demogrant;

2. derive the supply curve for labour;

3. explain the conditions under which the supply curve bends backward;

4. use income and substitution effects to analyze the work disincentives associated with income-security programs;

5. explain the impact of immigration and emigration on the supply curve for labour;

6. discuss the factors that influence the decision to migrate.

INTRODUCTION

All markets have a demand side and a supply side. The labour market is no exception. In order to analyze the workings of the labour market, it is necessary to study both sides separately. This chapter focuses on the theory behind the supply side of the labour market, with the aim of deriving the supply curve of labour. Some of the concepts discussed in this chapter, such as opportunity cost and elasticity, were introduced in Chapter 2.

At the level of the individual, the quantity of labour (number of hours of work) supplied to the labour market depends on the decision to work and for how long one is willing to work. At the level of society, the total supply of labour to the economy depends on the participation rate and the number of hours people are willing to work. This chapter begins with the theory behind an individual's decision to work for pay and discusses the factors that influence that decision, such as income-support programs, the presence of children in the household, the wage rate, and taxes. The chapter also discusses changes in the quantity of labour supplied to the market over a period of a person's life. A discussion about the impact of training and migration on labour supply concludes the chapter.

THE DECISION TO WORK

The theory about the decision to work relates to the use of one's time. It assumes that individuals can only do two things with their time: work for pay in the marketplace or participate in leisure activity. The definition of a leisure activity is very broad: It can range from participating in hobbies and sports to doing household chores, and includes attending school. Activities such as sleeping and eating can also be considered leisure activities for the purposes of our discussion. Basically, any activity that is not classified as work for pay is a leisure activity.

Some textbooks subdivide leisure activities into a number of categories. *Non-market work* would include the time allocated to household chores for which no compensation is received. It also includes work done on a volunteer basis. *Consumption time* refers to the time spent enjoying the purchases made in the marketplace such as watching television or playing golf. *Idleness* refers to the time allocated for rest and reflection during which no production or consumption is undertaken. The discussion of leisure in this text lumps the various categories of leisure together. There is no need to distinguish between the types of leisure in order to develop a workable theory of labour supply.

The theory of labour supply developed in this chapter assumes that individuals see work solely as an activity that takes them away from the pursuit of leisure activities. It assumes that individuals do not see work as an activity that provides satisfaction or pleasure, although many individuals do enjoy their occupation or profession and would choose to allocate many hours to work rather than to a leisure activity. However, for the purposes of establishing a theory of labour supply, the non-pecuniary aspects of labour supply will be ignored.

A number of factors influence the decision to work. One is the individual's demand for leisure. Leisure can be treated as a good that people desire; as such, the demand for leisure depends on the price of leisure, one's income and wealth, and one's preferences for leisure as opposed to working for pay.

What is the price of leisure? In order to take an hour of leisure, one must take an hour off work. The wage rate for that hour of work is the price of leisure. In other words, the price of leisure is the opportunity cost of not working. As the wage rate increases, the opportunity cost of not working (the price of leisure) increases. You will recall from the review of economic principles that as the price of a product increases, the quantity demanded of that product decreases. Therefore, as the wage rate increases, and the price of leisure increases, the individual will demand less leisure and will be encouraged to have less leisure time and to work more hours. This assumes that all other factors influencing the demand for leisure (such as one's preferences) remain constant. The fact that individuals substitute work for leisure as the wage rate increases is known as the **substitution effect (supply)**. The word "supply" is added to the substitution effect to distinguish it from the substitution effect discussed in the next chapter. For the remainder of this chapter, we will simply refer to the substitution effect.

The demand for leisure also depends on one's income and wealth. If leisure is a normal good, the demand for leisure will increase with an increase in income. The definition of a **normal good** is one for which demand increases with increases in consumer incomes. The ability to purchase more of all products, including leisure, in light of increases in income is referred to as the **income effect (supply)**.

When the wage rate increases, the income and substitution effects have an opposite influence on an individual's labour supply. The substitution effect encourages the individual to work more hours because the price of leisure has increased. The income effect encourages the individual to work fewer hours and purchase more leisure. Economists

substitution effect (supply) leisure and work hours are substituted for each other as the wage rate changes

normal good a good for which demand increases as one's income increases

income effect (supply) the change in hours of work caused by a change in income

say that the income effect has a negative impact on the decision to work while the substitution effect has a positive impact. If the substitution effect outweighs the income effect, an individual will decide to work more hours in response to a wage rate increase; if the opposite happens, an individual will decide to work fewer hours. If the two effects offset each other, there will be no change in the supply of labour.

The impact of the income and substitution effects can be illustrated with the help of the **labour supply curve**, which displays the number of hours of work offered in relation to the wage rate (see Figure 8.1). At low wage rates, individuals are not willing to offer many hours of work and the price of leisure is also low. As the wage rate increases, the substitution effect dominates the income effect. As the wage rate increases, the opportunity cost of not working increases. The individual wants to work more hours. The desire to work more hours gives a positive slope to the labour supply curve, as shown in the figure.

Figure 8.1 also identifies the **reservation wage rate**. This is the lowest wage rate that an individual is willing to work for; below this wage rate, the individual will not participate in the labour force. There is no supply curve below this wage rate. The reservation wage rate is influenced by factors outside the labour market such as the presence of

labour supply curve
graph showing the number of hours of work offered in relation to the wage rate

reservation wage rate
the lowest wage rate an individual is willing to work for

FIGURE 8.1 LABOUR SUPPLY CURVE

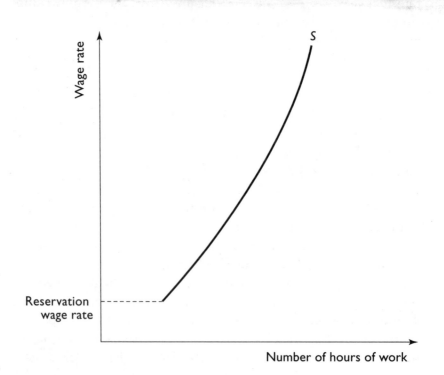

AN INTRODUCTION TO THE CANADIAN LABOUR MARKET

children in the family, the availability of income from sources other than work, and a person's preference for leisure.

As one's wage rate increases, one's income increases. That income may reach such a level that the individual decides to purchase more leisure. If so, the income effect will begin to dominate the substitution effect. With fewer hours of work, the slope of the supply curve will be negative. The switch in the dominance of the substitution effect to the income effect results in a **backward-bending supply curve for labour** (see Figure 8.2). The wage rate at which the income effect begins to dominate varies from individual to individual. Some may be willing to increase their hours of work at relatively high wage rates while others in the same situation will opt for more leisure.

One criticism of the work/leisure model points to the fact that the decision regarding the number of hours of work is not always in the hands of the individual. Employers may have established hours and employees must work those hours in order to remain employed. That is, if the company is open from 9:00 a.m. to 5:00 p.m. each day from Monday to Friday, those are the hours that the employee must work. It is not possible to choose fewer hours of work at this place of employment. In spite of this institutional restriction on hours, the individual

backward-bending supply curve for labour a supply curve for labour that switches from a positive slope at lower wage rates to a negative slope at higher wage rates, with the substitution effect dominating at low wage rates and the income effect dominating at high wage rates

FIGURE 8.2   THE BACKWARD-BENDING SUPPLY CURVE FOR LABOUR

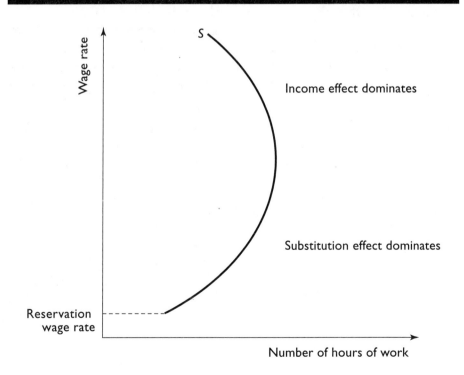

does have some choice in the selection of hours of work, for example by opting not to work overtime if it is voluntary. An individual may also have the option of switching from part-time to full-time employment in response to a wage rate increase. In other situations, individuals may select part-time work over full-time employment. Some flexibility in terms of the number of hours of work is also obtained through moonlighting. If it is impossible to acquire more hours of work at one's current job, a second job could be obtained. Thus individuals have some flexibility in their hours of work.

As discussed in Chapter 3, there are legislated requirements for payment of a premium wage rate for hours of work beyond a daily, or weekly, maximum. Many companies establish their own maximum hours of work beyond which a premium rate, or overtime rate, will be paid. What impact does a premium wage rate have on the number of hours offered for work by an individual, if we assume that working overtime is voluntary and not compulsory? Can employers encourage their employees to work more hours by offering a premium rate of pay for overtime? With a premium wage rate, the price of leisure will increase. Since the premium wage rate is likely to be at least 50% more than the regular wage rate, the price of leisure will increase substantially. The result is a strong substitution effect on the worker's behalf. Since in most cases, the number of overtime hours is limited, the income effect is likely to be small. The substitution effect will dominate and encourage the individual to work more hours.

To this point we have been discussing the individual's decision to participate in the labour force. We have ignored the fact that most adults marry and start families. Decisions about work and leisure are often made as a family and not by individual members of the family acting alone. Family income as opposed to individual income influences the work/leisure tradeoff. Furthermore, family responsibilities for such things as household chores are allocated to the various family members, keeping some members of the family from participating more in the labour market while allowing other members to devote more time to it. The spouse with the higher earnings potential may allocate more hours to the labour market.

So far we have been discussing the individual labour supply curve. We now shift our discussion to the market supply curve for labour. To get the curve for an occupation, it is necessary to find the sum of all the individual supply curves for people willing to work at that occupation. Since labour supply curves for individuals are normally positively sloped, the market supply curve is also positively sloped. The difference between the individual and market supply curves

BOX 8.1 Marginal Tax Rates and the Decision to Work

Canada has a progressive income tax system whereby individuals with higher incomes pay a higher proportion of that income in tax. The progressive nature of the income tax system increases the importance of marginal tax rates. The word "marginal" means extra, or additional. The marginal tax rate is the proportion of any additional income earned that is paid in taxes. With a progressive income tax system, marginal tax rates increase as income increases.

The following hypothetical example outlines how the marginal tax rate is calculated.

Income	Tax Rate	Taxes Paid	Marginal Tax Rate
$40 000	20%	$8000	
			> 4500/10 000 = 45%
$50 000	25%	$12 500	
			> 5500/10 000 = 55%
$60 000	30%	$18 000	

If one's income increases from $40 000 to $50 000 in one year, income taxes for that year increase from $8000 to $12 500, an increase of $4500. Therefore, 45% of the $10 000 increase in income was paid in taxes even though the individual is in the 25% tax bracket. Why is the marginal tax rate 45% when the individual is in the 25% tax bracket? When an individual moves from a 20% tax bracket to a 25% tax bracket, the $40 000 income that was previously taxed at 20% must now be taxed at 25%. Thus, when an individual receives an increase in salary and moves into a new tax bracket, any earnings to that point must be taxed at the higher rate.

Can the marginal tax rate influence one's decision to work? Assume that an individual is provided with the opportunity to work overtime at one and one half times the regular hourly wage rate. The price of leisure has increased since the hourly wage rate has increased. The substitution effect would predict that the individual would work more hours. However, when one considers the marginal tax rate on extra income, leisure is not as expensive as it would be without the tax. An individual will always bring home more money by working more hours. However, the individual may refuse overtime because the tax system has decreased the price of leisure.

appears on the horizontal axis. For the individual supply curve, the horizontal axis referred to hours of work (see Figure 8.1). For the market supply curve, the horizontal axis usually refers to the number of workers, although for some examples total hours of work is also recorded.

WAGE ELASTICITY OF LABOUR SUPPLY

The impact of increased wage rates on hours of work can be assessed by looking at the wage elasticity of supply. You will recall from our review of economic principles in Chapter 2 that the term "price elasticity of supply" refers to the responsiveness of the quantity supplied to a

price elasticity of supply
$= \dfrac{QS}{\Delta P}$

$\dfrac{\Delta QS}{\Delta WR}$

change in the price. In reference to the labour supply, wage rate elasticity of supply refers to the percentage change in the quantity of labour supplied in response to a 1% increase in the wage rate. Information on elasticity tells us more about the impact of wage rate increases on the quantity of labour supplied. What effects do wage rate increases have on the hours that individuals are willing to work?

wage elasticity of labour supply the responsiveness of quantity supplied to changes in the wage rate

The **wage elasticity of labour supply** is determined by dividing the percentage change in the quantity of labour supplied by the percentage change in the wage rate.

$$\text{Coefficient of wage elasticity of supply} = \frac{\text{Percentage change in quantity of labour supplied}}{\text{Percentage change in the wage rate}}$$

If the coefficient of wage elasticity of supply is positive, increases in the wage rate result in increases in the labour force participation. In other words, the substitution effect dominates. If the coefficient of wage elasticity of supply is negative, increases in the wage rate result in fewer hours of work being offered; the income effect dominates. The closer the coefficient is to zero, the smaller the impact of wage rate changes on the labour supply. As the coefficient moves further away from zero, either in a positive or a negative direction, wage rate changes have a greater impact on the quantity of labour supplied.

No two studies arrive at identical wage elasticities of supply. In general, the estimates of labour supply elasticity for women are positive. The estimates of labour supply elasticity for men are generally close to zero and some studies have indicated that the wage elasticity of supply is slightly negative. Overall, the positive wage elasticity of supply for women outweighs the low negative wage elasticity for men. Thus, any increase in wage rates is likely to result in an overall increase in the quantity of labour supplied.

ECONOMIC RENT

The labour supply curve to an occupation slopes up to the right. This implies that the more workers will be willing to work at a certain occupation, the higher the wage rate. An individual will be willing to work at this occupation for a relatively low wage rate. In other words, the individual's reservation wage rate is low. When an individual receives a wage rate in excess of his or her reservation wage rate, it is said that the person is receiving **economic rent**.

economic rent wage rate received in excess of the reservation wage rate

The concept of economic rent is illustrated in Figure 8.3. For some individuals the reservation wage rate is W_1: they are not willing to offer

AN INTRODUCTION TO THE CANADIAN LABOUR MARKET

their services to an employer for less than this wage rate. If the market wage rate were W_2, the individual would receive an economic rent of $W_2 - W_1$ for each hour worked. All individuals willing to work for less than W_2 are receiving an economic rent. The total economic rent paid to all individuals is shown by the shaded area in Figure 8.3.

FIGURE 8.3   ECONOMIC RENT

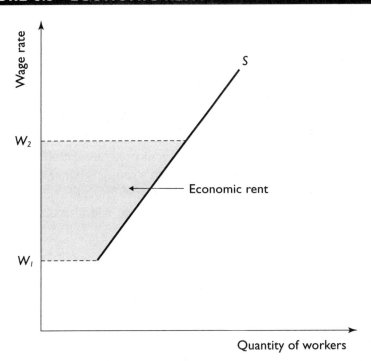

Why do employers not reduce an individual's wage rate down to the reservation wage rate for that person and eliminate economic rent? Reducing wage rates may not be possible. Minimum wage legislation may make it illegal to reduce the wage rate. Trade unions usually insist that all employers who perform a certain task get the same wage rate. Furthermore, an individual who is willing to work for a lower wage rate may not want to accept the lower rate if other employees receive a higher wage rate for the same work.

Rivalry among employers can lead to the payment of economic rent. This rivalry is evident in professional sports, where teams lure free-agent players away from the opposing teams. The desire to avoid paying economic rent has led, on occasion, to collusion among owners of sports franchises. The presence of salary caps (a maximum total pay-roll) in collective agreements between the players and the owners is a means of limiting the payment of economic rent.

POLICY ISSUES

The theoretical concepts of the income and substitution effects can be used to analyze how various income support programs influence the decision to work.

DEMOGRANT

demogrant a lump sum payment to an individual based on membership in a particular demographic group

A **demogrant** is a lump sum payment to an individual based on membership in a certain demographic group, such as being a senior. The current old age security benefit paid to all Canadians 65 years of age and over is a demogrant. The sole criterion for receiving it is age, not income or any other characteristic. All those who qualify receive the same lump sum payment. This program may not continue to operate as Canada is embarking on a plan to replace the current programs of old age security and guaranteed income supplement with a senior's benefit. This benefit will be tax free and will be tied to income. Individuals with higher incomes will receive less money than those individuals with lower incomes.

The former family allowance program in Canada was another example of a demogrant. Mothers received a monthly lump sum payment for each child under 18 years of age. The size of the payment was the same for all mothers regardless of family income. The family allowance benefit was taxable and was added to the income of the higher-income earner in the household. This program was replaced by the child tax credit, which gives more assistance to families with lower incomes.

What impact does a demogrant have on the decision to work? There is an income effect since one's income has increased. The individual can afford to purchase more leisure. There is no substitution effect associated with a demogrant since the price of leisure (the wage rate) has not changed. Thus, demogrants (that is, income from not working) would have a negative impact on the decision to work.

WELFARE ASSISTANCE

Governments pay welfare assistance to low-income individuals who are temporarily without work or who require financial assistance. Those who receive welfare must establish a need for that assistance.

Policymakers are concerned that such assistance reduces the incentive to look for work. That is, there is an income effect associated with receiving welfare assistance. With more income, an individual can purchase more leisure. Individuals who decline to look for work while receiving welfare assistance are not getting the work experience and training necessary to obtain long-term employment. The longer an individual remains out of the employed labour force, the more difficult it will be to obtain a job. In recent years, provincial governments have reduced the amount of welfare assistance benefits in an effort to improve the incentive to work. There is a negative income effect associated with lower benefits; lower benefits mean lower incomes and a reduced ability to purchase leisure.

Is there a substitution effect associated with welfare benefits? The substitution effect refers to the opportunity cost of not working. If there is no work available, the opportunity cost is zero. The price of leisure is zero. If employment is available, the opportunity cost of not working and relying on welfare benefits for one's income is the wage rate that is sacrificed. The structure of the welfare program can have an impact on the opportunity cost of not working. If the amount of one's welfare benefit is reduced by the full amount of any income from employment, there is no financial gain from accepting employment. The opportunity cost of not working, or the price of leisure, is zero. If the welfare program is structured so that an individual can keep most of the earnings from employment, the price of leisure increases. For example, assume that one's welfare benefit was reduced by 25% of one's employment earnings. In effect, an individual would keep 75% of any employment earnings. There would be an opportunity cost associated with not working. The higher the opportunity cost, the greater the incentive to seek employment.

The price of leisure depends on the wage rate an individual can command in the labour force. The higher the wage rate, the more expensive leisure becomes. In order to encourage labour force participation, governments have been insisting that individuals who receive welfare assistance continue to develop their labour market skills. If skill training can lead to higher paying jobs, there will be less incentive to continue receiving welfare benefits. In Ontario, welfare assistance is part of the Ontario Works program, which emphasizes providing work experience and upgrading the skills of those individuals receiving welfare assistance. They must agree to do community service jobs as a condition for receiving benefits. Single teenage mothers must attend school in order to receive welfare benefits.

BOX 8.2 Employment Earnings and Welfare Benefits

The strength of the substitution effect for those receiving welfare assistance depends in part on how much of one's employment earnings can be kept while continuing to receive assistance. The following examples and calculations are taken from the Ontario Support To Employment Program (STEP).

Example #1

A single person could be entitled to $520 per month under the Ontario Works program. Assume the person had $500 in employment income during the month. The monthly entitlement under the Ontario Works program will be reduced because of the presence of employment earnings. The individual is allowed a basic exemption of $143. The individual is also allowed an exemption of 25% of the remaining employment income ($500 − $143 = $357). This amounts to $89.25 ($357 × 0.25).

$$\$500 - \$143 - \$89.25 = \$276.75$$

The amount of $267.75 is the amount deducted from the monthly entitlement. The monthly entitlement from Ontario Works is $520 − $267.75 = $252.25. The total monthly income including earnings and entitlement is $500 + $252.25 = $752.25.

Earnings are up from $520 per month to $752.25 per month, an increase of $232.25. In effect, the individual keeps 46.45% of the $500 earned through employment.

Example #2

A family of two adults and two children under 12 years of age could receive a monthly entitlement of $1178. Assume the family earned $1000 of employment income in a month. The basic exemption of $346 is deducted from employment earnings. The family also has an exemption of 25% of the remaining employment income ($1000 − $346 = $654). This amounts to $163.50 ($654 × 0.25). The family may also be eligible for an exemption related to approved childcare expenses ($200). The amount to be deducted from the entitlement is:

$$\$1000 - \$346 - \$163.50 - \$200 = \$290.50$$

The monthly entitlement is $1178 − $290.50 = $887.50. Total monthly income from employment and from Ontario Works is $1000 + $887.50 = $1887.50, an increase of $1887.50 − $1178 = $709.50. Thus the family kept 70.95% of the employment earnings.

EMPLOYMENT INSURANCE

The federal government regulates the employment insurance program in Canada. Benefits are based on the number of weeks worked prior to unemployment and on the regional unemployment rate. Most recipients of employment insurance receive 55% of their insurable earnings for 14 to 45 weeks in a 52-week period. Individuals need a certain number of hours of work to qualify for benefits and must wait two weeks after applying before the benefits begin.

As mentioned in Chapter 3, the employment insurance program has undergone several changes since its introduction in 1941. Since

AN INTRODUCTION TO THE CANADIAN LABOUR MARKET

1971, changes have focused on reducing the work disincentives associated with the program by reducing benefits. There is an income effect associated with EI payments because high benefits increase the demand for leisure and reduce hours of work. Empirical evidence indicates that a positive relationship exists between the duration of unemployment and the size of the employment insurance benefits. That is, the higher the benefit, the longer individuals remain unemployed.

Is there a substitution effect associated with employment insurance? What is the price of leisure? Until recently, individuals who received benefits were not permitted to work and receive benefits simultaneously. As a result, the price of leisure was zero. The current program allows individuals to earn some money while continuing to receive benefits. The price of leisure is the wage rate sacrificed. It may include the expenses associated with looking for a job. A condition of EI is that individuals must look for employment. If good job opportunities are passed up while receiving benefits, the individual may be faced with a large drop in income when employment insurance benefits run out. The financial loss associated with not being able to find work in the future could also be part of the price of leisure.

Most studies on the impact of employment insurance on the labour market focus on the impact on the labour supply; however, there is also a labour demand aspect. Employment insurance is paid by employer and employee contributions. As such, it is a payroll tax and increases the cost of hiring a new worker. The increased cost of labour may reduce the demand for labour. On the other hand, employment insurance benefits can also increase overall labour demand, because they provide money for unemployed individuals to spend. The increased spending may prop up the demand for goods and services and the demand for workers.

The federal government has made an effort to provide EI recipients with access to skill training and upgrading. If training increases the potential wage rate for the individual, the opportunity cost of not working increases. The substitution effect would lead to more hours of work being supplied.

SUBSIDIZED CHILD CARE

As more women decide to enter or re-enter the labour force, the demand for childcare facilities increases. Accompanying the increased demand is an increase in the price of daycare or childcare services. Governments are pressured to provide financial assistance to families requiring child care. What is the impact on the labour force of government financial assistance to those with children? Will this assistance be provided only to those families that have more than one person in the labour force, or will it be provided to all families?

We can treat daycare expenses as a fixed cost. That is, assume that daycare expenses remain the same regardless of the number of hours an individual is employed during the week. Earnings from employment must be high enough to cover this fixed cost in order to make employment worthwhile. An individual's reservation wage rate is influenced by daycare expenses. The more expensive day care becomes, the more money an individual must command in the labour market. If day care is subsidized, the cost to the individual is reduced. The reservation wage rate will be lowered because less money will be required to meet daycare expenses.

The impact of subsidized day care on parents' labour market activity also depends on whether the assistance is available to all families or only to those with both parents employed or the only parent employed. If daycare assistance is given to all families with children, it will be a demogrant. The income effect will encourage the purchase of more leisure. If daycare assistance is provided only to families with employed parents, the possible presence of an income effect encouraging the purchase of leisure is more complicated. If the subsidy is given as a lump sum, it may encourage some individuals to work fewer hours. If the subsidy is tied to hours of work, there will be less incentive to reduce hours of work.

INFLUENCES ON LABOUR SUPPLY AND LABOUR FORCE PARTICIPATION

The decision to participate in the labour force and the number of hours of work supplied to the labour force are related to one's age. Youths are often too young to participate in the labour force. Mandatory requirement programs may mean others are too old to participate in the labour force. Apart from age, other influences help determine an individual's labour force attachment. These influences are discussed in this section.

THE WAGE RATE

The wage rate that one can expect to receive varies over one's working life. As discussed in this chapter, the wage rate can influence the number of hours of work. When one is young and inexperienced, the

AN INTRODUCTION TO THE CANADIAN LABOUR MARKET

wage rate is low. Therefore, with a low opportunity cost of not working, the substitution effect would indicate a high demand for leisure. Few hours of work will be offered. The lower opportunity cost of leisure for young people may help explain why younger people are more likely to take time for travel or to attend school than those in their prime working age. More experience comes with getting older, as does an increase in the amount of education and training that a person has. The opportunity cost of not working increases as one's labour market wage rate increases. Thus more hours of labour are supplied to the market. As one nears retirement, one's wage rate may increase slowly or start to decline. A decrease in the wage rate may be associated with supplying fewer working hours.

FERTILITY AND FAMILY SIZE

The life cycle theory connects the market wage rate to labour force attachment. The income and substitution effects are not the only determinants of labour market attachment. The presence of children affects the labour force participation of family members. The presence of preschool children in the family increases the reservation wage rate of at least one family member. Thus when preschool children are present, one family member is less likely to be in the labour force. What factors influence the decision to have children? The decision to start a family is not solely based on economic variables, yet economic variables do play a part in the decision.

There are costs associated with having children and the decision to have children is based to some degree on these costs. Some are direct in the sense that children must be fed and clothed. In order to raise children, certain goods and services must be purchased, such as child care, education, sports and entertainment, and medical care. The prices associated with these goods and services are part of the cost of raising a child. There are also indirect or opportunity costs if one family member, usually the woman, decides to stay at home to raise the children and forgoes income. In terms of the forgone income, the opportunity costs are often higher than the direct costs. The opportunity cost will be higher for women with greater earnings potential. This suggests that those women with greater earnings potential are less likely to have children, or are less likely to have a large family.

Does the number of children in a family depend on the income of the family? The income effect would indicate that higher income families have more children or spend more money on the children they have. However, not all high-income families are large families, so variables other than income must be more important in determining family size.

Attitudes toward family size have changed considerably over the years. These attitudes are influenced by culture, religion, the women's movement, and the increased educational levels in the population. Changes in birth control technology have also had an impact.

On the basis of empirical evidence, which of these factors are the most important determinants of family size? Research into the factors that affect fertility is complicated by the fact that some of the factors can be interrelated. For example, family income can be related to the level of education of the adults in the family. The higher the level of education, the higher the level of income. If one partner has a high level of education, it is likely that the other is also well educated. For research purposes, it may be difficult to divorce the family income factor from the educational level of the mother, who is likely to forgo income while raising children. If she is well educated, the opportunity cost is high. Nonetheless, empirical evidence indicates that as a woman's potential earnings increase, she has fewer children. There is also some evidence that the availability of government financial assistance to families in the form of tax credits, maternity benefits, and so on has a small positive relationship to the number of children in the family. That is, for some families, the increased income obtained through government assistance may result in more children.

RETIREMENT

Also associated with the life cycle is the decision to retire. This decision can be discussed in relation to the work/leisure model outlined in this chapter. If a pension is available before the mandatory or usual retirement age, an individual may find that the income effect dominates and choose to purchase leisure, or retire. If the wage rate continues to increase in one's later years, the substitution effect may dominate and one may keep working.

The retirement decision has been the focus of much research in recent years. It affects an individual financially and psychologically. It also affects the national unemployment rate and government income support plans. The decision to retire does not depend solely on economic factors, such as the wage rate and other sources of income. One's health, family, and leisure pursuits also influence the decision.

The decision may not be in the hands of the individual. Many companies have mandatory retirement policies. This topic is discussed in the accompanying box.

AN INTRODUCTION TO THE CANADIAN LABOUR MARKET

BOX 8.3 Mandatory Retirement

Many companies have mandatory retirement policies. Employees who reach the mandatory retirement age are required to retire from the company. Are such policies a violation of the Charter of Rights and Freedoms? Do they contravene provincial human rights legislation, which prevents discrimination on the basis of age? These questions were put to the Supreme Court of Canada. The Court ruled that mandatory retirement is discriminatory; nonetheless, it also ruled that the objectives of mandatory retirement were justified on other grounds. Are there any economic arguments that support mandatory retirement policies?

One argument for mandatory retirement centres on the belief that an employee's productivity declines with age. Faced with declining productivity from an employee, the employer may reduce the employee's wage rate or terminate the employment relationship. Since it may be impossible to reduce the wage rate of an older employee, the employer may terminate the employment relationship. If the company has a mandatory retirement policy, an end date is established for the relationship. The employee knows that he or she will not be fired or have their earnings reduced. The employer knows that the payment of a wage rate in excess of productivity will not last forever.

It can also be argued that mandatory retirement policies open up opportunities for younger workers. This argument often assumes that there are a fixed number of jobs in the marketplace. By forcing older workers to retire, younger workers can find employment and advancement opportunities. The number of

jobs in the labour market, however, is not fixed. Jobs can be created through more spending. If older workers continued on with their employment, they would have more money to spend, which would create new jobs. On the other hand, if the way is paved for young workers to get the employment opportunities, their earnings will increase and they will have more money to spend.

After retirement, a person need not drop out of the labour force. A person can continue to seek employment after reaching the mandatory retirement age with one company. People today live longer and may want to continue working past the mandatory retirement age. In the future, mandatory retirement polices may not substantially reduce the size of the labour force.

Human resources management within a company may benefit from a policy of mandatory retirement. The policy may assist in determining staffing and training requirements if it is known that employees who reach the mandatory retirement age will be leaving the company.

The main argument against mandatory retirement focuses on the discriminatory nature of the policy. As such, some jurisdictions in Canada prohibit mandatory retirement policies. From a financial viewpoint, a ban on mandatory retirement may ease the financial pressure on company and government pension plans. If individuals were permitted to work for more years, they would contribute more to pension plans and would collect from the plans for fewer years.

INVESTMENT IN EDUCATION

The overall supply of labour to the economy is affected by the number of individuals who decide to pursue further education and training. As more individuals enroll in post-secondary educational programs, the supply of hours for work is reduced. Some individuals may leave the labour force entirely while they pursue an education; others may switch to part-time work. Because individuals with higher levels of education stay in the labour force for a longer period of time, the reduction in the labour force that occurs while they are receiving an education is only temporary. The decision to further one's education will also have an impact on the supply of labour to individual occupations. More people will be qualified to do certain jobs and fewer workers will be available for other jobs.

When individuals undertake expenses to acquire a skill, further their education, or relocate to a new job, they are investing in themselves. Economists refer to this spending as investment in **human capital**. If the investment results in the individual acquiring new skills, these skills can be rented to employers just as other types of capital (such as machinery and equipment) can be rented out. The decision to undertake further education and training is an important one for analysts of the labour market. For this reason, Chapter 12 is devoted to the topic of education and training.

human capital human resources considered in terms of their contributions to the economy, as in skills, education, etc.

MIGRATION AND IMMIGRATION

To this point in the chapter, we have assumed that the individuals deciding to enter the labour force came from a fixed population. That is, the quantity of labour supplied to the market depended primarily on the wage rate and the response of individuals in the population to any changes in those wage rates. However, the distribution of the population is constantly changing. In Canada, there is internal migration as individuals and families move between provinces. Over the years, there has been internal migration away from the Atlantic provinces, Manitoba, and Saskatchewan to Ontario, Alberta, and British Columbia. Canada is also the destination of many international migrants. Canada's population and labour force have grown through international immigration but we have also lost labour force participants through emigration. In recent years, there has been substantial media coverage on the "brain drain" from Canada to the United States.

What impact does migration have on the supply curve for labour? The labour supply in the destination increases. The supply curve shifts to the right (S^2 in Figure 8.4). Regardless of the wage rate, more people are willing to work. Emigration shifts the labour supply curve to the left

FIGURE 8.4   THE IMPACTS OF MIGRATION ON THE
                     LABOUR SUPPLY CURVE

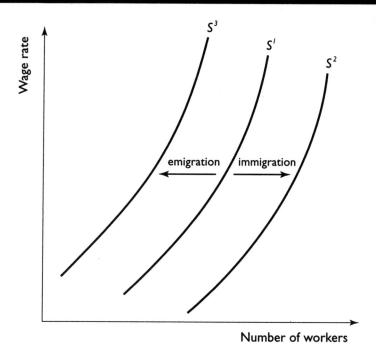

(S³ in Figure 8.4) in the country and province of origin. The supply curves in the figure can refer either to a regional labour supply within Canada or to the total domestic (Canadian) labour supply.

Why do individuals migrate internally within Canada or internationally? The literature treats the decision to migrate similar to the decision to invest in education and training. The individual expects certain benefits from the move, which must be matched against the expected costs. If the benefits outweigh the costs, relocation to another province or country is the outcome.

One benefit from migration is monetary in nature. Individuals expect to be paid a higher wage rate and receive more benefits in the labour market of their destination. They hope the increase in the wage rate is not temporary and will continue throughout their working life. The fact that benefits are measured over one's working life explains why young people are more likely to relocate. For young people, the benefit of higher wages will accrue over a longer period of time. However, not all benefits from migration are monetary; some individuals may relocate for reasons of weather, culture, language, or crime.

The expected costs vary depending on the distance of the move and the length of time required to find new employment. The costs also

BOX 8.4 The Brain Drain

In the fall of 1999, Canadian newspapers ran a series of articles on the large number of highly qualified Canadians leaving Canada to take up residence in the United States. This emigration was referred to as the "brain drain." The Conference Board of Canada stated that 16 900 highly skilled Canadians moved to the United States in 1986. By 1997, the number had increased to approximately 98 000. This estimate is likely too high since some of those included were on temporary work visas and had their visas renewed throughout the year; the renewal of visas may have resulted in some double counting. Nonetheless, there is a trend toward greater emigration to the United States. More Canadians are applying for temporary work visas: In 1996, 27 000 professionals were granted temporary work permits compared to 2700 in 1989. A study by the C.D. Howe Institute estimated the cost of emigration to the United

States to be in excess of $11 billion mainly from the dollars spent educating individuals who are taking their skills elsewhere.

Why do many Canadians want to migrate? Higher salaries in the United States attract qualified workers. Workers are also attracted by lower tax rates, exposure to leading-edge technologies, more opportunities for personal growth, and a warmer climate. Some analysts argue that emigration to the United States is less than it was in the 1950s and that the current concern over emigration is simply a smokescreen for pressure on government to lower taxes. Others believe that the brain drain is slowing down. Still other analysts point to the high number of qualified immigrants arriving in Canada. Ten times more migrants arrive in Canada than leave each year, and more than 30% of immigrants have a university degree.

depend on how many individuals in the family are relocating. It is less expensive for one individual to relocate than for a family. This also helps explain why many migrants within Canada are young people. In addition, there is an opportunity cost to moving. The individual may have to sacrifice a job or government social assistance payments in order to relocate. One also must consider the cost of living at one's destination. If the economy there is expanding, it is likely that house prices and living accommodation prices will be higher than they were back home. There are, of course, also non-monetary costs such as the difficulty in leaving family and friends.

The practice of comparing future benefits and costs will be discussed more fully in Chapter 12. In this chapter, let us simply state that the theory about the decision to relocate depends on expected benefits and costs. Do empirical results support the theory? Younger and better-educated workers are more likely than others to migrate, a finding that supports the contention that the benefits from migration accrue over a number of years. Within Canada, there is less migration between provinces that are further apart. This finding supports the discussion of the costs of migration. Other factors influencing migration include the level of employment insurance benefits and social assistance benefits, the unemployment rates in both areas, the climate, and the ethnic composition of the population.

SUMMARY

The decision to work is analyzed by studying the demand for leisure. The price of leisure is the forgone earnings, or the opportunity cost, of not working. As one's wage rate increases, the price of leisure increases. As the price of leisure increases, less leisure is demanded. The demand for leisure also depends on one's income. As the wage rate increases, and incomes increase, the demand for leisure increases. Thus, as the wage rate increases, there are competing influences on the decision to work. The substitution effect focuses on the opportunity cost of not working and encourages individuals to work more hours. The income effect focuses on the ability to purchase leisure and encourages individuals to purchase more leisure. A positively sloped supply curve incorporates both the income and the substitution effects with the substitution effect dominating.

The income and substitution effects can also be used to analyze the work incentives associated with income-security programs. A demogrant carries with it a pure income effect encouraging individuals to work fewer hours. General welfare assistance also encourages individuals to work fewer hours. However, if the assistance is accompanied by a subsidy for low-income workers, the substitution effect could dominate. The changes to the employment insurance program over the years have aimed at reducing the work disincentives associated with the program. Subsidized child care reduces the reservation wage rate for many women and could encourage them to enter or re-enter the labour force.

The labour supply is influenced by training and migration decisions made by individuals. For both training and migration, the decision to invest in oneself rests with a comparison of the expected benefits and the expected costs. Some benefits and costs are monetary while others are nonmonetary.

KEY TERMS

substitution effect (supply)   223

normal good   223

income effect (supply)   223

labour supply curve   224

reservation wage rate   224

backward-bending supply curve for labour   225

marginal tax rate   227

wage elasticity of labour supply   228

economic rent   228

demogrant   230

human capital   238

EXERCISES

1. Does personal wealth influence the dominance of the income or substitution effect with respect to the supply of labour? Explain.

2. Discuss the economic arguments supporting the policy of mandatory retirement.

3. Some occupations require a certificate in order to practise that trade or profession. For example, a professional accountant may be required to have a CA, CMA, or CGA. Physicians must be licensed to practise. Draw a graph that shows the impact of occupational licensing on the supply of labour.

4. A negative income tax system has been proposed as a form of a guaranteed income. Under this system, individuals whose income falls below a certain amount would receive a payment from the government. The size of the payment would vary depending on the individual's income. Above the income cutoff, individuals would pay income taxes as they do now. Using the concepts of the income and substitution effects, discuss the impact of a negative income tax system on labour supply.

5. What happens to economic rent in professional sports when rival leagues start up? (For example, the World Hockey Association was created after the National Hockey League already existed.) Explain.

6. A change in the normal retirement age could affect government programs other than the Canada Pension Plan. What other aspects of public policy could be affected by a change in retirement decisions?

7. A wage subsidy has been suggested as the best way to increase incomes of the working poor. The subsidy would involve government topping up the hourly wage rate of an individual. Discuss the possible income and substitution

effects associated with a wage subsidy.

8. Critics of the employment insurance program argue that the program discourages skill training and inflates the wage rate. Explain their reasoning.

REFERENCES

Ehrenberg, R. G., and Smith, R. (1997). *Modern Labor Economics: Theory and Public Policy,* 6th ed. Reading: Addison Wesley.

King, J. E. (1990). *Labour Economics,* 2nd ed. London: Macmillan.

Reynolds, L. G., Masters, S. H., and Moser, C. H. (1987). *Economics of Labor.* Englewood Cliffs: Prentice-Hall.

Schumacher, E. F. (1974). *Small Is Beautiful: A Study of Economics as if People Mattered.* London: Abacus.

9

LABOUR MARKET
DECISIONS OF FIRMS

OBJECTIVES

After completing this chapter, you should be able to:

1. define and describe each of the following terms: derived demand, law of diminishing returns, short run, long run, marginal productivity of labour, marginal revenue product, scale effect, substitution effect (demand), and quasi-fixed labour costs;

2. explain how the firm's demand curve for a specific occupation is derived;

3. explain how the demand curve for a specific occupation shifts;

4. discuss the factors that influence the wage elasticity of demand;

5. discuss the types of quasi-fixed costs and how they affect the demand for labour;

6. discuss the various factors that influence productivity in Canada.

INTRODUCTION

The demand side of the labour market is represented by employers who require employees to produce goods and services. Consequently, the demand for workers is derived from the demand for the final product or service. If there is no demand for the final product or service, there is no demand for the workers who make that product or provide that service. If customers want the final product or service, there is a demand for workers to provide that product or service. The demand for workers is thus said to be a derived demand. The price of the final product or service will also alter the ability of firms to pay wages. If the demand for a product increases, the price of the product will likely increase as well. The increase in price will likely be reflected in employees' wage rates. Chapter 10 will review the connection between the demand for the product and wage rates.

The demand for workers also depends on the productivity of the worker. The demand for workers who are more productive is greater than that for those who are less productive. More productive workers can produce more goods and services and are in greater demand from employers. Workers who undertake training and further their education in order to improve their productivity can expect the demand for their services to increase.

This chapter introduces the theory behind the demand side of the labour market. The objective is to derive the demand curve for labour. The next chapter will combine the supply curve from Chapter 8 and the demand curve from this chapter to draw a picture of the labour market. Wage rate and employment levels are determined in the labour market.

THE DEMAND CURVE FOR LABOUR

The demand for labour will be discussed within the framework of two time periods: the short run and the long run.

THE SHORT RUN

As mentioned in Chapter 2, economists refer to the short run as a period of time in which at least one factor of production cannot be changed. Factors of production are inputs into the production process such as the building, workers, equipment, and so on. There is usually a period during which some of these factors cannot be changed. For example, a company may have leased a building for a year, so it is locked into the lease. For the next year, the building, which is one of the factors of production, cannot be changed. In economic terms, the short run for this company is a year. The building, which is capital, is fixed, but the number of workers can be varied.

Assume that a garment manufacturing company has leased this building for a year. If its sales expand, it will need to hire more employees. As new employees are hired, some efficiencies in production will be possible. Workers can divide up the jobs and begin to specialize. For example, some employees will cut the cloth. Others will specialize in sewing on sleeves or sewing on collars. The productivity of the workers will increase. Unfortunately, the increases in productivity achieved by hiring more workers will not continue. The building is limited in size. There is only so much space in which the employees can work. At some point, the contribution of the next worker to the total output of the company will be less than that of the previous worker. The new employee has less of the fixed factor of production (the building) to work with than the previously hired employee. With less of the building to work with, the new employee's contribution to total output is less than that of the other employee. Economists refer to this reduction in the marginal output from the hiring of a new employee as the **law of diminishing returns**. As employment expands in the short run, a level of employment will be reached at which the next employee's contribution to total output will be less than the marginal contribution of the previously hired employee. Formally, the law of diminishing returns states that as more and more of a variable resource (workers) are added to a fixed amount of another resource (building), a point will be reached where the next worker's marginal contribution to output declines.

law of diminishing returns in the short run a point will be reached at which the extra contribution of the next worker to total output will be less than that of the previously hired worker

The law of diminishing returns only applies to the production time period known as the short run. In the long run, all inputs can be changed or altered. A new building can be rented, more equipment can be purchased, more employees can be hired, and so on. The contribution of the next worker to total output is referred to as the marginal productivity of labour (MPL), which is illustrated in Figure 9.1a.

The numerical example in Table 9.1 can help explain the law of diminishing returns. In this example, as more employees are hired the number of shirts produced each day increases. The increase in the number of shirts obtained by hiring one more employee is shown in the third column of the table. The MPL increases with the hiring of the second and third employees. The second employee adds eight shirts to the total output and the third employee adds nine shirts. The MPL increases as the work becomes more specialized. With the hiring of the fourth employee, the MPL begins to decline. At this point, diminishing returns from the hiring of more employees have begun to set in.

TABLE 9.1   CALCULATION OF THE MARGINAL PRODUCTIVITY OF LABOUR

Number of employees	Number of shirts per day	Marginal productivity of labour
0	0	
		> 5
1	5	
		> 8
2	13	
		> 9
3	22	
		> 8
4	30	
		> 7
5	37	
		> 6
6	43	
		> 5
7	48	
		> 4
8	52	

Although total output continues to increase with each employee hired, the increases are smaller and smaller.

Not all companies experience diminishing returns with the hiring of the fourth employee. In some situations, hundreds of employees can be hired before diminishing returns are experienced. Since all firms must always be operating in a short-run situation when at least one input cannot be changed, all firms will eventually experience diminishing returns. Figure 9.1a is a graph of the MPL from Table 9.1.

THE DECISION TO HIRE.   If the MPL of the next employee is less than that of the previous employee, should the new employee be hired? In order to make this decision, one must first convert the contribution of each successive worker to dollars. Since companies know how much they need to pay an employee in dollars, they need to determine the contribution of a new employee in dollars. The cost of the new employee and the contribution of the new employee can then be compared. In order to convert the contribution of a new employee to dollars, the MPL is multiplied by the **marginal revenue (MR)** obtained from the sale of the

marginal revenue (MR)
the extra revenue from selling one more unit of output

AN INTRODUCTION TO THE CANADIAN LABOUR MARKET

FIGURE 9.1A   MARGINAL PRODUCTIVITY OF LABOUR

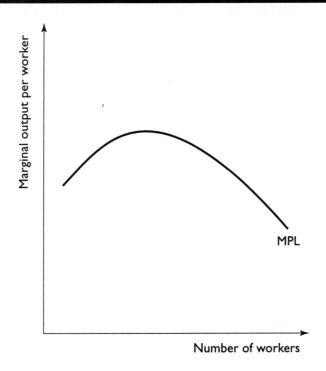

FIGURE 9.1B   MARGINAL REVENUE PRODUCT

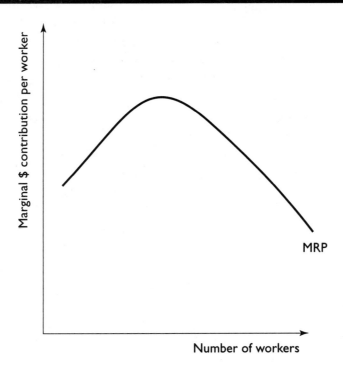

marginal revenue product (MRP) the extra revenue obtained from selling the output of an additional worker

extra output. The dollar value of the product is called the **marginal revenue product (MRP)**.

$$MRP = MR \times MPL$$

The marginal revenue product is the dollar value of the contribution of each successive worker. A graph of the relationship between the MRP and the number of workers is shown in Figure 9.1b. Since the MPL is a component of MRP, the shapes of the MPL and MRP curves are similar.

The decision to hire a new employee will depend, in part, on the value of the new employee. It will also depend on the cost of hiring the new employee, which is the wage rate paid. If the value of the new employee to the company is greater than the cost of hiring the new employee, the decision would be to hire the person. If the reverse is true, the person would not be hired.

Once the wage rate is known, the MRP curve can be used to determine how many employees are hired. By comparing the wage rate with the MRP, the following decision rule can be applied.

- If wage rate > MRP, do not hire the employee.
- If wage rate < MRP, hire the employee.
- If wage rate = MRP, the employer is indifferent about hiring the employee.

If the wage rate is W_1, the number of workers hired is L_1 (see Figure 9.2). If the wage rate is W_2, the number of workers hired is L_2. Thus, the MRP curve represents the firm's demand curve for a specific occupation. That curve displays the quantity of workers demanded in that occupation in relation to the cost, or the price, of one employee. More workers are demanded by employers at lower wage rates due to the decreasing marginal productivity of labour. Conversely, fewer workers are demanded at higher wage rates.

The demand for an occupation is influenced by the demand for the product, through the MR, and the MPL of the worker. If the demand for the product or service increases, its price will also likely increase. The MR from the sale of more of the product will increase, which results in increased MRP. If the MRP increases, the demand for labour increases, since the MRP curve represents the demand curve for labour. The demand for labour shifts to the right (MRP^2 in Figure 9.3a). A decrease in the MR shifts the demand curve for labour to the left.

If the productivity of employees (MPL) can be improved, and the MR does not change, the MRP and the demand for labour will increase (MRP^2 in Figure 9.3b). A decrease in MPL will shift the demand curve for labour to the left.

AN INTRODUCTION TO THE CANADIAN LABOUR MARKET

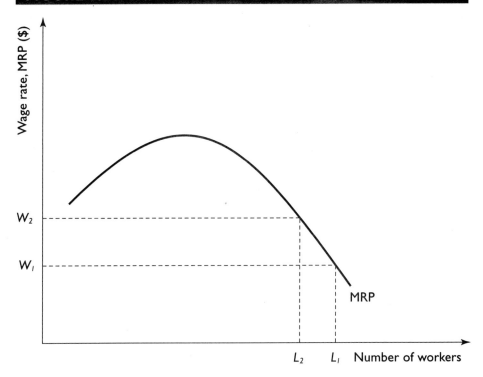

FIGURE 9.2   WAGE RATE AND NUMBER OF WORKERS

Employers do not usually talk of marginal productivity of labour and marginal revenue products. Since these terms are not used on a daily basis in business, one might assume firms do not use them in determining how many employees to hire. However, the lack of use in daily business practice does not make the concept useless or irrelevant. Firms that are successful in the marketplace must be following the principles discussed here. Employers must assess whether or not a new employee should be hired. That decision is based on a comparison of some measure of the contribution of the new employee to the firm and the cost of that employee.

Another criticism of the marginal productivity approach to labour demand stems from the fact that hiring is often accompanied by the purchase of new equipment. That is, the number of employees is not the only variable that changes in a firm as it expands. For example, a new employee may get a new personal computer to work with. If other factors of production are changing, the law of diminishing returns may not be relevant. You will recall that the law of diminishing returns applies only in the short run when at least one factor of production is fixed. If new equipment is purchased along with the hiring of a new employee, how is the productivity of the new worker determined? Although it is

FIGURE 9.3A   INCREASE IN MARGINAL REVENUE

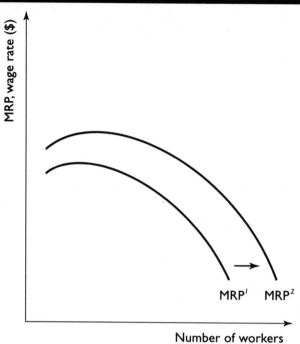

FIGURE 9.3B   INCREASE IN PRODUCTIVITY

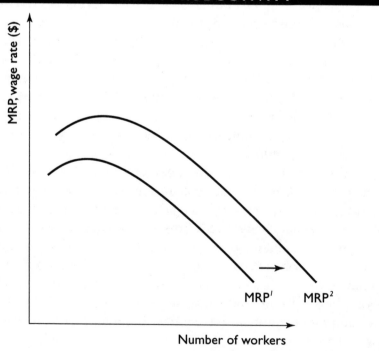

AN INTRODUCTION TO THE CANADIAN LABOUR MARKET

true that the hiring of employees and the purchase of equipment often go together, in many situations employees have been hired without any purchase of new equipment. In these situations, the marginal productivity of labour of the next employee can be determined.

THE LONG RUN

As with product demand curves, the demand curve for a specific occupation slopes down to the right (see Figure 9.4). That is, the quantity of workers demanded is greater at lower wage rates than at higher wage rates. The demand curve for labour has a negative slope for two reasons: the scale effect and the substitution effect. When wage rates paid to employees increase, the prices of products produced by those employees are likely to increase. Faced with higher prices, consumers buy less of the product. With less of the product being sold, the company needs fewer employees and cuts back the scale of its production. Conversely, if wage rates fall, the price of the product could be reduced. More of the product would be sold and more workers would be hired as the scale of production increases. The **scale effect** of a wage rate change refers to the change in the number of employees hired that results from changes in the amount of the product sold.

In some situations, employers can substitute capital equipment for workers. For example, robots may weld together pieces on an automobile. If wage rates increase, the substitution of capital for labour becomes more attractive. Fewer workers will be hired. Conversely, if wage rates decrease, there is an incentive to substitute workers for capital. More workers are demanded. The **substitution effect (demand)** refers to the substitution of capital for labour depending on the direction of the wage rate change. The substitution effect also applies when there is a change in the price of capital. For example, an increase in the price of capital could result in an increase in the number of workers employed as firms hire more workers instead of capital equipment. It is possible that workers in one occupation could be substituted for workers in another occupation. For example, labourers may be able to do the work of carpenters on a construction site. Nurses may be able to perform some of the duties assigned to physicians. Technologists may be substitutes for engineers and paralegals may be substitutes for lawyers.

Note the scale effect and the substitution effect for demand operate in the same direction with respect to the employment of workers. If wage rates increase, both the scale and substitution effects reduce the

scale effect the change in the number of employees hired as a result of changes in the amount of product sold

substitution effect (demand) changes in the wage rate encourage employers to substitute capital for labour and labour for capital

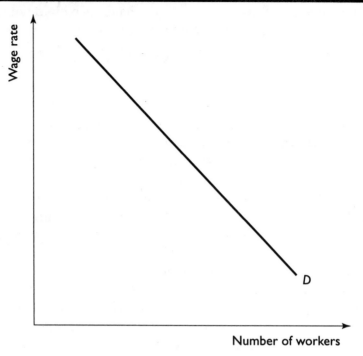

FIGURE 9.4 THE MARKET DEMAND CURVE FOR LABOUR

quantity of labour demanded. If wage rates decrease, both increase the quantity of labour demanded.

So far in our discussion, the demand curve for an occupation represents only one firm's demand for a specific occupation. In order to get the market demand for a specific occupation, such as plumber, one must add together the demand curves for the individual firms. The market demand curve is drawn with the wage rate on the vertical axis and the number of employees (quantity of labour) on the horizontal axis (see Figure 9.4). Note that the axes for the market supply and market demand curves are identical. In Chapter 10, the two curves will be combined on one graph to determine wage rate and employment levels.

WAGE ELASTICITY OF LABOUR DEMAND

wage elasticity of labour demand the change in quantity demanded in response to a change in the wage rate

As we have seen, the number of employees a firm hires depends in part on the wage rate paid. Changes in the wage rate will bring about a change in the number of employees hired. The **wage elasticity of labour demand** measures the degree to which changes in the wage rate

AN INTRODUCTION TO THE CANADIAN LABOUR MARKET

affect the quantity of employees demanded. The wage elasticity of labour demand is determined in a manner similar to the determination of price elasticity of demand:

$$\text{Coefficient of wage elasticity} = \frac{\text{Percentage change in quantity of workers demanded}}{\text{Percentage change in the wage rate}}$$

If the absolute value of the coefficient of wage elasticity is greater than one, the demand is said to be elastic. In an elastic situation, relatively small changes in the wage rate result in relatively large changes in the quantity of labour demanded. If the absolute value of the coefficient is less than one, the demand is said to be inelastic. In an inelastic situation, similar changes in the wage rate result in relatively small changes in the quantity of workers demanded. What factors influence the wage elasticity of demand?

PERCENTAGE OF LABOUR COSTS IN TOTAL COSTS. If labour costs are a relatively small percentage of the total cost of making a product or providing a service, the demand for labour is likely to be inelastic. Relatively large changes in the wage rate will not affect total costs significantly. As a result, changes in the wage rate will not significantly affect the number of employees. For example, in office tower construction, the cost represented by plumbers' wages is small compared to the overall cost of the project. An increase in the wage rate paid to plumbers will not significantly increase the overall cost of the project. Therefore, there will be little reduction in the number of plumbers in response to an increase in the wage rate.

Conversely, if labour costs constitute a significant proportion of total costs, any change in the wage rate will have a major impact on total costs. This impact will result in a relatively large change in the number of employees. For companies that clean offices after hours, the majority of the costs are labour costs. If the wage rate paid to these employees increases, the overall cost of providing the service will increase significantly. The number of employees would be significantly reduced by the wage rate increase.

NUMBER OF SUBSTITUTES FOR LABOUR. If there are no substitutes for a type of labour, the demand for labour tends to be inelastic. There may be no substitutes because of government regulation. For example, only physicians can prescribe prescription drugs. Only qualified pilots fly airplanes. If the wage rate were to increase for either of these occupations, the quantity of workers demanded would change very little. In other situations, unions may have negotiated restrictions on the introduction of new technology or restrictions on contracting out work to non-union workers.

However, if there are several substitutes for a type of labour, the demand is likely to be elastic. Capital is not the only substitute for labour. Substitutes can be employees in other occupations. If the duties of a lawyer can be performed by a law clerk, wage rate increases for lawyers may result in a reduction in the number of lawyers. The wage elasticity of demand will likely increase as time goes on. New technologies can be developed and introduced into the production process. For example, new technologies are continually being introduced in construction and medicine.

Even where substitutes exist, it may not be easy for employers to use a substitute in place of their employees when wage rates increase. Assume there is an increase in the wage rate for a certain occupation. If there is a substitute for that occupation, there will be an increased demand for the substitute, which will drive up the price of the substitute. Companies that planned to use a substitute for labour may have to adjust those plans in light of the higher price for the substitute. If the supply of the substitute is elastic, the price increase in response to an increase in demand will be small and it may be relatively easy to switch to a substitute.

PRICE ELASTICITY OF THE PRODUCT OR SERVICE. If the product or service produced by labour has an inelastic demand, price increases will not significantly change the quantity demanded of that product. If workers producing the product or service get a wage rate increase, the price of the product will likely increase. However, if consumers do not respond to price increases by reducing the quantity demanded, employees are in a better position to achieve wage rate increases. For instance, necessities such as health care tend to have inelastic demands, and the wage elasticity of labour demand for workers in health care occupations is also inelastic. Conversely, if the demand for the product is elastic, consumers will respond to increases in the price by significantly decreasing the quantity of the product demanded. Employees in these industries will find it harder to achieve increases in their wage rates. An example of an industry with an elastic demand curve is restaurants; with many restaurants for consumers to choose from, the demand for each restaurant's product is elastic, and increases in employee wage rates are difficult to pass on to consumers.

The price elasticity of demand for products is influenced by government trade policy. Successive federal governments have pursued a policy of freer international trade. The removal of trade barriers opens up more competition in the product market, and with more competition, the demand for Canadian products becomes more elastic. As a consequence, the wage elasticity of demand for Canadian workers becomes more elastic. Because workers have a better opportunity to get a wage rate increase in conditions of an inelastic demand, unions generally oppose any reduction in trade barriers.

Why is the concept of wage elasticity important? Knowledge of the wage elasticity of demand for labour provides an indication of the employment effects associated with wage rate changes. For example, governments legislate minimum wage rates that are in excess of the current wage rate for a group of employees. How many workers are likely to become unemployed as a result of the minimum wage rate? The answer depends in part on the wage elasticity of demand. When the demand for labour is elastic, more workers are apt to lose their jobs than when the demand is inelastic. Unions also negotiate base wage rates for their members. The negative effects of these increases on employment also need to be determined. Unions are in a more advantageous bargaining position if the demand for their members is inelastic. Government-legislated pay equity usually results in higher wage rates for female workers. The size of the potential reduction in the employment of female workers hinges on the wage elasticity of demand.

QUASI-FIXED LABOUR COSTS AND THE DEMAND FOR LABOUR

The costs faced by firms can be divided into fixed costs and variable costs. *Fixed costs* remain unchanged regardless of the amount of output, such as property taxes. The amount of money paid in property tax does not depend on the amount of output. *Variable costs* change with the amount of output. Examples of variable costs are wages and salaries, energy costs, shipping expenses, and so on. These costs increase with the amount produced by the company.

There are certain non-wage costs to hiring employees that are not related to the hours that an employee works, known as **quasi-fixed costs**. These are not fixed costs because these costs are not totally independent of the amount produced. That is, the greater the amount produced, the more employees are needed. On the other hand, these costs are fixed per employee. Quasi-fixed costs include hiring and training

quasi-fixed labour costs non-wage costs to hiring employees that are not related to the hours of work

expenses. Also included are government-legislated deductions from the payroll such as employment insurance premiums and Canada Pension Plan premiums. There are also some deductions specific to the company such as health plan deductions and company pension plan deductions.

Hiring costs include advertising for, and screening of, applicants, record-keeping, issuing paycheques, and so on. There are also costs to training new employees, which can be direct or indirect costs. The direct costs include materials and the salaries of the trainers. The indirect costs, or opportunity costs, include the lost production from employees who are in training and from the capital equipment used for training and not for the production of goods and services. Since these costs can be substantial, the firm would like to minimize these expenses by keeping their employees for a long time. If employees leave the company, the expenses occur again when new employees are hired. It should be noted that there may also be expenses associated with terminating employees, which may encourage firms to maintain their workforce in the face of changing economic conditions.

Once training and hiring expenses have already been incurred, the company may prefer its existing employees to work longer hours rather than hire new employees and incur new expenses. Existing employees may work longer hours in spite of the premium pay earned by employees working overtime. Firms may also contract out certain tasks, such as cleaning services, rather than hire and train a cleaning crew, or opt for temporary employees from temporary help agencies.

Labour Productivity

As mentioned in the beginning of this chapter, the demand for labour is influenced, in part, by the productivity of labour (MPL). If the productivity of labour increases, the demand for these workers increases. Chapter 10 will discuss the relationship between increases in the demand for labour and increases in the wage rate.

Much has been written in the past few years about the need for Canadian workers to improve productivity. Not only do productivity increases lead to wage rate increases, they also help to control price increases and improve the overall standard of living for Canadians. In this section, we discuss the concept of labour productivity and the factors that influence labour productivity.

The total production of goods and services in Canada varies from year to year. The value of the goods and services produced in a given year is referred to as **gross domestic product (GDP)**. The level of GDP in Canada depends, in part, on the resources that are available to Canadians. Canada's resources include land, labour, and capital. The land resource includes more than just the 10 million square kilometres that comprise Canada's land mass. It includes minerals, wild animals, vegetation, and water. Canada's population is the basis for the labour resource. The skills, levels of education, and training of the population are also part of the labour resource. The capital resource refers to human-made items that help us produce goods and services. Examples of capital are computers, factories, machinery, and airports.

Because this is a text on labour economics, the emphasis is on Canada's labour resource. An increase in the number of workers will increase the amount of goods and services produced. Production increases can also be achieved if Canadian workers become more productive. In economic terms, total production can increase if productivity increases. **Labour productivity** is a measure of the relationship between the quantity of inputs (workers) and the quantity of output. It is defined as the output per worker. For Canada, productivity is defined as the real GDP per employed person, or, to reflect changes in the hours of work, output per person-hour. The term "real" indicates that the GDP is adjusted for price increases. Because GDP measures the value of all goods and services produced in a given year, its value can increase simply by having prices increase. In order to reflect the goods and services actually being produced more accurately, real GDP is used to calculate productivity as opposed to nominal GDP.

If a small number of workers produces a relatively large quantity of goods and services, productivity will be high. If a large number of workers produces a relatively small quantity of goods and services, productivity will be low. The term "relatively" is used because we only know Canadian productivity is high or low when it is compared to the productivity in other countries or when it is compared to Canadian productivity in previous years.

Figure 9.5 shows Canada's performance in labour productivity in the manufacturing sector for the years 1975, 1985, and 1995 in comparison to other countries in the G-7 group of nations.[1] In this figure, Canadian productivity in each of the three years is given an index value of 100. The productivity indexes in the various countries are adjusted for differences in the values of the currencies of the respective countries. The bar graph shows how productivity in the other countries compares

gross domestic product (GDP) value of the goods and services produced in a given year

labour productivity the output per worker

---

1. The G-7 is a group of highly industrialized nations whose political leaders meet on a regular basis to discuss economic issues of common concern.

FIGURE 9.5 MANUFACTURING LABOUR PRODUCTIVITY LEVELS IN THE G-7

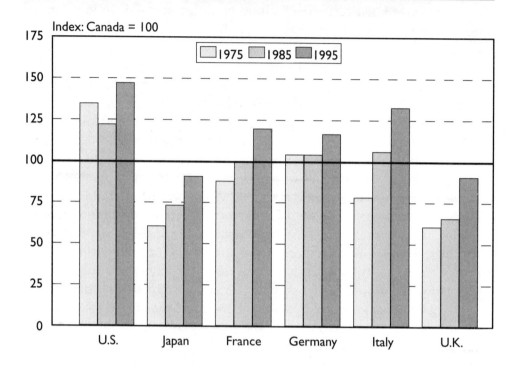

Index: Canada = 100

Legend: 1975, 1985, 1995

Categories: U.S., Japan, France, Germany, Italy, U.K.

Output per person-hour, based on purchasing power parity exchange rates.

Source: U.S. Bureau of Labor Statistics

to Canada. It is clear from the graph that manufacturing productivity in the United States exceeds that in Canada for each year shown. In 1995, Canada's manufacturing labour productivity also lagged behind France, Germany, and Italy.

The *level* of productivity is important for the Canadian economy, and so, too, is the *rate of* productivity growth. As indicated in Chapter 5, productivity growth is achieved when more output is produced with the same amount of inputs or, alternatively, the same level of output is produced with fewer inputs. In the late 20th century, productivity growth in Canada has slowed down.

The factors that influence productivity are the focus of this section. Why is productivity growth important? Total output of goods and services increases with increases in productivity. As the level of production increases, incomes generated in production increase. As a result, the standard of living of Canadians increases. It is difficult for incomes to increase when productivity is not increasing. Productivity increases also allow prices to remain stable or to rise less rapidly. If labour productivity increases, payments to workers can increase without being accompanied by price increases. Furthermore, if Canadian prices are not rising as fast as those in other countries, Canadian products are more attractive to foreigners. In order to sell more goods and services to foreigners, we need more workers. Thus productivity is not only related to incomes but also to employment.

Labour productivity growth may not be entirely due to improvements in the skill level of workers. Technological change, in terms of better machinery and equipment, can improve labour productivity. Studies of productivity in the United States have estimated that more than 40% of the increase in labour productivity can be attributed to technological change.

A more efficient use of resources can also improve productivity. That is, if resources are shifted to industries with higher levels of productivity, the overall level of productivity in the Canadian economy will increase. Decreases in the rate of productivity growth cannot be attributed solely to the fact that the workers are lazier than they previously were. As will be discussed shortly, many factors influence the level of Canadian labour productivity.

A summary of how productivity changes translate into changes in labour demand is shown below.

An increase in labour productivity $\Rightarrow$ a decrease in the price of goods and services $\Rightarrow$ an increase in both domestic and foreign consumption $\Rightarrow$ an increase in the production of goods and services $\Rightarrow$ an increase in the use of machinery and equipment $\Rightarrow$ an increase in demand for workers $\Rightarrow$ an increase in overall employment, real wages, and the standard of living.

The main influences on the level of productivity growth in Canada can be divided into three groups. The first group of influences affects productivity in the economy as a whole. These are referred to as *macro influences*. They are the following:

- the structure of the economy
- economic conditions
- government policies

The second group of influences primarily affects the productivity level of the individual business firm. These are referred to as *micro influences* and are:

- the scale of business operations
- management techniques

The third group of influences straddles both of the first two groups. These factors influence both Canada's overall level of productivity and the productivity of the individual business firm. They are:

- quantity and quality of capital
- the labour force

As the factors influencing productivity are discussed, you will notice that they are clearly interrelated. For example, the quality of management can influence the speed with which new technology is introduced. Economic conditions also affect the ability of the firm to produce on a larger scale.

THE STRUCTURE OF THE ECONOMY

The industrial composition of the labour force also influences productivity. The proportion of the labour force employed in both agriculture and manufacturing is continuing to decline. As mentioned in Chapter 5, most of the employment growth has been in the service sector of our economy, where it is more difficult to measure output than in either agriculture or manufacturing. It is more difficult to measure productivity in the service sector. Consider the difficulties associated with measuring the productivity of lawyers, nurses, and firefighters.

Much of the increase in agricultural and manufacturing productivity over the last century can be attributed to improvements in machinery and equipment. The productivity of workers in these sectors is increasing through the introduction of new machinery; however, these sectors account for a declining proportion of total employment. In many situations, new machinery has allowed for the increase in output with fewer workers. On the other hand, can you replace nurses, the police, and firefighters with machinery? Productivity increases are harder to come by in the service, retail, and government sectors, which are labour-intensive industries. Nonetheless, it is not impossible to get technical advances in the service sector. Examples of such advances are automated teller machines in banking and universal bar coding in the retail sector.

ECONOMIC CONDITIONS

Canadians are well aware of changing economic conditions. The economy expands when people, businesses, and government spend money. The level of economic activity eventually peaks and then heads toward a recession as the level of overall spending declines. Eventually, a trough is reached as the economy starts to pick up. How does the level of economic activity influence the measurement of productivity? When the economy slows down, employers cut back on hours of work. Employees no longer work overtime and some full-time employees are shifted to part-time employment. If productivity is measured as the output per employee, productivity will decrease. As employee hours of work and output decrease, the number of employees is unaffected and, as a result, the output per employee declines. Although some employee layoffs may take place, companies produce fewer products with almost the same number of employees. As the economy expands and spending increases, employees work more hours. Production per employee increases.

Slowdowns in economic activity affect goods-producing industries more than service industries and government. The demand for government-provided services and other services is more stable than that for manufactured products. Because recessions hit goods-producing or manufacturing industries harder than industries in the service sector, an economic slowdown will show drops in the overall level of productivity.

GOVERNMENT POLICIES

Governments can influence worker productivity in a number of ways. They can provide support through tax dollars or tax breaks for education and training. A better-educated labour force should be a more productive labour force. They could provide tax breaks for companies that provide skill training, or for companies that develop and introduce new technology. In addition, governments can ensure that school curricula are up to date and relevant to the workplace. The Organization for Economic Co-operation and Development (OECD) has stated that although Canada spends more on education than other countries, the competence of our workforce in terms of literacy and numeric skills is declining in comparison.

Government regulation of business has a large impact on productivity. For example, governments can restrict competition in some sectors of the economy by allowing monopolies to evolve in the public interest. The term "monopoly" refers to "single seller." The lack of competition in highly regulated industries may reduce the need to become competitive. The federal government has taken some steps toward deregulating industries such as energy, telephones, and trucking.

International trade polices also influence competition. Tariffs may be imposed on imports to protect certain Canadian industries. Tariffs

BOX 9.1 Literacy and Wages

Literacy involves three measured skills:

1. the ability to understand and use prose (e.g., reading newspapers and books)
2. the ability to use and understand documents (e.g., job applications and travel schedules)
3. the ability to use and understand numbers (e.g., balance a chequebook).

A study of 12 countries divided individuals into five skill levels. A level of three was considered the minimum level required to handle the everyday demands of work and life. In Canada, only 57% of the population rated a level three or above. This can be compared with 75% of the population in Sweden.

The number of years of formal education is not always indicative of literacy. For example, 60% of adults in Sweden who did not complete the equivalent of a Canadian secondary school education scored well in the second category (documents). Only 27% of Canadians scored well in this category without completing secondary school.

The number of years of schooling may help you get a job but in order to keep the job and receive promotions, you will need strong literacy skills. Employers associate literacy with productivity. More literate employees are better able to adapt to changing job requirements. Thus, more literate employees are higher paid employees and are less likely to be unemployed.

increase the cost of imported goods and thus help shift the demand from imported to domestic goods. Tariffs may temporarily help Canadian industries, but they make them less efficient in the long run. Continued tariff protection can prolong inefficiency. A major objective of the Canadian government in signing the North American Free Trade Agreement (NAFTA) was to increase the overall productivity of the Canadian labour force. It was hoped that the increased competition faced by Canadian companies would force them to be more productive. Also, Canadian companies would have a larger market where they could sell their goods and services. If companies could expand their sales and output, the productivity per worker should increase. Canada has had some previous experience with trade agreements and productivity. In 1965, Canada and the United States signed the Canada–United States Automobile Agreement, which permitted new cars to travel tariff-free between the two countries. This agreement resulted in greater output, employment, and productivity for the Canadian automobile industry.

A government's approach to managing the economy can also have an impact on productivity. Businesses that are comfortable with the government's economic policies may invest in Canada. If they do not agree with the government's policies, they may invest elsewhere. One aspect of economic management is taxes. The level of taxation is a major determinant of business confidence. Excessively high tax rates on both businesses and consumers may discourage investment in new plants and equipment. The monetary policies of the Bank of Canada with respect to stabilizing prices also increase the confidence level of business with respect to new investment.

The Scale of Business Operations

Rarely do companies begin their operations by producing a large output. As sales increase, the scale of the operation increases as well. Expanding output allows firms to take advantage of **increasing returns to scale**. That is, by doubling all their inputs (workers, size of building, etc.), output may more than double. Increasing returns to scale result in lower average costs and higher levels of productivity.

increasing returns to scale the percentage increase in output that is relatively greater than the percentage change in all the factors of production

What factors permit increasing returns to take place? As the scale of the company expands, more efficient machinery and equipment can be used. Workers can perform more specialized functions, becoming more productive. Consider the situation in the automobile industry: Workers have very specialized individual tasks that result in a completed car. Can increasing returns to scale be expected to influence productivity indefinitely? Unfortunately, increases in size are accompanied by communication difficulties between individuals within the company, which increase average costs and reduce productivity. Large size can lead to inefficiencies and cost increases. To ward off the inefficiencies of size, many companies are experimenting with decentralization and concentrating production in smaller units.

Since the population of Canada is less than that of its main industrial competitors, our companies have a relatively small domestic market in which to sell their products. The scale of operations for many Canadian companies is often less than that of similar firms in other countries. Many Canadian firms are branch plants of multinational companies and may only be producing for the Canadian market. Can Canadian companies hope to expand their sales? Governments have attempted to open up foreign markets for Canadian products. Initiatives in this area include Canada's participation in the World Trade Organization (WTO), NAFTA, and other free trade deals with countries such as Israel and Chile.

BOX 9.2 International Trade and the Labour Market

The Canadian economy relies a great deal on international trade. Approximately one in four Canadian workers produces a product for export. Thus it is important that Canadian companies have access to foreign markets in order to sell their goods. Conversely, foreign firms want access to Canadian markets. During the Great Depression in the 1930s many countries effectively closed their borders to foreign products. Many economists believe that the reduction in international trade extended the depression.

After World War II, 23 countries including Canada signed an agreement to promote international trade. That agreement was called the General Agreement on Tariffs and Trade (GATT). Over the years, this agreement has led to reduced tariffs and quotas as well as non-tariff barriers to international trade. In 1995, the GATT was replaced by the World Trade Organization (WTO), which has more than 130 members.

Canada's commitment to freer trade goes beyond its membership in the WTO. In 1965, the Canada-United States Automobile Agreement was signed. This agreement permitted the duty-free movement of new cars and car parts between the two countries. With access to the U.S. market guaranteed, the Canadian automobile industry has significantly increased employment. The demand for cars made in Canada increased and the number of automobile workers increased as well. When automobile production moved to a larger scale, the productivity of automobile workers increased, as did their wage rates.

In 1989, Canada signed the Free Trade Agreement with the United States. This agreement reduced trade barriers between the two countries over 10 years. Mexico has since signed the agreement, now known as the North American Free Trade Agreement (NAFTA). What impact have these agreements had on the labour market? For Canadian companies that now have better access to foreign markets, those agreements have resulted in greater demand for their products. The derived demand for labour has also increased. Other Canadian companies are now experiencing more competition than before. The demand for their products has declined. Their demand for workers has also decreased. Changes in international trade patterns have forced some adjustment on the Canadian labour force.

The foreign demand for Canadian products and Canadians' demand for foreign products also depends on the foreign-exchange value of the Canadian dollar. In the last 10 years, the value of the Canadian dollar has fluctuated between 66 cents and 89 cents of a U.S. dollar. When the foreign-exchange value of the Canadian dollar is low, Canadian products are more attractive to foreigners and foreign products are more expensive to Canadians. When the foreign-exchange value of the dollar increases, the reverse is true. Thus changes in the exchange rate also affect the Canadian labour market.

MANAGEMENT TECHNIQUES

In the last 20 years, Canadian companies have emphasized management style as a way of increasing productivity. Many books on management have been best sellers. How can management influence the level of productivity? It is the responsibility of management to organize production and to establish administrative and decision-making structures within the organization. Management's attitude toward innovation is significant — does it have a positive attitude or is it reluctant to innovate? Productivity can be improved by introducing better machinery and equipment and by creating a positive atmosphere in the workplace. Good labour relations policies are a reflection of a positive atmosphere. Canada can have the best-trained workers and the most advanced equipment but will not be competitive in the marketplace unless management does its job.

A criticism of management techniques is that Canadian companies have been slow to introduce new technology. Several reasons have been put forth to explain this tardiness in adapting to new technology. First, the cost of the new technology has discouraged Canadian companies from adopting it. Second, many Canadian companies are not big enough to use the latest technology. Third, Canadian industry is characterized by a large number of branch plants of multinational firms, which may not have the authority or the resources to invest in the new technology. Fourth, it has been suggested that Canadian firms are slow to find out about new technologies.

QUALITY AND QUANTITY OF CAPITAL

The amount of goods and services produced by an employee can increase if the employee has better machinery and equipment to work with. Farmers can be more productive tilling the land with a tractor as opposed to a manually operated hoe. Secretaries can produce more letters with a personal computer than with a typewriter. Automobile workers can produce more cars with the aid of robots. The more capital a worker has to work with, the more productive the worker is. The recognition of the contribution of capital equipment to productivity led Statistics Canada to calculate the Multifactor Productivity Index. This index indicates the level of productivity in an industry in consideration of all the relevant resources in the production process, not just labour. Employees are also more productive as the *quality* of the capital equipment improves. The speed of computers is constantly increasing and the software is constantly improving.

THE LABOUR FORCE

The characteristics of the Canadian labour force also affect productivity. These characteristics include the age, health, education, and skill training of the members of the labour force. The average age of the labour force is increasing. Older workers have more experience, especially managerial experience, but they often have less formal education than younger workers. The aging of the labour force may also have an impact on the health of the labour force. The health of the labour force is also influenced by health and safety legislation. Attempts to reduce workplace injuries will result in a healthier labour force.

Two other influences affect the labour force in Canada. Immigration has played a large role in the growth of Canada's labour force. Many immigrants enter Canada with needed skills; others need language training before they can become productive members of the labour force. Second, many skilled Canadians leave Canada for higher incomes in other countries, especially the United States, a phenomenon referred to as the "brain drain." The loss of skilled workers has a negative impact on productivity.

Summary

The demand for labour is a derived demand. That is, the demand for a specific occupation derives from the demand for the final product or service. The demand for labour also depends on the productivity of labour. The more productive the worker, the greater the employer's demand for the worker.

The firm's demand for labour is expressed in the marginal revenue product (MRP) curve. Changes in the demand for the final product change the price of the product and the marginal revenue (MR). Changes in MR change the MRP. Changes in worker productivity change the marginal productivity of labour (MPL). Changes in the MPL also change the MRP and thus change the demand for labour.

The demand curve for labour slopes down to the right. The negative slope is a result of two forces: the scale effect and the substitution effect (demand). Higher wage rates may result in higher prices for goods and services. Quantity demanded falls with higher prices, so fewer workers are needed. Higher wages may also encourage employers to substitute capital for workers.

The wage elasticity of demand measures the percentage change in the quantity of workers demanded divided by the percentage change in the wage rate. The wage elasticity is influenced by the percentage of total costs represented by labour costs, the number of substitutes for labour, the availability of substitutes, and the price elasticity of the final product or service.

Not all labour costs vary with the number of hours worked. Certain labour costs are non-wage costs that vary with the number of employees hired. These costs include training and hiring costs, termination costs, and payroll deductions such as Canada Pension Plan.

Increases in labour productivity allow for increases in incomes and for stable prices. The main influences on productivity can be divided into three groups; macro influences, micro influences, and factors that influence both the macro and the micro picture.

KEY TERMS

law of diminishing returns   247

marginal revenue (MR)   248

marginal revenue product (MRP)   250

scale effect   253

substitution effect (demand)   253

wage elasticity of labour demand   254

quasi-fixed labour costs   257

gross domestic product (GDP)   259

labour productivity   259

increasing returns to scale   265

EXERCISES

1. Describe the impact of freer trade between Canada and Latin America on the demand for labour in Canada and on the type of labour demanded.

2. Discuss how the productivity of employees can increase.

3. Why does the law of diminishing returns apply only in the short run?

4. State whether the wage elasticity of demand for each of the following occupations is elastic or inelastic: Explain your answer for each one.

   a. Dentist
   b. Data-entry clerk
   c. Chef
   d. Police officer
   e. Retail salesperson

5. Define two examples of quasi-fixed costs.

6. A payroll tax reduces the monetary contribution of each worker to the firm. Ontario has introduced a payroll tax to pay for health care in the province. Draw a diagram to show the impact of a payroll tax on the demand for

shift D curve to left wage rate will fall employees will decrease

labour. (Hint: The monetary contribution of a new worker is the MRP.)

7. a. Give an example of workers in one occupation being used as a substitute for workers in another occupation.

   b. Give an example of capital (machinery, equipment, etc.) being substituted for labour.

robot – painting cars
computers – designing rugs
mach – fence post

REFERENCES

Bruce, Christopher. (1995). *Economics of Employment and Earnings,* 2nd ed. Scarborough: Nelson Canada.

Ehrenberg, R. G., and Smith, R. (1997). *Modern Labor Economics: Theory and Public Policy,* 6th ed. Reading: Addison-Wesley.

Hamermesh, D. S., and Rees, A. (1993). *The Economics of Work and Pay,* 5th ed. New York: Harper Collins.

King, J. E. (1990). *Labour Economics,* 2nd ed. London: Macmillan.

Sharpe, Andrew. (1999, July). Measuring Up. In *Report on Business Magazine,* pp. 37–41.

10

....

WAGE RATE AND EMPLOYMENT DETERMINATION

OBJECTIVES

After completing this chapter you should be able to:

1. explain employment and wage rate determination in a competitive labour market and under conditions of monopsony;

2. use a graph to explain the impact of the minimum wage on the labour market;

3. use a graph to explain the impact of a payroll tax on the labour market;

4. explain the relationship between wage elasticity and the burden of paying a payroll tax;

5. explain how unions can influence the demand curve for labour;

6. distinguish between a craft union and an industrial union in terms of the ability to alter the supply of labour;

7. discuss causes of unemployment.

INTRODUCTION

In the previous two chapters, we discussed labour demand and labour supply curves as they relate to the individuals and firms in a competitive market. In this chapter, the individual labour demand and supply curves are aggregated and we analyze the overall labour market for a specific occupation. The labour market is where all the buyers and sellers of an occupation interact to exchange this service and establish a wage rate. Just as the firm's demand curve for a certain occupation slopes down to the right, so too does the market demand curve for that occupation. The market demand curve is simply the aggregation of the firms' demand curves. The factors that influence the demand curve for an occupation—the marginal revenue, or the price, of the final product or service and labour productivity—also influence the overall demand for that occupation.

The supply curve for an occupation slopes up to the right. As mentioned in Chapter 8, the opportunity cost of not working increases as the wage rate increases. Thus, as the wage rate increases more people will be willing to work at that occupation. For some occupations, however, there is a cost to becoming qualified to work in that occupation: a lengthy education or a lengthy apprenticeship may be required. A relatively high wage rate is also necessary to attract individuals to these occupations.

This chapter begins with a discussion of wage rate and employment determination in a competitive market. It continues with a discussion of wage rate and employment determination under less-than-competitive conditions, followed by an analysis of the impact of government and trade union activity on the labour market. In an ideal labour market, wage rates would adjust to balance the quantity of labour supplied and the quantity of labour demanded. Changes in wage rates would ensure that all workers find employment. In the real world, there are always workers who are unemployed. The chapter concludes with a discussion of why the labour market often fails to balance labour supply and labour demand.

WAGE RATE AND EMPLOYMENT DETERMINATION IN A COMPETITIVE LABOUR MARKET

The interaction between labour demand and labour supply in the market determines the equilibrium wage rate and the number of workers employed in that occupation. The determination of an equilibrium wage rate is identical to the determination of an equilibrium price, which we studied in Chapter 2. At the point of intersection of the demand and supply curves, the number of workers wanted by employers at that wage rate equals the number of individuals willing to offer their services at that wage rate. This state of affairs is referred to as *equilibrium* because it represents a balance in the labour market. If the wage rate is at the equilibrium level (W_1 in Figure 10.1), there is no tendency for either the wage rate or the level of employment (L_1) to change. If the current wage rate is below the intersection point (W_2 in Figure 10.1), the quantity of workers demanded by firms exceeds the quantity of workers who are willing to work. In other words, there is a shortage of qualified workers. The wage rate will increase as employers need to attract workers into this occupation.

If the wage rate is above the equilibrium level (W_3 in Figure 10.1), there is a surplus of individuals willing to work in this occupation. That is, more people are willing to do this job at the going wage rate than employers are willing to hire. There will be pressure on the wage rate to decrease. We saw in Chapter 2 that wage rates do not decrease as easily as they increase. Wage rates are often referred to as "sticky" in a

FIGURE 10.1   THE LABOUR MARKET

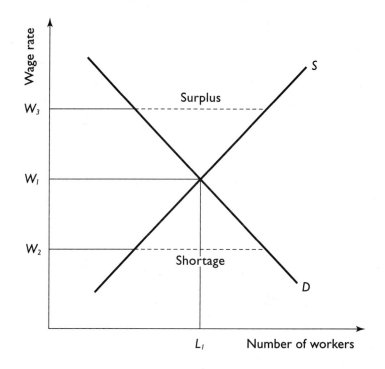

downward direction. Prices for goods and services tend to decrease more quickly than wages, under similar demand and supply conditions. The sluggish nature of wages in response to downward pressure ensures that the surplus of workers will continue for a while. Why are wages slow to decrease? The market wage rate may not fall towards equilibrium if the wage rate was set in a collective agreement between union and management. Changes in the wage rate may be negotiated only when the current collective agreement expires. Another possibility is the presence of a government-legislated minimum wage rate, which makes it illegal to pay or accept a wage rate less than the legal minimum.

Can employers respond to the surplus of workers in ways other than by reducing the wage rate? Employers may respond by raising hiring standards, which reduces the supply of potential employees. They may also reduce some of the benefits associated with the job that are not covered by the collective agreement or by legislation. For example, the length of coffee or lunch breaks could be shortened.

What causes market wage rates to change over time? Any factor that causes a shift in either the demand or supply curves for an occupation will result in a change in the equilibrium wage rate. For example, an increase in the productivity of employees performing this occupation will shift the demand curve to the right (see Figure 10.2). The increase in demand will increase the equilibrium wage rate from W_1 to W_2. As the wage rate increases, more people are willing to work in this occupation and, as a result, the equilibrium level of employment rises from L_1 to L_2. An increase in the number of qualified college and university graduates may shift the supply curve to the right for some occupations (see Figure 10.3). This will decrease the equilibrium wage rate from W_1 to W_2 and increase the equilibrium level of employment from L_1 to L_2. As the wage rate falls, firms are willing to hire more workers (a movement along the demand curve).

WAGE RATE AND EMPLOYMENT DETERMINATION UNDER CONDITIONS OF MONOPSONY

monopsony a market in which there is only one buyer

When one firm is the only buyer of a certain type of labour, the firm is referred to as a **monopsony** (single buyer). Examples of monopsony are present in the Canadian labour market, such as a paper mill or a mine in a small town, or electrical utilities that hire nuclear engineers. The main feature of a monopsony with respect to the labour market is that the wage rate must be increased in order to attract more employees to

FIGURE 10.2 AN INCREASE IN THE DEMAND FOR LABOUR

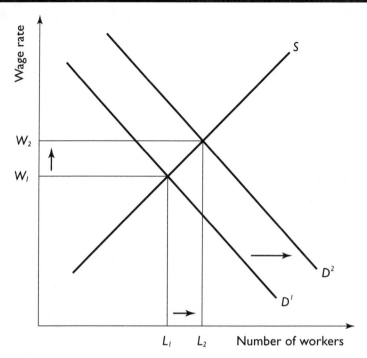

FIGURE 10.3 AN INCREASE IN THE SUPPLY OF LABOUR

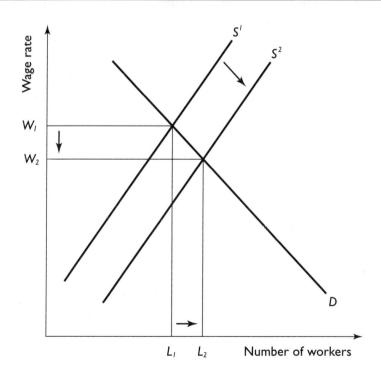

the firm. The supply curve for labour that the monopsony faces slopes up to the right. More workers can be hired only if the wage rate increases. Since the monopsonist is the only demander for a particular type of labour in that market, any desire by the monopsony to increase employment will increase the wage rate. If the wage rate paid to new employees is higher than the existing wage rate, all current employees in the same job category must receive the same compensation as the new employees. Therefore, the cost of hiring a new employee is not only the wage rate paid to that employee, but the increase in the wage rate paid to all existing employees as well.

The monopsony's demand curve for an occupation is identical to the market demand curve because the monopsony is the sole buyer of this type of labour. The supply curve of workers to the monopsony slopes up to the right. Under conditions of monopsony, wage rate and employment levels are not determined by the intersection of the demand and supply curves. A marginal labour cost curve, derived from the supply curve, must be introduced to determine the wage rate and level of employment. The **marginal labour cost (MLC)** is the cost associated with hiring one more worker and is higher than the wage rate paid to that worker.

marginal labour cost (MLC) the additional cost of hiring one more worker

The marginal cost of labour is calculated as follows. Assume a small electrical company in a remote geographical area has four electricians each earning $20 per hour. Business is improving and the company wants to hire an additional electrician. There are no unemployed electricians available so the company must attract electricians who are already employed elsewhere. It is possible to get another electrician if the wage rate is increased to $21 per hour. The extra cost of hiring one additional worker is $21 + 4($1) = $25 per hour since the four current employees need to have their wage rate increased by $1 per hour. Note that the MLC per hour ($25) is greater than the wage rate per hour ($21). The following table shows the calculation of the MLC. The MLC schedule in the last column shows the change in the employer's cost of labour per hour for each additional worker hired.

Figure 10.4 shows a graph of the labour market in the presence of a monopsony. It also shows the relationship between the MLC and the supply curve for labour.

The employment level under conditions of monopsony is determined by the intersection of the demand (marginal revenue product, or MRP) curve and the MLC curve (L_1 in Figure 10.4). In order to maximize profits, the monopsonist hires workers up to the point where

Marginal revenue product = Marginal labour cost

TABLE 10.1 CALCULATION OF THE MARGINAL LABOUR COST

WAGE RATE	QUANTITY OF LABOUR SUPPLIED	TOTAL LABOUR LABOUR COST	MARGINAL LABOUR COST (MLC)
$20	4	$80	
			> $25
$21	5	$105	
			> $27
$22	6	$132	
			> $29
$23 $+ ^\$6 =$	7	$161	

If the MRP > MLC, the contribution of the next worker to the firm is greater than the cost, and the worker should be hired. If the MLC > MRP, the cost of hiring one more worker exceeds the worker's contribution to the firm, so the worker would not be hired.

FIGURE 10.4 WAGE RATE AND EMPLOYMENT DETERMINATION UNDER MONOPSONY

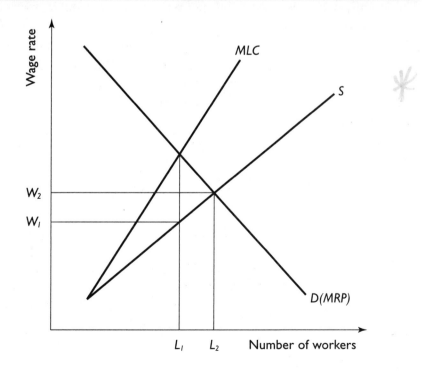

What wage rate is paid under conditions of monopsony? Once the level of employment is determined, the supply curve is used to determine the wage rate (see W_1 in Figure 10.4). Fewer employees (L_1) are hired under conditions of monopsony than under competitive conditions because the level of employment in competitive conditions is determined where the demand curve intersects the supply curve (L_2 in Figure 10.4). Workers are paid less in a monopsony situation (W_1) than under competitive conditions (W_2) and are often said to be "exploited." However, since they are paid more than their reservation wage rate, they are willing to accept W_1.

Examples of pure monopsony in the real world are not numerous. Some have already been mentioned. Another example of a Canadian monopsony is the Canadian Football League, the only employer of professional football players. The model explained in this chapter is useful in situations where the wage rate must be increased in order to attract more workers to this occupation.

The Impact of Government Policies on the Labour Market

The labour market is one of the economy's most regulated markets. A review of the legislation that impacts on the labour market was presented in Chapter 3. This section looks at the implications of three government policies with respect to the labour market: the minimum wage rate, payroll taxes, and wage subsidies.

Minimum Wage Rate

All provinces and the federal government have enacted minimum wage legislation. Not all employees are covered by minimum wage legislation but for those who are, the legal minimum wage rate is a *wage floor*. The wage rate cannot fall below the wage floor. Figure 10.5 illustrates a competitive labour market where the equilibrium wage rate is $6.50 per hour. Groups of employees may argue that $6.50 is too low and employees should not be required to work at that rate. In response to these concerns, the government imposes a $7 per hour minimum wage rate. At $7 per hour, the quantity of workers demanded falls to L_D while the quantity of workers supplied increases to L_S. There is a surplus of workers at the minimum wage rate. A surplus of workers in the labour market is referred to as unemployment. Thus, the imposition of a minimum wage rate has created some unemployment in the labour market.

The extent of job losses that result from the imposition of the minimum wage rate depends on the wage elasticity of demand for labour. If the wage elasticity of demand for labour is inelastic, wage rate increases will not have a significant impact on the number of workers employed. However, when demand for labour is elastic, the reduction in employment would be much greater because employers respond relatively more to wage rate changes. Since minimum wage rates apply mainly to unskilled and semi-skilled workers, it is unlikely that the demand for their services is inelastic.

When we predict the number of job losses that result from imposing or increasing a minimum wage rate, we assume that all other factors influencing the demand for labour remain constant. In the real world, however, a variety of changes can shift the entire demand curve to the right or to the left. For example, an increase in the overall demand for workers could come about as a result of an improvement in economic conditions, which would shift the demand curve for labour to the right. Such a shift would put upward pressure on the equilibrium wage rate. A shift of the labour demand curve to the right reduces the

FIGURE 10.5 THE MINIMUM WAGE RATE

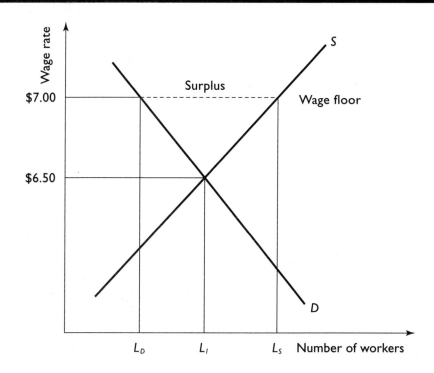

negative impact of the minimum wage rate on employment levels. Thus, governments increase the minimum wage rate when economic conditions are good, and freeze the minimum wage rate when the economy is in a slump.

Empirical studies measuring the extent of the negative impact of minimum wage rate increases on employment levels are inconclusive because so many factors on both sides of the labour market are changing over time. There is some evidence that increases in the legal minimum wage rate decrease employment opportunities for youth and for low-productivity groups in the labour force. As Figure 10.5 shows, the impact of the minimum wage is not felt only on the demand side of the labour market. Higher minimum wage rates encourage more individuals to enter the labour market, but if the employment opportunities are not available, the new entrants may find themselves unemployed.

Who earns the minimum wage in the Canadian economy? In 1998, Statistics Canada compiled a profile of minimum-wage workers. Some of the characteristics of minimum wage workers are listed below.

- Young people, aged 15 to 24 years, comprised approximately 58% of all minimum-wage workers.

- Close to 20% of all young people who have jobs are earning the minimum wage.

- Approximately 60% of all young minimum-wage earners are students living at home with their parents.

- There are more female minimum-wage earners than male. For those over 25, two thirds of the minimum-wage earners are women.

- Most minimum-wage earners are part of a family. About 14% of all minimum-wage earners are their family's sole income earner either because they have no spouse, or because the spouse is unemployed.

- Sixty-two percent of the minimum-wage jobs are part-time jobs.

- About 28% of all minimum-wage earners work in the beverage and food industry.

PAYROLL TAXES

In order to raise revenue, governments legislate payroll taxes to be paid by employers. That is, employers must pay a tax based on the size of their payroll. Well-known payroll taxes in Canada include the Canada Pension Plan and employment insurance. The conventional wisdom is that the payroll tax is a tax on employers. In fact, the burden of a

BOX 10.1 The Minimum Wage Rate and Poverty

The objective of minimum wage rate legislation is not always evident. When questioned about the objectives behind a legislated minimum wage rate, politicians and bureaucrats are often at a loss to explain the rationale behind increasing the legal minimum wage rate. Proponents of the minimum wage have listed the following as objectives of the legislation:

- to prevent employers who, in the absence of minimum wage rate legislation, may resort to the payment of sub-standard wage rates and exploit workers with little bargaining power;
- to force employers into making their operations more efficient;
- to help reduce poverty among the working poor.

For the purposes of our discussion here, we will focus on the minimum wage rate as a tool in the fight against poverty. In line with this goal, proponents of higher minimum wage rates argue that earnings from employment should be higher than the income received from social assistance. Earnings from employment at the legal minimum wage rate should exceed what a family of four receives on social assistance. If the minimum wage rate guarantees an income in excess of social assistance benefits, the extent of poverty among the working poor will be reduced.

However, there are a number of reasons why the legal minimum wage rate may not be an effective tool in the fight against poverty.

First, low hourly wage rates are only one cause of poverty. Poverty can also stem from low hours of work, unemployment, the size of the family, and the health condition of family members. Changes in the hourly wage rate are not sufficient to deal with all of these factors. For example, if someone is already unemployed, increases in the hourly minimum wage rate provide no assistance in the fight against poverty. In other instances, a large family may be the primary cause of a poverty-like existence. It is not likely that employers would pay those with large families a higher hourly wage rate.

Second, if increases in the minimum wage rate help alleviate poverty, why not increase the rate substantially, for example to $50 per hour? Increases in the legal minimum wage rate result in unemployment for some workers: the higher the minimum wage rate, the more unemployment. It is very difficult to determine exactly how many workers lose their jobs as a result of increases in the minimum wage rate. Still, economists know that some individuals become unemployed as a result of minimum wage rate increases. Higher minimum wage rates also pose a barrier to employment for other prospective employees. Those who become unemployed as a result of an increase in the minimum wage rate are often those with fewer employment skills. How can they acquire those skills if they are not working? Furthermore, how does one gain employment experience when one is unemployed?

Third, in many jurisdictions, several classes of workers are exempt from minimum wage coverage. For example, in some provinces, domestic servants and agricultural workers are exempt from coverage. Increases in the minimum wage rate do not help these employees.

Fourth, the impact of increases in the minimum wage rate on poverty depends on the characteristics of low-wage earners. A majority of low-wage earners are young people. The majority of these workers are single and have no dependants. They may also belong to a more affluent family. These individuals receive more money working than they would receive on social assistance since it is likely that they would be denied social assistance. Low-wage earners

payroll tax is also borne, in part, by employees in the form of lower wage rates and lower levels of employment.

The imposition of a payroll tax results in a shift to the left in the demand curve for labour. Firms will only hire the same number of employees if the payroll tax can be offset with a lower wage rate. Alternatively, firms will hire fewer employees if the wage rate cannot be lowered. Figure 10.6 is a graphical representation of the impact of a payroll tax on wage rate and employment levels. The equilibrium wage rate is W_1 before the imposition of the payroll tax. The demand curve shifts down by the amount of the tax. The new equilibrium wage rate (W_2) is determined by the intersection of the new labour demand curve (D^2) and the labour supply curve. The equilibrium wage rate has not decreased by the full amount of the tax. Because the equilibrium wage rate did not decrease by the full amount of the tax, both the employer and the employee share the burden of paying the tax. The employer's portion of the payroll tax is the difference between the amount of the tax and the reduction in the wage rate.

The proportion of the tax paid by employers and employees partly depends on the wage elasticity of demand and supply. If the demand curve for labour is inelastic (the demand is relatively steep), employment levels do not fluctuate greatly with a change in the wage rate. Both the wage reduction that results from a payroll tax and the corresponding decrease in employment are relatively small. If the demand curve for labour is elastic, the opposite occurs: the equilibrium wage

FIGURE 10.6   IMPACT OF A PAYROLL TAX ON THE
                LABOUR MARKET

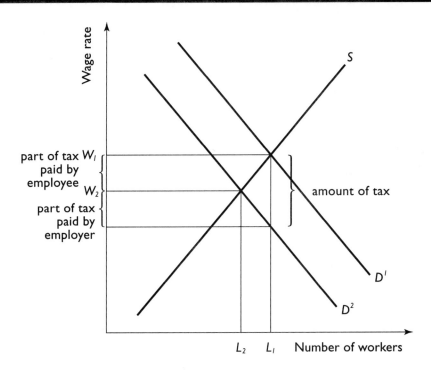

rate decreases to a greater extent and the job losses are also greater. In Figures 10.7a and b, an identical payroll tax is applied to situations of an inelastic demand and an elastic demand for labour. In both, the wage rate falls from W_1 to W_2. In the inelastic situation, the wage rate reduction is relatively small compared to the elastic situation. In the case of an inelastic demand for labour, the burden of paying the payroll tax falls mainly on the employer. In the case of an elastic demand for labour, the burden falls mainly on the employee.

The impact of a payroll tax also depends on the wage elasticity of supply for labour. If the labour supply curve is inelastic, the equilibrium wage rate decreases relatively more than under conditions of elastic supply. In Figures 10.8a and b, an identical payroll tax is applied in conditions of an inelastic labour supply curve and an elastic labour supply curve. The wage rate falls from W_1 to W_2 in both. The wage rate reduction is much smaller in the situation of an elastic supply curve. In terms of the reduction in wage rates, the employees bear the greater burden of a payroll tax under conditions of inelastic labour supply.

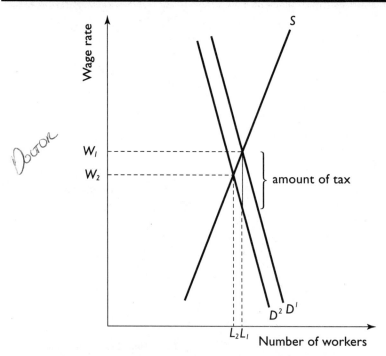

FIGURE 10.7A   IMPACT OF A PAYROLL TAX (INELASTIC DEMAND)

Doctor

Wage rate

S

W_1
W_2

amount of tax

D^2 D^1

$L_2 L_1$ Number of workers

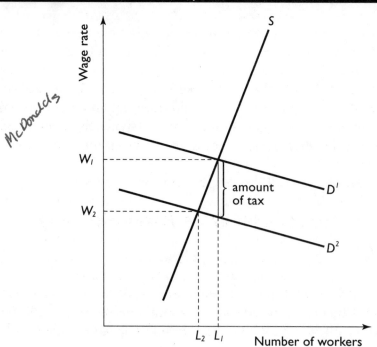

FIGURE 10.7B   IMPACT OF A PAYROLL TAX (ELASTIC DEMAND)

McDonalds

Wage rate

S

W_1

amount of tax

D^1

W_2

D^2

L_2 L_1 Number of workers

AN INTRODUCTION TO THE CANADIAN LABOUR MARKET

FIGURE 10.8A   IMPACT OF A PAYROLL TAX (INELASTIC
                SUPPLY)

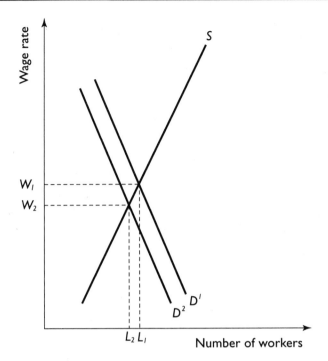

WAGE SUBSIDY

Consider the impact of a wage-rate subsidy paid to the employer on the labour market. A wage rate subsidy is the opposite of a payroll tax. If a payroll tax shifts the demand curve to the left, a **wage subsidy** will shift the demand curve for labour to the right. A shift of the demand curve for labour to the right will increase the wage rate and increase the level of employment (see Figure 10.9). The wage subsidy has increased the wage rate from W_1 to W_2. Government may use a wage subsidy to increase the employment levels of certain groups in the labour force such as youth.

wage subsidy   a payment by government to an employer to assist in paying wages

THE IMPACT OF UNIONS ON WAGE RATES AND EMPLOYMENT

One goal that workers have when voting to be represented by a union is to increase the wage rate. Obtaining wage rate increases from the employer is not the only objective for unions but for many unions it is

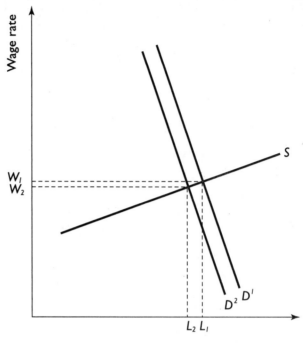

FIGURE 10.8B IMPACT OF A PAYROLL TAX (ELASTIC SUPPLY)

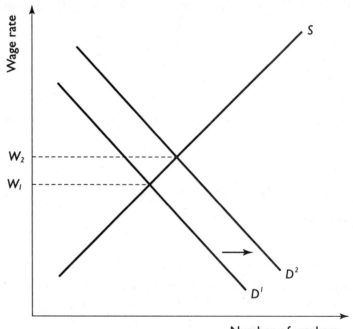

FIGURE 10.9 IMPACT OF A WAGE SUBSIDY ON THE WAGE RATE

the primary objective. This section describes how unions attempt to obtain wage rate increases for their members.

Wage rates are determined by the interaction of demand and supply in the marketplace. If unions are to be successful in obtaining wage rate increases, they must be able to cause a shift in either the demand or the supply curve, or both. We will first look at ways by which unions can increase the demand for the workers they represent.

The Impact of Unions on the Demand for Labour

The demand for any worker is derived from the demand for the product or service that the workers provide. Unions could increase the demand for the product by advertising it. Union advertising is not common since many people in the union movement believe that product promotion is the sole jurisdiction of the company. However, when an industry is facing increased competition, especially from imports, unions find it necessary to become involved in product promotion. For example, the International Ladies' Garment Workers Union ran advertisements on television promoting North American–made clothing. The union also set up booths in exhibitions that provided information on clothing and fabrics. The Canadian Automobile Workers union promoted the buying of cars "your neighbours help to build" in order to meet the challenge from imported automobiles. Labour organizations have also run "Buy Union Made" or "Look for the Union Label" campaigns. These campaigns aim not only to shift the demand curve for labour to the right but also to change the elasticity of demand for labour by making the demand for the product less elastic. In order to deal with the pressure from off-shore competition, unions have lobbied the federal government to create trade barriers. If the prices of imported products increase due to tariffs and other trade barriers, consumers may increase their demand for domestic goods— thereby increasing the demand for labour.

Unions can also help shift the demand curve for their members to the right by improving the productivity of their members. This can be done through upgrading courses and other training. Labour productivity may also increase if unions permit management to introduce the latest technology into the operation.

Unions have also used featherbedding to maintain the demand for their workers. That is, featherbedding techniques attempt to stop the MRP curve from shifting to the left. **Featherbedding** involves retaining jobs and workers who would otherwise be made redundant by technological change. For example, in the railroad industry, trains still had

featherbedding
retaining workers who would otherwise be made redundant by technological change

firemen long after steam engines had been replaced. It is only in recent years that the caboose was removed from trains. It is easier to maintain jobs through featherbedding when the industry does not face much competition. In construction, unions have resisted technological advances such as plastic pipe, which has reduced installation time. As competition in the marketplace intensifies, featherbedding disappears. Firms that face tough competition for their products are forced to introduce the latest technology.

THE IMPACT OF UNIONS ON THE SUPPLY OF LABOUR

craft union a union whose members all possess a certain craft or skill

industrial union a union whose members all work in the same industry

In order to examine the impact of unions on the supply side of the market, it is necessary to distinguish between craft and industrial unions. All the members of **craft unions** possess a certain skill, such as electricians or plumbers. The first unions in North America were craft unions. **Industrial unions** organize all workers in an industry such as steel or automobiles. Members of industrial unions can be skilled tradespeople or unskilled workers. Industrial unions represent a variety of skills.

Craft unions attempt to shift the supply curve to the left, thereby increasing the wage rate. For example, the supply curve will shift to the left if a lengthy apprenticeship period is required to acquire the skill. High initiation fees and union dues may discourage workers from entering this trade. Craft unions may pressure the federal government to limit the number of immigrants, especially those who possess the same skills as the union members. Some collective agreements call for a closed shop, meaning that the employer can only hire union members. Other collective agreements specify a journeyman-apprentice ratio. The number of apprentices that can work on a job are limited by the number of journeymen on that job. Governments can also help shift the supply curve to the left by legislating that only certain trades can perform certain functions. Professional associations in such occupations as law, accounting, and medicine operate in a manner similar to craft unions in order to restrict the supply of labour.

The impact of craft unions on the supply of labour is shown in Figure 10.10. A shift of the supply curve from S^1 to S^2 increases the equilibrium wage rate from W_1 to W_2, which decreases the number of workers from L_1 to L_2. The drop in employment affects union membership.

Industrial unions cannot control the supply of labour by insisting on long apprenticeships or bargaining for closed shops in collective agreements. These unions insist on a wage floor or else the members will go on strike to back their demands (see W_2 in Figure 10.11). The

AN INTRODUCTION TO THE CANADIAN LABOUR MARKET

FIGURE 10.10 IMPACT OF A CRAFT UNION ON THE SUPPLY OF LABOUR

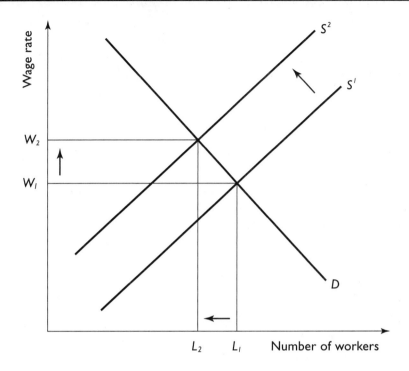

supply curve is altered as shown in the diagram. The new supply curve is W_2aS. Since no one is permitted to work for less than the wage floor, the section of the supply curve below that level does not exist.

The ability to get a wage rate increase depends on the wage elasticity of demand for labour. If the demand is elastic, an increased wage rate may result in a relatively large drop in employment and a decline in the total wage bill paid to members. The interests of union members anxious to get a wage rate increase must be balanced against the wishes of other members who are anxious to keep their jobs.

EMPIRICAL EVIDENCE

Do unions succeed in raising wage rates? Most studies indicate that unions do influence wage rates although the extent of that influence is difficult to determine. Many argue that the unions' ability to get wage rate increases for their memberships is contingent on the industry in which they work. Unions have accepted wage freezes when companies have been in financial difficulty. Some unions have negotiated lower wage rates in a new collective agreement in order to get their members

FIGURE 10.11 IMPACT OF AN INDUSTRIAL UNION ON THE SUPPLY OF LABOUR

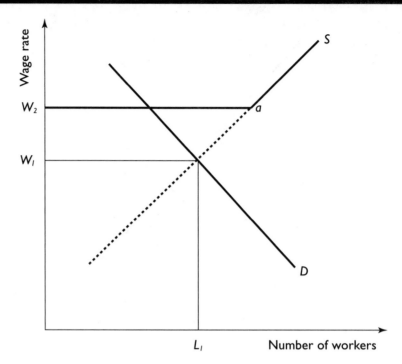

back to work. Some collective agreements contain the requirement that some jobs be paid at the minimum wage rate. Workers do not need a union to get the minimum wage.

Canadian studies conducted on the effects of unions on wage rates have estimated the union impact on wages to be an increase anywhere from 10 to 30%. One must be careful in interpreting these studies as many were conducted during the 1970s, when the labour market was different from today's. Some studies focused solely on manufacturing while others looked at all industries. The impact of unions on wage rates is likely to vary by industry and by individual firm within an industry. It is also possible that the presence of unions in an industry affects the wages paid to employees of non-union firms in the industry. Employers may increase the wage rate of non-union workers in order to ward off union organizing attempts. Increases in wage rates achieved through collective bargaining may reduce the number of workers employed. The terminated workers will then compete for jobs with non-union workers, increasing the supply of non-union workers. The increased supply of non-union workers may put downward pressure on non-union wage rates, which will widen the gap between union and non-union wages. Unions' success at improving the working conditions of their members cannot be measured solely by looking at the impact on wage rates, however. Unions also have an impact on the employment relationship by negotiating for fringe benefits, such as health plans, and by negotiating for some non-monetary benefits such as seniority and work assignments.

CAUSES OF UNEMPLOYMENT *WILL NOT COVER*

This chapter has explained how equilibrium wage rates and levels of employment are determined. The discussion now shifts to the question of why the labour market may not easily establish an equilibrium between demand and supply. In Chapter 6, we discussed various types of unemployment. Using our knowledge of how markets operate, we will now examine why there are always some workers without jobs. We have already seen in this chapter how minimum wage rate legislation can create an excess supply of labour (unemployment). In the following sections we will focus on three additional reasons for unemployment: job search, job rationing, and rigid wage rates.

JOB SEARCH

Job search is the result of imperfect information in the labour market. Unemployed workers often do not know where jobs are available and employers with vacancies are not always aware of all the individuals with adequate skills seeking work. **Job search** is the process of matching workers with appropriate jobs. Workers differ in their tastes and skills, jobs differ in their attributes, and information about job vacancies filters slowly through the various labour markets. It takes time to check want ads, inquire of friends and relatives, apply to companies, weed out acceptable jobs from unacceptable ones. Because it takes time to find an appropriate job, the process of job search usually involves periods of unemployment. What determines the length of search and thus the duration of unemployment?

job search the process of matching workers and available jobs

One key factor often singled out in the analysis of job search is the reservation wage rate. As mentioned in Chapter 8, the reservation wage is the lowest wage the unemployed worker will consider acceptable. Suppose an unemployed worker has searched vacancies and has received a job offer. The worker will compare the wage offered by the company with his or her reservation wage, and accept the job only if the wage offered exceeds or equals the reservation wage.[1] If a person has a relatively low reservation wage rate, suitable job offers will be received more readily and the period of unemployment will be short. A high reservation wage rate will result in a lengthy period of search and thus unemployment.

What determines a worker's reservation wage? In deciding upon a reservation wage, a person must balance the benefits versus the cost of each choice. The marginal or additional benefit that is associated with a higher reservation wage rate once a job is found is a higher rate of pay received in this job than in other jobs. In order to obtain a higher reservation wage rate, certain additional or marginal costs must be incurred. For example, a longer period of unemployment will usually be necessary before a job can be found at that rate. As long as the marginal benefit associated with a certain reservation wage rate exceeds the marginal cost, it is worth the wait to acquire employment at that wage rate, or at any wage rate where the marginal benefit exceeds the marginal costs. Realistically, factors such as the person's pay on the previous job, the customary standard of living, and wages earned by friends or relatives also affect the reservation wage rate.

A model of job search based on a comparison of the benefits and costs of search leads to the conclusion that any factor that reduces the costs of unemployment will increase the length of job search and the duration of unemployment. A major factor in the cost of unemployment anywhere is the unemployment compensation program instituted in a country. The cost of job search generally includes direct costs such as transportation costs, fax and phone bills, or fees of employment agencies as well as the opportunity cost of income forgone while being unemployed. An unemployed person with no income during the period of unemployment faces a high opportunity cost of job search. In this situation, the reservation wage rate is likely to be low and search to be short. The more generous unemployment benefits, or the longer the period over which benefits can be received, the lower the opportunity cost of job search will be. Low opportunity costs of job search result in a higher reservation wage rate for the individual and a greater likelihood of remaining unemployed.

---

1. Of course, the acceptance of a job offer depends on other factors as well, such as working conditions, reputation of the company, or commuting time.

AN INTRODUCTION TO THE CANADIAN LABOUR MARKET

Job Rationing

A second major explanation of unemployment is job rationing. **Job rationing** refers to the practice of employers paying wages that create an excess of workers seeking employment and a shortage of jobs. This practice may be legally required as, for example, by minimum wage legislation, or it may reflect the employers' decisions to pay wage rates that exceed the equilibrium level. The job search unemployment discussed in the previous section arises from a lack of information about where to find these jobs and how much they pay, not so much from a lack of jobs. Unemployment caused by job rationing is fundamentally different. Here the problem is not imperfect information but an insufficient number of jobs for the number of people who want one.

Another case of job rationing occurs when firms themselves may want to pay a wage higher than that mandated by supply and demand. Why would firms want to keep wages high even in the presence of an excess supply of labour? After all, higher wages add to their costs. The answer is that wages are not the only factor affecting labour cost. The other major factor is labour productivity. Firms want their workers to be productive because higher productivity lowers cost. Paying higher wages might prove profitable if the higher wages raise the productivity of workers. How can higher wage rates lead to higher labour productivity?

Higher wage rates can lead to a reduction in worker turnover. High turnover increases production costs; it is also costly for firms to hire and train new workers. Even after they are trained, newly hired workers are often not as productive as experienced workers. The higher the wage rate, the more financially attractive it is for workers to stay with that firm and the less likely they are to quit.

A second reason is that higher wages may reduce "shirking." In many jobs workers have some discretion over how hard they work. As a result, firms often try to monitor the efforts of their workers. Monitoring, however, is costly and sometimes even impossible. A firm can respond to this problem by paying wage rates above the equilibrium level. Paying a wage rate higher than the competitive wage rate makes it costly for workers to lose their jobs if they are found shirking. Also, when a firm hires new workers it cannot accurately assess the quality of those workers before they start working. By paying higher wages, firms can attract a pool of higher qualified applicants.

Economists refer to wage rates paid in excess of the equilibrium level as **efficiency wages** because wages have an effect on workers' productivity. Unemployment arising from efficiency wages is similar to

job rationing practice of employers paying wages that create an excess of workers seeking employment and a shortage of jobs

efficiency wages wage rates paid in excess of the equilibrium level in order to increase productivity

unemployment caused by minimum wage rates. In both cases, wage rates are higher than the level required to balance the quantity of labour supplied and the labour demanded. However, while minimum wage laws prevent firms from lowering wages, efficiency wage theory argues that firms deliberately keep wages above the equilibrium level.

RIGID WAGE RATES

A major explanation for unemployment is the downward inflexibility of money wage rates. As in the case of job rationing, rigid wage rates cause an imbalance between the number of people seeking employment and the number of vacancies available. The problem caused by rigid wage rates is illustrated in Figure 10.12.

To see how rigid wage rates cause unemployment, let us assume that Canadian households reduce their spending. As sales of consumer goods decline, firms reduce their desired level of employment, which is represented by the leftward shift of the labour demand curve to D^2. At the prevailing real wage of W_1, employment falls to L_3 (point A to point B), leading to deficient demand unemployment ($L_1 - L_3$). If wage rates were flexible downward, the excess supply of labour in the market

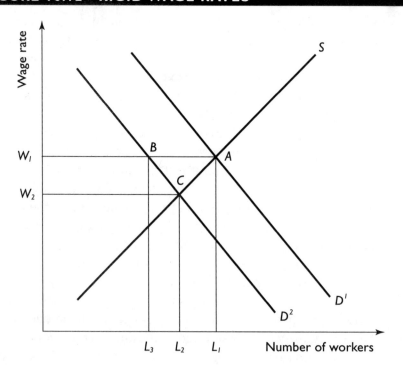

FIGURE 10.12   RIGID WAGE RATES

would result in a bidding down of wage rates until a new equilibrium were established at the wage rate of W_2, where the demand and supply of jobs are equal again (point C). The fall in the wage eliminates the amount of deficient-demand unemployment both by inducing firms to increase their hiring and by causing some of the unemployed to drop out of the labour force. Should wage rates be rigid in the downward direction, this equilibrating process would not take place, and unemployment would persist. Because wage rates are indeed sticky even in the face of substantial unemployment, this downward inflexibility offers an explanation for both cyclical and structural unemployment. The question, then, is why wage rates do not fall during periods of high unemployment?

One source of wage rigidity is labour unions. The majority of union contracts have two- or three-year terms, so wage rates in unionized industries cannot readily respond to short-run increases in unemployment. Why would firms bind themselves in such long wage contracts? One answer is the costs involved in collective bargaining, which is time consuming and expensive. There is thus a tradeoff between the costs of locking workers and firms into contracts for longer periods of time and the costs of wage negotiations. The optimal tradeoff seems to be between one and three years.

Even if longer contracts are preferred, they could be formulated in a way that allows wage rates to adjust downward in case the economy moves into a recession. Workers and firms could agree to a fixed employment level rather than a fixed wage level in their contract. However, contracts that guarantee jobs rather than wages are very rare. One reason is the application of the seniority principle in unionized firms. When layoffs occur, workers with seniority are usually the last ones out and the junior workers bear the brunt of layoffs. If senior workers hold most of the power in the union, they will prefer contracts that call for layoffs rather than wage rate cuts during hard times since they are less likely to be laid off.

Even labour markets unaffected by union wage rates exhibit downward inflexibility. Although non-union firms are not bound by any explicit, written agreement to follow a layoff policy over a policy of wage rate cuts, in most cases there appears to exist an unwritten agreement or implicit contract that such a policy will be followed. Implicit contracts are sometimes called the "invisible handshake." Because they are unwritten, it is difficult to confirm their existence; however, the fact that layoffs are the primary method by which firms adjust in economic downturns, even in non-unionized markets, speaks for their existence.

A related argument holds that workers are less concerned about their wages in absolute terms than they are about how they fare compared to other workers in other firms and industries. It is the relative wage rate that determines an individual's position in the income distribution. Because income comparisons largely determine workers' social status in society, workers will resist a reduction in their wage rates out of fear that it will lower their standing. The only way they would agree to wage rate cuts is if they knew that all other workers were receiving similar cuts. It is difficult to reassure any one group of workers that all other workers are in the same situation, and they, therefore, will resist any cut in their wages. There may thus be an implicit understanding between firms and workers that wages will not be lowered in order to avoid making workers worse off than their counterparts in other firms.

SUMMARY

The equilibrium wage rate in a labour market is determined by the intersection of the labour demand and the labour supply curves. If the wage rate is lower than the equilibrium level, the quantity of workers demanded will exceed the quantity supplied. Pressure will be put on the wage rate to increase. If the wage rate is greater than the equilibrium wage rate, downward pressure will be exerted on the wage rate. If the wage rate is at the equilibrium level, there is no tendency for the wage rate to change.

The imposition of a minimum wage rate on the labour market results in a surplus of workers. In the labour market, this surplus is called unemployment. The imposition of a payroll tax results in a lower wage rate and lower levels of employment. The impact of the payroll tax on wage rate and employment levels depends on the wage elasticities of demand and supply for labour.

Unions attempt to increase the wage rate paid to their members by shifting the demand curve for labour to the right or by altering the supply curve. Craft unions may be successful in shifting the labour supply curve to the left but industrial unions can only alter the shape of the supply curve.

Three main causes of unemployment are job search, job rationing, and rigid wage rates. The length of the job search is influenced by the person's reservation wage rate. The choice of the reservation wage rate is influenced by the marginal benefits of a high wage rate and the marginal costs associated with a larger job search. Job rationing occurs when wage rates are paid in excess of the equilibrium level. Rigid wage rates refer to the fact that wage rates do not fall that easily in response to an excess supply of labour.

KEY TERMS

monopsony   274

marginal labour cost (MLC)   276

wage subsidy   285

featherbedding   287

craft union   288

industrial union   288

job search   291

job rationing   293

efficiency wages   293

EXERCISES

1. Identify examples of monopsony (or near monopsony) in the economy.

2. What payroll taxes do employers pay in your province or territory?

3. Why are payroll taxes referred to as "job killers"?

4. Some newspaper editorials have recommended abolishing the minimum wage rate because of its negative impact on employment. What would be the consequences in the labour market if governments were to repeal minimum wage legislation?

5. Does an increase in the minimum wage rate result in a transfer of wealth from one group in the labour force to another? Explain.

6. Are employers likely to introduce labour-saving technology when faced with increases in the minimum wage rate?

7. There is a positive impact of increases in income associated with an increase in the minimum wage rate; this impact outweighs the negative impact of lost jobs. True or false? Explain.

8. Using a graph in your answer, discuss the impact of government paying $2 per hour toward the wages of each student hired for the summer by a private firm.

9. One reason for employees wanting to be members of a trade union is higher wages. List other possible reasons.

REFERENCES

Benjamin, D., Gunderson, M., and
Riddell, W. C. (1998). *Labour
Market Economics: Theory, Evidence
and Policy in Canada,* 4th ed.
Toronto: McGraw-Hill Ryerson.

Bruce, C. (1995). *Economics of
Employment and Earnings,* 2nd ed.
Scarborough: ITP Nelson Canada.

Chaykowski, R. P. (1994). *Modern
Labour Economics: The Canadian
Context.* New York:
HarperCollins.

McConnell, C. R., and Brue, S.
(1992). *Contemporary Labor
Economics,* 3rd ed. New York:
McGraw-Hill.

Appendix D

WAGE RATE CHANGES AND UNEMPLOYMENT

One factor that appears to have an impact on the wage rate is the unemployment rate. The British economist A. W. Phillips related the percentage change in wage rates to the unemployment rate for the years 1861 to 1957. He used percentage wage rate changes as the dependent variable and the unemployment rate as the independent variable. There was an inverse relationship between the two variables that seemed to last over the period covered by the study. That is, as the unemployment rate increased, the percentage increase in wage rates decreased.

Why does this inverse relationship hold? In times of low unemployment, there is a strong demand for labour. For many occupations, that demand exceeds the available supply. The shortage of workers at the going wage rate puts pressure on the wage rate to increase. The market adjusts to a higher equilibrium wage rate. The greater the excess demand for labour, the greater the increase in wage rates. When the demand for labour decreases, the unemployment rate increases and the pressure to increase wage rates is reduced. There may even be pressure for the wage rate to decrease, although, as we have discussed, wage rates tend to be more "sticky" downward than upward.

In Figure 10.13, the relationship between percentage increases in the wage rate increases and the rate of unemployment appears as P^1. Is this relationship a constant one? That is, does the line P^1 remain the same year after year? Research indicates that the relationship is not stable. Over the years, the graph of the relationship has moved to the right, as indicated by P^2. Unemployment rates are thus now associated with higher wage rate increases than in the past. Alternatively, the wage rate increases are associated with higher levels of unemployment. Why has the relationship changed?

Various reasons have been put forth to explain the fact that the tradeoff between the unemployment rate and increases in wage rates has deteriorated. These reasons include:

- A more generous employment insurance scheme, introduced in the 1970s, has allowed some individuals to remain unemployed rather than to seek work out.

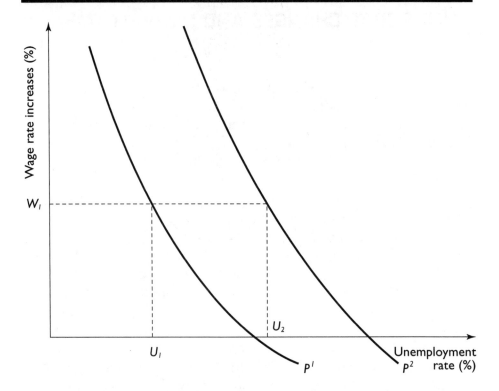

FIGURE 10.13 RELATIONSHIP BETWEEN PERCENTAGE WAGE RATE CHANGES AND THE UNEMPLOYMENT RATE

- Changes in the size and composition of the labour force have occurred, in part because of the entrance of "baby boomers" into the labour market and the increased participation rate of women.

- Canadians began to expect high levels of price increases through the 1970s and 1980s and these expectations found their way into negotiated wage rate increases.

- The decline in the foreign exchange value of the Canadian dollar caused prices for imports to increase, which also increased prices. Price increases have led to wage rate increases.

Since Phillips published his findings in the 1950s, the relationship between wage rate increases and the unemployment rate has been extended to price increases (inflation). Analysts have focused on measuring the relationship between price increases and the unemployment rate.

11

....

WAGE RATE
DIFFERENTIALS

OBJECTIVES

After completing this chapter, you should be able to:

1. explain how adjustment lags result in wage rate differences between occupations;

2. define the following terms: wage structure, compensating wage differentials, and equalizing differences;

3. list job characteristics that can contribute to equalizing differences;

4. describe how the presence of labour market barriers results in wage rate differentials;

5. discuss the personal characteristics associated with the wage structure;

6. describe various factors affecting the wage gap between men and women;

7. explain why discrimination occurs in the labour market;

8. discuss the government policies designed to combat employment and pay discrimination.

INTRODUCTION

Have you often wondered why your neighbour earns more than you do? Have you ever wondered why professional athletes earn so much money? Much has been written in recent years about the earnings difference between men and women—why are men paid, on average, more than women? Why is there a difference in wage rates between different occupations? This chapter will explain why the differences in wage rates exist.

occupational wage struc-
ture differences in wage
rates between occupations
in the labour market

We will focus here on the occupational wage structure. The **occupational wage structure** refers to the differences in wage rates among the occupations that exist in the labour market. Wage rate differences encourage workers to seek out occupations that are most productive. If we assume that most people want to earn a high wage rate, workers will move to those occupations that pay more. In this manner, workers gravitate toward jobs where they are most productive, which benefits society. Differences in wage rates also encourage individuals to develop their skills and invest in their training. If all occupations paid the identical wage, why would someone incur the expense of additional education or training?

Differences in wage rates can be explained by employing the principles of demand and supply. Those principles, previously explained in Chapters 8 and 9, were introduced to explain how wage rates are determined. The concepts of demand and supply can also be used to explain why a wage structure exists in the labour market.

Our discussion of wage rate differences is divided into three categories:

- adjustment lags
- compensating wage differentials
- labour market barriers

ADJUSTMENT LAGS

You will recall from the earlier discussion that wage rates tend to move toward equilibrium. That is, if the wage rate is currently above the equilibrium level (W_1 in Figure 11.1), there will be pressure to lower the wage rate toward equilibrium. As the wage rate is reduced, the quantity of workers demanded increases and the quantity of workers willing to work at that occupation decreases. At the equilibrium wage rate (W_e), the quantity of workers demanded equals the quantity of workers supplied to that occupation. The market is in equilibrium. Conversely, if the current wage rate is below the equilibrium wage rate (W_2), there is pressure to increase the wage rate to the equilibrium level. As the wage rate increases, the quantity of workers demanded by employers decreases and the quantity of workers willing to work at that occupation increases.

FIGURE 11.1 LABOUR MARKET EQUILIBRIUM

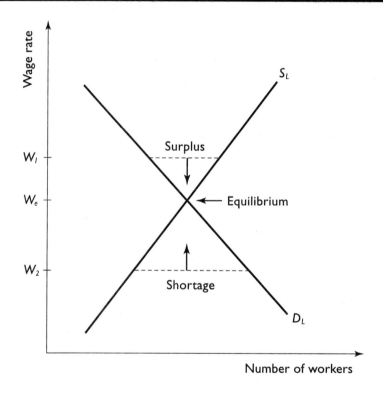

The difference in wage rates between two occupations may result from an **adjustment lag** as workers and employers react to changes in the wage rate. It takes time for the quantity of workers supplied to an occupation to increase. The period is extended if lengthy training is required to qualify for the higher wage occupation.

adjustment lag period during which workers and employers react to changes in the wage rate

It may also take time for employers to respond to changing wage rates. For example, where a collective agreement is in effect, wage rates may remain intact until it expires.

To further illustrate the concept of adjustment lags, imagine two occupations, A and B, with different wage rates (see Figure 11.2). The wage rate in occupation A is currently higher than the wage rate in occupation B. If we assume that workers want to earn more money and also that the jobs are similar in attractiveness, workers would move away from the occupation with the lower wage rate (B) to the occupation with the higher wage rate (A). In the market with the lower wage rate, the supply of workers would decrease. The reduction in supply (a shift of the supply curve to the left) would increase the wage rate for this occupation (see the graph for Job B). In the market with the higher wage rate the supply curve would shift to the right with the increase in supply of workers willing to do this job. The wage rate in this market would be reduced.

In the market for occupation B, the wage rate increases as a result of the flow of workers out of occupation B to occupation A. In the market for occupation A, the wage rate decreases as a result of flow of

Read.

FIGURE 11.2 WAGE DIFFERENTIALS BETWEEN TWO OCCUPATIONS

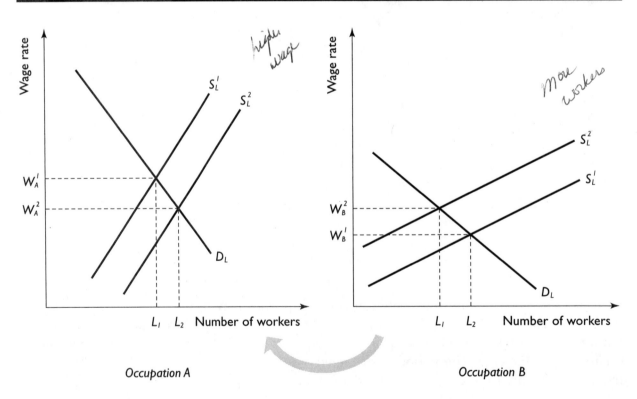

Occupation A

Occupation B

AN INTRODUCTION TO THE CANADIAN LABOUR MARKET

workers from occupation *B* into occupation *A*. The wage rate differential between the two occupations narrows.

As long as there is movement of workers from one occupation to another, the wage rates in the two occupations will get closer together. The wage rate differential will eventually disappear.

COMPENSATING WAGE DIFFERENTIALS

The theory of compensating wage differentials recognizes that jobs differ in terms of their attractiveness. Jobs or occupations with unattractive attributes will require a higher wage rate in order to attract individuals to those occupations. Attractive occupations may be desirable in spite of lower wage rates as the positive aspects of the job compensate individuals for the reduction in wages.

What are unattractive working conditions? The most undesirable attribute of an occupation is the risk of injury or illness. Studies that compared occupations on the basis of risk of death or injury found that, all else being equal, such risks are associated with higher wage rates. When studying the impact of risk on wage rates, we must assume that all other working conditions are the same, although this is not likely to be the case. It is difficult to find two jobs that are identical except for any one aspect. There are many variations in employment conditions. Also, it can be difficult to measure risk.

Other working conditions listed as undesirable are extensive physical effort, especially lifting; a stressful work environment, especially where the work must be performed at a fast pace; unattractive hours of work such as shift work and weekend work; the risk of unemployment; noise; smoke; and extreme temperatures in the workplace. Apart from the risk of death or injury, other unattractive working conditions appear to have a negligible impact on wage rates.

In theory, when the working conditions of an occupation are undesirable, the wage rate paid to workers in that occupation is adjusted upward. A higher wage rate becomes necessary to attract workers into that occupation. The increase in the wage rate that compensates workers for undesirable conditions is referred to as a **compensating wage differential**. The size of the differential in relation to each unattractive attribute of a job is difficult to measure, because it is difficult to single out the impact of certain characteristics on the wage rate. Furthermore, individual preferences play a role here. Some people prefer shiftwork to a regular 9-to-5 routine. Some prefer outdoor work

compensating wage differential increase in the wage rate that compensates workers for undesirable working conditions

BOX 11.1 Legislation Related to Risk in the Workplace

Empirical evidence suggests that higher earnings are associated with the risk of a fatal injury. However, the nature of employment is constantly changing and the amount of money necessary to compensate individuals for risk is changing as well. Occupational health and safety legislation has made many workplaces safer. In addition to better safety equipment and procedures, more information is available on hazardous substances. What impact does the presence of health and safety legislation have on the determination of wage rates?

If the risk of injury on the job is reduced through the use of better equipment or better procedures, the amount of the risk premium paid to workers is also reduced. On the other hand, the new legislation may make workers aware of dangers in the workplace. They are now aware that certain substances are hazardous and may want a wage premium to work there.

The presence of workers' compensation benefits may also reduce the compensating wage differen-tial associated with unsafe conditions. If workers believe that the loss of income due to injury is reduced because of workers' compensation payments, the premium required to work at a risky job is also reduced. In the absence of workers' compensation, employees may want to take out private insurance against wage loss. A wage rate premium would be required to pay for the insurance.

The availability of employment insurance benefits may reduce the compensating wage differential between jobs with varying risks of unemployment. That is, prior to the introduction of a federal employment insurance program, employees who worked in jobs where the risk of unemployment was high sought higher wages to compensate for this risk. Conversely, others would accept jobs with lower wage rates where the risk of unemployment was low. If employment insurance is available, workers need not seek out more secure jobs because they will receive some income in the event of a layoff or termination.

---

to office work. Although unattractive to many, some working conditions may appeal to others.

Wage differentials can also be viewed from the positive aspects of certain occupations. Some jobs are conducted in clean and safe conditions. Some jobs may be close to home, or they may have employment security. Some occupations have a degree of status associated with them, or flexible hours or long holidays. Where positive aspects of a job are present, individuals may accept a lower wage rate with the recognition that the positive aspects of the job compensate for the reduction in pay. These positive features of a job are referred to as **equalizing differences**. They act as a magnet, attracting individuals to lower paying jobs. The size of the equalizing difference can be measured by determining the amount of money necessary to convince someone to leave a lower paying attractive job for a higher paying unattractive job.

equalizing differences
the features of a job that compensate for wage rates that are lower than in other jobs

A survey of employees revealed the following attributes of a job to be the most attractive: job security, short hours and long vacations, promotion and training opportunities, low pressure/stress, lack of responsibility, prestige, superior geographic location, low danger, and non-monetary fringe benefits. There is some evidence that individuals will accept a lower wage rate to work in a location with a low crime rate, with less pollution, or with a lower population density. It also appears that individuals will accept a lower wage rate to avoid snow or to acquire extra sunshine.

In addition to non-monetary benefits of a job, there are also monetary fringe benefits. Employers may spend more than one third of their payroll on monetary fringe benefits such as company pensions, bonuses and profit sharing, and group health plans. Differences in monetary fringe benefits can also lead to differences in money wage rates.

LABOUR MARKET BARRIERS

As mentioned in the first section of this chapter, wage rate differentials may appear because of adjustment lags in the labour market. The wage rate differential is temporary. However, most wage rate differences between occupations are not temporary. As mentioned in the previous section, differences in the attractiveness of jobs lead to permanent wage rate differentials. The presence of barriers in the labour market is another factor that creates differences in the wage rate. The concept of labour market barriers is discussed in this section.

We have seen that workers move from lower wage jobs to higher wage jobs. This movement tends to equalize wage rates between occupations. If something interferes with the flow of workers from one occupation to another, the supply of workers in one occupation would remain high while the supply of workers in the other occupation would remain low. The wage differential between the occupations would continue to exist. If workers are restricted in their mobility from occupation B to occupation A, the wage rate will remain lower in occupation B than in occupation A. The restrictions on mobility of workers from one job to another are called **labour market barriers**.

The distinction between a labour market barrier and an equalizing difference is as follows. The equalizing difference acts as a magnet that keeps workers in lower paying jobs. Labour market barriers prevent workers who want to switch jobs from moving to higher paying jobs.

labour market barriers restrictions on the mobility of workers from one job to another

The following are labour market barriers:

- lack of information
- discrimination
- geography and language
- union-imposed regulations
- government regulations
- lack of education or training

The presence of labour market barriers means that the labour market is not as competitive as we assumed in our discussion of demand and supply. Removing them will make the labour market more competitive: Workers will move more freely between occupations and wage rate differentials will be reduced.

A discussion of each of these barriers follows. Note that some are easier to remove than others, for example it is easier to overcome a lack of education and training than it is to remove the barriers imposed by government regulation.

LACK OF INFORMATION. Thousands of different occupations exist in the Canadian labour market. It is virtually impossible for anyone to be aware of all the various occupations that one is qualified for. As long as people are unaware of other occupations that can utilize their skills they will remain in the lower paying occupation. The federal government has attempted to rectify this barrier with the establishment of Human Resources Development Centres. Private placement agencies fill a similar role in the marketplace.

DISCRIMINATION. People are often denied an equal opportunity to develop their potential capability, or they are denied a wage equal to what others of the same capability are paid. **Pre-market discrimination** occurs when people have been deprived of the equal opportunity to develop their natural abilities and talents during the early pre-employment years. Pre-market discrimination, for example, occurs when children of a minority group receive inferior schooling or inadequate health services. For example, children of aboriginal families living on reserves often encounter pre-market discrimination. **Market discrimination** occurs when job assignments, promotions, or wage rates are based on characteristics unrelated to job performance. These characteristics may be the person's age, gender, or colour of skin. The distinction between pre-market and market discrimination is important because differences in hiring, promotion, or pay often reflect pre-market discrimination

pre-market discrimination denial of equal opportunities to develop natural abilities and talents during pre-employment years

market discrimination different responsibilities and benefits based on characteristics unrelated to job performance

rather than market discrimination. If an aboriginal worker receives less pay than a non-aboriginal worker for the same job, it may be that the non-aboriginal worker has had more education or training, which makes that person more productive. In this case, wage rate differentials would not reflect market discrimination. Differences in educational attainment levels may reflect discrimination at the school level. But discrimination within the educational system is not the fault of the individual employer.

Labour market barriers that arise from discrimination are often not easy to detect. Ideally, we would compare men and women, or members of visible minorities and the majority, whose productivities are equal. In this case, if women receive lower wage rates than men with similar productivity levels, or if members of visible minorities receive lower wages than the other workers, we would clearly call it discrimination. However, discrimination normally takes more subtle forms than unequal wages for equal work. For example, employers can restrict women or members of visible minorities to inferior jobs, thus justifying the lower wages paid to them.

As long as individuals are prevented from access to certain jobs because of gender or skin colour, existing wage rate differentials are likely to remain. Governments address occupational barriers through human rights legislation that makes it illegal to discriminate on the basis of age, gender, creed, race, and other characteristics in hiring or promoting.

GEOGRAPHY AND LANGUAGE.   It may not always be easy to relocate to where the higher wage jobs are. There are costs associated with moving to another city or province. Furthermore, the higher wage job may be in a location with a higher cost of living. More expensive housing can be a barrier to the mobility of workers. There may also be social costs associated with relocation: it is often difficult to move away from friends and family. When children are involved in the move, their needs must also be considered. If one's spouse is also employed, relocation may be more complicated.

Language can also be a barrier to mobility. In Canada, the inability to speak one of the official languages may prevent a move to a higher wage rate job. Quebec's current language laws may not only discourage workers from moving to Quebec but may also inhibit francophone residents of Quebec from migrating interprovincially.

UNION-IMPOSED REGULATIONS.   Collective agreements between union and management can restrict the mobility of labour between occupations. In industries such as construction, the union practices of a closed shop and a hiring hall affect the labour market. In a closed shop, the company can only employ members of the union, so prospective employees must be a member of the union before being hired. In a hiring-hall situation, the union supplies workers to the employer and attempts to place local workers first.

GOVERNMENT REGULATIONS. Provincial governments have legislation that restricts the movement of workers from province to province. Restrictions have been imposed on the transferability of trade certification; that is, although a worker may be certified to practise in one province, the certification may not be valid in another province. The Canadian Constitution gives the provinces the right to pass legislation limiting the number of non-residents able to work in certain occupations.

Municipal governments can set regulations for such businesses as hot dog vending or taxicab driving. These restrictions often dictate who can work in that field and where they can work.

Provinces and municipalities can also issue licences for certain businesses and occupations. Licences provide revenue for governments and, if the fee is very high, restrict entry into the trade. The main argument in favour of licensing is that it promotes public health and safety. To ensure that standards are maintained, licence applicants may have to pass an examination or serve an apprenticeship. The difficulty of the examination and the length of the apprenticeship can act as labour market barriers: tougher examinations and lengthier apprenticeships restrict entry into the trade or profession. Because occupational licensing restricts competition, the cost of the services provided by licensed occupations is higher than it otherwise would be. The quality of the service may also be lower than it would be with more competition. Licensing arrangements exist for the following occupations, among others: dentists, veterinarians, physicians, architects, actuaries, lawyers, and optometrists.

Tax laws restrict the interprovincial movement of workers. Travel and living expenses are not deductible for temporary employment away from home.

LACK OF EDUCATION OR TRAINING. Many occupations have educational qualifications. Someone who does not have the required educational credentials cannot work at this occupation. Furthermore, if a specific amount of education is required to enter an occupation, employees want to be compensated for the time and expense involved in getting the education or training. Many studies have established the existence of a positive correlation between the level of education and wage rates. Expenditures on education and training are an important aspect of the labour market. Chapter 12 is, therefore, devoted to discussing the returns received from investments in education and training.

PERSONAL CHARACTERISTICS AND EARNINGS

A different approach to explaining wage rate differentials is to focus on the personal characteristics associated with earners of higher wage rates. These characteristics are discussed below.

QUANTITY AND QUALITY OF SCHOOLING. Higher education is assumed to provide more cognitive knowledge either in terms of general communication skills and problem-solving abilities or in terms of occupation specific competencies. It also may reflect a higher achievement motivation, discipline, and other personality traits often associated with productivity. Workers who are more productive are likely to be paid more. As mentioned earlier, empirical studies have confirmed the positive relationship between the amount of schooling and earnings.

Workers not only differ in terms of the number of years of schooling they received and the level of degrees or certificates they obtained, but they also differ in terms of the quality of schooling. Does it matter where someone got a degree or diploma? Given that employers grade academic institutions, there is clearly a perception that the school matters.

YEARS OF WORK EXPERIENCE. The longer an individual has been in the labour force, the more productive that person is likely to be.[1] There has been more opportunity for on-the-job training. When the relationship between training and wage rates is studied, the number of years of work experience is often used as a proxy for training, because it is difficult to measure how specific the training was. More years of service with an employer are likely associated with more opportunities for advancement within the company.

ABILITY. Not all individuals have equal ability. Some physicians are better than others. Some hockey players are better than others. In fact,

---

1. Increases in productivity are not directly related to years of work experience throughout all of one's working life. As an individual approaches the age of retirement, his or her productivity may start to decrease.

in professional sports, a small difference in ability may translate into a large difference in earnings. One player is not a perfect substitute for another.

SOCIOECONOMIC STATUS OF FAMILY. There is a positive relationship between the socioeconomic status of the family and earnings. If the parents are professionals, they may encourage their children to further their education. The parents may also have the finances to make that possible, and they may be able to introduce their children to people who can help them land a good job. Also, parents who are professionals expose their children to these types of jobs, so the children are aware that they exist.

Note that there is a great deal of interaction among these variables. For example, it is likely that individuals who come from a wealthy family will be able to afford more years of schooling. They may also be able to afford a higher quality education. Nonetheless, individual characteristics do matter when it comes to earnings.

DISCRIMINATION AND MALE-FEMALE WAGE DIFFERENTIALS

In discussing labour market barriers as a source of wage differentials we briefly discussed the subject of discrimination. We will now take a closer look at discrimination and how it relates to the gender wage gap.

EMPIRICAL EVIDENCE ON MALE-FEMALE WAGE DIFFERENTIALS

Statistics indicate that the earnings of women are less than the earnings of men. Does this mean that women are paid about one third less than men just because they are women? Obviously not. As we have seen earlier, there are many other factors besides gender that can affect earnings, such as the number of hours of work. On average, men work for pay more hours than women: 39.8 hours versus 35.2 hours per week. If one controls for differences in hours worked by men and women, for instance if one compares hourly wages, the gender gap is reduced to about 75% to 80%. Another factor is age: as the wage differential has narrowed over the years, one would expect that gender wage differences would be smallest among young workers. Indeed, that is what one finds. In the mid 1990s, women aged 55 and over who worked full-time earned on average 64% of the wages earned by male workers in the same age bracket. Their daughters and granddaughters, aged 15 to

24, earned on average 86% of the earnings of men in the same age group.

Marital status is another significant factor. The ratio of average earnings of females compared to males is very much reduced if one compares single men and women. The ratio is close to 90%. For single women in specific age groups or with certain educational levels, the difference is even less. The earnings of single women age 35 to 44 were almost 95% of those earned by single men of the same age. The wage gap disappears entirely when one looks at the most educated members of that age group—single men and women with a university degree. In contrast, earnings between married men and women differ significantly. This indicates that married men and women choose different life and career paths from those chosen by single men and women.

There are many other potential factors that can affect the wage gap: absenteeism, labour market experience, seniority, health, training. Economists have devoted considerable effort to disentangling the various effects and separating them from the effect of gender. The idea is to estimate the male-female wage differential that remains after controlling those factors that account for productivity differences between male and female workers. Wage rate differences that reflect productivity differences are considered non-discriminatory. The wage rate gap that remains after productivity related differences are taken into account is the unexplained or "residual" amount. It cannot be attributed to productivity differences and, therefore, is chosen as a measure of discrimination.

Theories of Discrimination

What does economic theory tell us about discrimination? In the following we will focus on market discrimination, not because pre-market discrimination is unimportant, but because its causes are largely beyond the field of economics. We look at two theories of discrimination. One is based on prejudice, the other on lack of information.

Prejudice by employers. Prejudice describes a subjective feeling of dislike for an individual or group. A common feature of prejudice is that the person tries to create a distance from the disliked individual or group, which can take several forms. One form is physical distance. What happens if employers distance themselves from individuals or groups by not hiring them, for instance by not hiring women?

Suppose we look at a group of firms that discriminates against women and a group that does not. Assume that the labour demand curves for both groups are identical. However, the supply curve of labour for the non-discriminating firms must lie further to the right than for the discriminating firms. Men and women can work for the non-discriminating firms whereas only men can work for the discriminating firms. Because of the larger supply of labour to the non-discriminating firms, wage rates will be lower. Women are restricted to work for the non-discriminating firms, so their wage rates are on average lower than those of men. Men's average wage rates are composed of the lower wage rates paid by non-discriminating firms and the higher paid wage rates paid by discriminating firms. The observed wage rate differential between men and women can be explained by the discrimination against hiring women.

Can these wage differentials persist over time? It depends. The discriminating firms pay a price for their prejudice: by excluding women they must pay a higher wage rate. The non-discriminatory firms have a cost advantage because they pay a lower wage rate. In competitive labour markets the discriminating firms will be driven out of business over time, and the gender wage gap will disappear. If, however, the discriminating firms have monopolies protected from competition, they will be able to remain in business. In protected industries such as government-regulated industries there is less competitive pressure to maximize profits. Thus firms that choose to do so can maintain their discriminatory practices. However, they will pay a price for discriminating by earning lower profits than they otherwise could have.

PREJUDICE BY WORKERS. Another source of discrimination may come from prejudice of fellow workers, which is often a more powerful source of discrimination because the motives are generally stronger. Employers are not always in contact with their workers; prejudice among fellow workers, on the other hand, is fuelled both by competition for jobs and close personal contact at work.

When employers are the source of discrimination, competitive forces tend to reduce discrimination over time. When workers are the source of discrimination, prejudice will remain for a longer period of time. Assume that men do not like to have women as their supervisors. If men fail to cooperate in the workplace, female supervisors will be less efficient in their work compared to their male counterparts. Hence the female supervisors will earn lower wage rates. The wage rate gap between male and female supervisors caused by the prejudice of workers can persist even in the long run. There is no mechanism in place that would force the gap to disappear over time.

DISCRIMINATION AS A RESULT OF IMPERFECT INFORMATION

A second explanation for market discrimination is the imperfect information that is available to employers when they hire workers. An employer can never be sure of a worker's actual productivity at the time of hiring. Employers, therefore, often use personal characteristics of workers in the screening process as indicators of their productivity. Some of these personal characteristics are individual in nature, such as years of education, previous work experience, or test scores. Others are group characteristics, such as gender or race. The use of group characteristics in screening job applicants gives rise to **statistical discrimination**.

For discrimination to take place, two workers of equal productivity must be paid different wages based on a criterion such as gender or race. How might this occur? Imagine a firm wants to hire a new worker. The firm's newspaper ad has attracted several male and female job applicants who have different levels of education and work experience and different labour force attachments. To choose the most productive worker, the firm will screen the applicants based on characteristics that it considers directly linked to a worker's productivity. Assume that the firm will use only two characteristics: level of education and gender. If the level of educational attainment were a perfect predictor of productivity, the firm might only hire college or university graduates. Male and female workers with equal educational attainment would receive equal wage rates. If education were an imperfect predictor of productivity, the employer would use additional characteristics that are correlated with job performance to improve the screening process. In our example, the only other observable characteristic is gender.

It is a fact that only women can give birth. It is also a fact that many, not all, women who have babies quit their jobs (at least for a while) to look after their babies. The employer knows this. However, what the employer does not know is which of the female applicants of child-bearing age is likely to withdraw from the labour force for this reason. If the employer knew, he or she would treat equally those male and female applicants with the same educational level and the same long-term job commitment. Instead, because of imperfect information, the employer presumes that all female applicants of child-bearing age are likely to quit to raise a family. Therefore, the employer would likely prefer to hire a male applicant.

Women whose careers have been interrupted to raise children may have a lower level of productivity than other women. Thus employers may systematically prefer male to female workers of equal educational

statistical discrimination
discrimination that results from imperfect information in the screening process of job applicants

level, giving rise to lower wage rates for women. Are these wage differentials discriminatory? On a group basis, they are not, to the extent that the differences in wage rates reflect actual differences in productivity. On an individual level, they are discriminatory. Those female applicants who are identical to male applicants in terms of personal qualifications, including job commitment, are rejected based on the fact that they are female.

POLICIES TO COMBAT DISCRIMINATION

Governments in Canada have enacted a wide range of legislation aimed at combating discrimination in the labour market.

EQUAL EMPLOYMENT OPPORTUNITY LEGISLATION. Discrimination, as we have seen, can affect different aspects of employment: hiring, promotion, dismissal, or pay. Equal employment opportunity legislation attempts to prevent discrimination in hiring, promotion, and dismissals. Provinces include this legislation in their Human Rights Code, so complaints regarding employment discrimination are considered by the province's Human Rights Commission. If the parties involved in a complaint cannot resolve the issue, a board of inquiry takes on the case and makes a final decision.

affirmative action
policy that promotes employment equity for women, members of visible minorities, people with disabilities, and aboriginal people

AFFIRMATIVE ACTION LEGISLATION. **Affirmative action** goes a step further than equal employment opportunity legislation. In addition to requiring that firms and other organizations end discriminatory practices, it requires them to demonstrate that they are actively making efforts to locate and to hire members of the following four designated groups: women, members of visible minorities, people with disabilities, and aboriginal people. These four groups have most frequently been subjected to discrimination. Affirmative action or equal opportunity legislation so far applies only to federal jurisdiction. Employment equity programs have also been adopted in some cities and for federal contractors.

Affirmative action legislation has not been without controversy. One criticism is that affirmative action really amounts to a system of employment quotas. Another criticism is that it forces companies and other organizations to hire unqualified workers simply because they belong to one of the designated groups. Proponents counter that, without affirmative action, employers who discriminate would simply claim they could not find qualified female or minority workers. The problem is that one cannot decide on purely objective grounds who is qualified and who is not. Supporters of affirmative action also argue that, even if some reverse discrimination is involved, it is justified as a compensation for past discrimination.

EQUAL PAY LEGISLATION. All Canadian jurisdictions have legislated equal pay for equal work. Under the provisions of this legislation, men and women who perform the same work within the same establishment must be paid the same wage rate. Equal or same work is generally interpreted in a rather broad sense, that is, as similar or substantially similar work. Differences can appear in the wage rate between men and women on the same job if a piece-work arrangement is in effect or if seniority is factored into everyone's wage rate in the firm.

Human Rights Code.

PAY EQUITY OR EQUAL VALUE LEGISLATION. The impact of equal pay legislation is limited because men and women are often not performing the same or similar work in a firm. To remedy the resulting wage disparities further legislative initiatives have been proposed and partly implemented. Legislation that ensures that men and women are paid equally for work of equal value is known as pay equity. Under this legislation, companies must pay the same wage rate to male and female employees performing different tasks if these tasks are deemed to be of equal value. The value of a job is determined by a job evaluation scheme, instead of being established in the market. Such a scheme compares male-dominated jobs with female-dominated jobs. The legislation establishes factors that attempt to determine the value of a job. These factors include physical effort, skill, educational requirements, responsibility, and working conditions. Points are assigned to each factor and

---

BOX 11.2 Bell Canada Settles Pay Equity Dispute

The employment practice of federally regulated industries such as airlines, banks, and telecommunications are regulated by the pay equity provisions of the *Canadian Human Rights Act.*

Since 1992, the union representing clerks and operators at Bell Canada has been at odds with management over the company's wage gap between male and female employees. In 1994, the union took the dispute to the Canadian Human Rights Tribunal. After an unsuccessful attempt to challenge the tri-

bunal's authority, Bell Canada agreed in 1999 to a $59 million pay equity settlement. The settlement applied to about 20 000 employees, mostly women, who worked or were working as clerks and operators at Bell Canada.

Many observers of the Canadian labour market believe that the case provides a wake-up call for other federally regulated companies where pay equity is an issue.

added up for each job. Male-dominated jobs are then compared with female-dominated jobs with the same total point score. If, for example, wages in female-dominated jobs are 20% lower than wages in male-dominated jobs with the same point score, the wage rates assigned to female-dominated jobs are adjusted upward.

In Chapter 3 we listed some of the jurisdictions that have implemented pay equity legislation. Here we will focus on some of the arguments that have been brought forward in the debate over pay equity legislation. Critics of the legislation charge that comparing the value of different jobs on the basis of a common set of characteristics is like trying to compare the value of oranges and apples on the basis of their nutritional value. In the case of oranges and apples, the subjective preferences of consumers play a large part in determining the demand for and, therefore, the prices of the two fruits. Even if oranges and apples had an identical nutritional value, the price of oranges might be much higher than that of apples if consumers preferred the taste of oranges. The same applies to different jobs. Critics point out that just because a job held by men has the same value in terms of point score for skills, responsibility, and so on, as a job held by women, this does not imply that the two jobs should have the same wage. If a majority of women prefer certain jobs, and therefore expand the supply of labour to these jobs, it can be expected that wage rates in these jobs are lower.

Another argument against pay equity legislation is that it would lead to serious inefficiencies in the labour market by creating chronic surpluses in some occupations and shortages in others. Job evaluations might give carpenters (a male-dominated occupation) and social workers (a female-dominated occupation) who are both employed in the public sector an equal point score; salaries in these two occupations would, therefore, be adjusted so that they are equal. If carpenters earned higher salaries than social workers before the implementation of pay equity legislation, the result would be an increase in the supply of people wanting social worker positions.

Opponents of pay equity legislation further argue that such legislation will cause many women to lose their jobs by raising the relative wage of women. The imposition of an increase in the wage rate brought about by pay equity legislation is similar to the imposition of a higher minimum wage rate. There will be fewer workers demanded, especially if the wage elasticity of demand is elastic. Also, there may be fewer job opportunities because employers who are faced with a major pay equity settlement may relocate to jurisdictions that do not have pay equity legislation.

AN INTRODUCTION TO THE CANADIAN LABOUR MARKET

Critics also argue that the process of determining the true value of jobs is inherently subjective. A job's evaluation score depends on which factors are included in establishing the value of a job and on the weights given to each factor. Both decisions are affected by the values and beliefs of the evaluator. Not surprisingly, the same jobs have received different ratings when evaluated by different people.

Proponents of pay equity legislation discount most of the criticism. First, they admit that in a competitive market, differences in supply and demand may lead to differences in wages for jobs that have the same measured characteristics. They maintain that real-world wage differentials between men and women do not arise from competitive market forces but are mostly the result of women being crowded into certain occupations due to discrimination and sex stereotyping. The fact that pay equity legislation negates market determined wage differentials is thus desirable because these differentials represent past and present discrimination. Second, they argue that job evaluation can be done far more objectively than the critics of the legislation seem to admit. The objectivity comes from standardized evaluation procedures.

Third, proponents dispute the negative effects of the legislation on economic efficiency and on the employment of women. They point to the experience of other countries such as Australia and Great Britain. Australia has had pay equity legislation since 1969. Since that time women's pay has risen from 66% to more than 85% of men's. Major labour market imbalances do not seem to have emerged. In Great Britain, pay equity laws were toughened in 1983. The legislative changes and their enforcement do not seem to have caused major market distortions in this country.

Empirical research on various aspects of pay equity legislation is still insufficient to draw firm conclusions on its pros and cons. Nevertheless, some tentative conclusions have emerged. In jurisdictions where pay equity legislation has been in force for some time, the gender wage gap has been reduced, in some cases considerably so. Negative employment effects for women seem to have been minimal.

SUMMARY

Occupational wage structure refers to differences in wage rates between different occupations. Wage differences between occupations may be the result of adjustment lags, as it takes time for workers and employers to adjust to wage differences. Wage differences arising from adjustment lags are generally of a temporary nature.

Occupations differ from each other in terms of both undesirable and desirable attributes. Jobs with undesirable attributes generally have to pay higher wages to compensate for the undesirable conditions. Jobs with desirable attributes often lead workers to accept lower wages. For the total of advantages and disadvantages to be equalized among occupations, wages must rise or fall by enough to equalize or compensate for the differentials, which are usually of a long-term nature.

Wage differentials between occupations generally cause workers to move from the lower paid to the higher paid occupations. Movements between occupations may be hindered by labour market barriers, which may be the result of discrimination, lack of information, different geographical location of employers and employees, language, or union or government imposed regulations.

Discrimination is often cited as the main reason for the wage gap between men and women. Although the gender wage gap has been decreasing over the last decades, men still earn on average more than women. There are many factors that affect the earnings differential between men and women such as differences in hours of work, work experience, training, absences from work, and seniority. It has been found that even if the major factors leading to productivity differences are taken into account, there remains a wage gap between men and women. This residual or "unexplained" part of the overall wage difference is often chosen as a measure of discrimination.

Labour market discrimination occurs when people of equal productivity are paid different wages, are hired into different jobs, or receive unequal training or promotion opportunities on the basis of characteristics such as gender, race, age, or religion. The source of discrimination can be found in prejudices of employers or fellow workers or in imperfect information regarding a worker's true productivity.

Several policies have been designed and partly implemented to reduce discrimination in the labour market. Equal employment opportunity legislation and affirmative action legislation address discrimination in hiring and promotion. Equal pay legislation and pay equity legislation address discrimination in pay. Equal pay legislation requires that men and women who perform the same or substantially similar work in the same establishment must be paid the same wage rate. Pay equity legislation prescribes that men and women receive the same pay in different jobs as long as these jobs are considered to be of equal value.

KEY TERMS

EXERCISES

1. Do jobs with undesirable attributes pay more than jobs with desirable attributes, or is it the other way around? Explain.

2. Occupation A and occupation B are identical except that occupation B requires people to work at night. Assume that some people prefer night jobs, but others do not. Will the wage in occupation B be higher, lower, or equal to that in A? Why?

3. Political pressure to pass occupational licensing legislation usually comes from the people employed in the occupation rather than from consumers. Why?

4. Draw labour market diagrams for two regional labour markets, A and B. In region A, a particular occupation is paid a higher wage than in region B. As a result, workers in that occupation move from region B to region A. Show the effect of the movement on the occupation's wage structure in both regions. What geographical barriers could prevent workers to move from region B to A?

5. Only a few women are employed as airline pilots, and only a few men are employed as dental hygienists. What could account for this pattern?

6. What is meant by statistical discrimination?

7. How can a seniority system perpetuate discrimination?

8. Some argue that the wages of equally productive men and women will converge over time in a competitive labour market and that wage differentials that result from discrimination will not persist in the long run. Discuss.

9. Why is equal employment opportunity legislation generally considered to be insufficient to abolish the segregation of women into female-dominated jobs?

10. Discuss the pros and cons of pay equity legislation. Which side of the debate do you think has the stronger argument?

REFERENCES

Becker, G. (1971). *The Economics of Discrimination*. Chicago: University of Chicago Press.

Cousineau, J., Lacroix, R., and Girard, A. (1992). Occupational Hazard and Wage Compensating Differentials. *Review of Economics and Statistics 74:* 166–169.

Friesen, J. (1996). The Response of Wages to Protective Labour Legislation: Evidence from Canada. *Industrial and Labour Relations Review 49:* 243–255.

Gunderson, M. (1995). Gender Discrimination and Pay-Equity Legislation. In L. Christofides, K. E. Grant and R. Swidinsky (Eds.), *Aspects of Labour Market Behaviour: Essays in Honour of John Vanderkamp*. Toronto: University of Toronto Press.

Kidd, M., and Shannon, M. (1994). An Update and Extension of the Canadian Evidence on Gender Wage Differentials. *Canadian Journal of Economics 27:* 918–938.

Meng, R. (1989). Compensating Differentials in the Canadian Labour Market. *Canadian Journal of Economics 22:* 413–424.

Meng, R. (1987). Equal Pay for Work of Equal Value. *Canadian Public Policy 13:* 445–461.

Moore, M., and Viscusi, W. (1990). *Compensation Mechanisms for Job Risks*. Princeton: Princeton University Press.

Weiner, N., and Gunderson, M. (1990). *Pay Equity: Issues, Options and Experiences*. Toronto: Butterworths.

12

....

EDUCATION, TRAINING, AND EARNINGS DIFFERENTIALS

OBJECTIVES

After completing this chapter, you should be able to:

1. describe the typical pattern of age-earnings profiles for different levels of education;

2. explain the cost-benefit analysis of investment in post-secondary education;

3. outline the changes in returns to post-secondary education over time;

4. discuss the impact of education and other factors on the distribution of individual earnings;

5. contrast the signalling approach with the human capital approach to investment in education;

6. distinguish between general and specific training.

INTRODUCTION

In Chapter 11 we looked at various factors explaining differences in wage rates. This chapter examines the role of education and on-the-job training as a source of earnings differentials. The study of the effects of education and training on the labour market is the core of what economists call human capital theory. The central idea of this theory is that expenditures on education and training are investments that individuals make in themselves in order to increase their market skills, productivity, and earnings. To explain earnings differentials, human capital theory focuses on individual differences in years of schooling and length of on-the-job training.

The chapter is divided into three sections. The first section examines formal education as a type of human capital investment. The concept of a rate of return to human capital investment is introduced and we explore why differences in years of education among individuals are expected to lead to differences in earnings. In the second section we focus more closely on the causes of individual differences in investment in schooling, particularly on factors such as individual ability, financial opportunity, and so on. The third section of the chapter is devoted to on-the-job training and the implications of different types of such training for earnings differentials.

THE PATTERN OF EDUCATION AND EARNINGS

age-earnings profile
average hourly or annual earnings for people of different ages with the same level of education

Is there any truth to the old maxim, "If you want to get ahead, get an education"? Consider the evidence shown in Figure 12.1a and Figure 12.1b, which make use of **age-earnings profiles**. Such profiles show annual earnings for people of different ages who have had the same amount of schooling. Profiles of average annual earnings for Canadian men and women in 1995 are drawn for five educational levels: (i) fewer than nine years of elementary schooling; (ii) nine to thirteen years of elementary and secondary schooling but no high school certificate; (iii) high school certificate; (iv) some post-secondary education such as trade certificates but not a college certificate or university degree; and (v) a certificate/diploma or degree from a college or university. The profiles are for year-round full-time workers only. We can see in these two figures that education and earnings are strongly related. Men and women with more education make more money, as shown by the successively higher level of each age-earning profile.

FIGURE 12.1A   ANNUAL EARNINGS BY AGE AND EDUCATION, CANADIAN MALES, 1995

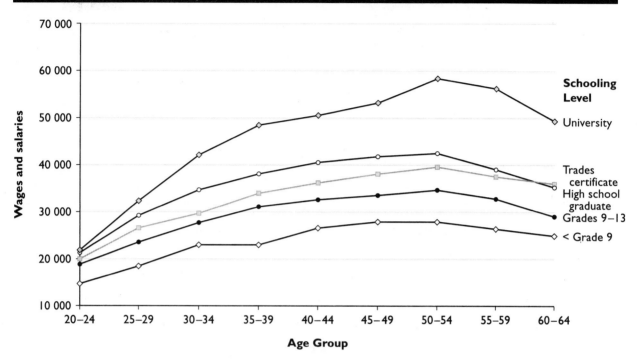

Note: Earnings are average wage and salary income of full-year (49+ weeks), full-time (30+ hours per week) workers.

Source: Authors' tabulations from the 1996 Census Public Use Microdata Files, Statistics Canada.

At first glance, these figures strongly support the belief that additional education results in higher earnings. Whether further education is a good investment, however, requires more analysis. It is necessary to compare the increased earnings from additional years of education and the additional costs. While a post-secondary degree or certificate does lead to higher earnings for most people, the investment nevertheless may not be worthwhile when one considers the rising costs of obtaining a post-secondary education.

INVESTMENT IN EDUCATION

When individuals incur expenses to further their education, to acquire a new skill, to relocate to a new job, or to improve their health, they are investing in themselves. Economists refer to this spending as

FIGURE 12.1B   ANNUAL EARNINGS BY AGE AND EDUCATION, CANADIAN FEMALES, 1995

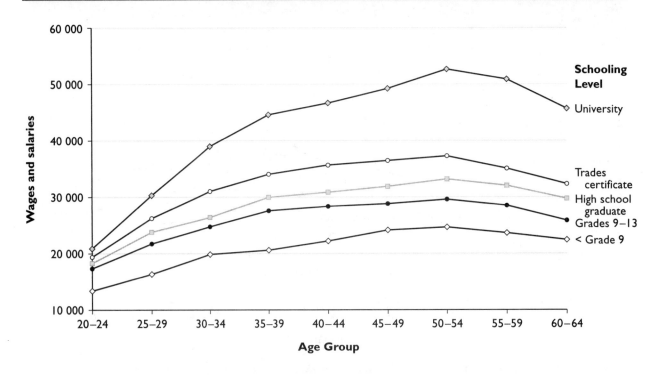

Note: Earnings are average wage and salary income of full-year (49+ weeks), full-time (30+ hours per week) workers.

Source: Authors' tabulations from the 1996 Census Public Use Microdata Files, Statistics Canada.

investment in human capital. Our discussion of human capital will focus on investment in education and training. While most individuals treat schooling as an investment in their future, schooling is also seen by many people as a consumption good. That is, individuals spend money on education for the pleasure and the satisfaction of the experience. There are certain psychic benefits associated with the learning experience and the social life while being at college or university.

THE INVESTMENT DECISION

cost-benefit analysis
a comparison of the costs and benefits of an investment

When is additional education a good investment? One way to find out is to compare the cost of the investment with the benefits derived from it. This is called a **cost-benefit analysis**. There are two types of costs accruing to the individual: direct costs and opportunity costs. Direct costs include tuition fees, books, and other educational expenses. They may also include the increase in living and travel expenses associated with living away from home. An opportunity cost is the lost income that a person could have earned had he or she been working rather than attending college or university. Opportunity costs depend on the labour force experience and skills of the individual who is sacrificing an income to attend school. A chartered accountant with 10 years' work experience who returns to school to earn a computer science degree will have much higher opportunity costs compared to a freelance writer with two years' part-time work experience who is enrolling in a certificate program in journalism. Balanced against these costs are the benefits obtained from spending on education. These benefits may be monetary or non-monetary. Pursuing more education may allow an individual to select a job that is associated with relatively higher wages, attractive working hours, or social status and prestige.

To apply the cost-benefit approach, consider the following. After finishing high school at age 18, should an individual seek full-time employment with the goal of working continuously until age 65? Or should the individual attend university for four years from age 18 to 21 inclusive and then work continuously from age 22 to retirement at age 65? From the perspective of human capital, the answer depends on the costs in comparison to the monetary benefits. Figure 12.2 illustrates the age-earnings profiles resulting from the two different investment strategies. Entering the workforce at age 18 produces the profile indicated by the label "High school." Pursuing a university degree is described by the profile labelled "University." The costs and benefits of attending university can readily be seen. The direct costs are shown by the area where the university profile lies below zero on the vertical axis. The size of the direct costs depends on such factors as whether the individual enrolls in a professional or liberal arts program, obtains a scholarship, lives in residence, and so on. The indirect costs or forgone earnings are indicated by the earnings that a high school graduate would receive in the first four years of employment. Had the individual not gone to the university, he or she would be earning this money. The size of these opportunity costs depends on the earnings that a high school graduate is able to make and whether or not the university student works part-time while in school. Although not shown in Figure 12.2, the opportunity cost of attending university may extend several years beyond age 22 if the university graduate begins work at a lower salary than what the high school graduate is earning at age 22. Finally, note that the opportunity cost of attending university outweighs the direct cost in Figure 12.2. The lost earnings from even a relatively low-skilled full-

FIGURE 12.2   BENEFITS AND COSTS OF FOUR YEARS OF UNIVERSITY EDUCATION

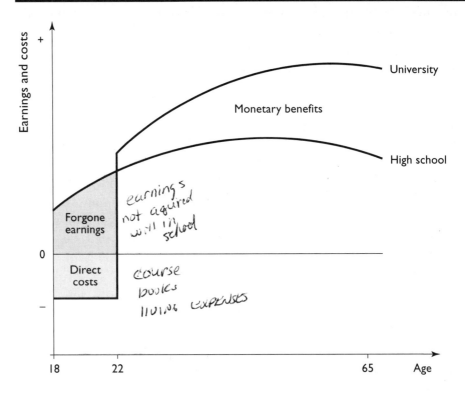

time job generally exceed the direct expenses of attending a post-secondary institution. With rapidly rising tuition fees and falling relative wages for less-skilled workers, the composition of total costs as described in Figure 12.2, however, may be reversed in the near future.

The monetary benefits of a university education are the higher after-tax earnings that the university graduate is able to command in the job market. In Figure 12.2, these monetary benefits are given by the difference between the age-earnings profiles for high school and university.

Following the cost-benefit approach, the question about the investment in four additional years of post-secondary education is resolved by the following criterion: If the benefits exceed the costs, the investment is worthwhile. If the area labelled "Monetary benefits" in Figure 12.2 is larger than the area indicated by direct costs and forgone earnings, the investment should be undertaken. Alternatively, if the costs exceed the benefits, the investment will not be advisable. This rule, however, is not as simple as it sounds. The dollar value of the costs and benefits are not directly comparable. Costs and benefits accrue at different points in time. The costs of acquiring the university degree in the example are incurred over four years, while the benefits are obtained over many years in the future. To compare the benefits with the costs, both must be calculated in terms of their present value.

Let us have a look at the procedure usually used to compare present and future receipts and outlays.

PRESENT VALUE. Would you rather receive $1000 now or $1000 a year from now? The answer is straightforward. If you had $1000 now, you could invest it in a savings account, term deposit, treasury bill, or bond, and receive interest. Suppose you invested $1000 for one year at a rate of interest of 10%. Then at the end of the year you would receive $1000 × .10 = $100, which, with the return of the principal $1000, would give you

$$\$1000 + \$1000 \times .10 = \$1000(1 + .10) = \$1100$$

The future value (FV) of $1000 received now would be worth $1100 a year from now.

If you invested the $1000 for two years at 10%, compounded annually, the future value of the $1000 at the end of that time would be

$$FV = \$1000\ [(1+.10)(1+.10)] = \$1000(1+.10)^2 = \$1000 \times 1.21 = \$1210$$

The future value of a sum of money (Y) in year (n) if invested at a given rate of interest (i) is given by the formula:

$$FV = Y\,(1 + i)^n$$

The formula tells us how much a sum of money invested today at a given interest rate will be worth in the future.

Let's turn the argument around and ask: What is today's worth of a sum of money received in the future? Or applied to the previous example: What is the **present value** (PV) of $1100 received at the end of a year worth now, given an interest rate of 10%?

Since the future value of $1000 at the end of the year is

$$FV = \$1000(1 + .10) = \$1100$$

the present value of $1100 is

$$PV = \$1100 / (1 + .10) = \$1000$$

Similarly, the present value of $1210 received at the end of two years is

$$PV = \$1210 / (1 + .10)^2 = \$1210 / 1.21 = \$1000$$

present value the current value of a future sum of money

The general formula for the present value of a future sum of money (Y) received in year (n) is:

$$PV = \frac{Y}{(1 + i)^n}$$

The formula permits us to translate amounts received at different dates in the future into their equivalent current value. Once we have translated those amounts into their current value we can add or subtract them directly. The present value of Y dollars is also called the discounted present value. The term "discounted" comes from the fact that the income received in a future year is discounted, with $1/(1+ i)$ being the discount factor. The interest rate (i) is sometimes called the discount rate. The discount rate is a measure of what we lose by receiving our money later rather than now. It is the *opportunity cost* of not having the money sooner. Since the interest rate is always positive, the discount factor is always less than 1. Having a dollar next year is worth less than having a dollar today.

The PV formula shows that the present value is determined by two factors: the length of time, indicated by n, and the interest rate. The more distant in time the payment is received, that is the larger n, the lower the present value of the same Y dollars. The higher the discount rate i, the lower the present value. For example, if $i = 5\%$, the value today of a dollar next year is $1/1.05 = 95$ cents; if $i = 10\%$, the value today of a dollar next year is $1/1.10 = 91$ cents. The interest rate, or discount rate, is influenced by current financial markets. If the interest rate on savings deposits at banks, for example, is high, the opportunity cost of spending this money on education is high.

Let us return now to our example of the decision whether to invest in a university or college education. Assume a person receives income after graduation each year until reaching age 65. To determine the monetary benefits from the investment in four years of post-secondary education requires calculating the present value of the income stream earned by the high school graduate and college graduate up to retirement.

For the high school graduate, the present value of the stream of income (PV^{HS}) is:

$$PV^{HS} = Y_{18} + \frac{Y_{19}}{(1 + i)} + \frac{Y_{20}}{(1 + i)^2} + \dots + \frac{Y_{64}}{(1 + i)^{46}}$$

where Y_{18} is the income received in the year of graduation, Y_{19} is the income received next year (when the graduate is 19), and so on. The last income received before retirement is Y_{64}.

The university graduate starts receiving income only at age 22. Since the decision of whether to invest in more education is made at age 18, the first income received at age 22 has to be discounted over four years. The income received at age 23 has to be discounted over five years, and so on. The present value of the stream of income for the university graduate (PV^U) is:

$$PV^U = \frac{Y_{22}}{(1+i)^4} + \frac{Y_{23}}{(1+i)^5} + \cdots \frac{Y_{64}}{(1+i)^{46}}$$

Converting the income streams of the high school and university graduate into their present value has a dramatic impact on the relative benefits of a post-secondary education. As we saw earlier, the more distant the receipt of income, the more heavily it is discounted and the less its present value. This fact clearly bears on the decision of whether to invest in post-secondary education. The high school graduate earns an income from age 18 to 22. Because of its immediacy, this income is discounted relatively little. The university graduate, on the other hand, forgoes current income for the promise of higher income in the future. Because these higher earnings are not realized for several years, they are worth considerably less in terms of their present value. Assume that the university graduate obtains a job at 22 years of age, that the student expects to retire at the end of age 64, and that the earnings estimated over that work life amount to $2 433 000 (in 1992 dollars). Using a discount rate of 5%, the present value of this income stream would be reduced to $629 000. Suppose the person had instead entered the labour market after graduation from high school and that the estimated earning stream from age 18 to the end of 64 would be $1 753 000. Discounted with 5%, the present value of the total income would be $503 000. While both income streams are greatly reduced in value, the income stream of the university graduate is reduced the most when converted to present value. The difference in total lifetime earnings of $680 000 ($2 433 000 – $1 753 000) is reduced to $126 000 ($629 000 – $503 000), once the earnings are discounted over the respective work lives.

So far we have looked only at the monetary benefits of pursuing a post-secondary education compared to entering the labour force directly after high school graduation. Since the investment decision is based on a comparison of benefits and costs, we now have to include the cost of university studies. The university graduate incurs costs over four years. The costs at ages 19, 20, and 21 must be discounted back to age 18. The present value of the (PV_C) is

$$PV_c = C_{18} + \frac{C_{19}}{(1 + i)} + \frac{C_{20}}{(1 + i)^2} + \frac{C_{21}}{(1 + i)^{46}}$$

Assume that the costs of pursuing a four-year degree are $15 000 for the first year, $16 000 for the second year, $18 000 the third year, and $20 000 the fourth year. The discounted value of the total cost of $69 000 using a discount rate of 5% would be:

$$PV = \$15\ 000 + \frac{\$16\ 000}{(1.05)} + \frac{\$18\ 000}{(1.05)^2} + \frac{\$20\ 000}{(1.05)^3}$$

$$= \$15\ 000 + \$15\ 238.10 + \$16\ 326.53 + \$17\ 277.12 = \$63\ 841.75$$

Subtracting the present value of the costs from the present value of the income stream in the previous formula yields the *net present value* of the income stream. In our example, the net present value of the income stream for the university graduate is $629 000 − $63 841.75 = $565 158.25. Once the net present value of alternative income streams is determined, the following decision rule can be applied: Select the human capital investment that yields the highest net present value. If the net present value of the investment in a university education is higher than the net present value of the income stream received after graduating from high school, then the investment in university education is worthwhile. In our example, the investment should be undertaken because the net present value of the post-secondary education, $565 158.25, is larger than the net present value of the income stream received by the high school graduate, $503 000.

INTERNAL RATE OF RETURN. An alternative way to decide whether post-secondary education is a good investment is to calculate the internal rate of return and to compare it with the market rate of interest. The **internal rate of return** is the discount rate (i), which equalizes the present value of the costs and benefits from a decision to invest in post-secondary education. If the internal rate of return of an investment is greater than or equal to the market rate of interest, the investment in education is profitable.

internal rate of return
the discount rate that equalizes the present value from both the benefits and the costs of an investment

Another way to look at the internal rate of return is to describe it as the discount rate that equalizes the net present value of two income streams. In our example, the internal rate of return would be the interest rate that makes the net present value of a high school graduate's lifetime earnings equal to the net present value of the lifetime earnings of a university graduate. The meaning of the rate of return can be illustrated with the help of Figure 12.2. If the discount rate were zero, the value of the income stream of the university graduate would far exceed the lifetime income of the high school graduate. As the discount rate increases,

AN INTRODUCTION TO THE CANADIAN LABOUR MARKET

the earnings of both graduates are discounted more than at a lower interest rate. As the discount rate increases, the earnings of a university graduate need to be much higher than those of a high school graduate in order for the net present value of the university graduate's earnings to be greater than those of the high school graduate. At some value of i, the present value of the age-earnings profiles of the high school and university graduate will be equal. This value of i is the internal rate of return: it is the minimum rate of return the university graduate needs to make on the investment in post-secondary education.

PRIVATE AND SOCIAL RATES OF RETURN

In addition to individual, or private, costs and benefits of post-secondary education, there are social costs and benefits. To assess the costs and benefits of spending on education, it is necessary to estimate both the private rate of return and the social rate of return. The **private rate of return** is the yield on the investment in education that is received by the person making the investment. The **social rate of return** measures the yield to society from the resources spent on education.

The cost used in calculating the private rate of return significantly understates the true cost of obtaining a post-secondary education. Education is heavily subsidized by taxpayers' dollars. Also, many students receive financial assistance from family members and scholarships from various organizations. To calculate the social rate of return, costs must include expenditures by government and non-profit institutions as well as expenditures by students and families.

On the benefit side, the returns from education are calculated on income before taxes. If we assume that firms pay workers an income equal to their productivity, the income received by graduates indicates their contribution to society. A more productive labour force is better able to provide higher quality goods and services at a lower cost. Society also receives other benefits from spending on education. Further education makes for better informed and more responsible citizens. This suggests that the social return calculated from pre-tax earnings is a minimum return—the floor of a true overall return. Some benefits may be difficult to measure in terms of dollars and cents.

private rate of return
yield on the investment in education received by the person making the investment

social rate of return
yield to society from the resources allocated to education

BOX 12.1 Who Should Pay for Higher Education?

Who should go to college or university? One answer could be those best qualified to benefit from higher education, regardless of family background, gender, or race. But there is the question of cost. Post-secondary education is expensive. Who should pay for it? There are two sides in the debate.

One side argues that higher education is essentially a private investment. People who undertake the investment benefit from it through higher lifetime income. Some also enjoy the learning experience. So why should post-secondary education be provided at public expense? Why shouldn't it be sold to cover cost?

Although tuition fees for college and undergraduate university studies have increased in Canada on average by 126% between 1990 and 1999 (the increases range from 43% in British Columbia to 194% in Alberta), students still pay less than 30% of the cost of their education. The largest portion is paid by government. Students thus receive a big scholarship and they receive this without regard to financial need: students from rich families benefit the same way as students from poor families do. Studies show that individuals from higher income families are more likely to attend post-secondary institutions than individuals from lower income families. Government subsidies to reduce tuition thus provide assistance to predominantly higher income families rather than to lower income families. Government spending on higher education involves an income transfer in the wrong direction, from the lower to the higher income families.

For these reasons, it is argued, the student, and not society, should bear the cost of higher education.

The other side argues that post-secondary education should be provided at less than full cost to all students because the benefits from education accrue not only to the individual student but also to society in large. A better educated labour force is likely to be a more productive one, which will result in more and better quality products. Scientific and medical advances are associated with a better educated population. Those who receive a post-secondary education are also likely to earn higher incomes and pay more taxes. Higher tax revenues allow governments to redistribute income to lower income families. There should be a higher standard of living for all Canadians. The argument that education benefits all of society is made to support free elementary and secondary education, so why stop at the end of high school? Why not extend the same reasoning through to college and university level?

If the price of higher education is closer to its full cost, students from low-income families will be less able to afford higher education. Someone who wishes to buy a major item, such as a car or a house, can save a certain amount of money over time and then can borrow the rest, putting up the car or the house as collateral on the loan. It takes time for a student to save the necessary funds, during which the student grows older and passes beyond the usual age of attending college or university. The option to borrow does not exist because, unlike in the case of a car or house, there is no collateral to put up.

But do the student loan programs offered by the government not provide sufficient funds for students? Studies indicate that students from low-income families are more risk averse. They are reluctant to take large loans because their families cannot be counted on if they run into problems to repay the loans later. Even if loans are available, high tuition set at or close to full cost will deter these students from attending a post-secondary institution.

Implications of Human Capital Theory

An objection sometimes made against human capital theory is that people do not really make decisions in the manner just described. Few college or university students would calculate the rate of return to a post-secondary education. Nonetheless, evidence suggests that the decision to attend college or university is significantly influenced by the benefits and costs of post-secondary education. The usefulness of this approach to educational expenditures can be determined by comparing its predictions with actual behaviour.

Effect of Costs on Enrolment.   One prediction is that any factor that reduces the cost of a college or university education should lead to an increase in post-secondary school enrolments. Scholarships, fellowships, and tuition waivers reduce the direct costs of higher education and should make educational investment more attractive. Increases in tuition fees or reductions in low-cost student loans would have the opposite effect. A reduction in the opportunity costs would also raise the rate of return to education, making college or university attendance more attractive. Many colleges and universities have recognized this fact by offering evening classes so that students may continue to work, either full-time or part-time, thus reducing the forgone costs of higher education. Research supports the prediction that college enrolments are sensitive to the costs of education.

Timing of Education over One's Work Life.   Another prediction is that investment in education will vary with age. Younger people will benefit more in monetary terms from a post-secondary education than older people. The reasons are twofold. First, older persons have fewer years of work life remaining during which to recoup the costs of the additional education. Second, as workers age, their earnings increase as a result of more work experience, training, and seniority. This increases the opportunity cost of leaving work to further one's education. The opportunity cost of leaving a job at age 40 to attend college or university is much higher than the opportunity cost at age 20. While educational patterns have been changing more recently, the vast majority of post-secondary students are still in younger age groups (18 to 24), as the theory suggests.

Labour Force Attachment.   A third prediction is that people with a weak labour force attachment will invest less in education. The fewer years spent in the labour force, the less time there is to recoup the cost of education. This prediction seems to be supported by the trend in labour force participation rates and university enrolment of women. In the late 1940s, about 25% of women were in the labour force, compared to 85% of men. At that time, most undergraduate degrees were awarded to men. Fifty years later, in 1998, 58% of women were in the labour force, many pursuing full-time careers. For these women, a post-secondary education became a much more attractive investment. The stronger labour force attachment of women has increased the attractiveness of educational expenditure. Today women obtain more than half of all undergraduate degrees in Canada.

EARNINGS DIFFERENTIALS.   Fourth, human capital theory predicts that people with more education should also have higher earnings in their peak work years. This prediction is supported by the age-earnings profiles shown in Figure 12.1a and Figure 12.1b. There are three reasons for this prediction:

- Higher earnings are necessary to compensate for the costs associated with additional schooling. If the earnings of a college graduate were no greater than those of a high school graduate, there would be little financial incentive to attend college or university. For the same reason, the annual earnings of a medical doctor must exceed those of a person with a four-year degree to keep the rate of return to a medical degree competitive.

- People with more education have fewer years in the labour force in which to recoup their investment in schooling. The high school graduate, for example, has 47 years of earnings between age 18 and 65; the person with a Ph.D. may have only 35 years or so (from age 30 to 65) in the labour force. Fewer working years plus additional costs require that actual dollar earnings be greater for people with more years of schooling in order to induce them to invest in human capital.

- Higher earnings from education are not received until relatively later in life and are heavily discounted in terms of their present value. The earnings of doctors or lawyers are received relatively far in the future compared to those of high school graduates. To make investment in education attractive, dollar earnings must be greater for persons with more years of education as a reward for postponing earnings and consumption.

CHANGES IN PRIVATE RETURNS OVER TIME

The rate of return on post-secondary education can vary over time. It is not a constant value. Using the supply and demand framework, in Figure 12.3 we show how changes in the supply and demand for workers with post-secondary degrees have affected the rate of return to post-secondary education from the early 1960s to the late 1980s. Notice the difference in notation on the axes of Figure 12.3 as compared to earlier labour market diagrams. On the vertical axis is the rate of return instead of the wage rate. The two variables are closely linked. As wage rates for college- and university-educated workers increase, so do rates of return, all other things remaining the same. On the horizontal axis is the number of workers who graduated from college or university expressed as a proportion of the total labour force.

   In times of a high rate of return to college or university education, many new students will be attracted to pursuing post-secondary education. Conversely, a low rate of return will deter many potential entrants. This response to changes in the rate of return is described by the supply curve S in Figure 12.3. The supply curve relates the fraction

FIGURE 12.3   SUPPLY AND DEMAND FOR COLLEGE/ UNIVERSITY GRADUATES

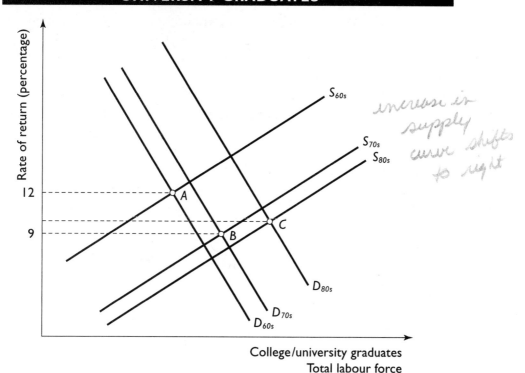

College/university graduates
Total labour force

of college or university students in the labour force to the rate of return to college or university education. The supply curve slopes upward. With a higher rate of return, more students will continue on to college or university. Corresponding to this supply curve is the demand curve D, describing employers' hiring plans for educated workers, which slopes downward. When the rate of return to post-secondary degrees/certificates is high, implying higher additional pay for college or university graduates, firms prefer to use fewer college educated workers.

Point A describes the equilibrium rate of return for an undergraduate university degree in the late 1960s. The rate of return was estimated at between 10% and 14%. The rapid growth in the population with post-secondary degrees or certificates during the 1970s shifted the supply curve to the right. The expansion of the educated labour force resulted from the entry of the baby-boom generation into the labour market. Since demand did not increase as much, earnings of college/university graduates dropped and as a result the rate of return to a college or university education declined significantly during the 1970s, as shown by the intersection at point B. Estimates of the private after-tax rate of return for the decade range from 7% to 13%. The decline in the rate of return was reversed in the 1980s, when the demand for workers with post-secondary degrees or certificates shifted out significantly. At the same time fewer educated baby-boomers entered the labour force. Post-secondary education became a better investment in the 1980s than it was in the 1970s, as is reflected in point C.

In Chapter 7, we noted the growing polarization of earnings between low-skilled workers and high-skilled workers. The polarization reflects the increasing returns to education in recent years. As employment has shifted from the primary resource and manufacturing sectors to the dynamic services industries, the demand for skilled, educated workers has increased. Other factors noted in Chapter 7 that are having a positive effect on the demand for skilled/educated workers are increasing international competition and continual technological change.

EDUCATION AND THE DISTRIBUTION OF INDIVIDUAL EARNINGS

One of the social issues that raises major concern is the inequality of income. Since the largest component of income for most people is the amount earned from work, income inequality reflects inequality of earnings. According to 1996 Census data, 8.9% of Canadian workers earned less than $15 000, while nearly 18% earned more than $50 000. What can account for this wide dispersion in earnings between individuals? Human capital theory suggests a number of important factors such as years of schooling, quality of schooling, age, mental ability, and family background. To isolate the impact of each factor on earnings, economists have used the statistical method of linear regression to estimate human capital earnings functions. The dependent variable in an earnings function is an individual's annual earnings; the independent or explanatory variables are all the factors thought to influence earnings.

The simplest earnings function would include only years of schooling, or highest educational level attained. Studies of that kind have found that differences in years of schooling among individuals can account for only a small portion of the overall difference in earnings—between 10% and 15%. As shown in the age-earnings profiles in Figure 12.1, individuals with the same level of education have very different levels of earnings depending on their age at the time the data are collected. By including an age variable in the earnings function, approximately 30% of the dispersion in earnings can be accounted for by differences in schooling and age. If differences in age and schooling account for only 30% of the differences in individual earnings, other factors must be important in explaining earnings differentials.

ABILITY. Particular attention has been given to the role of ability as a cause of individual earning differentials. People with greater ability often will invest more in education and training. If a measure of ability is not included in the earnings function, the higher earnings of the individual will be mistakenly attributed to the effect of extra schooling when, in fact, both the amount of schooling and earnings may be due to the individual's greater ability.

Disentangling the effects of ability and schooling on earnings is fraught with problems. One problem concerns the measurement of ability. Earning an income involves many different dimensions of ability, ranging from a soprano singer's ability to hold a high C to the quick reflex of a professional boxer to the ability of an electronics engineer to solve complex mathematical problems. Most often, however, ability is treated as synonymous with intelligence or mental capacity. To obtain an empirical measure of intelligence, most studies have used intelligence quotient (IQ) test scores, or scores on various types of aptitude tests. Whether or not IQ scores are a valid measure of intelligence is open to debate. Studies have found a strong positive relationship between IQ and educational attainment. People who are "smarter" also have generally more education.

The results of these studies have been criticized on several counts. One criticism is that measured IQ scores fail to capture many aspects of ability. This failure reduces the estimated impact of ability on earnings. A salesperson with a relatively low IQ may be highly successful and earn large commissions because of the ability to be a smooth talker. Second, ability itself may be to a large extent the result of another variable—family background.

FAMILY BACKGROUND. Family background includes such factors as parents' income, education, occupational status, and connections. Children raised in families of higher socioeconomic position may score better on IQ tests as a result of better care and parental instruction. This possibility is at the heart of the old nature versus nurture debate. How much is difference in IQ scores due to heredity or to the environment in which one is raised? The more important nurture is, the more important family background becomes as a determinant of both educational attainment and earnings and the less important inherited intelligence becomes.

How to disentangle the independent effects of family background, ability, and education on earnings is an unresolved problem. A novel approach to resolve the problem is to use large samples of identical and fraternal twins. The advantage of these samples are that identical twins do not differ genetically while fraternal twins do. This allows researchers to identify the effect of differences in ability on the earnings of persons who have identical family backgrounds. In one study that did not control either for ability or for family background among the twins in the sample, the rate of return to additional schooling was found to be 8%. When the influence of family background was controlled for, the rate of return fell to 6%. When both family background and genetic ability were introduced into the earnings function, the rate of return fell to 3%. The implication of these findings is that about two thirds of the estimated effect of additional education on income was really due the fact that those individuals who obtained more education were also of higher ability, or had a more favourable family background.

SCHOOL QUALITY. Another factor that might lead to differences in earnings is variation in school quality. If two people of equal ability made the same dollar expenditure on schooling, but one received schooling of higher quality, presumably that person would receive higher earnings and a greater rate of return. As with ability, there are obvious difficulties in obtaining a measure of school quality. One approach has been to include in the earnings function a variable for average expenditures per student in the individual's school district. Studies using this approach found that attendance in higher quality schools had a significant positive effect on earnings.

THE LINK BETWEEN EDUCATION AND EARNINGS

The age-earnings profiles and empirical studies convincingly show a strong link between years or levels of formal education and the earnings of an individual. Why does more education lead to higher earnings? The answer, according to human capital theory, is that more education leads to higher productivity, which in turn is reflected in higher earnings. Additional schooling is viewed as enhancing those abilities that make people more productive at work. These abilities include logical reasoning, communication and writing skills, as well as more specific job skills learned in accounting, engineering, and other professional courses. The reason a community college graduate earns more than a high school graduate, or business majors earn more than history majors, is that they have skills that employers consider to enhance productivity and are willing to pay extra for.

EDUCATION AS A SIGNAL

Some economists disagree with the argument that more education makes a person more productive. They maintain that the primary reason that education and earnings go hand in hand is because employers use educational credentials such as degrees and certificates as a *screening device*. According to this view, the educational system is a means of finding out who is productive rather than a system that increases the productivity of workers. Remember that at the time of hiring, employers are not sure of the actual productivity of an applicant. To improve the probability that the best worker is chosen, prospective employees can be given aptitude tests or other tests. References can be checked. In addition, firms use educational credentials as an indicator to sort or screen prospective workers into those most likely to be high- and low-productivity employees. When employers use the level of education as a signal of an applicant's potential productivity, it is known as

signalling the use of educational credentials as an indicator of a worker's potential productivity

signalling. According to the human capital approach, education and earnings are positively related because education itself increases a person's productivity on the job. Following the signalling approach, more education leads to higher earnings because employers have found that educational credentials are a reliable signal concerning trainability and subsequent productivity on the job.

THE JOB COMPETITION MODEL

An example of the screening view of education is provided by the job competition model. Most job skills are not acquired before one enters the labour market. Rather, they are obtained through on-the-job training and learning by doing. One can view the labour market as primarily a training market where firms have training slots to be filled at the bottom of the job ladder and workers compete to be hired. From the firm's perspective, the decision regarding which worker to hire is not based on who will work for the lowest wage, but rather on who is most trainable. Because the firm is uncertain about which applicant can be trained at the least cost, it must screen or sort the applicants into a queue, from highest expected productivity to lowest based on each worker's signals. From the viewpoint of the applicants, the competition in the labour market is over obtaining access to the firm's job ladder (hence the name job competition model). To obtain access sets off a race among workers to acquire the background characteristics and credentials that employers value most.

The role of education in the job competition model is quite different than in the human capital model. According to the job competition model, education does not itself lead to greater productivity for workers. Rather, it identifies the workers who possess the character traits such as intelligence, discipline, perseverance, and communication skills that are necessary for success on the job. As in the human capital model, additional years of education result in additional earnings. These extra earnings from education, however, are *not* a payment resulting from the productivity of the person's human capital. Instead, they are a payment for the individual's pre-existing ability and intelligence that education signals.

These two views of schooling have created considerable debate over the social benefits of additional expenditures on education. According to the human capital approach, additional resources devoted to education are an important source of economic growth because they represent an investment in upgrading the work skills and productive capacity of the nation's workforce. From a screening perspective, the social benefits from additional expenditures on education are more dubious. At its best in this context, education adds to productivity by enabling firms to identify superior-quality employees. At its worst, the main effect is to set off a "paper chase" as workers invest in ever higher educational degrees in order to compete for jobs. An example is the trend toward increasing professionalization of occupations that ties professional status to educational certificates. Access to a growing number of occupational positions is monitored through educational credentials. The increasing dependence of occupational status on educational certificates causes individuals to make higher educational investments in order to achieve these certificates. As more and more people satisfy the educational entrance requirements for certain occupations, firms respond with educational upgrading of these occupations. This process has been called the "inflation of educational certificates."

EMPIRICAL EVIDENCE

A number of studies have attempted to sort out to what degree the positive relationship between education and earnings is caused by screening and productivity. The results are not clear cut. Some empirical tests conclude that years of schooling and various types of academic credentials raise a person's income regardless of any productivity that may have been acquired in the educational process. For example, one study looked at the starting salaries of university graduates who majored in economics. The authors' idea was that if earnings are strictly related to productivity, then economics majors who took jobs that used their academic training should be paid more than those who took jobs unrelated to their field of study. They could find no difference in the starting salaries of the two groups, leading them to conclude that employers were using a university degree in economics as a means of screening applicants. An additional piece of evidence that education is used as a screening device is the so-called "sheepskin effect." Studies have typically found that the rate of return on the last year of high school (for example, the 12th year) is much higher than the rate for the penultimate year (the 11th year). Such findings suggest that acquiring a high school certificate or diploma has a large effect on earnings that exceeds whatever additional knowledge was gained in that one extra year of education.

Other studies conclude that education has direct effects on productivity. One study compared the years of schooling obtained by self-employed workers with those of contractually employed workers. If education were only used as a screening device, one would expect self-employed people to have lower educational levels. People who planned on being self-employed would invest in only the amount that could be justified from a productivity point of view, while salaried workers would invest in additional schooling for its value as credential. The study, however, found only negligible differences in educational levels between these two groups.

Independent of empirical evidence, there is a sound economic reason to doubt that education serves only as a signal for screening purposes. If education had only a signalling function, firms and workers alike would probably have found a less costly method of identifying worker productivity. The fact that education continues to be used as a central screening device indicates that it improves the skills of workers in a way that firms value.

On-the-Job Training

Formal education is one type of human capital investment. On-the-job training (OJT) is another one. OJT offered by employers varies from formal programs that are very much like classroom instruction to the simple forms of learning by doing, e.g., observing others. Relatively little is known about the extent of employer-based training in Canadian industry. This is partly due to the problem of defining what constitutes training. A recent "survey of surveys" suggests that roughly one third of firms in Canada provide formal training. Estimates of the incidence of training (percentage of employees who received training) are considerably higher—between 60% and 70%—when informal training is included.[1] A few studies have compared the training efforts in Canada with those in other countries and concluded that Canadian firms train employees less than their counterparts in other major industrialized countries. These conclusions are based on a range of indicators including the percentage of employees receiving training, the percentage of firms providing training, private sector expenditures on training, and the incidence of apprenticeship training. A recent Statistics Canada study using average training hours per employee concludes

---

1. What is the distinction between formal and informal training? Two examples of definitions: The Human Resource Training and Development Survey defines formal training as programs that have "an identifiable structured plan and objectives designed to develop a worker's skill and competence." Informal training, as defined by the Small Business Panel Survey, includes training "acquired by working under normal work or production conditions, either with an experienced worker or under the direction of a supervisor."

AN INTRODUCTION TO THE CANADIAN LABOUR MARKET

that Canada's training effort is average when compared to that of other countries.

On-the-job training is as much a form of human capital investment as a college or university education since it involves costs and benefits. Where the training is clearly a separable activity, these costs can be identified fairly straightforwardly. The direct costs include the salaries of training staff and the operating and capital costs of equipment used in training. Where training takes place concurrently with production, the costs, although of the same general kind, may be more difficult to measure. Some of the trainees' time and that of their supervisors or co-workers is used in training; output is therefore less than it would be if all workers were fully trained. For the same reason, capital cost may be higher than normal. Material may be wasted or products may be defective due to the trainee's inexperience. Workers may also bear some of the costs of acquiring OJT by agreeing to work at reduced wages during the training period. The benefit to the firm is that its workforce becomes more productive, which will result in greater profits. Workers benefit

---

BOX 12.2 A Training Tax to Solve the Free Rider Problem

Employer-based training is an investment in human capital. Firms will undertake the investment only if the net present value of the investment is positive. During the training, the cost of training, which includes the wage the trainee receives, often exceeds the value of that trainee to the employer. Firms are thus faced with a loss if the trainee goes elsewhere after a short term of employment. Unlike with investments in physical or financial capital, many employers do not want to take the risk of investing in training. They want a free ride in the training system. "You train, I'll hire," they say.

As for the employees, faced with a dwindling number of jobs with career ladders, how can they rationally plan a training investment? What skills will pay off? As jobs become less permanent, employees switch employers more frequently. As a result, they do not know what skills they will need or how long those skills will be relevant. Who wants to waste money on skills that will go unused?

There is no shortage of policy proposals to overcome the lack of training opportunities in the private sector. The recommendations range from general subsidies to firms' training costs to special grants for training programs designed to train workers in fields of critical shortage to accelerating the depreciation of machinery used in training to tax credits.

Another proposal is a training tax. France levies a training tax of 1.5% of payroll. The purpose is not to raise tax revenue for the government but to make it rational for an employer to train, because employers can deduct their expenditures for training. Thus if they spend 1.5% of their payroll on training their workers, they pay no training tax. Since the firm would lose the money if it did not train, training becomes a free good as far as the firm is concerned. Employers are not told what skills to teach their workers, but they are effectively told that they must teach some skills. If all employers are obliged to invest, no one gets a free ride.

because they gain additional skills and experience that increase their earning power and bargaining strength in the labour market.

GENERAL AND SPECIFIC TRAINING

general training
training that increases the worker's productivity not only in the firm providing the training but also in other firms

specific training
training that increases the worker's productivity only in the firm providing the training

It is conventional to draw a distinction between general and specific training. **General training** is training that increases a worker's productivity not only in the firm providing it, but also at other firms. An example is apprenticeship training for crafts such as electrician or carpenter where the skills learned are of general value throughout the industry. Computer skills or supervisory skills are also often transferable. Less formalized types of training such as how to operate a word processor or a bulldozer also work to enhance an employee's productivity both in the firm providing the training and in other firms. **Specific training** increases the worker's productivity only in the firm providing it, such as training in the operation of a firm's wage payment system or an assembly line job. Skill specificity may arise out of unique features of the firm's product. A computer engineer employed by IBM, for example, would develop many skills of value to IBM, but this knowledge may be of far less value to another company with computers of different design. Although few types of OJT are truly specific in nature, many job skills do have a firm-specific component. Furthermore, regardless of whether a person is a clerk, salesperson, or manager, with experience on the job each worker in the firm acquires a detailed knowledge of the organizational structure and operation of the firm that is itself a valuable but very firm-specific type of training.

BENEFITS AND COSTS OF ON-THE-JOB TRAINING

For OJT to be undertaken, it must promise a rate of return competitive with other investments. The rate of return is a function of the benefits and costs of training, which are illustrated in Figure 12.4.

The horizontal line EG at W_A gives the wage and marginal revenue product (MRP) of the untrained worker over a work life. The stepped line $ABCD$ gives the wage and marginal revenue product of the worker who undergoes training. During the training period, the worker's wage and marginal productivity (W_0) is lower than it would have been had the worker chosen alternative employment. After training the wage rate and marginal productivity increase to W_1.[2] The cost of training is the

---

2. For simplicity, it is assumed the worker receives one "dose" of training and that the economic value of the training does not depreciate over time.

FIGURE 12.4   BENEFITS AND COSTS OF ON-THE-JOB TRAINING

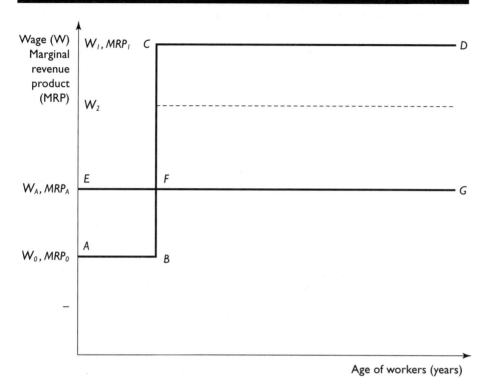

value of production forgone during the training process, shown by the area *AEFB*. The economic benefit is the increase in production that training makes possible, shown by the area *FCDG*. For training to be a good investment, the present value of the stream of output (in dollars) generated by the worker receiving training (the profile *ABCD*) must be at least as large as that of the output stream if no training were provided (the profile *EG*).

If we assume that training is a good investment, who bears the cost and reaps the benefit: the firm or the worker? The answer depends on whether the training is general or specific in nature. With general OJT, it is the worker who bears the cost of training. Without training the worker's marginal productivity is MRP_A. Competition among firms insures that the worker is paid a wage rate W_A corresponding with this level of productivity. If the firm were to bear the cost of training, it would have to continue to pay the worker W_A even though productivity during training is only MRP_0. What inducement does the firm have to do this? In the case of general training, the answer is none. The productivity of a worker who completes the training rises to MRP_1. If the firm were able to still pay a wage of only W_A, the difference between the value of output produced and wage paid (the distance FC) would provide it with a return on its investment. Because general training is transferable, however, were the firm to pay less than W_1 the worker would quit and find employment at a firm willing to pay a wage equal to his or her productivity. Competition for labour and the transferable nature of general training make it impossible for the firm to pay a wage less than W_1. At this wage, the firm is unable to recoup its investment, so it is unwilling to bear the costs of general training. Because firms have no incentive to pay for general OJT, the workers must pay for it. The cost of general training is the drop in productivity from MRP_A to MRP_0. A worker can pay for general training by agreeing to work during the training period for a wage of only W_0. Workers have an incentive to bear this cost since once training is completed, the wage they can demand in the market will rise to W_1, providing the return on their investment.

If on-the-job training is firm-specific, it is the firm that bears the cost. Because specific OJT is non-transferable, once training is completed the productivity of the worker at any other firm in the labour market is still only MRP_A. Even though the firm that provided the training receives a level of production worth MRP_1, it need not pay the worker more than W_A since that person can do no better elsewhere. In this case the worker has no incentive to work for a lower wage of W_0 during training since it is the firm that reaps the benefit. To induce workers to acquire specific training, the firm must bear the cost of training by paying the original unskilled wage of W_A even though the worker's productivity is only MRP_0. The return on its investment is the difference between the worker's higher productivity MRP_1 and the wage W_A that it pays after training.

In practice, the post-training wage rate paid by the firm in the case of specific training is generally higher than the minimum W_0. One possible wage might be W_2, shown by the broken line. The reason for the wage increase is that specific training creates a situation where the firm and the worker have some power over the other. Should the worker quit, the firm will lose its investment in training, so the firm is induced to share a portion of its return ($W_1 - W_A$) with the worker. The firm, however, also has power over the worker. Should the worker demand a wage rate so high that it would eliminate the firm's return on its investment, the worker would be laid off. This would cause a financial loss on the worker, who could only earn the lower wage rate of W_A at any other firm.

IMPLICATIONS OF ON-THE-JOB TRAINING

Whether training is general or specific has a number of implications for understanding the pattern of several labour market outcomes.

EMPLOYEE TURNOVER. Specific on-the-job training provides a strong incentive to both firms and workers to reduce turnover from quits and layoffs. Employee turnover is costly to a firm because the firm loses its investment in specific training. Workers with specific training also stand to lose by leaving (or being forced to leave) because there is no other employer at which their productivity and their wage will be as high. One would expect, therefore, fewer quits and layoffs among workers who have relatively more specific training.

MINIMUM WAGE. A frequent criticism of minimum wage laws is that they may lead firms to reduce the amount of general OJT provided to workers, particularly younger workers. An employer has little incentive to bear the costs of training youths because of their relatively high turnover rates. To make training attractive to the firm, the young worker must invest in himself or herself by working at a relatively low wage rate such as W_0 in Figure 12.4. The incentive to do so is that with some experience the young worker can move to a better job with higher earnings. A minimum wage law may prevent the provision of training if it places a wage floor at a level W_A. At this wage rate, the employer no longer finds it profitable to provide general training because the cost exceeds the worker's productivity.

JOB LADDERS AND INTERNAL RECRUITING. Firm-specific training is also an important factor in explaining the development of job ladders and internal recruitment within firms. For many types of production processes, a vertical or hierarchical set of job tasks builds on one another. They are often sufficiently unique to a firm that they can only be learned by workers starting at the bottom and working up. If all job skills were acquired through general OJT, there would be no internal labour markets since firms could readily hire a worker in the external labour market. The more important specific training is as a source of job skills, the less reliance the firm puts on outside recruitment. Internal promotion and advancement will be the preferred means of filling job vacancies.

AGE-EARNINGS PROFILES. If employers expect workers to stay with them for a longer period, they will be more willing to offer specific training because there is a longer pay-out period on the investment. Workers will also be more willing to undergo training if they expect to stay with the firm longer or if they are younger. In both cases, they too have a longer time over which to reap the returns on the investment. These considerations suggest that the fraction of time spent on training will be highest early in a work life. Some time late in the work life, it will neither pay for them to accept nor for the firm to offer any more training. There is not sufficient time left in the work life to make the investment pay off.

The pattern of declining investment in OJT during the work life carries specific implications for the age-earnings profiles observed in Figure 12.1. A worker's earnings capacity rises rapidly early in the work life because of the large investment in OJT. Actual earnings reflect this rapid rise in the earlier stage of the work life. A worker's stock of human capital is depreciating all the time. As time devoted to training is decreasing, the negative effect of the depreciation of skills begins to outweigh the positive impact of the diminished additional investment in additional skills. Earnings drop more rapidly near the end of the work life when the stock of skills is still depreciating and is no longer augmented by additional investment in OJT.

SUMMARY

Education is an important investment in human capital. It entails costs and benefits to the individual and to society. The costs to the individual are the direct cost of tuition, books, and other expenses and the indirect cost of the forgone earnings. The monetary benefit is the higher income the person expects to earn. For society, the costs are the opportunity costs of the tax dollars spent on education. The economic benefits are the increased production made possible by a more skilled (educated) work force.

There are two methods one can use to find out whether or not an investment in education is worthwhile: the present value method and the internal rate of return method. The private and social rates of return are likely higher than those estimated with these two methods since education yields also non-monetary benefits.

Private rates of return to post-secondary education in Canada were relatively high in the 1960s. They declined in the 1970s and rose again during the 1980s. The increase in the 1980s has been mainly due to an increase in the demand for higher educated workers.

To quantify the effects of education on earnings, economists estimate earnings functions. There are individual factors other than education affecting earnings. Among these factors are age, ability, and family background. In estimating earnings functions it is difficult to separate the contribution of these interrelated factors to earnings.

There is some debate about why earnings and education are closely related. According to human capital theory the reason is that education increases productivity and higher productivity is reflected in higher earnings. The signalling approach argues that education is used by firms as a screening device to separate the more able from the less able applicants. Empirical evidence supports both views.

Investment in human capital can also take the form of on-the-job training. General training increases an individual's productivity to many potential employers. Because skills from general training are transferable between companies, the trainee bears the cost of general training. Specific training increases an individual's productivity only in the firm that provides the training. Since the skills are not transferable, the firm bears the cost of specific training. The distinction between general and specific training is useful in understanding employee turnover, the effect of minimum wage legislation on firms' training efforts, recruitment policies of firms, and the shape of the age-earnings profiles.

KEY TERMS

age-earnings profile   324

cost-benefit analysis   326

present value   329

internal rate of return   332

private rate of return   333

social rate of return   333

signalling   342

general training   346

specific training   346

EXERCISES

1. The age-earnings profiles in Figure 12.1a and Figure 12.1b rise steeply early on, then flatten and eventually fall. Explain the falling part of the earnings profile.

2. Use the human capital approach to explain why medical doctors work on average more hours per week than most other professions.

3. Empirical studies have found that the rate of return declines with additional years of education. How could you explain this? Does the "sheepskin effect" contradict the findings of a diminishing rate of return?

4. In Canada post-secondary education is heavily subsidized by the government. Students do not bear the full cost of their education. What are the reasons for public subsidies? While there may be good reasons for subsidizing post-secondary education, there are also drawbacks. Explain what these drawbacks are.

5. Human capital theory predicts that people with weak labour force attachment will invest less in education. Why?

6. Suppose educational certificates and degrees are used as a screening device by firms and are responsible for the higher earnings of college and university graduates. Why might the private rate of return to college or university be relatively high, yet the social rate of return be relatively low?

7. Why are the costs of general training most likely to be borne by the trainee, whereas in case of firm-specific training the costs are shared by the employer and the trainee?

8. Which type of vocational training will most likely require more government subsidies: general training or firm-specific training? Explain.

9. If firms fill most jobs by promotion from within, what does this tell about the type of training they provide their employees?

10. Assume that after graduating from high school you had to decide whether to enroll in an apprenticeship training program or to enroll in a certificate program at a community college. What economic criteria would you apply in making this decision?

REFERENCES

Bar-Or, Y., Burbridge, J., Magee, L., and Robb, A. L. (1995). The Wage Premium to a University Education in Canada, 1971–1991. *Journal of Labour Economics, 13:* 762–794.

Becker, G. S. (1975). *Human Capital,* 2d ed. New York: National Bureau of Economic Research.

Betcherman, G. (1992). Are Canadian Firms Underinvesting in Training? *Canadian Business Economics, 1:* 25–33.

Betcherman, G. (1993). Research Gaps Facing Training Policy Makers. *Canadian Public Policy, 19:* 18–28.

Dooley, M. (1986). The Overeducated Canadian? Changes in the Relationship among Earnings, Education and Age for Canadian Men: 1971–1981, *Canadian Journal of Economics, 19:* 142–159.

Economic Council of Canada. (1992). *A Lot to Learn: Education and Training in Canada.* Ottawa: Minister of Supply and Services Canada.

Ehrenberg, R., and Smith, R. S. (1997). *Modern Labour Economics,* 6th ed. New York: Addison-Wesley.

Freeman, R., and Needels, K. (1995). Skill Differentials in Canada in an Era of Rising Labour Market Inequality. In D. Card and R. Freeman (Eds.), *Small Differences That Matter.* Chicago: University of Chicago Press.

Kapsalis, C. (1998). An International Comparison of Employee Training. *Perspectives on Labour and Income, 10:* 23–28.

Kaufman, B. E. (1991). *The Economics of Labour Markets,* 3rd ed. Chicago: Dryden Press.

Vaillancourt, F., and Henriques, I. (1986). The Returns to University Schooling in Canada. *Canadian Public Policy, 12:* 449–458.

GLOSSARY

actual working hours

total hours actually worked (5)

adjustment lag

period during which workers and employers react to changes in the wage rate (11)

affirmative action

policy that promotes employment equity for women, members of visible minorities, people with disabilities, and aboriginal people (11)

✓**age-earnings profile**

average hourly or annual earnings for people of different ages with the same level of education (12)

aggregate labour demand

the total number of jobs made available by firms and government agencies (5)

average labour productivity

the output produced per worker in a given period (7)

backward-bending supply curve for labour

a supply curve for labour that switches from a positive slope at lower wage rates to a negative slope at higher wage rates, with the substitution effect dominating at low wage rates and the income effect dominating at high wage rates (8)

base wage rate

the wage rate that applies to the lowest-paid classification for workers in a bargaining unit (7)

birth rate

the number of births per 1000 of population (4)

Canada Labour Code

labour standards and practices for industries that fall under federal jurisdiction, and for their employers and employees (3)

circular flow model

a visual model of the economy that shows how goods and services and money flow between households and firms via markets (2)

command system

a system in which the decisions about resource use are made by the state (2)

compensating wage differential

increase in the wage rate that compensates workers for undesirable working conditions (11)

Consumer Price Index (CPI)

a measure of the overall cost of the goods and services bought by a typical family (7)

cost-benefit analysis

a comparison of the costs and benefits of an investment (12)

craft union

a union whose members all possess a certain craft or skill (10)

cyclical unemployment

unemployment that arises because the economy does not generate enough jobs for those seeking one (6)

demand curve

a graph of the relationship between the prices of a good and the quantity demanded (2)

demand-deficient unemployment

see "cyclical unemployment" (6)

demand for labour

the stocks of job vacancies and employed workers (2)

demogrant

a lump sum payment to an individual based on membership in a particular demographic group (8)

derived demand

the demand for workers that is derived from the demand for goods and services (2)

diminishing returns

additional output decreases as a result of hiring one more worker, when other factors are fixed (2)

discouraged workers

persons who want a job but have given up the search for a job (6)

duration of unemployment

the average time each person spends unemployed (6)

economic rent

wage rate received in excess of the reservation wage rate (8)

efficiency wages

wage rates paid in excess of the equilibrium level in order to increase productivity (10)

employed

describes a person who works for pay or profit during the reference week of the Labour Force Survey (4)

employment equity

a work environment in which all barriers to employment have been removed and equitable treatment of employees exists (3)

employment rate

the ratio of employment to working-age population (5)

Engel's law

expenditures on necessities such as food are a decreasing proportion of one's income as real income increases, while expenditures on rent and clothing remain constant and expenditures on luxuries increase in proportion (5)

equalizing differences

the features of a job that compensate for wage rates that are lower than in other jobs (11)

equilibrium price

the price at which the quantity demanded equals the quantity supplied (2)

factor market

the market in which factors of production are exchanged (2)

factors of production

the inputs used to produce goods and services (labour, land, and capital) (2)

featherbedding

retaining workers who would otherwise be made redundant by technological change (10)

fertility rate

the number of births per 1000 women aged 15 to 49 years (4)

flow variable

a variable whose quantity is measured per unit of time (2)

Fordism

a mass production system that combines a small group of highly skilled managers and technically trained personnel with a workforce of relatively low education and vocational skills organized in a vertical hierarchy (2)

free-market system

a system in which the decisions about resource use are made by individuals (2)

frictional unemployment

unemployment that is inevitable even in a well-functioning labour market (6)

full employment

when the actual rate of unemployment equals the natural rate of unemployment (6)

functional flexibility
>internal labour market rules that give employers greater freedom to move employees from one job to another within the firm (5)

functional income distribution
>the share of national income going to the owners of the factors of production, labour, and capital (7)

general training
>training that increases the worker's productivity not only in the firm providing the training but also in other firms (12)

globalization
>the integration of countries through the growth in foreign trade and foreign investment (2)

gross domestic product (GDP)
>value of the goods and services produced in a given year (9)

gross national product (GNP)
>the total income earned by Canadians in a given year (7)

hidden unemployed
>discouraged workers who do not show up as unemployed on the Labour Force Survey (6)

hours paid
>hours for which workers are paid regardless of whether they were working or not (5)

human capital
>human resources considered in terms of their contributions to the economy, as in skills, education, etc. (8)

hypothesis
>tentative generalization that tends to fit the facts (1)

incidence of unemployment
>the proportion of people in the labour force entering the state of unemployment in a given period (6)

✓ **income effect (demand)**
>the effect of changes in price on how much a consumer can buy with a given income (2)

income effect (supply)
>the change in hours of work caused by a change in income (8)

income elasticity of demand
>the relationship between changes in real income and changes in the quantity demanded (5)

increasing returns to scale
>the percentage increase in output that is relatively greater than the percentage change in all the factors of production (9)

industrial union

a union whose members all work in the same industry (10)

inflation

an increase in the overall level of prices in the economy (7)

internal rate of return

the discount rate that equalizes the present value from both the benefits and the costs of an investment (12)

job rationing

practice of employers paying wages that create an excess of workers seeking employment and a shortage of jobs (10)

job search

the process of matching workers and available jobs (10)

labour force

the total number of workers, including both the employed and unemployed (4)

labour force participation rate

the percentage of the working-age population that is in the labour force (4)

labour income

earnings and supplementary labour income combined (7)

labour market

the interaction of buyers and sellers of labour services (2)

labour market barriers

restrictions on the mobility of workers from one job to another (11)

labour productivity

the output per worker (9)

labour's share

labour income as a ratio of total income (GNP) (7)

labour supply curve

graph showing the number of hours of work offered in relation to the wage rate (8)

law

a regular and repeatable pattern of events (1)

law of diminishing returns

in the short run a point will be reached at which the extra contribution of the next worker to total output will be less than that of the previously hired worker (9)

long run

a period of time during which all factors of production can be changed (2)

marginal labour cost (MLC)

the additional cost of hiring one more worker (10)

marginal productivity of labour (MPL)
> extra output obtained by adding one more worker or having a worker work one more hour (5)

marginal revenue (MR)
> the extra revenue from selling one more unit of output (9)

marginal revenue product (MRP)
> the extra revenue obtained from selling the output of an additional worker (9)

marginal tax rate
> the proportion of any additional income earned that is paid in taxes (8)

marginal workers
> workers with a weak attachment to the labour force (6)

market
> the interaction of buyers and sellers, in which a price is established and a product or service exchanged (2)

market discrimination
> different responsibilities and benefits based on characteristics unrelated to job performance (11)

mixed economy
> a combination of the command system and the free-market system (2)

monopsony
> a market in which there is only one buyer (10)

moonlighting
> multiple jobholding (5)

mortality rate
> the number of deaths per 1000 of population (4)

natural population growth
> the balance between the number of births and deaths (4)

natural rate of unemployment
> the unemployment rate that exists when the economy is functioning at full capacity (6)

net wages
> gross wages minus taxes and other payroll deductions (7)

nominal wage
> the rate of payment to workers in current dollars (7)

non-standard employment
> employment that is not full time for a full year (5)

√ **normal good**
> a good for which demand increases as one's income increases (8)

normative statement
a statement about how the world ought to be (1)

not in the labour force
describes a person who is neither employed nor unemployed (4)

numerical flexibility
a company's practice of contracting out and making greater use of temporary or part-time workers to improve flexibility in its workforce (5)

occupational licensing
the requirement that individuals practising in an occupation have a licence or certification

occupational wage structure
differences in wage rates between occupations in the labour market (11)

open economy
an economy in which imports and exports represent a large percentage of overall economic activity (5)

opportunity cost
value of the best forgone alternative when a decision is made (2)

own-account self-employment
entrepreneurs without employees (5)

pay equity
equal pay for work of equal value (3)

personal income distribution
the share of national income going to groups of families or individuals (7)

positive statement
a statement about how the world is (1)

pre-market discrimination
denial of equal opportunities to develop natural abilities and talents during pre-employment years (11)

present value
the current value of a future sum of money (12)

price elasticity of demand
the responsiveness of quantity demanded to a change in price (2) $\frac{QD}{\Delta P}$

price elasticity of supply
the responsiveness of quantity supplied to a change in price (2)

private rate of return
yield on the investment in education received by the person making the investment (12)

product market
the market in which goods and services are exchanged (2)

quasi-fixed labour costs
> non-wage costs to hiring employees that are not related to the hours of work (9)

real average labour income
> total annual labour income, adjusted for inflation, divided by average annual number of paid workers (7)

real wage
> the quantity of goods and services that can be bought with the nominal wage (7)

recession
> a period during which the total production of goods and services falls (4)

reservation wage rate
> the lowest wage rate an individual is willing to work for (8)

salaried worker
> worker paid by the week or longer time period (7)

scale effect
> the change in the number of employees hired as a result of changes in the amount of product sold (9)

scarcity
> limitation of a society's resources (2)

scientific method
> experimentation and explanations about the outcome of experiments (1)

seasonal unemployment
> unemployment resulting from the decline in the number of jobs at certain times of the year (6)

severance pay
> a lump-sum payment to an employee upon termination of employment (3)

shortage
> a situation in which quantity demanded is greater than quantity supplied (2)

short run
> a period of time during which at least one factor of production remains fixed (2)

signalling
> the use of educational credentials as an indicator of a worker's potential productivity (12)

social rate of return
> yield to society from the resources allocated to education (12)

social science
> the study of the ways in which people behave (1)

specific training
> training that increases the worker's productivity only in the firm providing the training (12)

standard working hours
> the number of hours in a standard work week as established by law, collective agreement, or company policy (5)

statistical discrimination
> discrimination that results from imperfect information in the screening process of job applicants (11)

stock variable
> a variable whose quantity is measured at a given point in time (2)

structural unemployment
> unemployment resulting from a mismatching of workers and job opportunities based either on skills or geography (6)

substitution effect (demand) (labour market)
> changes in the wage rate encourage employers to substitute capital for labour and labour for capital (9)

substitution effect (demand) (product market)
> changes in price encourage consumers to substitute one product for another (2)

substitution effect (supply)
> leisure and work hours are substituted for each other as the wage rate changes (8)

supplementary labour income
> non-wage benefits received by an employee (7)

supply curve
> a graph of the relationship between the price of a good and the quantity supplied (2)

supply of labour
> the stocks of employed and unemployed workers (2)

surplus
> a situation in which the quantity demanded by consumers is less than the quantity supplied (2)

technological unemployment
> unemployment due to advances in technical and organizational know-how occurring at a faster pace than the ability to find new uses for labour (6)

theory
> an idea or set of ideas that can be generalized to explain many kinds of events (1)

total factor productivity

the increase in output obtained from the same amount of inputs into the production process (5)

total income

the total of labour compensation and unearned income (7)

Toyotism

an organizational model involving flexible management forms of semi-independent groups linked laterally rather than vertically (2)

underemployed

describes workers who are obliged to take part-time jobs although they prefer to work full time (5)

unemployed

describes a person without work, available for work, and looking for work (4)

unemployment rate

percentage of the labour force that is unemployed (6)

union density

ratio of the number of employees belonging to a union to the total number of paid employees (3)

wage earner

worker paid by the hour or the day (7)

wage elasticity of labour demand

the change in quantity demanded in response to a change in the wage rate (9)

wage elasticity of labour supply

the responsiveness of quantity supplied to changes in the wage rate (8)

wage rate

the price established in the labour market (2)

wage subsidy

a payment by government to an employer to assist in paying wages (10)

working-age population (labour force source population)

the Canadian population aged 15 years or over, excluding members of the Armed Forces, institutional residents, persons living on Indian reserves, and residents of the Yukon, Nunavut, and the Northwest Territories (4)

INDEX

To the owner of this book

We hope that you have enjoyed *An Introduction to the Canadian Labour Market,* by Helmar Drost and H. Richard Hird (ISBN 0-17-616772-2), and we would like to know as much about your experiences with this text as you would care to offer. Only through your comments and those of others can we learn how to make this a better text for future readers.

School _____ Your instructor's name _____

Course _____ Was the text required? _____ Recommended? _____

1. What did you like the most about *An Introduction to the Canadian Labour Market?*

_____

_____

_____

2. How useful was this text for your course?

_____

_____

_____

3. Do you have any recommendations for ways to improve the next edition of this text?

_____

_____

_____

4. In the space below or in a separate letter, please write any other comments you have about the book. (For example, please feel free to comment on reading level, writing style, terminology, design features, and learning aids.)

_____

_____

_____

Optional

Your name _____ Date _____

May Nelson Thomson Learning quote you, either in promotion for *An Introduction to the Canadian Labour Market,* or in future publishing ventures?

Yes _____ No _____

Thanks!

You can also send your comments to us via e-mail at
college@nelson.com

PLEASE TAPE SHUT. DO NOT STAPLE.

TAPE SHUT

TAPE SHUT

- - - FOLD HERE - - -

MAIL ▶ POSTE
Canada Post Corporation
Société canadienne des postes
Postage paid   Port payé
if mailed in Canada si posté au Canada
Business Reply   **Réponse d'affaires**

0066102399   01

TAPE SHUT

TAPE SHUT

0066102399-M1K5G4-BR01

```
NELSON THOMSON LEARNING
HIGHER EDUCATION
PO BOX 60225 STN BRM B
TORONTO ON M7Y 2H1
```